Franz Baermann Steiner

SELECTED WRITINGS

Volume II

Methodology and History in Anthropology

General Editor: David Parkin, Director of the Institute of Social and Cultural Anthropology, University of Oxford

FRANZ BAERMANN STEINER

Selected Writings

*Edited and with an Introduction
by Jeremy Adler and Richard Fardon*

Volume II

Orientpolitik, Value, and Civilisation

With a Memoir by M.N. Srinivas

Berghahn Books
New York • Oxford

First published in 1999 by
Berghahn Books

Editorial Offices:
55 John Street, 3rd Floor, New York, NY 10038 USA
3, NewTec Place, Magdalen Road, Oxford OX4 1RE, UK

Library of Congress Cataloging-in-Publication Data
Steiner, Franz Baermann, 1909–1952.
[Selections. 1999]
Selected writings / Franz Baermann Steiner : edited by Jeremy Adler and
Richard Fardon.
p.   cm. -- (Methodology and history in anthropology : v. 3)
Includes bibliographical references and index.
Contents: v. 2. Orientpolitik, Value, and Civilisation / with a memoir by M.N. Srinivas.
Volume 1: ISBN 1-57181-711-5 (alk. paper). -- ISBN 1-57181-712-3 (alk. paper)
Volume 2: ISBN 1-57181-713-1 (alk. paper). -- ISBN 1-57181-714-X (alk. paper)
GN471.4.S622 1999   99-15631
306--dc21   CIP

British Library Cataloguing in Publication Data
A catalogue record for this book is available from the British Library.

Printed in the United States on acid-free paper.

CONTENTS

LIST OF ILLUSTRATIONS

(All photographs by Franz Steiner, Summer 1937)

PREFATORY NOTE TO
VOLUME II

Stay on the border ...
Franz Steiner

Franz Baermann Steiner occupies a unique place in modern anthropology. The fact that his contribution has been recognised by only a handful of influential contemporaries is attributable to his tragically short life, which ended just when he had embarked upon his most mature and innovative writings. Working at the confluence of many of the most significant theories and methodologies of the twentieth century, in the early post-war years – and especially in the all-too-brief period he enjoyed as a Lecturer in Social Anthropology at the Institute of Social Anthropology at the University of Oxford from 1949 until his untimely death in 1952– he had begun to select among these various currents. At this time, he was developing an unprecedented synthesis in mid-century anthropological thought. Broadly speaking, Steiner's thinking stakes out a territory between German post-Enlightenment philosophy, modern linguistics, Marxism, Central European ethnology, German sociology, British social anthropology, and early structuralism. He deploys these resources with a passion for accuracy – which for Steiner is never far removed from an almost Biblical passion for truth, albeit he is often careless of scholarly details – allied to an overriding concern for the right to self-determination of non-Western peoples, among whom he includes his own Jewish people. In their equal concern for geopolitics and detailed local ethnography, his writings foreshadow trends in anthropology that were to become apparent only as the twentieth century wore on. In their deep aversion to the imposition of Western values on non-Western peoples, his writings relentlessly expose biases brought by Western reporters to their texts.

The present volumes hope to promote a re-evaluation of Franz Baermann Steiner's thought by presenting his ideas in their most complete form to date. Volume I reprints Steiner's classic study *Taboo* together with three uncollected essays on truth and religion. A newly researched introductory essay places Steiner's development into biographical context, explores his relations with contemporaries like Malinowski, Evans-Prichard, Elias Canetti and Iris Murdoch, details his affinity with various intellectual schools, and indicates a synthesis of the ideas that he seemed to be working towards. Volume II prints other texts by Steiner which saw their way into print, together with many published here for the first time. Besides his articles on labour and economics, it includes hitherto unknown political writings, a section from Steiner's dissertation on slavery, unpublished lectures on Aristotle, Simmel, and kinship, a selection of aphorisms, and extracts from the poetic cycle *Conquests*. A detailed introductory essay relates Steiner's thought to current concerns. Whilst this body of work does not aspire to completeness, we trust that it represents Steiner fairly, and will lead to a new appreciation of him as an encyclopaedic figure: poet, aphorist, social critic, ethnologist, anthropological and philosophical theorist, Zionist, political activist, friend, colleague, and mentor. Each volume is introduced by a memoir specially written by one of Steiner's Oxford colleagues, Mary Douglas and M.N. Srinivas.

J. A. and R. F.

ACKNOWLEDGEMENTS

It is possible to appreciate Aristotle's sociological thought much better now than during the last few centuries; and this is very significant, not only for the stage reached in the development of sociological reasoning but generally for our cultural situation.

Franz Steiner on Aristotle's sociology

In the conviction that today's intellectual climate also is a more auspicious moment for their appreciation, we have collected Franz Steiner's more important anthropological writings in two volumes. Steiner would have recognised with approval the origins of many of the changes in our sociological reasoning and cultural situation that have occurred in the fifty years since he settled in Great Britain and set about transforming himself into an English-speaking anthropologist, though we can presume he would have expressed his inimitable doubts about others. It is a conducive moment, therefore, to consider his ideas together and to contextualize them in two essays on his biography and his intellectual projects. We are fully aware that what we have to say cannot be definitive, but we trust that it may hold surprises even for those familiar with Franz Steiner's published works.

That we are able to do this is thanks, in the first instance, to those without whom Steiner's anthropological writings would not have been been preserved in a usable fashion: H.G. Adler, as Steiner's literary executor, preserved Steiner's papers and devoted himself tirelessly to the promotion of his *Nachlaß*. Steiner's close friend Dr Esther Frank typed up an invaluable three-volumed selection of his aphorisms for Steiner which we have used with profit. Laura Bohannan and Paul Bohannan each prepared two essays and one book of Steiner's for publication. Sadly, one of the books never appeared. Other than introducing uniformity into the styles of referencing and bibliography, in Volume I we have entirely relied upon Laura Bohannan's editorship of *Taboo* and 'Enslavement and the early Hebrew Lineage System', and have incorporated her edition of 'Chagga Truth' into our new text of that paper, and in Volume II we have relied entirely on Paul Bohannan's editorship of 'Notes on Comparative Economics', 'Towards a Classification of Labour', and we are also indebted to his unpublished edition of *A Prolegomena to a Comparative Study of the Forms of Slavery.* We are grateful to the Bohannans both for permission to reprint their work and for their staunch encouragement of our editorial project. We also wish to record our debt to Alfons Fleischli, whose doctoral dissertation provides an invaluable starting-point for the study of Steiner's life and works; he kindly made his correspondence available to us, and we are pleased to record our debt to his biographical chapters on Steiner.

We have been overwhelmed by the personal response from friends and colleagues of Steiner's Oxford period. Of his three surviving colleagues at the Institute: Mary Douglas's enthusiasm sustained our conviction that a re-edition of Steiner's anthropological writings was intellectually important; we are grateful also for her eager contribution of a memoir in Volume I; M.N. Srinivas graciously consented to provide a memoir to introduce Volume II; and the late Louis Dumont wrote us a moving private letter. Several other of Steiner's contemporaries at Oxford or in London have been kind enough to respond to written or personal enquiries, sometimes at great length: Paul Baxter, David Brokensha, Kenelm Burridge, Anand Chandavarkar, Ian Cunnison, Sir Raymond Firth, Ioan Lewis, John Middleton, Rodney Needham, William Newell, Julian Pitt-Rivers, and David Pocock.

Iris Murdoch, one of the few readers familiar with his private writings, profoundly encouraged us in our aim to revive interest in the writings of Franz Steiner, and particularly championed the plan to publish his aphorisms. Thanks to her generosity and that of her husband, John Bayley, we are able to quote extracts from Miss Murdoch's private journal on Steiner written in 1952-3, which have kindly been made available to us by Dame Iris's official biographer, Peter Conradi. Elias Canetti responded to our request to write a memoir on Steiner, published elsewhere, which has proved invaluable. Johanna Canetti kindly provided us with copies of Steiner's letters to her father, Sybille Miller-Aichholz generously transcribed for us Steiner's letters to her, and the late David Wright kindly lent us Steiner's letters to him. Michael Hamburger has been unfailing in his support of Steiner, both through his translations and his own writings. Mary Donovan thoughtfully shared her personal memories with us, and Franz's cousin, Lise Seligmann, kindly wrote and talked to us about Franz Steiner, and has taken a constant interest in the publication of his works.

Franz Baermann Steiner's *Nachlaß* has been housed at the Schiller Nationalmuseum, Deutsches Literaturarchiv, Marbach, since November 1997. We are grateful to Herr Jochen Meyer and Dr Ingrid Belke for making these papers available to us.

The wide-ranging nature of Steiner's prodigious scholarship would have overcome our flagging attempts to follow his footsteps to an even greater degree without the help of: David Arnold – Professor of South Asian History at SOAS; Professor Yehuda Bacon – Bezalel Art School, Jerusalem, for help with a reference on Hugo Bergman; Christian Bartolf – Director of the Gandhi-Informations-Zentrum in Berlin; Matthew Bell – Goethe scholar and historian of eighteenth-century German anthropology at King's College London; D.C.K. Glass, also at King's College London – German scholar and bibliographer extraordinary; Professor Sir Ernst Gombrich – formerly of the Warburg Institute, University of London; Linda Greenlick – Chief Librarian of the Jewish Chronicle; Michael Knibb – Samuel Davidson Professor of Old Testament Studies, King's College London; Jeremy Lawrence – Professor of Spanish, University of Manchester; Mike Morris – Librarian of the Institute of Social and Cultural Anthropology of Oxford University; Robert Pynsent – Professor of Czech Language and Literature at the School of Slavonic and East European Studies, who kindly helped remove some of the worst errors from a draft of our Introduction to Volume I; David Riches – of the University of St. Andrews as an ethnographer of the Arctic and sub-Arctic; J.W. Rogerson – emeritus Professor of Theology at the University of Sheffield who gave us his views on Steiner's 'Hebrew Lineage' article; Gabor Schabert – freelance scholar and linguist who provided us with an evaluation of Steiner's unpublished first dissertation, on which we have relied for our assessment; Erhard Schüttepelz – scholar of Elias Canetti who filled some interesting bibliographical gaps and kept us up-to-date with current developments in Germany; Chris Thornhill – scholar of German social and political theory, King's College London, for whose views on Steiner's Simmel lectures and German social science we are grateful; Zdeněk Vašiček – historian of archeology, political scientist, and expert on all things Czech and Slovak, who commented in detail on our Introductions to Volumes I and II; Bernard Wasserstein – President of the Oxford Centre for Hebrew and Jewish Studies, who read the sections in our Introductions concerned with Steiner's Zionism and Steiner's relevant texts; Shamoon Zamir – scholar of English and American literature at King's College London, who helped us with ethnopoetics. Professor David Parkin, formerly of SOAS and now Professor of Social Anthropology at the University of Oxford, first saw the link between our interests, brought us together, and helped us through the sources at Oxford. Chris Rojek grasped the point of our project quickly and supported it consistently. Marion Berghahn put us in her debt by taking the risk of allowing full rein to our ambitions for a two-volume edition. This has enabled us to include both the published papers we had originally intended to edit and selections from the large body of unpublished or hitherto untranslated material, including aphorisms and poems, which we believe are essential to a full grasp of Steiner's work. Needless to say, we alone are responsible for the remaining errors.

Michael Mack's doctoral research at the University of Cambridge will relate Franz Steiner's work to that of Steiner's friend Elias Canetti. We are grateful to Michael for his sincere support of this project and for permission to make use of his draft translation of 'On the Process of Civilisation'. Nicolas Ziegler, doctoral student at King's College London, who is writing a thesis on Steiner's poetry, has been a constant support, too; he kindly made copies of many of Steiner's letters and unpublished manuscripts for us, and also made available two unpublished research papers, which we cite. We look forward keenly to reading their completed accounts of Steiner's work.

A word about our editorial principles may be in order. In editing Steiner's writings, we advanced from a decision to re-edit *Taboo* into preparing a one-volumed collection of Steiner's published papers, but this also expanded the more we became familiar with Steiner's ideas and the more we began to recognise the interdependence of his different productions, including minor writings and fugitive texts. Whereas the Bohannans edited some of Steiner's major writings as 'papers', almost half a century later, now that the period in which he wrote has itself assumed historical interest, we were forced to come to terms with his newspaper articles, private writings, and the character of some 'papers' as 'lectures' delivered to an audience at Oxford. His views are firmly embedded into his time, not just intellectually, but politically. This can be seen in the different possible approaches to Steiner's classic paper on 'Chagga Truth'. Laura Bohannan singled out the lecture's central intellectual achievement for editing, which implicitly puts Steiner's work into the context of contemporary philosophy. In printing the full version, without, we hope, risking the impact of its points about 'truth', we include the contextual opening, which contains a polemic on the German view of society: Steiner's anthropological ideas take on a new focus against the background of Zionism, Nazism, and the Shoah. This simple fact has also dictated our inclusion of personal and more occasional writings.

As to the texts. We began by making exact transcriptions, with emendations in square brackets, conjectures, footnotes, and so on of Steiner's unpublished writings. It soon became clear that such an exact rendition would divert attention from what Steiner said. We have therefore adopted the method used by Laura Bohannan and Paul

Bohannan in their editions and silently emended inconsistencies, un-English word order, and so on, keeping editorial comment to a minimum. Wherever necessary and possible, we have supplied missing references and bibliographies in the currently accepted format. Full reference to our sources and to the previous publication of Steiner's works can be found in the footnotes and in the select bibliography of Steiner's writings at the end of each volume.

In rendering extracts from Steiner's *Conquests*, Jeremy Adler has been helped by Franz Wurm, who checked the translations against the originals, and made many suggestions that have been gratefully adopted. The aim has been to reproduce Steiner's idiosyncracies to the maximum extent compatible with English usage. In translating Steiner's German prose, we have taken a different route. *Orientpolitik* is written in an exceedingly clipped style, and Steiner never prepared his 'Letter to Georg Rapp' for the press or fulfilled his plan of revising the text of his *Essays and Discoveries*. Indeed, the extant text reveals occasional omissions and infelicities. The style, cut off from the German mainstream, is sometimes idiosyncratic. Occasionally we have silently emended the remarks, and have in all the prose writings aimed to make an idiomatic English version, in the belief that fluent English, such as Steiner wrote so well himself, will do more for the reception of his ideas at the current stage of research than an apparatus, square brackets, explanations, and the other devices at an editor's disposal. The remarks aim at immediacy, and this is the effect we have tried to reproduce. We trust that in the process the ideas are rendered accurately.

For permission to republish 'Enslavement and the Early Hebrew Lineage System: An Explanation of Genesis 47: 29-31, 48: 1-16', which first appeared in 1954 in *Man* 54 (article no. 102): 73-5, we are grateful to the Royal Anthropological Institute; to republish 'Chagga Truth', which first appeared in 1954 in *Africa* 24 (4): 36-49, we are grateful to Professor Last, Editor of *Africa*, the Journal of the International African Institute; to republish 'Notes on Comparative Economics', which first appeared in 1954 in *The British Journal of Sociology* 5.2: 118-29, we are grateful to Routledge and *The British Journal of Sociology*; to republish 'Towards a Classification of Labour', which first appeared in 1957 in *Sociologus* NS 7,2: 112-39, we are grateful to the Editor, Professor Georg Elwig of the Institut für Ethnologie, Freie Universität, Berlin, and the publishers, Duncker & Humblot; and to republish 'The Steps Swings Away' and 'The Heart', which first appeared in 1994 in *Comparative Criticism* 16: 157-60, we are grateful to the Editor, Dr Elinor Shaffer and the Press Syndicate of the Cambridge University Press. For permission to reproduce photographs from their collections, we are grateful to the Deutsches Literaturarchiv, Marbach am Neckar, and the Marie-Louise von Motesiczky Charitable Trust, London.

We are grateful to our Colleges for granting us periods of sabbatical leave in the academic year 1997-8 which has enabled us to complete our research and editing. Grants from the Research Committees of the School of Humanities, King's College London, and the School of Oriental and African Studies (both of the University of London) allowed us to engage the services of Carol Tully and Lisa Rowland as research assistants and of Christel Ahmad and Mary Warren, without whose help we could not have brought this project to completion. David Yeandle and Rita Pannen's keyboard wizardry have ensured that our intentions took the correct electronic format. A special word of thanks goes to our departmental colleagues. Eva Adler and Catherine Davies have both been a constant support.

We learned more than even we expected from the privilege of editing and thinking about Franz Baermann Steiner's writings and formed a friendship in the process. As a general rule, Richard Fardon initially edited the previously unpublished works in English and Jeremy Adler those in German. However, with the exception of the translations of Steiner's *Conquests*, we each revised and commented upon the other's work. In this respect, as in the Introductions, our efforts have been fully collaborative.

J.A. and R.F.
University of London 1999

A NOTE ON QUOTATIONS

All quotations in F.B.S.'s works have been standardised and checked wherever possible. His sources are listed in the bibliographies attached to each article. Printed sources used in the Editors' introductions are given at the end of each volume. A list of F.B.S.'s cited unpublished writings, letters to F.B.S., and Ms writings about F.B.S., are also included, and individual items referred to in the Introductions may be sourced in this list. Quotations from letters and verbal communications to the Editors by F.B.S.'s friends and colleagues are signified by 'PC' (= personal communication). A list of other such sources is contained in the bibliography.

Fig. 1.   Ruthenian Shepherd

Fig. 2.   Flautist

Fig. 3.   Ruthenian Girl

Fig. 4.   Ruthenian Girl

Fig. 5.   Romany Girl

Fig. 6.   Romany Youth

Fig. 7.   Hassidic Youth

Fig. 8.   Romany Settlement

Fig. 9.   *Ruthenian Farm*

Fig. 10.   *Uniate Religious Procession*

Fig. 11.   Ruthenian Wedding

Fig. 12.   Watermelons

Fig. 13.   Town Marketplace, Ruthenia

Fig. 14.   Town Marketplace, Ruthenia

Fig. 15.   Romany School

Fig. 16.   Romany Girl

PART I: INTRODUCTIONS

FRANZ STEINER. A MEMOIR

M.N. Srinivas

I became a student of Professor A.R. Radcliffe-Brown in May 1945, a few months after he had returned to Oxford from a two-year British Council Fellowship to São Paulo in Brazil. Franz Steiner was very much my senior at Oxford, having joined the Institute of Social Anthropology in 1938, two years after he had moved to London from Prague. When in London, he was a student at the London School of Economics, where Malinowski's lectures and seminars were attracting students from all over the world. It is not known, however, what prompted Franz to move from London to Oxford.

I kept a diary of sorts during my first eight months in Oxford, from April to December 1945, and Franz figures in it on a few occasions. The diary is too scrappy and desultory, and I am embarrassed to quote from it, but then I suppose any sort of record is better than none. According to my diary, I first saw Franz on Friday 15 June, when he walked into the main room on the ground floor of 1 Jowett Walk, after R.-B. had finished his lecture. (The Institute was located on the ground floor of the building of the department of Geography.) I find that I refer to Franz as a 'foreign-looking', small man, wearing a 'shabby' mackintosh over his suit. He was writing a thesis. He asked R.-B., 'I have just come to inquire if you had defined work or labour anywhere. When a professional footballer is playing in a match, is he playing or working?'

'Is there anything in your *Andamans*?' (*Andaman Islanders*, Cambridge, 1922).

R.-B.: 'There is nothing in the *Andamans* though I used to be fond of definitions once. By the way, look up Malinowski.'

F.S.: 'There is nothing in Malinowski's *Argonauts*.'

R.-B.: 'Oh, got any letter from home?'

F.S.: 'Both my parents are dead, that's what I hear.'

R.-B.: 'Oh dear! Have you looked up Firth?'

F.S.: 'There is nothing in Firth.'

R.-B.: 'Were they in Prague?'

F.S.: 'Yes, I expected the news rather. The real trouble is I have to write a brief note on labour, and I just cannot skip it.'

R.-B.: 'Oh yes, you cannot.'

Even when I was writing the above, I felt that it was a greatly abridged account of the actual conversation but what I found bewildering was the interweaving of work and personal tragedy in the conversation. The seeming casualness of the references to the death of Franz's parents, I found strange. Work was all-important and should go on, personal tragedies notwithstanding. But I was to experience something similar in my own case later in October. A week or so prior to the beginning of term I had a letter from home informing me that my elder brother Gopal had died suddenly of pneumonia. He was in his thirties, and he had given me money to proceed to Oxford, and had told me that he would be sending me another instalment in September. The news of his death was devastating, and further I felt trapped in Oxford as I could not go home at short notice. A passage in a boat going home was difficult and would not be available for months. After the initial shock which lasted a few days, I started attending to my work, and it helped to take my mind away from my brother's death. I told R.-B. about this and he replied that when one is doing something important one forgets other problems. I think R.-B. was trying to be helpful but the way he said it I had the impression that he thought work was the only thing that mattered.

The next entry concerning Franz was on Friday 5 October 1945. Franz had invited me to the house he was living in, in North Oxford. I reached his place in late afternoon and rang the bell. A scholarly-looking and bearded gentleman opened the door and told me that Franz was delayed at the dentist's but that he would be back soon. I was invited to take a chair and, while I waited for Franz, my host talked about Warde Fowler, an authority on ancient Rome. As it happened, some months previously, I had hunted up several references in Warde Fowler for my teacher in Bombay, Ghurye, who was planning a book on Indo-European kinship. Franz's host told me that Warde Fowler was deaf from childhood, but that he was able to distinguish the calls of birds except those of the cuckoo which he dismissed as 'shoutings'.

During our conversation, Franz's host told me several things: That he had seen Edward Tylor, whom he described as 'the father of anthropology' and that Franz's parents had been murdered by the Nazis. I was also told that Franz had lost the manuscript of his thesis on slavery ('servile institutions') while travelling from Oxford to London. It meant the loss of four years' work, and Franz had had to start again from scratch. Franz walked in while we were talking, and he took me upstairs to his room where books and papers were strewn about in total chaos. After both of us had sat down, Franz talked about many things. He referred to his fieldwork in the Carpathian Ukraine for his Ph.D. (in Ethnology and Semitic languages) from the University of Prague. He told me that he wrote poetry (in German), and that Stephen Spender had liked it very much. He also talked of many other things. He must have been in an unusually chatty mood, for by nature he was reticent and did not open up easily. His chattiness invited me to talk about myself and my current worries and problems. And it was 7.15 p.m. when I left him and his host to catch a bus to the bottom of Iffley Road where there was a 'British Restaurant', one of those war-time institutions, where I dined frequently. It was popular with students, and my 'digs' were only ten minutes' walk from it.

Franz's loss of notes cropped up occasionally in our pub conversations during my stay in Oxford (1945-51). There was great sympathy for Franz in his loss while his pluck and his determination to start once again from scratch were admired by all. However, the matter was never discussed when Franz was present, and Franz himself never referred to it.

When I knew him in 1945-47, Franz was in the habit of catching the 8.40 a.m. from Oxford to London every morning, and returning by an evening train, spending the working hours in the British Museum Library. The 8.40 a.m. from Oxford was a popular train, and if one missed it, one caught a later train which required one to change trains at Reading to get to London. It was when Franz was changing trains at Reading that he lost his manuscript and some notes: Franz got off the train at Reading and headed for the loo. He deposited his briefcase at the entrance to the loo, and when he returned a few minutes later, the briefcase was missing. And all his efforts to trace it were in vain.

It is interesting to recall that T.E. Lawrence lost the manuscript of his *The Seven Pillars of Wisdom* while changing trains at Reading, around Christmas time 1919. And like Franz, he too rewrote *The Seven Pillars of Wisdom* from scratch.

Professor Evans-Pritchard, in his Preface to Franz's posthumously published book, *Taboo* (Cohen and West, London, 1956), wrote: 'His scholarship and remarkable breadth of learning had long been the admiration of his colleagues ...'. This was a richly deserved tribute but it is not known that it was Radcliffe-Brown who first drew E.-P.'s attention to the erudition of Franz. I was present when R.-B. talked to E.-P. about the depth of Franz's scholarship, his knowledge of languages, etc. R.-B. wanted his favourite students to be supervised by E.-P. He thought very highly of E.-P., in a class higher than Meyer Fortes. Franz himself did not care much for Meyer Fortes and this I know from a talk which Franz had with me after both of us had attended a seminar by Dr Meinhard which was chaired by Meyer. Much later, on the day when Franz had his *viva voce* examination, Meyer made a tactless remark about Franz's visit to London on the following day and this upset Franz no end. If I remember rightly, Meyer and Firth were Franz's examiners.

Franz's thesis on servile institutions was, however, an outstanding one, and E.-P. lost no time in appointing him to a University Lectureship in Social Anthropology.

I had been appointed University Lecturer in Indian Sociology in January 1948, and E.-P., with characteristic forethought and generosity, had provided for my spending the first year of my Lectureship doing a field-study of a village of my choice in India. After spending ten months in Rampura near Mysore in South India, I returned to Oxford in January 1949 to find that both the faculty and student body had increased markedly. In a little over two years after taking over as Professor, E.-P. had transformed the department. The students were very bright and keen, and classes were lively, students carrying on discussions even after the classes had ended. There was excitement in the air, and one felt privileged to be part of the Institute.

Franz had a coronary sometime in 1949 and had to be treated at the Radcliffe Infirmary in Oxford. Luckily, he recovered quickly, and E.-P. was told by the specialist who treated Franz that Franz's problem was 'only functional and not organic'. But illness was not the only enemy Franz had to fight; poverty was also there. I think that it was some time after his illness that Franz needed £200 badly, and it was suggested to me by a friend of Franz's that I should approach E.-P. for a loan on Franz's behalf. I broached the matter with E.-P., and he agreed to give the money, making it clear, however, that he did not like to have financial transactions with his colleagues. He was annoyed, and I felt that I had been foolish to have approached him for the money. I must mention here that an impression seemed to have grown in the Institute that I was one of those close to E.-P.. I do not know how it had arisen: perhaps the fact that on a few occasions E.-P. had asked me to convey a message to a student was responsible for it. In retrospect, it is possible that this even created some resentment against me among my colleagues. Once or twice E.-P. wanted me to convey a message to a colleague who, he felt, was getting distracted from serious work by broadcasting frequently on the BBC, but I refrained from passing on the message. I greatly valued my friendship with that colleague, and I did not want to lose it.

Submitting his thesis must have lifted a huge load off Franz, while his appointment as Lecturer so soon after obtaining his doctorate, must have given him relief and pleasure. He was seen more frequently at pub sessions where E.-P. used to meet a few of his students and colleagues. Franz was a welcome figure, and his wit and wisdom were much admired. For instance, when a few Oxford graduates who had offered PPE (politics, philosophy and economics) at the B.A. Honours, moved to the Institute to study social anthropology, Franz commented that they were 'moving from PPE to EEP'. English intellectuals usually look down upon punning, or pretend to look down upon it, but Franz had a gift for punning which he occasionally indulged in. For instance, once when he heard a couple of puns during a pub session, he said, 'we are all pundits here', a remark which attracted both groans and laughter from his colleagues.

Franz had been advised by E.-P. to approach Cohen and West, who had published E.-P.'s BBC lectures *Social Anthropology* (London, 1951), to find out if they would be interested in publishing Franz's thesis on slavery. Franz journeyed to London on the following day to meet Sir Cohen, and returned to Oxford by an afternoon train. He then made his appearance at the pub and when he was asked how the meeting had gone, Franz's face broke into a grin, and then he danced a minuet, saying 'Cohen is Cohen and West is West'.

Some time after recovering from his illness, Franz moved to a house located on a corner of Woodstock and Thorncliffe Roads. This move made him a close neighbour of mine as I lived at 14, Thorncliffe Road, only about two hundred yards away. Franz was being looked after by a young Jewish couple with a child, and the couple seemed very respectful if not in awe of their learned guest. I dropped in on Franz occasionally, and I had the impression that my visits were not unwelcome. Franz ate early in the evening whereas I ate at about eight and I found that food was often served while we were talking. The arrival of food, however, slowed down our conversation, but did not stop it. And it was during one such conversation that Franz told me that the Jews had made a profound historical mistake in moving to Europe from their ancient home in Asia. Had they turned east their history would have been very different, and not marked by persecution and pogroms. This was a basic conviction of his but totally new to me. I was very recently reminded of the depth of Franz's conviction when I received a long, unpublished letter which Franz had sent to Mahatma Gandhi, a response to Gandhi's somewhat ill-considered advice to the Jews published in the *Harijan* of 20 July 1946. Franz sent his typewritten reply to Gandhi through a friend. The letter is written in anguish and anger, and I quote an extract from it (see pp. 141-42, below):

For, me, the decisive point in assessing a people, are the observable relations between individuals and the value attached to *them*, as differing from the value attached to the achievements of the individuals. It is the social structure which I consider as decisive. And never, never have I found in all the literature the opinion that the Jews prior to their emancipation were an European people. Their contributions to civilisation, their medieval philosophy and science, their share in the development of scholasticism, have been claimed as European contributions. But through the ages the Jewish communities and the Ghettos of Europe have been regarded as foreign bodies. Their very confusion – confusion from a European point of view – of the political and religious community marked them as foreign to European civilisation. Their strictness in their dietical prescriptions which amounted to the impossibility of inter-dining, their severity against intermarriage was disgusting to the European. *Had we come to your country ... surely all this would not have been extraordinary. We would have settled down as one of the many castes of India, we would have worshipped the God of all mankind, and as your castes do, we would have strictly preserved our ways of worship, our seclusion and tradition. If there are two ways of life, there is no question to my mind for which of them the Jews are fitted.* (emphasis mine)

It was only when I read Franz's letter to Gandhi that I learnt that Franz had been deeply influenced by the Bhagavad Gita. It is possible that Franz's friendliness towards me was at least partly due to his affection for Indian culture and society, including the Bhagavad Gita. This also explains to me my meeting him at a house in north Oxford (17, Polstead Road) on a Sunday afternoon during the academic year 1945-46. It was the residence of four or five middle-aged English women and an elderly Indian philosopher, Mr B.K. Mallik. The women kept open house on Sundays, serving a lavish tea to everyone who came. (The place also served as a meeting point for Indian students.) The tea was followed by a discussion led – and dominated – by Mr Mallick. In Isaiah Berlin's language, he was a hedgehog out to demolish all sceptical foxes. Mr Mallick thought India stood for the group while the West stood for the individual, and the gulf between the two was unbridgeable. India was also superior. I met Franz at one of the Sunday tea sessions and found him listening to the debate but not uttering a word. When the discussion ended, we both walked out, and Franz remarked on the beauty of the lone Indian girl who was there and how she was like a porcelain doll. I knew the girl slightly: she was petite and very brown, and had thick, black hair, arched eyebrows, very dark eyes, and a friendly smile.

Franz was, as could be expected of a poet, highly sensitive to beauty everywhere, but I have a feeling that he found brown and black women particularly attractive. I remember another occasion when both of us met at the YMCA recreation room in London, and found a few young people playing table tennis. Among the players was a lively and slim West Indian girl, and after we went out of the recreation room, Franz commented on the beauty of the girl we had seen.

Franz became more and more orthodox as time went on. His Jewish hosts kept a kosher household, and he started observing the *shabbath* strictly, keeping away from the Institute on Saturdays. E.-P. came to the Institute even on Saturdays, and occasionally held informal meetings with his colleagues. And Franz's growing orthodoxy upset him. E.-P., who had once boasted in my presence that there was not a single English name in the department (1946-51) – he himself was Welsh – and who was also religious, was irritated by one of his colleagues practising his faith!

Paul and Laura Bohannan, American students studying for the D.Phil. in Oxford, were both close to Franz, and Franz was an occasional guest at their flat on Banbury Road. Franz thought highly of their work on the Tiv of West Africa but unfortunately he did not live long enough to see the publication of the results of their field-research.

During term time, seminars were held on Friday evenings, and after the seminars had ended, most participants moved to the King's Arms to continue discussions there. These pub sessions were usually brief, the participants going home after a drink or two. But there were other sessions, presided over by E.-P., either at the White Horse at Headington, the Peacock at St. Giles, or some other pub, and these often continued till closing time. When I lived on Thorncliffe Road, either E.-P. or Godfrey Lienhardt would phone me to tell me where we would be meeting. These were intimate sessions where we discussed not only matters anthropological but many others. Religion came up frequently, not only the religion of the peoples we were studying, or knew about, but our own personal beliefs as well. On rare occasions such discussions became heated but displays of temper led to apologies on the following morning, in the form of gifts of books or other things we had come to value.

I visited Oxford briefly in June 1982, and stayed with Godfrey in his flat. In the evening, he took me to a pub off Walton Street, and while we were talking, someone pointed out to a lady and said that she was Iris Murdoch. She was engaged in conversation with a few people around her. Godfrey had studied English literature at Cambridge with F.R. Leavis before moving on to anthropology and he maintained his contact with Leavis even after he became an anthropologist. It is likely that it was Godfrey who had introduced Franz to Iris Murdoch.

Franz smoked only cigarettes, and I once asked him why he preferred it to a pipe. He told me that when he got on the boat to England in 1936, all the fellow Jewish refugees had given up smoking cigarettes to start puffing on the pipes they had bought on board the ship. Franz was put off by this, and stuck to cigarettes.

I remember a New Year's Eve party with the Bohannans, either in 1949 or 1950. Franz and I, bachelors both, were the guests. We were not easy to cater for, Franz eating only kosher food while I was a vegetarian. But the Bohannans were thoughtful and generous hosts, and we enjoyed ourselves immensely. I remember emerging from their flat at about two in the morning, to find the roads and hedges dusted liberally with snow. But we both walked home cheerfully, unmindful of the cold.

I remember another walk with Franz, either on Banbury or Woodstock Road, and Franz telling me, pointing to the hollyhocks in some compound, 'when the hollyhocks come I know my summer has ended'.

I left Oxford for Baroda on 13th June 1951 to take up the newly established Chair in Sociology in the M.S. University. The decision to leave Oxford was a difficult and painful one, and even after a year in Baroda I often felt out of place in the local academic atmosphere. But I had plenty to do and I was determined to establish in Baroda the kind of sociology that I wanted to.

Some time in November or December of 1952, I received an aerogramme from Phyllis Puckle, Secretary in the Institute, telling me that Franz had died suddenly of a heart attack. He was on the phone speaking to someone when the attack came, and he collapsed, leaving the receiver dangling on the line.

ORIENTPOLITIK, VALUE, AND CIVILISATION: THE ANTHROPOLOGICAL THOUGHT OF FRANZ BAERMANN STEINER

Jeremy Adler and Richard Fardon

Beyond Culture Circles: The Field Trip

Hammering, cymbals, the dusk of brown violins,
Frugal beauty of the wood's strong edge,
Balancing breath on the acrid hill
And the sheen of birches around the teeming life of the streams,
Windy prospect and rattling caravans
On a rough road,
Pictures and sounds, molten into pure metal....

Conquests, IX, 'The Bear in the Coat of Arms'

By the standards of mid-century anthropological enquiry, which required the modern scholar to engage in fieldwork, Steiner might be thought a literary anthropologist. To the extent that he never visited Africa, Asia, or the Amazon, there would be some truth to this view. However, it would be wrong to conclude that Franz Steiner was not fully acquainted with the methodology of fieldwork, or that he had not absorbed this into his thinking. Like so many of his contemporaries, it was through Malinowski that Steiner came to know about participant research. To judge by his journal entry (Volume I, p. 64, above) and his aphorism on Conrad and Malinowski (pp. 239-40, below), Steiner was from the outset – at least privately and in some respects – intellectually condescending towards the master of Trobriand ethnography. But against this must be set both Steiner's admiration for Malinowski's views on language (reiterated in his lectures on 'Tabu' and 'Language, Society, and Social Anthropology'), and the indirect evidence which suggests another picture. First, we need to consider the fact that Steiner was drawn to study in London not just by the Library of the British Museum but by Malinowski's presence at the LSE. Secondly, as we may deduce from H.G. Adler's detailed description of the anthropological method he used to survive the death camps (volume I, p. 85 above) and his reference to the practice of the Trobriand Islanders in an unpublished short story which pre-dates the war, Steiner transmitted an enthusiasm for Malinowski to his closest pre-war friend: it is most likely that Adler's knowledge of Malinowski was mediated via Steiner, and that if he read Malinowski, as seems probable, it was at Steiner's prompting. Thirdly, Steiner's choice of an area in which to try out his fieldwork technique for the first time, the Carpathian Mountains, is a territory that belongs to the common Central European heritage from which both he and Malinowski emerged, i.e., a region on the eastern border of what, before its demise at the end of the First World War, had been the Austro-Hungarian Empire, and by then lay at the intersection between Czechoslovakia, Hungary and Russia.

The Carpathian trip may have been a surrogate for Steiner's original plan, which had been to study Siberian ethnology and to learn Russian for this purpose. An anthropological field trip to Stalinist Siberia seems a somewhat unlikely project by this time; but a visit to Sub-Carpathian Ruthenia (on the westerly borders of the Russian domain) would at least have allowed Steiner to extend his knowledge of a region of easternmost Czechoslovakia. Ruthenians and gypsies were members of the same political entity as the cosmopolitan citizens of Prague, so the field trip could not but have impacted on Steiner's sense of the culture and politics of his own Central European home; and thus, indirectly, on his own identity. Nonetheless, the differences between Sub-Carpathian Ruthenia and Prague (economic, cultural and linguistic) were sufficient for it to qualify as a fieldwork site, in the sense usual in the British anthropological tradition that Steiner was to endorse in his later lectures. The journey would have given Steiner his first opportunity to compare how Malinowski's ideas and the 'culture circle' theory he had studied in Vienna fared in practice. Our discussion, in the context of Steiner's biography, of the single, brief article of 1938 predominantly concerned with gypsy education (see Volume I, pp. 55-58) strongly suggested that, so far as contemporary societies were concerned, Steiner accepted a – modified – Malinowskian approach. Moreover, the field trip will have added a further perspective to Steiner's growing familiarity with scenarios involving co-residential and co-modernising peoples: after Prague and Palestine, Sub-Carpathian Ruthenia will have confronted him with a third multi-ethnic community. In 1936 to 1938, the evidence is that Steiner still held out hope for an 'emancipation' that allowed co-modernisers to recognise common interests and thus exist compatibly. Education remained crucial to his thinking in this regard. However, this optimism did not survive the early war years, and so his poems on the Ruthenian experience – written during the personal deepening and suffering of the middle years of the war that transformed his thought – cannot be interpreted as direct evidence of how he might have understood his fieldwork had it been written up contemporaneously.

In fact, we know very little about Steiner's experience as a fieldworker in Ruthenia. It is not even clear whether he was primarily concerned to study the gypsies, or Ruthenians, or the wider society. We suspect the last, which he envisaged as a modernising, plural social and cultural formation, integrated – insofar as it was – through the market for commodities, including labour. However, there is good reason to believe that Steiner did not need intensive, long-term fieldwork in some distant spot in order to think like an ethnographic researcher. Perhaps the Ruthenian experience reinforced in him that habit of observation by which anthropologists both meld with their surroundings, in order to absorb local practices and beliefs as if they were their own, and at the same time learn to distance themselves, in order to analyse, interpret, and represent local phenomena within the terms of their own discipline. But this way of relating ethnographically to the world seems already to have been habitual for Steiner, and was increasingly to become his second nature, affecting the way he saw himself and his friends. It may be a legacy of an upbringing as a German-speaking Jewish Czech between the wars, for Ernest Gellner seems to have shared it in large measure (D. Gellner 1997). We meet it in his aphorisms on the English (Steiner 1988: 64-66), in the poetry he wrote on English life such as 'Kafka in England' (p. 81, below) and it may not be going too far to say that his own characteristic method of interrogating the ethnographic record, the reciprocal subordination of opposite values, may be connected to his experience of the multi-ethnic societies of Prague, Palestine, and Ruthenia before the war. In weaving between self and other, the fieldworker *practises* a methodology which Steiner made part of his theory; but Steiner's self was such a complex amalgam of cultures, histories, languages and places that he really had no need of an exterior other with which to enter an ethnographic dialogue. As his poetic cycle *Conquests* both demonstrated, and exploited, these resources existed in abundance within himself.

In his wartime *Conquests*, Steiner planned to present his experience of Ruthenia, including his memories of Romany life, but little more than the fragment describing the Romanies which we used as an epigraph for this section was written. The unwritten poem was to have been called 'The Bear in the Coat of Arms'; the punning reference to his middle name (Baermann) would have placed himself within Ruthenia. The plan reads as follows:

1. 'Anticipation', evocations of the land, simultaneous memory of its occupation by the Magyar hordes.
2. General description of the landscape, campsites, the peoples of the land: Ukrainians, Jews, Gypsies.
3. Whirling together of the two songs: the Wallachian and the Yiddish (Esther the Green).
4. Gypsies – travelling people – eternal movement – poverty. Knowledge of the future no contradiction.
5. Conversation with a Gypsy. The future is foretold: travelling, travelling, travelling ... no home anywhere. No manual work. Insight, but no happiness. (Steiner 1964: 102).

The plan indicates an ethnographic poem – about twenty-five years before Jerome Rothenberg defined his 'ethnopoetics' ([1968] 1985; Schiffer 1979), which have now been formulated systematically by A.T. Hatto (1995). Steiner's poem is centred on an evocation of Ruthenia's multi-ethnic society, into which he inserts a description of his own fate, a fate that proves to be essentially cognate with the gypsies' – and that of the country as a whole, which had successively belonged to different nations, without achieving autonomy. Another poem, entitled 'Ruthenian Village', which Steiner did complete between 1941 and 1942, also looks back to his Ruthenian experience. This time Steiner addresses the rootedness of the peasantry rather than the gypsies' motion:

> The inn's lust-reddened eyes have been extinguished,
> The flute of the lonely hill-shepherd is silent,
> Wind and his lullaby's softness,
> Gently have led him dreamward, flocks are asleep at his side.

> The faces of the houses were locked by their thatches
> From moon to the floor, and beneath every gable
> Girls' voices surging in their singing.
> Slowly each tree in turn entwines with clouds and the night.

> The sows have been dismissed to their meal all in darkness
> And wheezing they root up the daytime's remainders,
> Mightily roll in the ditches.
> Puddles all milky splash their bodies, the stones and the path.

Across the mossy centre the stars are in transit,
The walls and small gardens are merged in one blackness;
Slavering mongrels are turning
Spotted wry heads and, howling, mount their guard against night.

(Steiner 1992: 27)

Steiner effectively rewrites Western European pastoral poetry by extending it to a peasant village on the eastern margins of Central Europe: the familiar trope of the flute-playing shepherd, derived from the Greek pastoral poets and transmitted via countless Arcadias, gains a new meaning in Steiner's poem, because of his lived experience. Compare his photograph of a Ruthenian shepherd (Fig. 1) and a flute-player (Fig 2). Steiner reinvents the empty shadow of the arcadian shepherd by placing him into a recognisable environment – a village with an *inn*. This essential requisite of village life has no place in ancient Greek poetry and its renaissance imitations. Yet its presence lends facticity to Steiner's poem. Or take the reference to the *straw roofs* of the village houses. Again, Steiner is recording the material culture of a Ruthenian village (Figs 7-8), just as his evocation of the gypsies began (as had his brief descriptive article) with their tinkering and musicianship. As the wind fills his gypsy poem, so do the sows and the mongrels in his Ruthenian poem fill out the scene with the sounds and smells of village life. The German poems explore the (recalled) sensuous aspects of Steiner's Ruthenian experience, which are so markedly absent from his English-language account of 1938.

Reflection on the Ruthenian field trip may have enriched Steiner's conception of the polarities of East and West, which came increasingly to structure his applied and critical social thought. Ruthenian peasants might be regarded as Eastern Europeans by people whose existence was centred in the cosmopolitan capitals of Prague, Vienna and Budapest; and the same people might regard Romanies as Orientals in relation to Eastern Europeans. However, Steiner's poems, reportage and photographs present a complementary picture of the local relations between these categories, as well as Jews. The photographs are concerned with two main themes: in the first (Figures 1-11) characteristic ethnic 'types' are suggested through divergent material cultures (such as basketry and house-types), ritual acts (such as a Uniate wedding and processions – the church preserved Greek rites, but acknowledged the supremacy of the Pope; see Krejčí and Machonin 1996: 40), and ethnic dress (both formal and everyday, the latter including the working-dress of shepherds, etc.); and in the second (Figs 12-14), the town marketplace is represented as the single location – at least in Steiner's depictions – upon which these different strands of Ruthenian local society converge. Compare his photographs of local women and Hassidim (Figs 12-13), a market photograph (Fig. 13) showing the Hassidic Jew probably bargaining with a peasant woman. A sign in the background appears to be a German name (Guttman). Another photograph illustrates piles of watermelons for sale (Fig. 12). The shared economic situation involves a collaboration between very different ethnic elements. Steiner's 1938 written account (see our discussion in Volume I, pp. 55-58) is largely preoccupied with a description of the successes and failures of the segregated education of gypsies which he also records visually (Figs. 14-15). In short, while not using the term, Steiner presents Ruthenia as a socially and culturally *plural* society, loosely integrated only by the reliance of its different components on the marketplace and market principle. Together the poems, the photographs and reportage project a nuanced picture of the themes which interested the young Franz Steiner as an emerging ethnographer. In terms of his anthropological development, we seem to witness Steiner combining the Viennese interest in material culture with a Malinowskian attention to synchronic functional connexions. Moreover he does so with particular attention to ethnic pluralism and its visual cues. Whilst we would make no grand claim for Steiner's photographic record, it is perhaps worth remarking as an aside, that the pictures of Uniate processions prefigure the work of the Czech photographer Markéta Luskačová, who began her career in the 1960s with a series of pictures which record the religious processions in neighbouring Slovakia.

Zionism, Political and Cultural Critique

No non-European power has ever built a colonial empire.
'Letter to Mr Gandhi'

The attempt to reevaluate Steiner's anthropology must also reassess his Judaism: his Jewish identity, the *galut* and the sufferings of the *Shoah* form the experiential and intellectual centre of his work. They are the fulcrum around which his other interests turn. Although these issues do not explicitly intrude on his anthropology (Steiner is too self-aware an epistemologist for that), they do inform his writings in countless ways, whether in the choice of the Romanies as a subject for study (as fellow Orientals), his thesis subject (which recalls the Jewish fate in Egypt), his grasp of taboo behaviour (which correlates to Jewish law), or his use of biblical exegesis; arguably, his critical method of weighing the value of opposing critical voices has a Talmudic streak. Steiner was active in the Zionist movement, co-founded a left-wing Zionist group in Oxford (volume I, pp. 55-58, above), and involved himself in Zionist politics before, during, and after the war. This side of Steiner's activities has yet to be studied, and at the present state of research, the available evidence is scanty. Yet even so, it must be considered, since Steiner's political writings, notably the essay on 'Orientpolitik', the 'Memorandum' and the 'Letter to Mr Gandhi', are intellectually inseparable, though methodologically distinct, from his anthropology. Indeed, the connexions fall further into place when one considers Steiner in the Oxford context. Steiner's 'Letter to Mr Gandhi', as a political text, comes into biographical and intellectual focus when one recalls Steiner's close friendship with another student of Radcliffe-Brown, M.N. Srinivas; Srinivas's *Religion and Society among the Coorgs of Southern India* (1952), like Steiner's thesis on slavery, derived from a Radcliffe-Brown-supervised dissertation. In his argument in the 'Letter', Steiner appears to foreshadow elements of Louis Dumont's contrast between *Homo Hierarchicus* (in India) and *Homo Aequalis* (in Europe). Whether or not a direct link can be made between Steiner's thought and Dumont's theory remains open. Although Steiner and Dumont were Oxford colleagues and friends in the final year of Steiner's life, Dumont informed us that the brevity of their time together precluded serious intellectual influence (PC). Steiner's 'Letter to Mr Gandhi' gains additional interest when we recognise that as an anthropologist he was situated between two foundational figures in the sociology of the sub-continent.

An untitled, undated and unsigned proclamation in German, beginning 'We, the Oxford group of the "Association of Jewish Refugees"' which survives in Steiner's *Nachlaß* offers us a moment from which to survey Steiner's Zionism. Judging by the typeface, the document appears to have been produced on Steiner's typewriter; further context is largely surmise. Judging from its content, the proclamation belongs to the middle years of the war: presumably later than the publication of Vladimir Jabotinsky's *The Jewish War Front* which appeared in February 1940, and earlier than the formation of front line Jewish Brigade Groups in 1944 (Gilbert 1998: 109-10, 117). Some time around 1943 seems likely, the year in which Steiner became a founder-member of the Oxford Branch of Poale Zion (the Jewish Socialist Labour Party). The proclamation was probably produced for Poale Zion and is the closest account we possess to a public statement of Steiner's political views during the war. However, just because this document has come down to us as an anonymous joint proclamation, its views may well represent a compromise. The proclamation invokes its signatories' 'individual' relation to 'political' Judaism by defining the Jews as a 'community of fate' or *Schicksalsgemeinschaft* – a term which has since gained some currency in Holocaust studies. As a consequence of this 'fate', the text asserts that 'political collective measures' (*politische Kollektivmaßnahmen*) are required. The link to Steiner's writings appears in the stress on 'suffering', central to the 'Letter to Georg Rapp' (pp. 115-22, below), which here provides the rationale for collective political action. The document makes three key points which were typical demands of the period: (1) The extremity of the suffering that the Jews are currently experiencing as a community; (2) That the attacks causing this suffering are directed at the community as a whole; (3) That the relevant non-Jewish authorities in Britain have recognised the nature of their attackers and the collective nature of the Jewish plight. These assertions are then followed by three key demands: (1) That the post-war 'rehabilitation' of the Jews be effected by coordinated relocation of Jewish refugees in Palestine; (2) That Jews be permitted to fight during the war with 'human dignity' *'as Jews in Jewish fighting units'* and be permitted to participate in Civil Defence and the Home Guard; (3) That the group will fully assist in, and wishes full consideration of, what in English are called 'Training schemes for post-war relief for Jewish refugees'. Several points stand out: the rejection of outright opposition to fighting of any kind, contrary to the anti-war posture Steiner endorses when speaking as a poet in *Conquests* (Steiner 1964: 47); the identification of the individual with a suffering collective; the dual wartime perspective directed at both the host nation and the enemy; and the long-term Zionist goal.

We have already referred to the impact made on the youthful Steiner by his study of Arabic at the Hebrew University of Jerusalem (Volume I, pp. 38-42, above). The School of Oriental Studies which he attended had been founded in 1926, and its Acting Director at the time of Steiner's studentship was Professor L.A. Meyer – a specialist in the art and archaeology of the Near East (Spiegel 1950). Franz Steiner's host in Jerusalem, Shmuel Hugo Bergman, was a member of *Brit-Shalom* (Covenant of Peace), and Steiner may even have been present when meetings were held at Bergman's home. It is noticeable that Steiner's own views seem broadly to have accorded with the views of this organisation and it is, therefore, to Brit Shalom that we turn first as the context for Steiner's political writings.

Brit Shalom had been founded in 1925 by Arthur Ruppin and proposed binationalism with equal rights as a solution to the conflicting aspirations of Arabs and Jews in Palestine. While recognising that 'the significance of Brit Shalom lies in its failure', in his history of Zionist thought David Goldberg adds that 'it represented the one brief, genuine attempt to bridge the chasm between Zionism's aims and recognition of the indigenous population's rights' (1996: 164). Among other notable spokesmen for Brit Shalom were Martin Buber and Judah Magnes (Goldberg 1996: 165) who, like Steiner, were to address corrective letters to Mahatma Gandhi protesting his statements about the rights of Jews in Palestine (Shimoni 1977: 40-46). Although Brit Shalom petered out in the mid-1930s, several of its members – including Buber, Gershom Scholem and Magnes – continued to advocate rapprochement between Jews and Arabs during the following years. These may be the specific strands of Zionism hinted at in Michael Hamburger's general account:

> It seems that ever since his stay in Palestine in 1930 and 1931 Steiner had been a Zionist of a sort, believing or feeling himself to be an 'Oriental' on grounds of descent, though he had grown up in a largely assimilated family and, as a writer in German or English, could not have been more indebted culturally to precedents and traditions that were not Jewish. [However,] his Zionism differed from the prevalent one in positing the integration and partnership of the Arabs in any Jewish nation established in the common homeland of these ethnically related 'oriental' peoples. ... The Palestine in which he had felt more at home than anywhere else was that of the pioneer settlers and the 'kibbutz' movement. (Hamburger 1992: 13)

Although Hamburger's view seems valid, it tends to conflate Steiner's pre- and post-war ideas. The question of Steiner's Jewish and Oriental identities also needs to be addressed with a little more precision, not least since these were the grounds of his identification with the objects of anthropological investigation. Notwithstanding a consistency of his concerns, the more than two decades between Steiner's Palestinian sojourn and his death could not, indeed did not, pass without effect upon his Jewish identity, his Zionism or his notion of Orientalism. Clearly something more than 'descent' is at issue here. In his post-war 'Letter to Mr Gandhi' Steiner approvingly cites the vision of Asher Ginsberg or Ahad Ha-am ('One of the people'), an advocate of Jewish cultural regeneration and critic of Jewish nationalism modelled on the West. Ahad Ha-am was disturbed by the attitude of Jewish settlers towards Arabs, which he thought resulted from the prejudices of European-assimilated Jews. The particular target of his opposition was Theodor Herzl – founder of political Zionism – to whom, he believed, the Jewishness of a Palestinian state was less important than its statehood. One implication of Ahad Ha-am's views was to make European cultures appear alien to Jews, although many of them had lived within and contributed to European cultures for centuries. His supporters on some of these issues included Martin Buber, hence a link with Brit Shalom (Goldberg 1996: Chapter 7). Integration in some kind of 'Semitic symbiosis' seemed a logical implication of these views, and was explicit in the views of Dr Nissim Malul, a Palestinian-born Sephardi Jew, who maintained that immersion in Arab culture was a prerequisite to the revival of Hebrew culture (Goldberg 1996: 163). Steiner's advocacy of the idea of Jews as an Oriental people, as well as his decision to study Arabic at the Hebrew University of Jerusalem, seem very much at home in this intellectual company. But the modernising programme of his pre-war writing about Palestine seems somewhat at odds with his later championing of a theocratic state.

Between 1933, at Hitler's accession to power, and 1936 an influx of more than 164,000 Jews into Palestine had almost doubled the Jewish population. The Arab response was a six-month general strike, an economic boycott, demonstrations and what came to be known as the 'Arab-revolt' in which hundreds of Arabs, Britons, and Jews were killed or wounded (Goldberg 1996: 201). Jewish opinion was sharply divided over an appropriate reaction. The article published under the title 'Orientpolitik' in 1936 (pp. 107-11, below) first appeared in the periodical *Selbstwehr* (Self Defence) which had been founded in 1907 to propagate a new, Jewish assertiveness, albeit without proposing a single fixed ideology (Kieval 1988: 119-23). This provides a local context for Steiner's reflections: we find him in his mid-twenties, reacting to British policy towards the Palestine Mandate and Nazi propaganda in Europe by advocating a policy of Jewish cultural propaganda to appeal to modernising elements in the Arab world, especially Egypt. His analysis falls into line with the prevailing mood of the times: 'The Yishuv, the Jewish community [in Palestine], prided itself on the modernity of its life and culture' (Gilbert 1998: 78). Steiner argues that Jewish scholarship, learning and science should be directed towards the solution of Oriental agrarian problems; Egyptian culture should be represented by an Egyptian Institute in Tel Aviv. The acceptance by Jews in Palestine both of their Oriental environment and their shared cause with modernising, nationalist Arabs was superior to violent action against either Arabs or British. In short, in 'Orientpolitik' Steiner advocates a search for solidarity with Arabs as fellow colonised peoples aspiring to modernity, and in this he envisages a special scientific and cultural role for the Hebrew University. Steiner advocated a *realpolitik* of Arab-Jewish rapprochement, apparently as co-modernising, colonised peoples, rather than as fellow Orientals. Thanks to his Palestinian sojourn, Steiner was aware of current, and practical, considerations. As in his paper on Ruthenian gypsies two years later, education is crucial to his modernising vision. The University on Mount Scopus is central to his argument – no doubt on the basis of his experience in Hugo Bergman's company as well as in the university itself; and in this connexion, he advocates *agrarian* studies at a University level as a prerequisite of the rapprochement between Arabs and Jews, with the Academy as a meeting-place. In terms of then current concerns, intensive farming for Palestinian Arabs would also have removed one of the arguments in favour of restricting Jewish immigration: land shortage. In 1940, the University School of Agriculture was indeed founded (Reifenberg 1950); however, in contrast to Steiner's goal, the School does not appear to have set much store by cooperation with the Arabs in setting its agenda.

Between 'Orientpolitik' and the 'Letter to Mr Gandhi' lie the war years: the experience of the attempted annihilation of the Jews in Europe and the murder of Steiner's own family. As we recounted in Volume I, the darkest years of his life wrought a transformation in the optimistic, confident young scholar, and eventually hastened his death. Without an anthropological mentor after 1942, and upon the loss of his dissertation and research that same year, Steiner gave himself over to intensive recasting of his identity in the process of writing his *Conquests* and a torrent of aphoristic – often scathing – observations on art, life and science. His intense and taxing friendship with Elias Canetti provided him with an intellectual partner who in many ways shared his fate as the full horror of the *Shoah* became apparent. Canetti abjured creative writing during the war. Steiner internalised the suffering of his people. His views were to emerge more profound but also more extreme.

This is the background to Steiner's letter of 1946 to Gandhi. The immediate political context of Steiner's letter to the Indian leader concerned comments published in Gandhi's English-language journal *Harijan* for 21 July 1946 (p. 229) on the day before the bombing in Jerusalem by Irgun of the south wing of the King David Hotel in which ninety-one people (Arab, British and Jewish) died (Gilbert 1998: 134-35). These comments were reprinted elsewhere, and the London *Jewish Chronicle* for 26 July 1946 carried an abridged version of Gandhi's comments on a front-page dominated by negative reaction to the bombing. Although the action occurred after Gandhi's comments had been written, it could hardly have failed to be part of the context of Steiner's own 'Letter'.

Gandhi's 1946 pronouncement in *Harijan* was to be the last of his published contributions devoted specifically to the debate on the Jews and Palestine. However, it was far from being the first, nor – as we have noted above – was Steiner the first Jewish intellectual provoked to address a response. Although Gandhi's views are not our central concern here, a few words about them may be in order. Gandhi's first public statement on Zionism was made as early as 1921 after the abolition of the Caliphate in the wake of Turkey's defeat in the First World War. He was concerned that Muslim sovereignty of the Holy Land should not be ceded as a result of the war, a stance that Gideon Shimoni suggests cannot be dissociated from Gandhi's desire to demonstrate solidarity with fellow-Indian Muslims (1977: 22-23). In terms of its fundamental morality, Gandhi's opposition to Jewish violence was part of his uncompromising opposition to all violence (Brown 1989: 321).

On the basis of his experience of British colonialism (in both South Africa and India) Gandhi proposed *satyagraha* 'the active nonviolent resistance of the strong' as a means to overcome domination. The principled and the pragmatic met in Gandhi's belief that nonviolence would work only if practised as 'an article of faith' (Dalton 1993: 137). It is difficult not to believe that in matters of fact Gandhi knew less than he believed. Consider for instance his statement of 20 November 1938 printed in *Harijan* of 26 November (ten days after Kristallnacht) that 'The Jews of Germany can offer Satyagraha under infinitely better auspices than the Indians of South Africa' (quoted extensively in Chadha 1997: 366; full text in Bartolf 1998: 14 f.). This suggests that the British Empire and the German Third Reich would react similarly to nonviolent resistance.

Martin Buber and J.L. Magnes responded from Jerusalem to Gandhi's ideas in February 1939 (Bartolf 1998: 16-40). It now seems established definitely that Gandhi received neither of their letters (Dalton 1993: 229-30, fn 172). Given that the letters were published in the same year as a single volume in Jerusalem and in the context of his strong Zionist links, it is probable that Steiner knew, or at least knew about, these initiatives (Shimoni 1977: 40, fn 88). Following the break-up of Brit Shalom, Buber and Magnes became members of a 'small nonconformist circle of Zionist intellectuals in Palestine who called themselves *Ha'ol* (the Yoke). ... They were untiringly devoted to Jewish-Arab rapprochement and peaceful co-existence, some of them had long admired Gandhi' (Shimoni 1977: 40-41). On many grounds, they seem conducive intellectual and moral company for the exiled Steiner in England. Buber and Magnes raised a variety of points with Gandhi including the Jewish claim to land in Palestine, the unviability of nonviolent resistance to Nazism, the incomparability of the Indian and South African situations with that in Germany, and the lack of even-handedness with which the Mahatma treated Jewish and Arab interests (Shimoni 1977: 41-46). A further effort at dialogue made by the American Hayim Greenberg, and pointing out – among other arguments – that 'a Jewish Gandhi in Germany' would function for about five minutes before being murdered, elicited a principled reply from Gandhi that the truth of his position was unaffected by this (Shimoni 1977: 47-49). Numerous further personal contacts were organised subsequently to try to effect a change of heart on the part of the Indian leader, but without success.

Steiner's letter is therefore a late contribution – one written in 1946 after unequivocal revelation of the facts concerning the virtual annihilation of Jewry in Europe – to a tradition of persuasion in which Jewish intellectuals sought to influence a major and admired figure in public life who, they felt, ought to have been more understanding of the Jewish plight. It is a contribution, moreover, completely unre-marked in the literature. We do not know whether, like the letters from Buber and Magnes, it failed to reach its intended recipient. Steiner had no doubt that it did arrive, relying on an Indian intermediary, though our attempts to identify him have so far failed. Steiner, as we have seen, was an admirer not only of Gandhi but of Indian civilisation, and not just as a subject of his academic curiosity but also because Indians enjoyed a kinship with Jews under Steiner's very broad definition of Oriental peoples. In contemporary terms, Steiner's critique of Gandhi might seem to come from a perspective identifiable in certain respects as 'subaltern' or 'Orientalist'; but his position is complex, as is that of Zionism within such a politics. Steiner's argument – which is notice-ably more philosophical than that of Gandhi's previous correspon-dents – has two main strands. One might be considered the more fundamental since it rejoins Steiner's understanding of the particu-larities of the growth of Western civilisation: a civilisation that he sees as fundamentally predatory, in terms both territorial and epistemic, upon civilisations that differ from it. His other arguments might be termed contingent in that they relate to twentieth-century political tactics involving Europeans, Arabs and Jews: or more broadly Euro-peans and non-Europeans. The link is made when the contingent issues are seen as symptomatic of the long process.

Steiner's argument rests on his proposition that the Jews are an Ori-ental people. In treating them instead as a European people, Gandhi accepts by default the position of the West, and sees them through Western Christian (specifically English Protestant) eyes. This proposi-tion asks us to accept a series of essentialisations which later scholar-ship finds intensely problematic. Steiner, however, draws upon an argument we shall find at greater length in the earlier extended apho-rism 'On the Process of Civilisation': the Jews as a collectivity consti-tute an alterity internalised by the West in the course of its expansion. Like Adorno and Horkheimer, Steiner claims that anti-Semitism is a feature of modernity, and here there is a signal convergence between his work and the near-contemporary thinking of the Frankfurt school; but whereas Horkheimer and Adorno – to single out only one possible connexion – locate the origins of what they call 'bourgeois' anti-Semi-tism – Marxist fashion – in a 'specific economic cause' (1988: 182), Steiner treats anti-Semitism generally as a function of European impe-rialism. Steiner goes on to argue that a long process of European, lat-terly Christian and Western, expansion (imperialism and colonialism) is the unifying thread from the expansion of the Roman Empire (described as its first brutal shape: 'European might is built up on the ruins of our temple'; see p. 144), to later Christendom (including the Crusades) and Western Imperialism. Territorial aggression and civilisational domination have gone hand in hand both externally and internally. Gandhi's sense of the Jews as a European-sponsored people in conflict with an Asiatic (Arab) people derives from a misrecognition of this process in its *longue durée*. Aside from this fundamental argument, Steiner's contingent arguments concern the Balfour Declaration, legality, military capacity, the attitude of particular Arab statesmen and so on that, albeit historically interesting, are of less intrinsic complexity as sociological ideas.

It is in terms of his fundamental argument that Steiner counters Gandhi's assessment of the viability of nonviolence as a tactic for the Jews. In order to adopt nonviolence one would need to be assured of the commitment on the part of the dominant – who were to be resisted – to the continued existence of those they oppressed. Only under such a circumstance can nonviolence be an effective expression of the moral coherence and fortitude of a collectivity. But the West has no such commitment to the cultural or physical persistence of the Jews within its domain. Christianity depends intrinsically on a superior understanding of Jewish tradition; a cultural and epistemic violence is the foundation of the relation between the two traditions. Furthermore, Christians do not wish to use Jews to their own ends but to eject and eradicate them. Thus the conditions under which passive resistance strengthens the moral will of the community (while the use of violence necessarily weakens it) cannot hold (as they did in India or might have done had the English employed passive resistance against the Germans during the Second European War). Victorious martyrdom is no option. Steiner's friend, Anand Chandavarkar, was struck that:

> Steiner was a great admirer of general Yigael Yadin, Commander of the Haganah and valiant defender of Israel whom he regarded as a splendid exemplar of the Zionist ideal of the life of thought (archeology and biblical studies) allied to the life of action ... .(Chandavarkar Ms 1996: 2)

How could Franz Steiner maintain that the Jews in Europe are an Asiatic people? Steiner introduces an original perspective onto the question of Jewish identity by examining the issue in sociological terms, focusing on the issue of 'value' and comparing Indian and Jewish society. The Jews' 'Asiatic' character, Steiner argues, is not a matter of race, but a matter of 'the observable relations between individuals and the value attached to *them*, as differing from the value attached to the achievements of the individuals' (original emphasis). Steiner's invocation of 'values' here indicates a convergence between his religious, anthropological and political views. Jewish custom, he claims, was 'disgusting' to the European: the Jews did not distinguish between the political and religious, they strictly maintained their dietary laws to prevent interdining, they severely forbade intermarriage. In India, this would have been unremarkable since Jews would have been treated as another caste. According to Steiner, it is the nature of the process by which alterity is encompassed, dominated and rejected that constitutes the specificity of Western civilisation. Increasing individualism, technological capacity, and expansionism are intrinsic processual characteristics of this civilisation, as also are its human and cultural consequences. Power and domination are defining features of Western civilisation.

The next step in Steiner's argument follows logically from his having derived contrary civilisational forms – European and Asian – and argued that the former tended to encompass and dominate the latter: Jewish 'emancipation' has to be conceived as a mistaken assimilation of alien, European values. Now, 'emancipation' had been the very term Steiner used with taken-for-granted, positive, connotations when discussing the plans for the emancipation of gypsies in Ruthenia a decade earlier; the critique of modernisation on which Steiner now launches is also a critique of his own earlier views:

> With the Ghettos we left a world that 'belonged to the past' – as many of us imagined. Such delusions we shared with many of our brethren of the other Oriental nations, in Turkey, in Syria, in Egypt, and in your own country. Like they did (though later) we thought of loosening the burden of our tradition, of opening up to 'modern' life; but while they, with the new misconceptions stood after all on their own ground, and in their own social reality which sooner or later must call them to order and to a creative compromise – we stood naked, unprotected in foreign, in European societies which we tried to imitate. (p. 142, below)

From this followed another mistake: the attempt to achieve a European-style state in Palestine, which amounted to no less than the adoption of an 'alien fanaticism' (p. 142, below). Comparing Theodor Herzl's desire to imitate the European state (even if in East Africa) with Ahad Ha-Am's project of cultural revivalism, Steiner argues that the outcome to this fundamental struggle between emulation and withdrawal will depend on struggles between East and West in a triple sense: between Eastern and Western Jewry, the Jews and Europe, and between solidarity with other Asian nations 'against the European ideology in us'. Steiner's analysis now seems innocent of the many problems entailed by the assertion that the contemporary authenticity of cultures can be secured by reference to their historical differences, and correlatively that their contemporary 'inauthenticity' can be derived counter-factually from the way an authentic tradition should have developed were it not dominated by or imitative of alien influences. None the less, his analysis proceeds powerfully to foresee the decline of

European civilisation and to explain European fear of the revival of Hebrew voices in terms of this decline. His conclusion – the 'new village communities … and noncompetitive economic units' hailed as Asiatic achievements of both India and Palestine (p. 145, below) – seems to hark back to 'Orientpolitik' a decade earlier; but there the reference to collectives and cooperatives had been made within a wider framework of Jewish (socialist or social democratic) modernisation; here the appeal is to Oriental collectivism. The 'Letter to Mr. Gandhi' represents a considerable radicalisation of Steiner's ideas. A positive theory of Orientalism now occupies the argumentative space previously filled by endorsement of Arab modernisers. As we know from another source, by the 1950s Steiner believed in the necessity of a theocratic state in Israel: Kenelm Burridge records that on this point, 'Franz was adamant, surprisingly sweeping and firmly assertive: "Israel must be a theocracy," he declared very forcibly. "Not a secular state: a theocracy" or it was "doomed, would founder"' (Burridge: PC). Looking ahead to our discussion of Steiner's lectures on 'Tabu', it will be difficult in the light of this evidence for future readers again to imagine that his motivation in exploring the investment of boundaries with dangers was exclusively scholarly. Scholarly it may have been, but *Taboo* was also one of Steiner's most considered statements in critique of Western modernism and in defence of non-Western values. The theory of civilisational growth that undergirds Steiner's 'Letter' as well as *Taboo* find its fullest expression in what is by far the longest and, judging by the fact that Steiner placed it among the first in his own selection of aphorisms, among the most considered of his short essays, reprinted here as 'On the Process of Civilisation'. This essay offers a sweeping view of the development of Western civilisation which further clarifies the broad intellectual context in which Steiner conceived the posthumously published Oxford lectures on 'Tabu'.

Pending further research, our account of Steiner's developing Zionist views depends on a few explicitly political writings connected with a background knowledge of his anthropology: a published 1936 appeal to fellow European Jews, a war-time proclamation apparently addressed to British authorities (was it read or even sent?), and a letter to Mr Gandhi (did he receive it?). A final view derives from an undated 'Memorandum', which can be placed by the reference to its having been written 'two months' before the Asian Relations Conference which took place from 23 March-2 April 1947 (Gopal 1975: 344-45). Steiner refers to 'invitations' to attend this conference being sent to the Yishuv (Jewish settlers in Palestine) in September 1946. To what audience Steiner submitted this hitherto unrecorded document we do not know; presumably an Oxford- or London-based Zionist organisation. It bears all the signs of Steiner's authorship: the Orientalism, the cultural Zionism, the appeal to India – all this is familiar. What is new, is the added dimension of the Chinese connexion, which brings yet another of Steiner's long-standing cultural enthusiasms into precise political play, but also reflects the appointment of the Chinese to the United Nations' Trusteeship Commission (which had responsibility for Palestine). Steiner has reverted to the enthusiasm for educational plans that he evinced in 1936; however, this time the plan is not for initiatives involving Muslim Arabs, but rather a programme that is targeted globally towards the major (non-Muslim) Asian nations (India and China), and locally towards the non-Muslim minorities in the Middle East: the Chinese are to be informed about 'our post-biblical moral teachings'; India is to be enlightened by 'a book "Jewish Women of Palestine"' and so on. For an 'Asiatic Monroe Doctrine' to work to the advantage of the Jewish community in Palestine, the Jews had to be accepted as an Oriental people. Steiner's views on civilisational development now converged with his *realpolitik*. The State of Israel was not to be founded until following year, but by comparison with the 1936 'Orientpolitik', the 1947 'Memorandum' makes little positive reference to Muslim Arabs in general, or the Palestinian Arabs in particular. Something of the distinction between modernising and fundamentalist Arab states may survive in Steiner's reference to the 'surprise' of immediate success in negotiations with Egypt, but the tone of the document derives more from the pervasive threats associated with Pan-Arabism and Islam. If, as seems attested by our contemporary witness, Steiner's advocacy of a modernising state in Israel had yielded to promotion of a 'theocratic state', then it is not difficult to understand why he has little to say about Arab-Jewish co-operation. On the other hand, it needs to be considered that the 'Memorandum' singles out the work of the socialist A.D. Gordon to be spread among the Arabs. Gordon's belief in a cosmopolitanism that encompassed individual nationalisms, what he called *ad-adam* ('people humanity' or 'people incarnating humanity') was the basis for an inclusive approach to Arab-Jewish relations (Bergman 1961: 114-17). In practical terms, Gordon believed that 'wherever settlements are founded, a specific share of the land must be assigned to the Arabs from the outset'. This rapprochement, in Gordon's view, rested on universal foundations: the cosmic integration of man within nature represents the universal order within which individual nations should cooperate. Perhaps one here glimpses an intimation of Steiner's own, never formulated linking of his political beliefs within a wider religious context. Yet, Steiner never wholly turns his back on the modernist project: his scholarly work remains wedded to methods of rational argument, to logic and scientific standards. Even his pan-Asianism becomes grounds for another educational programme. Steiner never visited the

State of Israel founded in 1948, despite invitations to do so. His attitude towards it remains a closed book to us, although we might infer
his support from the fact that the Hebrew University of Jerusalem was
left his collection of scientific books under the terms of his will. We
cannot say for certain whether Steiner's advice, either before or after
the war, made much impact, but there is no evidence it did. Where,
especially before the war, he advocated rapprochement with the Pales-
tinians, the rifts then deepened; and where, particularly after the war,
he advocated an alignment of Israel with the Asian world, and a
recognition by Jews of their Oriental identity, the State has remained
tied to the West. In this sense, his politics have remained as unfulfilled
as all the other projects he left incomplete.

Steiner on Slavery

Everying grows silent.

Conquests, X, 'The Wheels'

Lost in the early years and resurrected after the peace, one project
spans Steiner's war years. Perhaps it was not his central concern during the war, but there are indications he continued to work towards its
recuperation. The Oxford doctoral thesis, 'A Comparative Study of the
Forms of Slavery', begun in 1939 and submitted in 1949, was the
chief object of Steiner's anthropological labours for a decade, and had
the widest ramifications for his mature social anthropology. It would
be fascinating to be able to follow the tortuous path from its genesis to
what is more accurately called its 'submission' than its 'completion'.
The dissertation is a turning point in his anthropological studies, and
branches out into numerous areas that occupy his mature thought:
topics like method and comparison, kinship relations and the problem
of labour all find a recognisable treatment here, not to mention
Steiner's preoccupation with the history of his discipline or Aristotle as
a sociologist.

The papers on slavery comprise four large files (DLA, S 24)[1] containing a great number of notes, which are certainly enough for a
major book. Besides this collection, there are two more convolutes
(DLA, S 25 and S27) containing several folders on servile institutions.
Among these we find the following:

---

1. As Steiner's papers have yet to be catalogued, we refer to them according to the
   archive box numbers (S24, S25 etc.) in which they are currently housed in the
   Deutsches Literaturarchiv (=DLA), Schiller Nationalmuseum, Marbach am Neckar.
   We indicate some of Steiner's folders by their numbers, others by colour.

Folder I: Asia, including Mongolia, Tibet, China, Korea, and Japan.
Folder II: Africa: North Africa to West Africa (subdivided by people).
Folder III: Africa: West Bantu (subdivided geographically), Nilotic, Nilo-Hamitic, non-Bantu Lacustrine and sub-Lacustrine area.
Folder IV: Africa: South Bantu (sub-divided geographically and by people).
Folder V: Aboriginal North America.
Folder VI: Terminology of servility (including derivation of 'slave').
Folder VII: General Sociological Problems bearing on Inequality (including definition of labour; division of labour; division of labour by gender; artisanship; class, exchange, wealth, luxury, capitalism, etc.)
Folder VIII: Servile symbiosis, extra-tribal patronage and similar relationships. (S 25).

This is a major body of systematically organised notes and excerpts. The approach indicates a detailed scientific method – effectively an eighteenth-century taxonomy, enriched by a Goethean understanding of life-forms as displaying a living morphology. If this pattern of arranging materials follows that of the lost draft, we may infer that Steiner will not only have read widely for the first version, but will have developed some form of analytic. The structure of the folders stands in close relation to the thesis which Steiner submitted: folders I-V are organised by geographical region. Folder VI corresponds to the opening discussion of slavery which we reprint, folder VIII corresponds to the closing section of the dissertation on this subject, and folder VII indicates material relevant not only to the dissertation but also to several lecture series (notably that on labour). There does not here seem to be much evidence of the 'missing' five sections of the *magnum opus* on slavery that Steiner planned. To judge by the working method apparent here and elsewhere, it seems that the manner of Steiner's systematic, reading, excerpting, organising and classifying material itself implicated an analysis, which laid the foundation for the discursive representation. There is practically never any evidence of drafting, writing, rewriting, etc. All the emphasis therefore falls on a quasi-scientific collection of materials. On this point, at least, Steiner will have been with Radcliffe-Brown regarding the 'scientific' character of his discipline. From the evidence concerning Steiner's working method, we can also understand how Radcliffe-Brown could be so confident that the thesis was almost finished at the time when it was lost, even though there is no evidence of actual writing. Writing-up will have been a relatively simple procedure for one as versed in writing as Franz Steiner, and indeed it is attested by H.G. Adler that Steiner penned the final version extremely quickly (H.G. Adler Ms 1953: 10v). Yet if the organisation of material seems a throw-back to the comparative ethnology of an earlier age, inspection of the thesis itself shows how far the study departed from Steiner's previous ethnological mode. What we appear to have lost is the encyclopaedic account of slavery, since some topics mentioned in terms of his 'loss' are missing from the 1949 dissertation; yet other points are probably new including, perhaps, the focus on Africa, the concern with the anthropological investigation of systems of inequality, and with formal sociology – specifically, with the treatment of attachment/detachment.

It is necessary to say something about the thesis in its entirety since we are able to include only a short excerpt from it. One of the surprises in store for any reader of Steiner's thesis is the fact that its content scarcely matches its title – or the material in the notes. For his abridgement of Steiner's work, Paul Bohannan added the words 'A prolegomena to ...' to the original title. And this is just since, as both Bohannan and Steiner note, the thesis never actually gets as far as 'a comparative study' at all! The sheer variety and extent of theories and materials about slavery, writes Steiner, were so considerable that he eventually submitted only the first three introductory sections of a planned eight-part comparative survey. We doubt the others were ever written. The *Nachlaß*, which contains so very complete a collection of materials, contains no evidence of further passages. Of the projected eight parts, then, only three survive. Part I involves a discussion of:

> the meaning of the word <u>slave</u> and the way contemporary conditions had impressed themselves on the various definitions attempted; then the object of inquiry is as far as possible narrowed down and the question is asked, and to some extent answered, how institutions could be, for the purpose of *formal sociology*, fitted into a system of the institutions of social inequality. ... As labour functions matter very much in servile institutions, a short survey is made of theories about labour, and the organisation of labour is analysed in reference to servility. (Steiner Ms 1949a: ii; underline original, italics added.)

In the section from Part I we reproduce, Steiner offers a lucid explanation of the relation between the ethnographic and anthropological uses of the term 'slavery'. This echoes his earlier account of 'superstition' (Volume I, pp. 223-29) and anticipates his later method in treating 'taboo'. In contemporary parlance, he notes what might be called the 'partial connexions' between different phenomena identified as 'slavery' from a particular starting point – namely the Western concept. What remains interesting about Steiner's treatment is that he is able to recognise the historical, perspectival and thus interested character of his starting-point – the term 'slave' – without embracing an entirely deconstructive logic that would dissolve the category as a focus of investigation. Instead, he situates his concern with slavery within the scholarly discourse more broadly concerned with forms of social inequality.

The succeeding sections aim to classify some of the characteristic ways in which 'labour' may be organised, and so draw attention to the more common features of slave labour. Many of these ideas have become more widely known than the thesis itself thanks to being included in the Oxford lectures from which Paul Bohannan edited the article 'Towards a Classification of Labour' (pp. 174-90, below).

The two remaining sections of the thesis (II and III) do not deal with slavery at all. They are about institutions which are easily confused with slavery because they have 'some elements in common with servile institutions'. It is somewhat unhelpful that Steiner, contrary to his own insights, persists in calling these institutions 'pre-servile' – presumably thinking of the German prefix '*vor-*' and using his term in a typological, not a genetic sense accordingly – while vigorously denying any necessary developmental link between them and servile institutions themselves.

Two pages of Steiner's short introduction outline the remaining, unwritten (or perhaps lost), parts of the intended eight-section work. Comparing this organisation of materials with Steiner's arrangement of reading notes in files, readers will recognise a more advanced stage of composition in that Steiner's presentation has moved on from a purely geographical taxononomy into a systematic representation in terms of specific social institutions:

IV. Institutions outside class and caste structures (African, Indonesian, slave laws of the Pentateuch, early Mesopotamia).

V. Slavery conditioned by rank systems (Ashanti, Dahomey, NW American); pawning and debtor slavery of West Africa and Indonesia.

VI. Slave concubinage, as complementary marital institution and as institution of luxury; 'racialism' to be discussed, especially in the context of societies where dual descent means that 'emancipated slaves continue to be a different kind of human being and offspring by slave concubines are regarded as inferior'.

VII. Caste and slavery: Nepalese, Ancient Indian, Somali and Mauretanian institutions.

VIII. Complex class societies and their kinds of slavery: Ancient East, Roman slavery, the Aztec laws, and modern European plantation slavery.

A discourse will deal with the relation between the system of punishment existing in a society and its servile institutions, while another will indicate the social structures incompatible with slavery, comparing chiefly Southern Bantu cattle economy with the money economy of later capitalist society. (Steiner Ms 1949a: iii)

Comparing the files in Steiner's *Nachlaß* with the finished project, one senses a fault-line running through this work which may separate the lost dissertation's comparativistic ambition to include every available culture – a kind of ethnographic monumentalism, possibly conceived competitively as a counterpart to both Malinowski's intensive encyclopaedism and Radcliffe-Brown's partial comparativism, but also exhibiting a thoroughly scientific ambition towards completeness – from what his anthropology later became: a more sociological enterprise, focused less on empirically verifiable data than on conceptually graspable categories.

Even so, the outline is encyclopaedic and goes far beyond what might reasonably be contemplated for inclusion in a doctoral dissertation. Steiner intended to show through a typological analysis how *forms* of social inequality, including whatever it might make sense to call slavery in such different contexts, differed according to the most fundamental *institutions* of social inequality within a given society: rank, status, caste and class. The three completed sections constitute only a preamble to this – investigating forms of social inequality that fell short of slavery. But they resume the argumentative thread of both 'On the Process of Civilisation' and 'The Letter to Mr Gandhi'. By investigating 'pre-servile' institutions, Steiner develops his analysis of the social conditions under which *enduringly* servile relations might, or might not, be institutionalised. In so doing, he seeks to comprehend the West and (at least some of) its Others dialectically. In purely typological terms, 'pre-servile' institutions are anterior because the inequalities on which they rest are routinely overturned; servile institutions surmount these subversions with the effect that inequalities are permanently entrenched.

Drawing on his training in comparative philology and his expertise in ethnographic regions including those of Slav speakers, Steiner opens with the term 'slave' itself (Ms 1949a: 9ff.). He notes that 'slave' and 'slavery' entered various European languages during the Middle Ages and derive from the ethnic term *Slav*. They came to be applied to lawless, or 'a-legal', institutions that differed from then dominant servile institutions of serfdom, which were closely regulated in terms of rights and duties. Thus the term 'slavery' was used to label diverse historical phenomena with reference to an already existing field of values and differences. As the field of meanings changed so did the sense attributed to slavery: for instance, the campaign for the abolition of slavery occurred in the context of a general espousal of the contractual establishment of rights and duties – of which slavery seemed the antithesis. The development of the modern concept of 'slavery' thus appears as a dialectical correlative to the emergence of 'rights'. As

Steiner shows, the highly contextual character of the term made it very difficult to attribute to it an essentialised sense. It seemed thus intensely problematic to theorists naïvely trying to devise evolutionary accounts of the origins of slavery or of its original form. This opening is reflexive in the most valuable sense: it examines the shifting situatedness of the ordinary language term from which the comparative study both begins and departs.

Next follow the pages we reprint (Ms 1949a: 29-34). Here Steiner argues that the ambiguity of words like 'slavery' is a logical aspect of their very function. We use the same terms with a greater or lesser range of allusions. Moreover, this is affected by whether we know the term from our immediate social contexts (as we know 'marriage') or only from instances remote in time or space (as 'slavery'). We ought to realise that we cannot define the essence of marriage, we can ask only what our term 'marriage' signifies when we follow a skein of resemblances that lead from our initial word to a term in another social and cultural context. Because we know 'slavery' less immediately, Steiner claims, it is easier to fall into the trap of believing that it has some essential meaning. Steiner's linguistic analysis deftly homes in on a fundamental problem in sociological discourse that his contemporaries at Oxford had yet to realise. In the context of 1940s British social anthropology, the assurance of his analysis and its methodological sophistication are remarkable.

Steiner prefers to begin from a typology, or formal sociology, of power and social inequality and then to describe general patterns of association and the structural principles, such as rank, caste, class and servile institutions, which may be found jointly, and even conflictually, in specific societies. There are various affinities here. Focusing on 'power' may recall Steiner's shared concerns with Canetti, but quite unlike Canetti, and in a manner reminiscent of Weber, Steiner proceeds from one definition to the next in order to narrow the range of phenomena necessary for study; yet, despite the logical, deductive character of his analysis of concepts, Steiner actually proceeds in the body of his thesis by substantive (and it must be admitted wearyingly detailed) presentation of cases.

His definition of 'slavery', like his method, is innovative in its context, though fifty years on readers may be less quick to spot the originality. Definitionally, Steiner maintains that servile institutions are found wherever there are relations between two or more people in which one person exercises rights over the other that are not derived from kinship obligations and where these rights 'are maintained to the exclusion of similar rights of other people'. Such rights may concern only particular activities or they may approximate to whatever is the prevailing notion of ownership in the society: 'The only feature[s] common to all the institutions is that the relationship ... between the two people in question, establishe[s] the social status of the servile person' (Ms 1949a: 74), that this status has 'total social range' (i.e., is recognised throughout the society in question) and that it refers primarily to the relationship to a master (Ms 1949a: 74).

The servile institutions that fall within such a definition are much too varied to fit into a simple dichotomy between 'slavery' and 'serfdom'. However, it can be generalised that a slave is a kinless person: someone who has been detached from a kinship grouping and attached, on different terms, to another grouping. From this follows the need to look in particular at those societies where such processes were normal and occurred without supplies of slaves from outside that society. The degree both of inequality and its institutionalisation are variable (Ms 1949a: 77). In order to speak of servile institutions, inequalities must apply throughout a 'total social range'; it is not enough if they are limited to subgroupings as, for instance, when the status of a junior sibling is relevant only among family members. By 'institutional', Steiner seems to mean what we would describe as 'a necessary feature entailed by the structure of a social unit'. This can be explained by his own example: declassed women may become servile, but it is not obligatory for a family unit to have one such servile woman attached to it. There is no *institutional* requisite for family units to include a declassed, servile woman member. More generally, Steiner says that the rank-scale within the domestic unit is extended at both extremes of its range to attach both servile people and honoured guests without, however, incorporating them as members of the unit.

In addition to a typological account of social inequality, Steiner's analysis requires a 'typology of labour' as 'an activity, interdependent with other activities of other people' (Ms 1949a: 86), that has a 'socially patterned associative character' (Ms 1949a: 103). Following Malinowski's distinction between the organised co-performance of differentiated tasks and communal labour (that is identical common tasks performed by people together), Steiner generalises that servile labour is strongly but not wholly associated with the latter; as it is with a lack of control over the process of labouring, and with an abrogation of the normal gendered division of tasks such that servile men may find themselves performing tasks otherwise gendered as women's work. The relationship between servility as a social status, on the one hand, and the economic functions of kinds of labour, on the other, is not simple. As with the origin of slavery itself, Steiner argues that there exists a range of phenomena and relations requiring study rather than a set of *a priori* propositions to be illustrated.

To open Part II Steiner observes that there exist 'a number of institutions which have among themselves very little in common, while they have particular affinities to kinship organisation on the one hand, to servile institutions on the other' (Ms 1949a: 141) – i.e., the 'pre-servile relationships and institutions'. These differ from servile institutions most importantly in that 'they lack certain other structural elements that would make the *potestas* exercised, the rights enjoyed, a permanent institution of social inequality which is inherent in a social system' (Ms 1949a: 141). Steiner's completed account consists almost solely of such pre-servile institutions (although, as noted above, he makes no assumption that servile institutions necessarily develop from them). What transpires is a survey of mechanisms related to kinship which underwrite forms of social inequality.

Paul Bohannan's abridgement of the work (Ms 1957) organised Part II into four sections, the first three of which give a good sense of the content covered by Steiner:

VI. Detached persons: orphans and widows.
VII. Detached persons: captives.
VIII. Detached persons: outcasts and the problem of asylum.

In this formal delineation of social types and exploration of their entailments, Steiner's approach is highly reminiscent of Simmel. A familiar feature (e.g., widowhood) is shown to belong to a broader recognisable form of sociation (detachment and reattachment) which also includes familiar forms that we might otherwise have thought dissimilar (e.g., outcasts). The analysis here (as, for instance, in Simmel's excursus on 'The Stranger') reveals similarity at the level of a sociology of forms, and shows that the form described exists in a tension of opposites (for 'The Stranger' the conjunction of closeness and distance; for the widow the conjunction of detachment and attachment) (see Green 1988: 133). Chapters proceed by ethnographic illustrations rather than abstractly: we learn about the sacrificial status of the captive among Tupinamba, and the regulations concerning orphans in ancient Athens, the laws governing concubinage with prisoners in Deuteronomy, etc., as much as anything, to demonstrate the different ways that the processes of detachment and attachment may be institutionalised without involving slavery.

Steiner draws upon a vocabulary about to be introduced to a wider anthropological readership by Laura Bohannan to distinguish different sorts of rights in women (L. Bohannan 1949). Laura Bohannan's analysis had been presented to considerable acclaim at a seminar – probably one run by Meyer Fortes in 1948 (Mary Douglas: PC). We know that she and Franz Steiner enjoyed an especially close intellectual relation, not least because she spoke German, shared his wider reading in German, and read Simmel and other sociological texts in the original (Laura Bohannan: PC). Steiner may have been present at her seminar presentation, and his thesis (submitted in the same year as Bohannan's article was published) acknowledges her permission to use the unpublished manuscript. Bohannan herself termed control over the sexual, domestic and labour functions of a woman rights *in uxorem*, the filiation of children she distinguished as a right *in genetricem*. This distinction was a significant step towards the more general recognition of the partibility of the person into elements – a point that both Steiner and Bohannan could have developed from Simmel's *Soziologie* – and therefore of the ways in which such elements could be transacted. This is what Steiner calls the 'apportionment of detached persons' (Ms 1949a: 251). In the case of a female captive who is made kinless, all rights accrue to her husband; the case of a free wife differs because she is not rendered kinless by the transferral of all rights in her. However, as Steiner rightly notes, there is a close relation between the mechanisms of kinship and servility in such cases; both belong to the regime of circulation of values, in this case valued rights in people, within the society. A similar relation might be noted between the transference of male slaves and palace servants in those chiefly societies in Africa where boys are transferred to the *potestas* of the chief. The way in which Steiner generalised Laura Bohannan's distinction between rights transferred in marriage was of a piece with his view of the person as a complex entity (in itself akin to a small society diverse in origin and complex in structure). We revert to this aspect of his thought, which recalls Goethe's morphology and Mach's psychology, when we discuss Steiner's *Conquests*.

Steiner's 'Discourse on Aristotle's "theory of slavery"', one of the several somewhat loosely integrated, long 'discourses' – i.e., excursions – in his dissertation, considers Aristotle's theory of powers and its relation to the types of authority a person could exercise over others (Ms 1949a: 304ff.): thus serving legionaries were allowed to exercise rights *in uxorem* but not *in genetricem* in their consorts; this situation is the obverse of wealthy African women exercising rights *in genetricem* over other women while not themselves enjoying all rights *in uxorem*. Such partibility of the person, and classification of rights subject to apportionment, occupies a typological position on the very margins of regulation through the idiom of kinship.

The concluding chapter of Part II (Slavery and Kinship) subsumes all the foregoing examples under the category of 'domestic slavery' – which also exists in class-based societies but is 'nevertheless not part of the class structure' (Ms 1949a: 279). Where domestic slavery exists in the absence of a rank system, Steiner argues there is no reason to anticipate the development of full slavery; for:

> ... we can see, how close the institutions under discussion still are to the life of kinship groups and their jural idiom. There is no doubt, we have been

describing kinship mechanism[s] acting on a higher level of social organisation. (Ms 1949a: 262-63)

Detached from his clan, a man may be attached to another clan,
otherwise:

> As soon as the man finds himself severed from his clan, he is situated in a
> social no-man's-land, a space which is not structured by clan life and clan
> spheres. This space is the domain of the other social force, the chief. Thus
> his expulsion from his clan is tantamount to a transfer into the charge of
> the chief. (Ms 1949a: 263)

Steiner's style of thought is particularly clear here: he envisages a
structuring of social spaces by institutional forces. Kinship and clan-
ship are mechanisms that, among other things, classify people and
determine their mutual rights and responsibilities. An extension of
this idiom can be made to attach and eventually assimilate non-kin.
Unlike Western civilisations, which on Steiner's account use differences as pretexts for domination or expulsion, or Eastern civilisations,
which make difference the enduring basis of association, here are societies in which status differences tend to be transitory and devoid of
enduring and general social significance.

Part III of Steiner's thesis deals with the 'Servile Symbiosis' (also
described as extra-tribal patronage) which may occur when societies of
differing complexity are in contact (Ms 1949a: 327-70). This can be
passed over relatively quickly. Steiner is thinking, for instance, of the
sort of relations that existed between pygmy gatherer-hunters and
Bantu farmers in Central Africa. Such relations are examples of social
asymmetry because of the different degree of involvement of the two
social structures in the arrangement, and the differing scale of the
groups directly involved in the relations between the two social structures (in Steiner's example: a single Bantu and numerous pygmies). A
similar situation exists in the symbiosis of the Negritos of Northern
Luzon with the Malay neighbours who supply them with rice in
exchange for jungle products. Employing a model of the plural economy, Steiner argues that the groups belong to two essentially separate
economies. At this point, Steiner's thesis simply breaks off; Paul
Bohannan's abridged version supplies a conclusion by the expedient of
turning the 'Introduction' into a concluding chapter. But if his dissertation is one of histories' longer fragments – albeit somewhat shorter
than one of the novels he much admired, Musil's *The Man without
Qualities* – then his intention is clear: to document a gradation of forms
of increasingly radical detachment from kinship-relations and enduringly servile attachment in terms of inequalities of broadening social
scope. In the course of his investigation, he would broach questions of

the disposition of labour and the creation of value. The significance of kinship is clarified in one of the shortest of Steiner's fragments, an introduction to kinship studies in which he refers to kinship as the most social of our possessions (below). By implication, alienation from our possession of kinship (rather than say our labour), is what makes us slaves. A poignant conclusion for someone whose life had been scarrred so deeply by the confiscation of his kin.

Steiner's surviving fragment works in a dialectic mode. By a strong contrast to the (only relatively) more benign, instances of servile insti- tution – the outcast, the widow, the domestic slave – Steiner is leading us towards an understanding of the most malignant institutions of captivity. This is why he could describe his study as a sympathetic act of suffering in the context of Jewish captivity in Europe. The thesis's governing and related antitheses explore kinship and kinlessness, attachment and detachment, community and exile, those who belonged and those who remained strangers, and by implication those who would be allowed to live and those who would be allowed to die.

Radcliffe-Brown and Evans-Pritchard

A society no more consists of individuals than a net consists of
knots. The net is made with the help of knots. But no knot is a
piece or a unit of anything that in any sense could be called a 'net'.
                                    Essays and Discoveries, Ms 1948

Franz Steiner brought formidable experience and qualifications to the close circle of men and women who were about to reshape the nature of the discipline of social anthropology in the immediate post-war years. His anthropological thought had passed through various stages – and two doctorates – in Central Europe (via studies in Prague and Vienna, and research in Sub-Carpathian Ruthenia) and Britain (as a familiar of both Malinowski's and Radcliffe-Brown's seminars). He had sojourned in Jerusalem, and had a command of a striking variety of languages and their literatures matched by an encyclopaedic knowledge of global cultures from his ethnological training. In Rad- cliffe-Brown's absence during the war, we caught sight of him briefly as virtual representative of the 'Oxford School' of social anthropology in his public lecture on 'Superstition' (Volume I, pp. 223-29, above). But such forthrightly anthropological subject matter was not typical of his war-time writing, devoted in greater part to his aphorisms, poetry, letters and political thought. The war years had, as we have empha- sised, been the crucible in which the later intellect was forged. Often passed over as an interruption to the development of the discipline of social anthropology, in Steiner's case particularly – but this goes for the Oxford Institute generally – the direction that anthropological thought was about to take is inconceivable outside its post-war setting.

In addition to their anthropological interests, the Oxford scholars with whom Steiner now associated appear to have shared with him a temperament attuned to both his literary and his religious forms of expression. According to Paul Bohannan, Evans-Pritchard had a great regard for poetry, and admired Steiner for being a poet (Paul Bohannan: PC). Many Oxford anthropologists were practising members of the world religions (as Mary Douglas reminded us in her preface to Volume I of this edition); and the strong affinity between the Roman Catholicism and the broadly philosophical anthropology of several post-war members of the Institute is well-known (Fardon 1999). We also know from several witnesses that Evans-Pritchard considered Steiner the 'most scholarly' of the members of the Institute; he told Rodney Needham so in these words (Needham: PC). However, on the evidence of the same Oxford contemporaries' testimonies, Steiner the polymath was not just at the intellectual heart of the Institute but embodied its moral soul. Although one of the few who had not been a combatant in the war, more than the others Steiner was the war's survivor: damaged in body but apparently indomitable in spirit. The experiences of the war, and of the holocaust, were the broader context in which we feel it necessary to situate the questioning of the status and purpose of anthropology which ensued at the Institute. And this questioning provided some of the grounds for twentieth-century anthropology's subsequent bouts of intensive self-questioning – first, in the close aftermath of decolonisation, and then again as the relation of exteriority between the West and its others lost credibility in the light of post-colonial globalisation.

The status of social anthropology as a 'natural science of society' was key not only to the discipline's epistemological standing but, at least for many of those involved, its moral standing. It is well documented, at least in general terms, that once Evans-Pritchard succeeded Radcliffe-Brown in the Oxford chair relations between the two men deteriorated from the collaboration they had enjoyed at the time of their co-sponsorship, with Meyer Fortes, of the seminal collection *African Political Systems* (1940). The exact date of Evans-Pritchard's epistemological falling out with Radcliffe-Brown has remained contentious, and we would not revisit the issue did it not have so obvious and immediate a bearing on Steiner's Oxford lectures.

Such facts as there are about the disagreement between Radcliffe-Brown and Evans-Pritchard have been reported elsewhere (Stocking [1995] 1996: 435fn; Kuper 1996: 124-25). In 1948, Evans-Pritchard's Inaugural Lecture at Oxford had been, in Adam Kuper's words, 'an orthodox Radcliffe-Brownian performance' (1996: 124). Yet as Kuper

goes on to note, quoting *in extenso* from a letter Evans-Pritchard wrote
to the journal *Man*, he later called this lecture a dutiful restatement of
Radcliffe-Brown's position – an expression of his 'personal regard,
though less intellectual sympathy or appreciation' for his predecessor
(Kuper 1996: 125). In the light of what happened in the following three
years, this motivation seems strange indeed. Only two years later, in his
Marrett Lecture of 1950 (1962a), Evans-Pritchard strongly repudiated
Radcliffe-Brown's entire epistemology of anthropology. These views
were repeated in a series of broadcast lectures for the BBC Third Programme that year (published as *Social Anthropology* 1951b). Radcliffe-
Brown took the public opportunity of his own 1951 Huxley Lecture to
restate his conviction that social anthropology was a natural science of
society; and he addressed narrower criticism to Evans-Pritchard in a
review of *Social Anthropology* (Radcliffe-Brown 1951a, 1951b). Such a
public falling out between professors past and present cannot but have
set the tone for debate in the Institute. Steiner must have been alive to
this situation: he had worked closely with both men, and owned Evans-
Pritchard's *Social Anthropology* (1951b) *ex dono autoris* as he noted in his
copy, which is dated May 1951. Steiner was one of the few colleagues
with whom Evans-Pritchard might have discussed the changes his
views underwent between 1948 and 1950; and it is notable that
Steiner's earliest Oxford lectures address the same issues that Evans-
Pritchard was to contest with Radcliffe-Brown.

In repudiating Radcliffe-Brown's natural science of society, Evans-
Pritchard accelerated that complex (and by no means clear-cut) process
in British anthropology that David Pocock epitomised as a move from
'function' to 'meaning'. An identification of anthropology with the
humanities, particularly history, and an emphasis on the translation of
comparative religious sensibilities are well-known elements of this
movement. Steiner's diary for 21 October 1952 finds him having read
a belatedly published 1951 issue of the *Journal of the Royal Anthropological Institute*, a copy of which survives in his library; here, Evans-
Pritchard's 'excellent' RAI presidential address ('Some features of Nuer
religion' – a disquisition on the complexities of translating Nuer conceptions of God that later became chapter 1 of *Nuer Religion*) was followed by Radcliffe-Brown's 'ridiculous' 1951 Huxley Lecture (a
depiction of classificatory logic feted by Lévi-Strauss (1963: 158) as a
genuinely structuralist analysis!).

That Steiner's thought concurs with Evans-Pritchard in so many
respects is unsurprising given that the two men worked closely together
and respected one another. For example, Evans-Pritchard argued that,
because societies were not natural systems, they did not undergo necessary developments, and therefore these could not be stated as general
principles or laws. While it might be possible to find logical consistencies

in the analysis of societies or cultures, these were neither real nor necessary connexions (Evans-Pritchard 1951b: 17). This idea closely matches Steiner's remark (of October 1948) in which he analyses the relations between chronological and morphological series (p. 241, below). Evans-Pritchard proposed three levels of analysis: the translation of overt cultural features, the detection of the underlying form in a society or culture, and the comparison of these forms (1951b: 24-25). Steiner's analysis of units of comparison in his aphorisms locks into this debate: and like Evans-Pritchard, he stresses that the *analytical categories* of the investigation must be understood *in relation to the act of comparison*.

Radcliffe-Brown's vigorously critical review of the lectures Evans-Pritchard published as *Social Anthropology* argued that Evans-Pritchard's ideas were confused and ill-formed. Radcliffe-Brown accepted that historical and ethnographic studies were both 'sociographic', but denied that social anthropology (or for that matter history) consisted entirely of such studies. What Radcliffe-Brown understood by 'laws' and Evans-Pritchard by 'patterns' was no more than a matter of 'verbal quibbling'. Sociography, on Radcliffe-Brown's understanding, provided:

> the data for systematic comparative studies, which can give classifications of the various features of social life and typological classifications of societies, and can also reveal the existence of regularities in social phenomena, thus enabling us to begin building up a general body of theoretical knowledge about human societies. (Radcliffe-Brown 1951b: 365-66)

While Steiner's explicit statements on this professorial wrangle leave no doubt that his sympathies lie with Evans-Pritchard, some of his interests (notably in Simmel's formal sociology) have a hue that may reasonably be considered Radcliffe-Brownian. Personalities aside, Steiner's views may have been less clearcut; an aphorism he thought worth collecting at the time seems to undercut any clear grounds for opposing comparison of social forms to translational understanding. It simply runs '"Meaning and structure" seem to me about the best translation of *Tao te King*' (Steiner 1988: 25). And while his close associates argued whether anthropology was 'science' or 'art', Steiner's 'universal mathesis' sought integral relations between practices of knowledge and forms of writing that in the West might be classified as religion, mysticism, poetry and philosophy.

One of Steiner's closest friends in the Oxford group, M.N. Srinivas (himself an admirer of Evans-Pritchard) feels in retrospect that Evans-Pritchard did anthropology a 'service' by arguing it to be a 'moral not natural science'; however, Srinivas regretted certain 'side-effects' of the polarisation: a downgrading of the achievements of modern social anthropology and of the fieldwork tradition (correlating with an overemphasis on the fieldworker), and a 'denigration of Radcliffe-Brown as thinker and man' that ignored his historical contribution to the discipline (1973: 143). Had he lived as long, Steiner might also have concluded that personal antagonisms had removed some of the nuance from scholarly disagreement.

The arguments between Radcliffe-Brown and Evans-Pritchard had a well-established history in German social thought which Steiner controlled with a native's grasp. For him, presumably, the conflict between *Geisteswissenschaften* and *Naturwissenschaften* was not an issue. As we have remarked, H.G. Adler describes Steiner as having a 'universal mathesis', or procedure for expressing knowledge transformatively, rather than a systematic method, and certainly not a 'system' (Volume I, p. 36, above). In this commitment to the shifting grounds on which knowledge is transformed, Steiner seems very much our contemporary. Committed to a translational approach to ethnography, to the formal study of types of sociation, and to comparative anthropology, Steiner nonetheless considered the outcomes of all of these activities to be provisional and problematic. These three methods provided the means to examine pressing problems; but the problems felt pressing because investigators were themselves situated in specific historical and political circumstances. The interests that propelled curiosity about social phenomena were themselves just as much social phenomena.

For all these reasons, our reading of Steiner's Oxford lectures in their entirety suggests he might have been uncomfortable with the crudity of the terms on which the argument between the two eminent scholars was developing. Steiner strongly advocated empirical sociographic studies, but unlike Radcliffe-Brown saw these as theoretically informed rather than as 'data' to be submitted to inductive analysis. He concurred with Evans-Pritchard that social anthropology was unlike natural science by virtue of the questions it posed. However, he was more strongly attracted to formal sociological comparison (à la Simmel) than the later Evans-Pritchard. For Steiner, the most pressing problems concerned the possibility of translation between sociographic idioms, a translation which could only derive from intensive study across ethnical or historical distance and which could only be conducted by means of comparative analyses. This in itself entailed exploring the epistemological limits of the concepts and language that made such studies possible. Likewise, it entailed continuously analysing the comparability of social phenomena and negotiating differing standards of truth and different concepts of value. Binary distinctions between the 'sciences' and 'humanities' were of no use in thinking through the situated nature of knowledge, whether sociographic or comparative, and in evaluating the ideas of those who had sought such knowledge. How to achieve sociographic knowledge, and how to use such knowledge in comparative analyses, what transformations were involved, are the recurrent themes of Steiner's Oxford lectures. Throughout, he argues against any stable or simple solution to the dilemmas such disciplinary ambitions posed. Although Evans-Pritchard returned to questions of comparison in anthropology and of the relation between anthropology and history in lectures long after Steiner's death ((1961) 1962c, (1963) 1965a), his later statements only draw out some of the implications of his 1950 lecture leaving the fundamental questions unanswered – indeed, even unposed. It is, therefore, to Steiner that we must turn for the most subtle probing of these issues in Oxford anthropology around 1950-52.

For Steiner, the relationship between sociographic and comparative study was as problematic to history as it was to anthropology. Declaring anthropology to be like history pointed to a shared dilemma rather than to its solution. Although his training in Central European ethnology and philology, an influential source of American cultural anthropology, pre-dated the sociological insights he gained in Britain, Steiner added sociological perspectives to these earlier approaches, while yet retaining the comparative and historical commitment of ethnological scholarship. And to both Schools – as we have argued – he added an appreciation of the politics of anthropology that derived from his identification with Oriental civilisation and his solidarity with the colonised.

Many of the lectures which Steiner left in fragmentary form (and which we reproduce for the interesting light they shed both on Steiner and on a particulary influential Oxford pedagogy), begin with fully formed paragraphs that are evidently considered and almost complete. As the lecture outlines go on, it seems as if Steiner ran out of time, interest or both. And time and again, these well-formed paragraphs are devoted to attempts to delineate the nature and purpose of anthropology. Take the lecture we reprint here under the title 'Language, Society, and Social Anthropology' which probably dates from 1950. Rather than worrying over the definitions of language or society, Steiner homes in on 'social anthropology' which he defines by repeatedly splitting the idea of interest in social phenomena, as if by wittling away what was not anthropology he might be left with something that was. Thus our interest in social phenomena is less constant than that in natural phenomena; no secure body of knowledge of social phenomena grows through the ages. We become interested in social phenomena when we are challenged in some way: either by social change or by 'confrontations'. Taking now confrontations, these are of two types: internal to the social formation (and here Steiner derives American anthropological interest in 'culture and personality' directly from the nature of American society) and external, when the lone ethnographer intrudes upon an entire and different form of life. From a position of unfamiliarity, the ethnographer goes on to learn linguistic and social forms together and to make his experience more predictable (both in terms of language and social behaviour). All language is socially embedded (and here, as in *Taboo*, Steiner pays generous tribute to Malinowski's anticipation of what would later be formalised as speech act theory). Ethnography then is the translation of this experience, and fundamentally to do with meanings.

Turning to the roughly contemporaneous lectures on kinship (also fragmentary) we find again that the most developed paragraphs are those concerned with the standing and particularity of anthropology. He begins, 'Our problems are shaped by the situations which gave rise to our enquiries. ...', and again distinguishes 'social change' from 'confrontation'. But then he develops the same line of thought with a slight difference:

> ... both kinds of situation can give rise to either abstract theorising or empirical investigation ... in both ... detachment and involvement [are] possible. And both situations are profound: the one [social change] can make one realise the basic insecurity of social existence, the other is apt to infuse all observation of social phenomena with that questioning bewilderment, *taumazein* as the Greeks called it who believed it to be the mainspring of all our more important knowledge. Thus both kinds of situation are 'existential' ... (pp. 197-98 below).

'Insecurity' and 'bewilderment' are the reasons for our curiosity and the grounds for our existential situation being questionable. One recalls that Iris Murdoch was writing on Sartre at this time, and that Steiner here refers problems that were pressing in the past to the 'fascinans' or *taumazein* of those who were concerned passionately by them. Does this mean that the ensuing analyses reflect only the local grounds for a thinker's fascination? Sometimes yes, as in the case of thinkers who could find nothing but their own prejudices in the other. But Steiner, adhering to relativity of a kind informed by both Mach and Einstein, sees difference as prerequisite to knowledge. As he puts it in his second lecture on Simmel:

> ... the conundrum – what objectivity can there be in an enquiry where subject and object are identical: socially conditioned man and the social conditions of man? – that conundrum is solved by us as far as it can be resolved at all: we are investigating kinds of social life quite different from the one which conditioned us (p. 216, below).

Some of the implications of this for comparison in anthropology are explored in a scathing review of George Murdock's *Social Structure*, a work Steiner found unscholarly and thoroughly erroneous 'a stream-lined self-service buffet of culture items' (1951: 367). The review opens with a broad statement of the state of the art that points yet again to a problematic absence:

> It does not serve a reasonable purpose, nor has it ever been attempted with any measure of success and accuracy, to distinguish sociology from social anthropology, and particularly the more general research of 'pure' sociology from 'the' comparative method which at any time is being given a free hand in the anthropological realm. One of the features in the relationship between these partly overlapping fields of knowledge, and perhaps not the least irri-tating one, is that social anthropology, which has given rise to new methods of analysis and discoveries, but has left its comparative functions awkwardly undeveloped (the more so where a structural outlook prevails), still bears the burden of comparative research and exposition without receiving (since the days of Durkheim) contributions from 'pure' or general sociology.
>
> Instead of talking of Social Anthropology, a simple distinction could be made between analytical and descriptive sociology on the one hand and comparative and general sociology on the other, subdividing analytical sociology into research with a necessary ethnological bias, and without it. (1951: 366)

The problematic posed here will be taken up in the lectures on taboo: individual instances of ethnographic description are written up in ways that are not commensurate with their comparison. This seems to argue an initial distinction between description and comparison that must later be bridged. However, Steiner – his circumspection recalls both Kafka and T.S. Eliot's prose as literary models – immediately and typically qualifies his own distinction:

> Unfortunately, this is not possible, because the necessary ethnological bias involves the sociologist in some of the complexities of ethnology – viz. the configuration of spatially distinct types and the historical character of the features defining the types, or else the ethnological bias becomes confused with social history, or with the genuine sociological problems of the analysis of small-scale communities, or again the latter with the fascinans of other-ness and with ethnical distance as a condition of research. (1951: 366-67)

If it is not possible to separate description from comparison, then this is because the criteria for distinguishing types of social phenome-non are themselves historically produced and depend upon the partic-ular situation of the analyst. To ask Steiner for a general resolution to this problem is to mistake his argument; rather than an easy resolu-tion, the tension between ethnographic description and comparison is an essential condition of the comparative sociologist's calling. Anthro-pology requires a methodology, a way of going on. To face this tension simply *is* to be a comparative sociologist. Later, in this otherwise entirely critical review, he speaks of the Durkheimian heritage emphasised by Radcliffe-Brown; the need for a 'social Linneanism' in 'systematic sociology' based on features such as segmentation. Descriptive and comparative sociology are engaged in the same quest for features that will permit comparison. Methodologically, it is essential to distinguish, as Steiner claims Murdock has failed to do, between:

> cultural elements – which are not necessarily sociological isolates and which are used for the identification in space and time of a culture aggregate – and social institutions – which by their nature are parts of systems and interdependent with other social phenomena. ... (1951: 367)

Like Radcliffe-Brown, Steiner believes that comparison needs to occur in terms of social rather than cultural aggregates; and his last writings explore two axes of comparison – economy and cosmology – which are interrelated through notions of value and danger.

Labour and Value

> *My greatest ambition is to write a comparative economics of primitive peoples. I have completely new theories of value formation in noneconomising [nichtwirtschaftenden] societies, especially about the formation of value in the procedure of sacrifice-exchange.*
> Franz Steiner to Paul Bruell, 13 April 1947 (Fleischli 1970: 24)

Steiner's thesis opened up to him the sphere of his mature anthropology, taking him into the areas of economics, labour, and value where his work was to leave a more noticeable mark on the discipline than in the study of slavery itself. Paul Bohannan's best efforts failed to find a publisher for his carefully prepared, abbreviated version of Steiner's dissertation, and since, understandably, Bohannan did not attempt to truncate the text still further into article form – in itself a highly questionable procedure – it was left almost untouched by later scholars, albeit some key ideas filtered through via Bohannan and others. But the immediate products of the thesis fared better, although here, too, we are dealing with fragments of larger projects, the relations between which are not entirely clear. We learn from Evans-Pritchard of Steiner's proposed book on 'the sociology of labour' that it 'would have been his thesis rewritten for publication' (1956b: 12); but Paul Bohannan also mentions 'a book on the economics of primitive peoples' (in Steiner 1954b: 118 fn.1): it is not clear whether these references apply to the same or to different works, and in either case, one is left to speculate what would have happened to the ideas on 'slavery'.

'Towards a Classification of Labour' derives from the notes Steiner made for a lecture series under the title 'Division and Organisation of Labour'. It both continues the concern in Steiner's thesis to classify forms of labour, and adds intriguing comments about the nature of economics. It is the only one of his articles to have been reprinted in English after its journal publication, having been recognised by its subsequent editor as 'one of the more definitive studies of its topic', and therefore suitable to introduce a collection of essays on *The Social Dimension of Work* (Bryant 1972: 3).

We have already noted the essential reflexivity of Steiner's address to a new problem: a stocktaking of the terminological and conceptual resources defining the subject of study, followed by interrogating both the origins and interestedness of these resources, and asking how they structure questions askable within that domain. This was his approach to 'slavery' and it will be repeated for 'taboo'. Likewise, for Steiner economics is a way of looking: 'economics stands for an approach and a terminology, not for facts' (p. 174, below). In his own draft, he formulates this more radically than in the published version: 'There is no such thing as an economic fact' (MS 1951b: fol.1). He immediately moves – in both versions – to add some more substantive content to his definition: 'We can define economic relations as those relationships existing between human individuals and groups which can best be described in terms of values and non-human quantities' (p. 174, below). Although economics is an approach to analysing some aspects of social life, those aspects yield themselves up to being understood in this way. Thus economics, while a point of view, is nonetheless to some degree answerable to the way the world is independently.

Casting around for a specifically sociological definition of labour produces a similar argument. Steiner rejects any attempt to distinguish particular sorts of activity as labour: any activity may be labour at one time and something different at another. Labour is any socially integrative activity concerned with human subsistence (p. 188, below). Adding that, 'By "integrating activity" is meant a sanctioned activity which thus presupposes, creates and recreates social relationships' (p. 188, below). On this definition, for Steiner as for Durkheim, labour comes to mean virtually 'all social activities' (p. 180, below). Labour, like economics – although Steiner does not put it this way – refers both to a way of looking at the world and to the aspects of the world that yield best to this way of being seen. The remainder of this essay (before it peters out) proposes the promised 'classification of labour' using such criteria as the sexual division of labour (which may gender tasks by reference to places or tools), and the organisation of collective labour (according to the degree of authoritative direction of allotted tasks, the differentiation or not of tasks and so on). Although Steiner's account contains valuable insights – for instance, into the relations between servile and gendered labour tasks, as noted in the dissertation, or the persistence of uniform labour as a sphere of activity after an economy has become monetised – the fragment gains greater interest when read in conjunction with Steiner's notes for the proposed book on economics, on which he was working at the time of his death.

Although also fragmentary, Steiner's ideas on value, published as 'Notes on Comparative Economics' by Paul Bohannan, offer more substantial indications of the ambitious work he planned. Peter Bumke, introducing the German printing of Steiner's paper (1983), argues for its importance in drawing 'the most radical' of all conclusions from overturning the distinctions between economic and noneconomic values (1983: 50). Neither Durkheim nor Mauss are cited in the surviving article, but Steiner's friend Godfrey Lienhardt, who drew on this article to conclude the chapter concerned with 'Economics and Social Relations' in his survey *Social Anthropology*, helpfully notes two resemblances with the French masters: in Steiner's proceeding from 'concrete example', and in his interest in 'the link between notions of economic and of religious value' (1964: 88, 90). In a broad sense, Steiner's speculations concern the link between the values of things and people's other values. As usual, Steiner's specific concern with relatively undifferentiated societies is contextualised within a broader concern with cultural criticism; it draws implicitly on his readings of Marx and Simmel, before concluding explicitly with the analyses that Weber and Tawney made of the relation between the ideals of Protestantism and capitalism, and the collapse of this value relation in the disaster of the Weimar Republic.

Steiner's argument is condensed and some exegesis is warranted. 'By an economy', Steiner tells us, he means 'a system of production and distribution of units of value'. Although Paul Bohannan speculates (in a footnote) 'value' should probably read 'utility', to us the original here seems more plausible (see p. 173 fn. 2, below). To analyse a society economically is, therefore, to look at social actions from a particular perspective: the investigator examines the making and circulating of values. Steiner goes on to distinguish two common configurations of values in non-capitalist economies.

First, Steiner presents Type A. Three groups of goods are here distinguished:

1. Foodstuffs and raw materials;
2. tools and clothing;
3. personal treasures.

Personal treasures, in Steiner's neat formulation, are valued by their owners 'because of their rarity or because of the *memorably inten-*

sive attention given to them during their production' (p. 161, below; emphasis added). Eskimo carvings are cited as an example – and some of these survive in his estate. The argument that follows may first introduce the distinction of 'spheres of exchange' later commonly made by anthropologists. In non-capitalist economies of Type A, personal treasures have no universal value and do not circulate; only raw materials circulate and 'members of the society respond to the distribution by actions of solidarity enabling further production'. The effect of adding labour to raw material is to *remove* the object from the primary economic cycle; its further circulation can only be as a gift in alliance or booty in war. Steiner's choice of words carefully distinguishes this circumstance from the Marxist assumption that value derives from labour. Rather, value depends upon people's classification of things. One senses here the substantive importance that Steiner attaches to the apparently purely analytic concept of 'classification' in his work; in a related aphorism, Steiner suggests that the whole 'form' versus 'content' distinction despite being unsustainable remains necessary (p. 240, below). Turning next implicitly to liberal economics, Steiner notes that the laws of supply and demand operate only within the sphere concerned with foodstuffs. Such societies have no accumulation and no markets. Put another way, the regime under which value is created in such societies is particular to their type.

Secondly, Steiner considers Type B. A second type of non-capitalist economy is distinguished from the first in that there are no 'personal treasures' standing entirely apart from the primary economic cycle. Treasures have general value which derives from their importance in ritual or from their exchangeability. These are subdivided according to 'the various modes by which people integrate, classify and interrelate the different groups or categories of objects' (p. 162, below). Such economies may be analysed in the terms of a distinction between goods whose value derives from use and those whose value is non-utilitarian. Some utilitarian objects may also be used as means of exchange if their supply is limited in some way.

Implicitly, Steiner's definition of two forms of non-capitalist systems of value creation contrasts with the capitalist system, in which a general standard of value is recognised. Thus, he rejoins the problem central to Simmel's *Philosophie des Geldes* (1900; *Philosophy of Money*): that of the relation between a general-purpose money and the expansion in range of general standards of value. It is the collapse of monetary values within this nexus that precipitates the disastrous progression from Weimar to the Third Reich (as Lienhardt noted of Steiner's analysis above). If economic systems are concerned with the creation and distribution of economic values, when they collapse as systems they bring down entire shared systems of value more generally. The comparison between economics and religion as systems of ultimate values is pursued via an analogy that borders on theories of sacrifice. The collapse which marked the transition from the Weimar Republic to the Third Reich – to indicate Steiner's own situatedness – may have been as significant for his understanding of the rise of Nazism as it was central to Canetti's analysis of crowd phenomena (1960: 207-12).

Steiner next elaborates a symbolic terminology to distinguish the usefulness, exchangeability and value of objects that refines the crude conventional distinction between use and exchange values. He then runs through the possible types of exchange his terminology permits.

1. Useful objects can be *bartered* directly.
2. A useful object can be *traded* for a useful object that is gained only because it is exchangeable for another useful object. This is trade through an intermediary useful object.
3. A useful object can be *traded* for a non-utilitarian object (a treasure or a ritual object) on account of its exchangeability against other useful objects. This is trade through an intermediary non-utilitarian object.
4. An exchangeable object (treasure or ritual value) can be *exchanged* for another exchangeable object. This is *a financial transaction akin to trade*.

Running systematically through the various possibilities of a fairly simple combination of his terms (to yield barter, trade and exchange of various types), Steiner's attention comes to rest on the remaining forms: the *translation* of all or any useful properties of objects into ritual objects.

5. *Negative translation* occurs when all the useful, Steiner says *empirical*, qualities of objects (both their actual use and the usefulness of their exchangeability) are relinquished so that the giver retains their ritual value which henceforth attaches to his status. Negative translation may or may not involve splitting the value of the original object. If the value can be split, then, when the object(s) are given, the owner relinquishes only their empirical value while retaining their ritual value. Alternatively, the object may be destroyed so that its ritual value is all that remains (as in the final stages of potlatch).
6. *Positive translation* differs from the previous type in that value from exchangeability is classified together with ritual value. Things are specially valued because they retain their ritual value when exchanged. Under these circumstances, the different spheres of exchange (of useful and treasure objects) are not entirely disjoined, but there is no common standard of value between them. Terms of trade can change in one sphere without necessarily affecting the other.

Steiner's notion of 'translation' perhaps needs to be located some-where between a strictly scientific concept on the one hand, and Canetti's affective concept of 'transformation' or 'metamorphosis' on the other, namely his key idea of *Verwandlung* – a German word Steiner also uses in similar contexts (p. 240, below). Translations of value have economic, aesthetic and moral aspects and occur in definite social formations. Each of the above forms of exchange has different consequences for sociality, and several forms often occur together in a single society seen from the perspective of its economy. Steiner notes in correction of his own distinction between empirical and ritual values, that there are cases in which the sheer quantity of utilitarian objects confers on them a value qualitatively different from the aggregate value of the individual objects that make up the whole. He calls this *assembly value*, and notes it may involve abstention from consumption (as in the case of Trobriand yams used for display).

As empirical values are rejected, the economic model of value may approximate the model of sacrifice. The contrary peculiarity of the West, which accounts for the tragedy of Weimar, was the 'conquest of Western civilisation by a total money economy [which] meant the bestowing of transcending values on money' (p. 171, below). On the one hand we find an 'ascetic rejection of the uses of goods', whether in relation to the Protestant ethic or the accumulation of yams in the Tro-briand Islands that Malinowski reported. On the other hand, the loss of property of the German middle classes under the Weimar Republic which led to the disintegration of their work ethic and the 'ideals and codes of the middle classes. No short-lived hardship, however severe, can account for a loss of confidence on such a scale' (p. 172, below). The collapse of Weimar was evidence of the fragility of a regime of social values founded on the economics of possessive individualism. Or, following Simmel, it might be in the spirit of Steiner to attribute the calamitous consequences of the general collapse in value to the secular process through which money became concrete and goods abstract.

As these observations indicate, Steiner's German ethnological and philosophical training, the political background and his religious com-mitments provide an essential context for understanding his social anthropology. Specific ideas on 'economics', 'labour', 'value', and 'taboo' impinge directly on large complexes like 'culture', 'politics', 'society', and 'civilisation', but because Steiner's personal and political writings have remained unpublished, and he does not elaborate the wider consequences of his specific arguments in his scholarly work, it has been hard for readers to grasp the way in which quite detailed, as it were 'abstract' arguments, like that on economics and value, impact directly on the wider, so to speak 'substantive' debates on issues like the rise of Nazism.

Civilisation and Taboo

The process of civilisation is the conquest of man by the natural
forces, the demons.

Franz Steiner, 'On the Process of Civilisation'

The reception of Steiner's Oxford University lecture series on 'Tabu' is a case in point. The longest of his works republished here, *Taboo* has particularly suffered for want of placement in this larger context of Steiner's social thought. Evans-Pritchard, in his well-intentioned Preface to the original edition, understated the book's concerns and achievement in the eyes of its potential readers by presenting the work as a critical examination and close scrutiny of previous theories: 'useful' to teachers and 'of great value' to anyone interested in taboo. Most damaging was the insistence that the author 'does not reach any positive conclusions himself' (1956b: 12-13). Reviewers largely followed Evans-Pritchard's assessment of his late colleague's work. The anonymous reviewer for the *Times Literary Supplement* praises Steiner's critical insight but, like Evans-Pritchard, regrets that 'his [lecture] notes seem to have come to an end before his positive contribution to this very complex subject had been adequately developed' (1956: 38). The state of the manuscript does not support such a contention: Steiner's final lecture is not fragmentary, and ends with a strong conclusion, which is sufficiently clearly stated in Laura Bohannan's edition (*Taboo* Lecture L, fol.3). The anonymous reviewer for *The Listener*, while noting that the book was almost 'entirely critical' did, however, add that as 'a pious practising Jew for whom the Mosaic prohibitions were a living part of a living religion [Steiner] avoids the condescension which is a feature of the writing of his predecessors' (1956: 281). Cohn (1957) concludes his review by lengthy quotation from Evans-Pritchard; and Raglan (1957), Lanternari (1957), and Branden (1958) also echo Evans-Pritchard's assessment. Only Cora Dubois (1957) is more appreciative of Steiner's positive contribution in linking the institutional localisation of danger, classification, value and behaviour. It took a second wave of reception to recognise the significance of Steiner's text. Mary Douglas's *Purity and Danger* makes due acknowledgement of Steiner's ideas, though the link has rarely been commented on: exceptions include Needham's early review of Douglas's book (anon *TLS* 1967) and J.C.Winter's perceptive comments (1979: 26). The conclusion that Steiner reaches at the end of his lectures is as follows:

> it is a major fact of human existence that we are not able, and never were able, to express our relation to values in other terms than those of danger behaviour. Social relations are describable in terms of danger; through contagion there is social participation in danger. (Volume I, p. 214)

In Steiner's own words, the first version of his key sentence runs, more inclusively, as follows:

> we human beings are not able and never were able to express our relations to values in other terms than danger behaviour. (*Tabu*, Lecture L, fol.3).

Taboos (or rules of avoidance) classify and localise dangers and transgressions. Instead of being bizarre or exotic, taboos are one of the forms taken by a universal propensity to express the value of classification by imbuing the world of social relations with inherent and contagious, thus potentially shared, dangers. The social anthropologist needs to investigate how generally recognised dangers are distributed in different sorts of human society, and to ask what social pressures are brought to bear in order to fix a shared scheme of dangers. Societies differ according to the ways in which dangers are identified and classified. The significance of the broadest terms of this contrast is made explicit in Steiner's essay 'On the Process of Civilisation'.

'On the Process of Civilisation', to which we have already had occasion to allude, belongs to a line of German-speaking thought that engages specific social criticism with a wider cultural critique: Lichtenberg's *Sudelbücher* (Waste-Books), Nietzsche's *Zur Genealogie der Moral*, Karl Kraus's social satire and Freud's *Das Unbehagen in der Kultur*, to name a heterogeneous but not unconnected set, each belonging to a very specific cultural and historical context – Enlightenment Germany, *fin de siècle* Europe, modern Vienna – share a critical attitude towards Western civilisation which moves from opposing (and often satirising) specific institutions and beliefs into a more fundamental critique of the culture itself. However, though sharing ideas with Nietzsche and Freud, Steiner lacks Nietzsche's iconoclasm and stringently avoids Freud's psychology. In this respect, his critique is more linked to Mach's cool analysis of global categories into their smaller parts, and would have been at home among practitioners of Oxford's linguistic philosophy. Steiner's style, as elsewhere, lies in accepting a conventional starting point but developing from it an analysis that subverts the conventional narrative. What is conventional about his essay on civilisation is the category 'civilisation' itself, which Steiner seems to invite the reader to accept in its nineteenth-century self-evidence. Steiner is not using the term in the way in which Norbert Elias's similarly entitled work was to do (with reference to a specific European culture of civility). However, the questioning of the very idea of 'civilisation' takes place in both their cases against the backdrop of the holocaust. Although first written in 1938, when Elias's *The Civilizing Process* was published in English, in 1968, its dedication was to his parents who both perished in concentration camps. Steiner likewise invites us to reflect on modern man's inhumanity. He does not make his reader examine the concept of civilisation definitionally. Rather, he puts the ideological character of the concept in question by following an alternative logic which discloses the nature of civilisation in process, 'civilisation's' positive connotations are shown to hide a more ominous will to domination.

What sort of intensifying process differentiates the uncivilised and civilised states? Steiner rejects the obvious notion that civilisation grows in direct proportion to man's power over nature. Pre-modern societies were capable of technological control over the relevant aspects of their environments. What changes among 'civilised' people is that power is predominantly power over other people. Concurrent with this change, the location of dangers also changes: cultures differ in the way that *danger* is localised.

Steiner takes two contrasting instances. By the application of detailed practical knowledge and a tried technology, Eskimos (we recall Steiner took a specialist's interest in Arctic ethnography) master a perilous environment entirely surrounding their world. The dangers exist, and remain, outside Eskimo society. Christian-European or modern society, however, has been engaged from the time of the Romans through the Crusades and up to modern science in extending the boundaries of society in several senses. Dangers outside human society are increasingly few and inchoate. The greater dangers now lie within the society in the form of uncontrollable economic crises, catastrophic wars, massive means of destruction, and the attack on difference (e.g., in the concentration camps). All this, according to Steiner's argument, is not accidental. Human society has overwhelmed and thus absorbed the demonic sphere and this progressive expansion of boundaries *is* the form taken by 'the process of civilisation'. The *external* demons are now *internal* and can only be repressed by organisational achievements. Even then, they may continue their inward migration to the divided self. Steiner – along with contemporaries like Kraus, Wittgenstein, and Canetti – strenuously resists a psychologisation of the problem in Freud's terms. His 'demons' are not to be translated into the symbolic projections of psychoanalysis. Like Weber, he notes that the ancient gods or powers have reappeared as impersonal forces ([1919] 1951: 589), and like Weber he sticks firmly to a sociological grasp of the human subject, which in his case is not at variance with a religious view. His conclusion states that only a society in the image of God acting according to the covenant may be able to arrest these demons, or (to formulate this less strongly) a society within which boundaries are clearly marked and patrolled by dangers. The grounds for his espousal of a theocratic Jewish state are immediately clarified. Likewise, the lectures on 'Tabu', it can now be seen, belong to a long-standing, deeply unsettling preoccupation with danger, and with its avoidance, creation, and resolution by different forms of society.

Analysing 'danger' behaviour as an institution involves under-standing the society it occurs in, contrasting it with different types of danger behaviour, and comparing similar practices in other societies. 'On the Process of Civilisation' and *Taboo* thus belong to a wider con-cern with danger, and with the correlation between danger behaviour and particular social forms. As both the essay and the lectures make clear, *comparison* is central to his analysis of danger behaviour: whether Eskimos and the West, or the Orient and the West, Steiner always has at least two possible types of practice in view. This is impor-tant in *Taboo*: to enquire about 'taboo' is also to ask about the func-tioning of societies that – despite the fact all societies must localise danger to agree on values – do not demonise and destroy sections of humanity; by implication, we are being invited to look at alternative social models, in which 'dangers' are not treated as they are in the West. The critique of the West emerges clearly from Steiner's analysis of its signal failure to understand 'otherness' as represented by the Polynesian concept of 'tabu'.

Altogether, *Taboo* seems to encompass many of the themes in which we have seen Steiner to be interested. Specifically: how is agreement to regimes of value stabilised? How do relatively undifferentiated soci-eties deal with alterity? How do they value difference? Why did 'taboo' become a 'problem' for Western scholarship? What are the different ways values are maintained under different forms of society? Method-ologically, can one compare taboos across cultures?

Apparently, it was Evans-Pritchard who suggested the subject of taboo to Steiner at a time when the latter had intended to deliver a series of lectures on Marx. One wonders whether there is anything to the tim-ing: Steiner's lectures on taboo were delivered against a background of deteriorating relations between Evans-Pritchard and Radcliffe-Brown, and the critical momentum of Steiner's account peaks in his destruc-tive analysis of Radcliffe-Brown's pre-war lecture on 'Taboo' (1939). Steiner's account also opens with Radcliffe-Brown: a recollection of his teaching, at the Institute in 1938, that social anthropology and com-parative sociology were 'the same thing'. 'Comparative sociology referred to a body of theories and concepts concerning the social life of human beings' that were based on the 'observation' of various, pre-dominantly simpler, societies. As such it differed from the type of soci-ology that derived from philosophical concerns. On the other hand, 'Social anthropology was an empirical pursuit. It was represented by field monographs, written chiefly by contemporary British students.' For the present-day reader, it may clarify the argument if what Steiner calls comparative sociology is translated as 'social anthropology', while we understand as 'ethnography' what he calls 'social anthropology'. By comparative sociologists (read social anthropologists), Steiner meant theorists like Durkheim who 'took over whole vistas of foreign societies' rather than plundering such accounts for apt illustrations. 'In those days it seemed as though field data had to undergo two scrutinies, that of the collector and that of the theorist, and the second could not dispense with the first' (Volume I, p. 103, above). He goes on to argue that as theorists became ethnographers, so comparative studies became rare. With an increasingly detailed descriptive inventory of foreign societies, comparison of 'whole societies' as Radcliffe-Brown had proposed had to contend with 'such a wealth of detail, such a complexity of abstractions, that comparison becomes an impossibility'. This is why, Steiner concludes, no recent comparative studies had been made. Here we approach that recurrent theme at which all Steiner's lecture worry: how the accumulating ethnographic record can be put to the service of a comparative social anthropology.

Generalising the point examined in relation to slavery, his argument continues with reference to terminology. The broad concepts and categories anthropologists use are left over from an earlier period of comparative sociology, but when ethnographers try to employ these categories for description they are found wanting. The ethnographer reacts to this situation by redefining the comparative concept to fit the ethnographic context. But in the process, the term becomes too specialised to serve any longer as a tool of comparison. The specific example he chooses to illustrate his point anticipates Lévi-Strauss's later argument in his celebrated *Le totémisme aujourd'hui* (1962). Totemism as a general category was meant to cover a plethora of cases; totemism as a term of ethnographic description must be tailored to fit a particular society. If we dismantle a general category by reference to its inadequacies in particular ethnographic descriptions – however virtuous a task in some ways – we also abrogate the attempt to explain totemism as a stage in human evolution or as a 'solid block of "otherness"' (Volume I, p. 105, above).

> But the question remains: How far can we, for our purposes today, use terms developed for such [comparative] purposes? And if we strip our vocabulary of these significant terms of the comparative period, what are we going to put in their place, not only as labels for pigeon-holes, but also as expressions indicating the direction of our interest? We do retain them and, sooner or later, each of us in his own way makes the unpleasant discovery that he is talking in two different languages at the same time and, like all bilinguals, finds translation almost impossible. (Volume I, pp. 105–106, above)

This problem has become no less perplexing in the almost half-century since Steiner spoke, and his own treatment of 'taboo' is all too readily treated as a demolition of earlier theories. However, his painstaking deconstruction of earlier views exposes the West's inability to grasp the 'otherness' of the Polynesian concept. By implication, the Western scholar's inability to understand *Polynesian* danger behaviour lays bare the inadequacies of the West's own institutions for dealing with the problem: it has no satisfactory way for treating 'otherness' as Polynesian, Jewish and Indian civilisations (in their different ways) have or had. As Steiner promises, his lectures will first deal with the ethnographic usage of the term 'taboo' – initially in relation to Polynesia and then more widely – before proceeding to 'find a basis for a general criticism' of the 'diverse theories perpetrated in the name of taboo' (p. 107).

Having grouped existing definitions of taboo, Steiner generalises – 'tentatively' – that 'taboo is an element of all those situations in which attitudes to values are expressed in terms of danger behaviour' (p. 108). Values, and the situations in which they are expressed, vary widely between societies, so there is neither sociological nor psychological unity that might allow a solution to a problem of taboo. Instead, Steiner is suggesting that there is a valid viewpoint from which values and the attribution of dangers prevalent in a society can be seen to intermesh, and this tells us important things about that society and its difference from others. This is the specific debt Mary Douglas acknowledges in the opening pages of *Purity and Danger*. Whatever his reservations about the difficulties that have beset those who have previously attempted to define taboo, Steiner does not abjure the idea that a general concept is required for his comparative sociology. He immediately rejects what might seem an obvious strategy for anthropologists faced by a term that threatened to become too broad: to narrow its meaning by reference to particular cases. For this falls back into the trap against which Steiner already warned: deriving social anthropological concepts from ethnographic instances. Generalising a rebuke to Margaret Mead, Steiner writes:

> one cannot expect much success of such an attempt [to restrict the sense of a term]; the world accepts an extension of meaning much more readily than it allows any loss of connotation. (Volume I, p. 109, above)

As Lévi-Strauss was later to dissolve 'totemic thought' as an instance of a style of thought in general, so Steiner intends to dissolve 'taboo' within a broader analytic category of relations between socially shared conceptions of value and danger. The fact that the entire discussion appears as a preamble to a first chapter entitled 'The Discovery of Taboo' – after which follows a discussion of the historical circumstances of Cook's report of the term from Polynesia – means its importance as a framing device can easily be lost. The next thirty pages are devoted to historical scholarship and a close textual analysis of the early reports.

That 'taboo' struck Cook as odd but passed unremarked by Spanish visitors might, Steiner speculates, be accounted for by the former's northern Protestantism. As Europeans began to speculate why eating should be considered an intimate activity by people who went largely unclad, he begins to detect 'that ... irritated indulgence which some people have for others who cannot think clearly' (p. 112). With Steiner, the strangeness of the representing Western subject is never far from view. From the writings on Polynesia, as he relates, the word rapidly gained general currency in English with a sense of 'sacred prohibition' or 'forbidden'. The idea of 'taboo' as a 'problem' emerged from this Western appropriation of an exotic term.

Two following chapters attempt to recontextualise the specifically Polynesian senses of the term. Speculating from etymological accounts and usage, Steiner supposes that 'taboo' most likely derived from 'marked off' and was used of things, circumstances and characteristics that were indivisibly 'holy' and 'forbidden', the two senses not being separable as they are in modern European languages. Put the other way, no European term was available to translate the undivided sense of the Polynesian original. Referring to Malinowki's 'brilliant essay', Steiner notes that the meaning of the term can be found only situationally 'in the manifold simultaneous overlapping and divergent usages of the word' (p. 119).

The particularities of the Polynesian concept were related to Polynesia's political organisation and notions of power, *mana*. Power was measured by the recognised capacity to restrict, and chiefs of greater power could delegate some specific ability for interdiction to their inferiors. *Mana* and *tabu* therefore classified and energised what was otherwise inchoate, indeterminate or of no significance, *noa*, and did so by imputing to the Polynesian world dangers that were of a piece with Polynesian political ideas and practices. The breach of taboos was strongly sanctioned. Taboo, in its Polynesian context, thus exemplifies the broad thesis already presented in 'On the Process of Civilisation'.

From this ethnographic and close textual analysis, Steiner moves to the second part of his promised account – a survey of existing theories of taboo – via the observation that taboo was a 'Protestant discovery' and a 'Victorian problem'; clear indication that it is the category and problem, rather than the Polynesian ethnography, which are to be deemed problematic, and its observers who are to be construed exotic. Indeed, Steiner moves directly to discussion of Victorian ethnography. The very rationalism of Victorian thought made the remaining 'little islands' of 'do's' and 'don'ts', dubbed magic and religion, problematic (p. 133). Yet Victorian society was itself intensely, and from a mid-twentieth century perspective amusingly, taboo-ridden; a phenomenon Steiner relates to a middle class simultaneously threatened by industrialisation and swollen by new wealth. When he turns to consider the Scots, Robertson Smith and Frazer, it is apparent that one task to be pursued by Steiner's – on the surface highly digressive – disquisition will be an ethnography of Western intellectuals. Ironically, Steiner seeks to make the exotic taboo theories of the Western intellectuals comprehensible to later readers. But he has at least two other irons in the fire.

Robertson Smith and Frazer's preoccupations with 'taboo' have to be understood in terms of their interests in evolutionism: the former being concerned to trace the path of revelation to true religion, the latter being interested in the advent of science and the modern aspects of his own society. Both want to place Hebrew religion within their whiggish schemes. Steiner is preoccupied with both the what and the how of their doing this; and on both issues sides, as did his Oxford contemporaries, in broad terms with Robertson Smith against Frazer. Robertson Smith is interestingly wrong but Frazer is ridiculously muddle-headed. Robertson Smith takes religion seriously, Frazer treats it dismissively. Robertson Smith thinks, as far as one could expect of his generation, sociologically; Frazer's thought is marked by specious psychologism, faulty logic and unacknowledged free-association. Steiner might feel this less keenly if he did not find himself to belong as much on the subject's as on the analyst's side of a discussion of the ideas of the Hebrew Bible. 'The name [of God] is, in the framework of the doctrinal logic of the Pentateuch, always *qodesh* because it establishes a relationship; it has, *so we primitives think*, to be pronounced in order to exist' (p. 163, emphasis added). Steiner deftly changes masks to produce a perspectival reversal – an ironic phrase which captures Western prejudice against the Jews – they are 'the primitives': in his extended analysis of Biblical tradition, Steiner occupies the place of the native.

For Steiner, the Pentateuch evidences a 'universe of values' which can be interrogated in two main ways: in terms of its relationship to the society that conceives it and in terms of its own conceptual ordering (p. 148). The Pentateuch's values should not be teased apart to distinguish progressive from primitive strands (whether in the religiously musical manner of a Robertson Smith or in the fashion of a secular progressive like Frazer), rather it should be granted its own conceptual richness and functional relationship to a form of society. Thus, for instance, the scapegoat of the Pentateuch needs to be analysed not just as a mechanism for the external transmission of impurity but in terms of its specific expulsion into the desert where the forebears of those taking part in the rite had undergone a collective exodus until the desert had absorbed their sins and a fresh generation taken their place (pp. 142-43). A sympathetic portrait of Robertson Smith's intellectual environment may explain why he sought to distinguish between what was crude and what sublime in the Old Testament. However, Robertson Smith's (Volume I, pp. 145-46) attempt to distinguish between the holy and the superstitious was not only doomed but inexplicable outside his Protestant religious concerns. Moreover, it was demeaning to other religions that their elements be morally evaluated according only to the degree they contributed, or failed to contribute, to the ideas of a later religion.

Frazer is portrayed without redeeming features. Most notably, he lacked the sociological sense to realise that things become meaningful in determinate social contexts. When Frazer tries to argue some positive sense to taboo: that it supported rights in property and marriage, thus providing the stem to which 'were grafted the golden fruits of law and morality', Steiner's impatience is clear, this is:

> a justification, to a point, of what he regards as the most horrible superstitions, because they produced, according to his belief, a law of property and sexual propriety. All that fear and self-inflicted torture, all that pondering about life and death, all those proud and humble and desperate patterns of obedience in order to produce the *summum bonum* of the late nineteenth-century bourgeoisie. (Volume I, p. 170, above)

Behind its donnish irony, this is a passage of real anger and passion. The remaining survey chapters change tone markedly, as if Steiner could not become as agitated by mere argument as by questions of ethnographic representation. Marrett's positive contributions to taboo are such as to make even Frazer seem worthy of admiration; Radcliffe-Brown's analysis is shown to chase after the most vicious of tautologies, and his notion of ritual value is ridiculed in the process; having toyed with the notion of being unable to comment on Freud because he had not undergone psychoanalysis, Steiner concludes that it would be ungrateful to expect cogent sociological theorising from him. All is set for the denouement. Yet, as we have indicated, the conclusion withholds its theory. Fundamentally, we have seen, Steiner concludes that *tabu* is not the basis upon which to generalise about 'taboo', rather it is an instance of something far wider. 'Instead of explaining danger behaviour in terms of negative values, we may – and should – explain value behaviour in terms of positive danger' (Volume. I, p. 196, above). This approach is particularly apparent from the full draft of the lecture's concluding paragraph:

> I feel that the institutional localisation of danger can be studied apart from that function of taboo which is the classification and identification of transgressions; and this again can be separated quite well from a major fact of human existence: that we as human beings are not able and never were able to express our relations to value in other terms than danger behaviour. These things are more or less connected in various societies. To study these various problems connected as taboo means to go into the social structure

quite thoroughly, while the isolated problems may be studied as general rules of social grammar, basic social attitudes. (*Tabu*, Lecture L, fol.3).

Laura Bohannan's sensitively edited version (Volume I, p. 214) is clearly the more elegant, but Steiner himself orders the ideas slightly differently. He emphasises the potential distinctness between three considerations: the way that danger is localised institutionally, the function of identifying and classifying transgressions, and the fact about our collective lives that value is expressed in danger behaviour. Steiner invites a comparative sociology attentive to the way danger and transgression interact in differently structured forms of human existence and, in doing so, create value. Steiner's use of the phrase 'human existence' in the context of taboo behaviour may be significant since – as we have noted – his friend Iris Murdoch was at the same time engaged in writing on existentialism. But if so, it would also be significant that Steiner's approach pluralises the 'fact' of an existential situation by reference to the differing institutional contexts within which values are created: as ever, Steiner's ideas are sociologically grounded. 'Taboo' classifies and localises danger and transgression; the task of the social anthropologist is to question how this is done institutionally and what social pressures are brought to bear through this process.

Even in isolation, the text of *Taboo* tells a richer story than its first critics allowed: as the conclusion makes clear, it is a book concerned with human existence, and should be read as a treatise on classification and value understood as aspects of all human societies. Steiner's monograph might be seen to lack a theory relating different regimes of danger to different types of society and, true, for the broadest terms of such a correlation we need to go back to 'On the Process of Civilisation' and its account of Western civilisation as an internalisation of dangers. But *Taboo* itself sets up some important markers for a comparative account of the localisation of dangers – for instance in the comparison of Polynesian cases, and in the comparisons between (particularly) Polynesian, Indian and Jewish ideas o f sacrality and transgression.

Taboo's epistemological critique of the misappropriation of indigenous values by European scholars is inseparable from its comparative, descriptive ambition. Steiner asks his readers (or listeners) to grasp the Polynesian and Western conceptions of taboo relationally; so it is precisely through the history of Western *failure* to comprehend *tabu*, and via the different category of 'taboo' that Westerners devised from their misunderstandings, that a sense of the relational standing of these different situated practices becomes present to the reader. The literary anthropologist thus conveys his own sense of 'being there' as meanings are made. This is also the sense that Steiner seemed himself to experience in reading – and lecturing on – two of his own favourite social thinkers.

Simmel and Aristotle

To Simmel

River of representation
Without footnotes, delight
Nourished from its own sources
That travels far
Yet flows into no foreign seas:
Much have I enjoyed exploring you...
Your lack of footnotes
Will trouble only professors,
But I sometimes ask myself,
How to imagine or picture
A river flowing like yours
Yet well-annotated and subject to one's wish.
Academic language is a very curious beast.

January 1952 (Steiner 2000)

The very idea of stable theoretical synthesis seems foreign to Steiner's method; and problems of method – what it means to think anthropologically – allied to a sense of what deserved to be thought about – the proper discovery of a subject matter for social anthropology – are the object of his enquiries. He constantly confronts these issues in dialogue with scholars past and present. Steiner's lectures on Aristotle and Simmel deserve our close attention, since these two thinkers epitomise for him the processes by which sociological problems are posed and addressed; his sense of identification with both is strong. Aristotle was a recurrent point of reference for Steiner. Evans-Pritchard noted that one of the three books on which Steiner was working at the time of his death concerned Aristotle's sociology. Apart from his 'Discourse on Aristotle' (Ms 1949a: 304-326), a draft lecture on Aristotle survives, which we reprint here (pp. 202-207, below). In this paper, Aristotle is presented as the founder of formal sociology, one whom it has again become possible to appreciate. Between the Renaissance and the First World War, social thought was held in thrall by the interests of the European middle classes, for whom the individual was taken for granted as a locus of needs to be satisfied within society. Aristotle's brilliance was really something quite simple: he saw the social phenomenon in terms of the relations between relationships and institutions, and the combination of these relationships. Steiner continues that 'it is possible to grade European sociologists of later times according to their similarities in interests, outlook and approach with the master'.

What is the most characteristic feature of this approach? Like all things of genius it is something very simple. It is the refusal to regard the human being and human society as two separable things, or, in the philosophical idiom, they are not 'given' separately: they may belong to different levels of reality, but within every human being, society is given. The human individual himself is a social phenomenon, and human beings cannot be abstracted from society, just as for us it is nonsensical to separate word-language from thought, as if there was something in our thought that is not words but can be thought and eventually expressed in words. Aristotle refuses to regard man as anything but a societal creature, a *zoon politikon*. (p. 203, below)

Since man is a societal creature it is part of his being to belong to associations, such as the *polis*, which are themselves social activities. Associations exist for a purpose, although their growth is not of necessity a function of this purpose. Steiner's lecture ends peremptorily by noting Aristotle's achievement as the source of the distinguishing features of different social forms. However, Steiner's lectures on Simmel – his final lecture course – follow seamlessly from his reading of Aristotle. We print them for the light they throw on Steiner's thought in the last phase of his life – when he was already a dying man: he died before the final lecture could be written – and *not*, we must stress, as an introduction to Simmel's work. Students who wish to acquaint themselves with Simmel would be advised to consult the more recent literature. However, as a reflection on Steiner's thought and the position of anthropology at Oxford in 1952, we believe they are an essential part of the story we wish to tell.

Steiner's work probably represents the first lecture course devoted to Simmel held within a British department of social anthropology. We know that Steiner worked at Oxford and at the British Museum Library in preparing the lectures, and assume that he had bibliographical problems. This may have caused some of the difficulties in his lectures. Others may be the result of the colossal pressure under which Steiner was working. Many issues would all be treated differently today, some of which we list here. Plain errors appear to include Steiner's comments on Simmel's attitude to his family and to the war. His relation to Judaism also deserves more attention (Liebersohn 1988: 152). Simmel supported the war and was widely associated with Jewish thought, even on occasion being the object of anti-Semitic criticism. The observation of Simmel's reliance on eighteenth-century ideas of reification and objectification, though interesting, would need further analysis, and the section on the German Kant-revival is sketchy. Steiner's comment 'never lectured on Hegel' would need to be set against Simmel's knowledge of Hegel and the critique of Hegel's teleology that informs so much of his work. The relation to Nietzsche needs clarification, as does that to Weber. Regarding Simmel's ideas, it can be argued that Steiner appears to neglect that the 'form'/'content' distinction grounds many aspects of Simmel's thought; and it may also be objected that Simmel's theory of value needs greater attention in the concluding lecture, where the links need to be drawn between value-formation and Simmel's theory of structure and system – 'value' might well have formed a topic for the unwritten, final lecture.

Against all this, one needs to set Steiner's originality in presenting Simmel at Oxford in 1952. The earlier interest of the Oxford School in Simmel is apparent from Radcliffe-Brown's attention to him (Volume I, p. 65, above) as well as from the fact that Laura Bohannan gave a talk on him to one of the Oxford Friday seminars attended by Mary Douglas and others around 1948 (Mary Douglas: PC). Also, one is struck by the personal identification Steiner seems to evoke with many elements of Simmel: the polymath, the unclassifiable scholar, the Jewish outsider, above all Simmel's sense of the 'problem':

> Not that the problems Simmel saw were more important than the answers he found to them – but the problem is the thing that remains in the mind of Simmel's readers, it is carefully constructed, grows, diminishes, disappears, to make place for a hydra of other problems. The problems are the lumps in a slowly moving river of arguing. We watch them dissolving. (p. 200, below)

Steiner appears to be treating Simmel as his ancestor when recalling the German-Jewish scholar's career; and what Steiner says of the problem in Simmel will be echoed after his death by Canetti's comments on the 'question' in Steiner (Volume I, p. 79, above). Uncannily, Steiner even appears to forsee his own end, juxtaposing the death of the sociologist with the end of a European war; Simmel moved from Berlin to the University of Strasbourg in late middle age, 'this appointment, and life in the war-overshadowed and war-congested city, was a painful anti-climax to his active teaching life, and he was a sick man already. He died a month before the end of the war which had destroyed all he stood for' (p. 209).

There are other respects, however, in which Simmel seems less admirable, which may mean only that there are aspects of Simmel with which Steiner could not (or did not want to) identify. Simmel, according to Steiner, was of a 'typical Berlin Jewish bourgeois family', 'steeped in German middle-class culture'; this Steiner might let pass, but Simmel's family 'had gone as far as accepting the Lutheran creed', and Simmel himself 'was brought up a Protestant'. As we know from Steiner's letter to Georg Rapp, constancy in religious affiliation was not something negotiable (at least for others) so far as the post-war Steiner was concerned. Simmel, in Steiner's view, was a stranger to religious insight.

However, philosophically it is this resistance to transcendence that Steiner admires: as, for instance, in Simmel's refusal to find an 'underneathness of the true meaning' of historical facts. Whether the following comment is addressed to Evans-Pritchard one can only wonder:

> The historical fact is its own true nature, nothing factual can be abstracted from it. We can conceive it as a configuration of events and split this to obtain component parts, which, however, have no more true nature than the whole. The abstractions are due to our categories of thought and to value judgements. (p. 213, below)

Like Radcliffe-Brown, Simmel could fall into the trap of distinguishing between historical (chronologically causal) and scientific accounts of a phenomenon. But the givenness of the historical sequence is illusory. Radcliffe-Brown's favoured example (why did a girl drop the glass; in chronological terms because she was startled, in scientific terms because the law of gravity dictates that unsupported objects fall) simply plays on a confusion of different senses of the term 'why?'. Better known examples (for this one with a derogatory reference to a 'blackman' as the cause of the girl's alarm presumably derives from R.-B.'s lectures), are R.-B.'s assertions that the contemporary race horse can be understood aside from its evolution, as can the contemporary political constitution of the United States. The distinction R.-B. seeks to make, wrongly for Steiner, is between historical and functional understandings (1952: 3; [1935] 1952: 185). To his credit, Simmel was to abandon this search for laws similar to those that (erroneously) sociologists tend to believe sanctify the results achieved by scientists.

Again, similarly to Radcliffe-Brown in his distinction between observable social structure and structural form, Simmel believes:

> society as a concept has two meanings which we must distinguish carefully: one meaning is that of the whole complex of associated individuals, the 'human material societally formed'; the other meaning is the sum total of all those forms of relationship with the help of which the individuals become (or we would say: are) the society in the first sense. ... He uses the analogy of geometry, saying that a sphere too has two meanings: a part of matter shaped in a certain way – spherically – but also the shape itself, the mathematical concept which we abstract (or as Simmel, the idealistic philosopher says: through which mere matter becomes the sphere in the first sense). And Simmel maintains that legitimate enquiries are related to both these concepts of society, hence there are two different social pursuits. The first, attending to the 'human material societally formed' must yield a multiplicity of contiguous but otherwise independent disciplines, following the diversified nature of the subject matter, the social content. Here we find the cluster of social sciences again, ranging from economics to the sociology of religion. General sociology, however attends to forms only, it is formal, could not be general without being exclusively formal. (p. 217, below)

Simmel, therefore, would appear to be the source of Steiner's distinction between general and specific sociology (albeit he does not believe the distinction to be water-tight, as we saw earlier). Like

Durkheim, Simmel eschews the psychological explanation of social forms but, with Steiner's apparent endorsement, his reasoning is different. Whereas Durkheim argued that social facts were qualitatively different from, therefore not reducible to psychological facts, Simmel argues that all social forms are part of the whole society, but that statements cannot be made about society in a formal sense. Claiming that what Simmel conflates as 'forms' would be what anthropologists are accustomed to distinguishing as either 'patterns of behaviour or structural principles' Steiner resolves an apparent contradiction:

> we can better appreciate now the peculiar accident which creates an affinity between our empirical endeavours and this most abstract of all sociologists: we confront whole social entities and our analysis brings out the overall features of their institutional life. ... For any fact, any attitude, any principle we try to find all the social contexts in which they are operative, Simmel comes to a similar method as a result of abstraction. (pp. 218, 219, below)

Essentially, Steiner seems to be using Simmel as a source in the German sociological tradition from which to create a genealogy for the 'Oxford School' which supplants that via Radcliffe-Brown and Durkheim while retaining the primacy of the social. The following observation is critical to Steiner's approach to the social phenomenon and marks a crucial departure from Durkheim:

> This leads to the central sentence, which is most difficult to translate:
>
> > 'Nowhere does "society" exist as such; that is to say: in such a way that it could form the premises under which special (discrete) phenomena of relationship could be formed. This is because mutual influence does not exist as such, but only special kinds of it; when they occur, there *is* society; they are neither cause nor effect of society – they immediately are society.'
>
> What does this mean? It means the avoidance of insecure tautologies, such as those with which every reader of Durkheim is familiar. When it is said that the function of an institution or social activity is to create social solidarity – and the implication of 'solidarity' is the cohesiveness of society – and when the cohesiveness of a social system cannot be imagined without social activities: what else is Durkheim then saying than 'Society is society'? (p. 220, below)

Steiner's third lecture on Simmel proceeds, after some consideration of the social forms identified by Simmel, to disavow Simmel's attempt to produce a conjectural history of the evolution of such forms but notes that it is possible to use his terms comparatively, as when one compares the depth and normative character of various authorities in one society. Unfortunately, Steiner's fourth lecture – if, as seems unlikely, it was ever written – does not survive. The third ends abruptly. Two quotations from its closing pages may suggest, however, a sense of a summation:

> Behaviour is socially formed; behaviour enacts social relationships; and what we call society, social structure, social system, etc. are different types of abstractions made from the observed behaviour. There is nowhere (neither for Simmel nor for any twentieth-century sociology) a private individual that can be seen apart from society; there is nowhere the glove of social convention fitting the live and different and private flesh of a hand. (pp. 223-24, below)
>
> The question [for sociology] is: how is what appears to be, able, how does it manage to appear? Thus, the question: 'How is it possible that subordination and submission constitute, on the one hand, a form of objective organisation of society, on the other hand, the expression of personal qualities among men?' is a specific manner of asking the Simmelian question: 'How is society possible?' We know a group of data, and the proof of our knowledge is our ability to frame in terms of that group of data the basic question concerning the societal phenomenon. That is really Simmel's way of discussing sociology. And, as we cannot ask in the same way (as 'How is society possible?'), how the physical is possible, sociology is not a natural science. (p. 224, below)

Steiner's final synthesis of his concerns suggests an analytic interdependence of the general sociology of (abstracted) social forms, an ethnological investigation of cultural complexes, and an empirical sociography (indebted to both of the foregoing) as the privileged means to investigate what appear as pressing problems to an investigator necessarily situated in specific historical and political circumstances. In Steiner's hands they also constituted tools of political and personal engagement. However, these tools constitute a methodology for examining values, not a set of ultimate values in themselves.

The Poet as Anthropologist: Religion, Truth, and Myth

> *When you get lost in yourself, you don't go round in circles – oh dear, no: you go round in circles when you are on the right track.*
> *Essays and Discoveries* (1988: 116)

Franz Steiner pursued his poetry and his anthropology as two separate enterprises, conforming strictly to the rules of genre, style and aesthetics in the former, whilst adhering to the laws of evidence, logic and the specifics of his discipline in the latter. Yet his work in each area was from the very beginning deeply enmeshed with the adjoining field, such that his poetry became ever more deeply informed by his scholarship, and his mature anthropology came to display numerous markers of his poetic avocation. Although he never went so far as Evans-Pritchard to regard anthropology as an 'art', his most finished productions, notably the lectures on *Taboo*, even in their unedited form, display a remarkable command of English idiom and voice. Laura Bohannan has ironed out some stylistic infelicities, yet the printed voice is recognisably Steiner's own, with its modulations and ironies, its facticity, its equivocations, its appeals to the reader, its rhetoric: Steiner the alien enjoys nothing better than the chance to go native among the British. We see him, the incorrigible exile, gleefully donning the skin of a senior common room speaker. It pleases him to play the role of a donnish tutor while going about his business as a head-hunter who proudly displays the lifeless heads of earlier scholars, from Frazer and Malinowski to Freud and Radcliffe-Brown, among his collection. He is, then, an intimate of the poetic method, of empathies and transformations, even when engaging in the most rigorous discourse. Indeed, as we shall suggest, even at the terminological, conceptual, and methodological levels of his discourse, recognisably 'literary' elements assume a pivotal role, to the extent that they enter the substance of his thinking.

We do not here wish to explore all the ramifications of the dialogue between poetry and anthropology in Steiner's work. That would lead too far. But some understanding of the way in which anthropology enriches his verse is helpful, and we believe: essential for an understanding of his scholarship (not to mention the ways in which 'literary' ideas entered his theories). Whether in the adoption of ethnic materials in the poetic *Variations*, of anthropological subject matter in poems like 'Capturing Elephants', or of anthropological notions like 'purity' in 'Leda', we are faced by a consistent deepening of the lyric by scholarly insight. Twentieth-century poetry, from T.S. Eliot's *The Waste Land* to Jerome Rothenberg's ethnopoetics and the work of Nathanael Tarn, has been rich in such dialogues, which hark back to Vico and Herder (Rothenberg and Rothenberg 1983). Steiner stands out, however, as being one of the few practitioners in both fields. From 1942 to 1943 onwards, the aphoristic form enters into dialogue both with Steiner's poetry and with his anthropology, on the one hand anticipating and reacting to his scholarship, and, on the other, overlapping with his verse, to the extent that some aphorisms read like short scholarly disquisitions, whilst others read like lyrical texts. In some, like that we print as 'Conrad and Malinowski', we find a surprising prefiguration of later concerns (Clifford 1988: 92-115; Fardon 1990). Steiner's concern with 'margins' also entails extending the boundaries of genre, discipline, and thought. His *margins* – like Prague, like Sub-Carpathian Ruthenia – are also, crucially, unexplored *centres*, areas of *overlap*, points of *intersection*. When, in *Taboo*, he briefly adopts the voice of a 'primitive', he permits his religious viewpoint to intersect with his scholarly discourse; and when, in *Conquests*, he introduces the myth of Robinson Crusoe, he foregrounds himself as a child – first reading the myth – as a literary man – recalling the myth – and as an intellectual explorer – revalidating the myth; correlatively, echoing Marx in *Das Kapital*, he also refers to Robinson Crusoe at the end of 'Towards a Classification of Labour': the literary reference fits to the pursuit of scholarly learning. A key contribution of Steiner's lies in probing such intersections, margins, borders, and boundaries – whether thematically, as in examining the rules governing danger behaviour, or generically.

Two or three leading ideas from German Romanticism appear to have left their mark on this aspect of Steiner's method. One is Friedrich Schlegel's notion of a 'progressive universal poetry' (Eichner 1970: 57 ff.), a mode that encompasses poetry and prose, literature and philosophy, rhetoric and criticism. 'Progressive universal poetry', according to Schlegel, was to unite all forms of expression into a single whole. Another idea is Novalis's connected fragmentary 'encyclopaedism' (Neubauer 1980: 51 ff.), in which a totality is invoked by fragmentary aphoristic texts (O'Brien 1995: 145), each of which chemically (Schlegel's notion) connects diverse ideas. Yet another related idea is Friedrich Schlegel's call for a 'new mythology', so close to the demand for a 'mythology of reason' in *The Oldest System-Programme of German Idealism* (Jamme and Schneider 1984; anon 1988; Volume I, pp. 81-82, above). Steiner's aphorisms, to some extent, recall this romantic idealism, but by and large his work exhibits a generic stringency informed by, but wholly at variance with, this romantic 'mixture' (to use another Schlegel term): linking the fields of scholarship, poetry, personal communication and aphorism never means merging the forms, let alone confusing them; for Franz Steiner, each utterance follows its own rhetoric, which links the statement to its own realm of discourse. In looking to see how some of these different areas interconnected, therefore, we do not propose to collapse their differences, but simply to consider how the sundry parts of Steiner's oeuvre hang together in a concern with religion, truth, and myth. We begin with the poetry.

From the outset, a close link can be observed between poetry and anthropology in Steiner's work. To each poem he attaches the exact date and place of composition. As a result, his typescript 'Collected Poems', with its careful chronology and geography, takes on the appearance of a notebook from the field, in which the observer chronicles his own spiritual development against the parameters of a constantly changing scenery. The staging posts in this quest include Bohemia, Palestine, Austria, Dalmatia, the Carpathians, England, Wales, Scotland, and Spain. The starting point that Steiner sets is Palestine. This is where the earliest pieces in his 'Collected Poems' originated. By treating Palestine in this way, it functions for him as origin in more sense than one. Palestine, with its melons and sands reappears in the *Conquests*, too, the central autobiographical poem which is his *magnum opus* and which preoccupied Steiner during the war years, when he was engaged in writing his thesis on slavery. From this poem we print the first seven sections (pp. 247-66, below).

Steiner's *Conquests* are conceived in the tradition of Wordsworth's *Prelude* as an extended autobiographical poem, and are equally set against the background of the great poetic cycles of the twentieth century, Rilke's *Duineser Elegien* (Duino Elegies) and Eliot's *Four Quartets*. Steiner began the cycle at Oxford in 1940 (Parts I, II, IV, XIII), continued it over the next two years until mid-1942 (Parts III, V, VII, VIII), and added a further section in 1943 (X), concluding with a final piece in 1945 (XII). By then, he had settled on the poem's definitive structure of thirteen parts. However, IX and XI remain unwritten. Steiner explicitly rejected a ten-part poem. 'That must be avoided on every account because of the [ten] commandments. After all, that would also be bad because of the [Duino] Elegies' (J. Adler 1994a: 148). As Wordsworth called the *Prelude* 'a long poem on the formation of my own mind', Steiner describes his text as 'a metaphysical autobiographical poem' (1994a: 148). Elsewhere, he expands on his plan, and underplays the autobiographical content:

> The *Conquests* are an extended, and in a sense autobiographical poem, which introduces and repeatedly seeks to reanimate a sequence of memories from childhood into adulthood with the aim of self-examination and with a generalising purpose. By repeating and varying combinations of the elements, different configurations emerge, which are intended to explore the remembering self and the nature of memory. The actual content: the affirmation of 'repetition' in life and the demand that memory be sacrificed. (After Fleischli 1970: 42)

The term 'conquests' in the poem is used for the 'memories' which the subject constructs of the world, and ironically intimates the violent colonialism which understanding the world entails. For memories, which are the 'heaped-up stacks of past experience', are ultimately no more than 'worn-out remnants from the past', 'the debris of formerly collected bliss' (I, l.16ff.). In deconstructing memory, Steiner also deconstructs the Western subject, who is 'master of so little'. 'How far', the poem asks, does a human being's 'dominion extend?' (IV, I, l.21ff.). The reply to this rhetorical question implies the vacuity of all human 'conquests' and 'dominion'. By adopting the word 'conquests' for his own experience, Steiner draws an extreme consequence from his critique by internalising the very idea of Western colonialism that he abhors. He is thus able to take it apart in a consistently nonviolent manner, since it is only his own putatively dominating subjectivity that he destructs. The device of 'repetition' that he uses in his explorations is a key idea in his work. The notion also has a strong deconstructive force in that it points to the underlying feature of memory in a simple, formalistic, and therefore non-prejudicial manner. A 'memory' is *a priori* nothing other than a certain form of 'repetition'. The beauty of the concept is that it contains none of the auratic overtones that the term 'memory' normally entails. It begs no questions about 'mind', and none about 'time'. Nor does it possess the law-like quality of a 'regularity'. In Steiner's thinking, life itself consists in a series of such repetitions, just as rituals and customs are also simply 'repetitions'. The apparent dullness of the idea hides its radical power. The apparent lack of insight it offers is the very insight that it permits. For 'repetition' clearly denotes a simple category anterior to notions such as 'ritual'. As a constitutive factor in natural and human life, the notion links very diverse areas of experience ranging from mental phenomena ('memory') and social ones ('customs') as comparable entities, entirely avoiding issues such as causality, mentalism, intention, and so on. 'Repetition' is, then, one of Steiner's modestly deconstructive terms by which he excavates to reach a less elusive if apparently trivial layer underlying human behaviour. It is also a less loaded term for 'law'. Finally, the 'sacrifice' of 'memory' and 'conquest' at the conclusion of the *Conquests* brings about the end of 'repetition': life ends, and the subject renounces its 'conquests'. This final renunciation recalls the Jewish loss of self in God after death, but is no less indebted to the spirit of the *Gita* and the Hindu *nirvana*.

The architecture of Steiner's cycle is conceived on the grand scale. It may therefore be helpful to summarise the main features of each poem: I. *The step swings away* forms a prelude which introduces the speaker in a landscape and reflects that all that remains with a person are memories or 'conquests', the individual's exclusive possessions; II. *Memories* recalls the speaker's childhood and his reading of Robinson Crusoe – that key text for Steiner's persona as traveller and anthropologist – and finally reaches an aporia, the inexplicable 'closing of the heart'; III. *The heart* defines the organ of human life and understanding, questions its governance, yet fails to resolve the aporia; IV. *To retain a little* examines a sequence of memories or conquests associated with the landscapes of Dalmatia and Palestine, raising the question of memory's governance; V. *The lonely man* reaches the nub of the argument: questioning the earlier aporia, it constructs a myth of time, the soul, and the 'lonely figure' in order to account for the heart's closure; VI. *With a sleeping woman at his back* presents the speaker after a sexual encounter, confronted by the Way, 'the writing on the wall', and death; VII. *The leaf of the ash* is a turning point that meditates on the black and deadly bud of hope; VIII. *The dying man* establishes a counter-type to the 'lonely one' and quests for certainty ('exactness'), which is ultimately found, hesitantly, in memories, and more positively in hope; IX. the unwritten *The bear in the coat of arms* (punning on 'Baermann' Steiner) was planned to describe the Carpathians and the various peoples there – Ukrainians, Gypsies, Jews; X. The unfinished *The wheels* locates the speaker in exile in London, understood as Babylon, and develops the theme of exile, of which Hölderlin as wanderer is understood as an exemplar; XI. the unwritten *At the time of the flood* was planned as a meditation on a flooded meadow at Oxford, completing the cycle's mythic staging posts, it was to introduce the myth of Noah, and possibly justify the superiority of myth over speculation; XII. *The spider and the moon* treats the figure of the exile and the act of prayer; XIII. *The step ceases* recapitulates the central themes and reaches a resolution in the end of the human subject: the ultimate telos of the 'conquests' is to disintegrate.

The *Conquests* evoke a multiplicity of cultural references to map their spiritual concerns, welding them into Steiner's own new mythology of the self. The writer works as a 'myth-maker' in Steiner and Canetti's senses (Volume I, pp. 80-83, above) in that he *transforms* diverse materials from different cultures into a new whole. If Rilke's *Duino Elegies* provide a major locus in modern German poetry, the cycle also looks back to Hölderlin, whom Steiner celebrates in an early version of X, ii. as the 'wanderer' – an epithet Hölderlin here shares with Simmel's 'stranger'. Steiner's vatic persona recalls the priestly voice in Hölderlin's oracular late hymns, just as his attempt to splice together various religions recalls Hölderlin's grand scheme to unite monotheism and polytheism in a new synthesis of Greek and Christian thought. Indeed, Hölderlin's continual play on the interrelations between West and East provide a significant poetic reference for Steiner's own concerns. The *Gita*, as mentioned, provides a key to the philosophy of renunciation that the *Conquests* invoke, but other religious texts are equally implicated: the use of parallelism recalls the Hebrew Bible and the Psalms, and the calmly distanced, apparently objective style is also much indebted to Lao Tse. Steiner had known the *Tao Te Ching* in Wilhem's celebrated translation since his youth in Prague, and heavily annotated his copy later, possibly when writing the *Conquests*. In 1942 he also bought the translation into English by Ch'u Tao-Kao, and Arthur Waley's *The Way and its Power*, both of which appeared in London that same year. Besides the gnomic impersonality of the *Tao Te Ching*, some of Lao Tse's leading ideas will be found again in *Conquests*. In literary modernism, Eliot's 'The Waste Land' provides an exemplar of a poem linking Western and Eastern cultural materials, though Steiner is perhaps more intimate with Eastern religion than Eliot, and for the verse form, too, Steiner is indebted to the Eliot of 'Ash Wednesday' and after. Eliot's English verse provided a model for a style which could seamlessly accommodate the most diverse cultural materials.

The relation betweeen Steiner's *Conquests* and Eliot's *The Four Quartets* is not as simple as it first appears. Steiner's poem looks like an amplification of the *Quartets*, but this is not the case. Steiner's admiration for Eliot is implicit in his fine translation of *Marina*, and Eliot clearly provided a significant inspiration for him as a modern *poeta doctus*: a learned poet in the Renaissance style. However, the work of Eliot's which the *Conquests* most obviously resemble, *The Four Quartets*, was not yet published, let alone completed, at the time Steiner began his *magnum opus*. The first poem, *East Coker*, only appeared as a pamphlet in September 1940, about a month after Steiner had begun work on the *Conquests*, though he may not in fact have encountered the poem before November 1941, when he bought the fifth impression (February 1941). He marked several passages in pencil in his copy and that same year acquired 'Burnt Norton' which then appeared (February 1941). Here too he marked several passages in pencil and began work on a translation of the poem, producing versions of sections I and III. It seems likely that around this time he began to take issue with Eliot's ideas. He counters Eliot's memorable reflections on 'Time past and time present' in his own notions of the time (or seasons) of the soul in *Conquests*, V: 'The lonely man' (1942). Intriguingly, the vocabulary of Eliot's reflection – that 'only through time time is conquered' – seems to be echoed in Steiner's single word title; but Steiner depersonalises Eliot's notion: time is the object of the 'lonely man' and his 'conquests', 'debris' of 'formerly perfected bliss', are the memories he must relinquish to attain *nirvana*. After this linguistic convergence the *Conquests* and the *Quartets* diverged. The *Dry Salvages* appeared in 1941, *Little Gidding* in 1942, and in each case Steiner bought his copy after a year's delay. The publication of the *Four Quartets* as a single volume followed in 1944, confirming the work as a major new poetic cycle. The similarities between Eliot's work and Steiner's are not, then, to be explained in terms of a direct influence of the completed *Quartets* on the *Conquests* as might at first appear. The intertextuality is more complex. Steiner, like Eliot himself, began with the verse line and the style of meditative poetry that Eliot had pioneered in *Ash Wednesday* and, independently of Eliot, recognised its suitability for a grand meditative poem. He began his poem almost simultaneously with Eliot, reacted to Eliot's composition, and continued work for about a year after Eliot's poem had appeared in print. Because of his failure to complete this grand project, Steiner's dialogue with Eliot remained tantalisingly open-ended, unless we count 'Prayer in the Garden' as a late rejoinder to Eliot's religiosity.

In the absence of any material from the first draft of Steiner's dissertation, the *Conquests* are among the most important records we possess of Steiner's intellectual development during the war years, when he was moving beyond his first assimilation of structural functional anthropology (largely owed to Radcliffe-Brown) and forging a more personal methodology and epistemology through his political and poetic writings, as well as his aphorisms. The *Conquests* probably are the closest that Steiner came to producing a grand synthesis of his thought during this period. Interpreting them is tricky partly because of their hermetic style, partly because they are unfinished, yet it may not be going too far to recognise in them certain characteristic features of Steiner's social anthropology. The Robinson Crusoe myth of Steiner's youth is firmly embedded in the second poem as a starting point for his intellectual life:

> Lashed to the mast ...
> ...
> You make me pious.

Steiner reverts to the Robinson Crusoe myth in the final poem in which he adopts Crusoe's persona for the poem's 'I' (X, l.26ff.). But he rewrites the myth and the geography of the original voyage. The 'feathered tree', which recurs at key points in the poem, does not appear in Defoe's novel and serves Steiner as a powerful if deeply enigmatic symbol, variously conveying both the biblical tree of life and the tree of knowledge, and also Rilke's more concrete 'tree' in the first of the *Duino Elegies*. Steiner's 'tree' may recall the shape of the palm-tree, and it may also be a reference to the plant *iberis semperflorens*, which is at home throughout the mediterranean region and as far as the coast of Palestine and is in German called *Federbaum* or 'feathered tree' (Ziegler Ms 1996). Its habitat may therefore here connect the biblical land with the south seas and the West as a mythic culture circle. The captain 'lashed to the mast' and with his 'bleeding forehead' recalls Christ. A strong set of parallels seems to connect the natural botanical life ('feathered tree') with Western material culture and religion ('mast'). A sense of sacrifice pervades this scene: the captain as 'sufferer' seems mysteriously to be re-enacting the Passion, and the 'foundling' on the distant isle appears to have merged with the 'wilderness', and to return as a renewer of Western culture and religion. Steiner's thought is here utterly concrete, and lacking in the normal auratic quality one associates with poetic symbolism. In this instance, the concrete symbol evokes the mutually exclusive worlds of civilisation and savagery. It is interesting to note that the only violence in the scene is introduced by the ship's crew and is perpetrated by Westerners on one of their number, the captain, whereas the Westerner-turned-'savage', Robinson, is at one with his environment.

The new myth tells of the meeting between primitivism and civilisation in an act of renewal. This bears directly on Steiner's fate. Robinson Crusoe's sojourn on the island, as a moment of isolation and exile, in renewing 'piety', recalls other 'memories' in the poem, and specifically those in the incomplete section, *The wheels*, namely: the historical exile of the Jewish people in Babylon, which itself rehearses their wanderings in the desert, and the speaker's own exile in London, the poem's modern Babylon. Just as the Jewish people emerged purified from the desert, so Robinson Crusoe comes from the island to restore faith. Steiner's handling of myth here differs considerably from that in earlier twentieth-century German poets like Rilke and Trakl: whereas they tend to witness a quasi-timeless mythical moment, e.g., in the Egyptian landscape of Rilke's tenth *Duino Elegy*, Steiner envisages a quite distinct diachronic sequence, each involving particular moments; but instead of observing a historical *process*, time consists in a sequence of mythic *reenactments*. His notions of 'time' and 'selfhood' signally abjure the all-pervasive language of 'growth' introduced into German literature and the human sciences by Herder and Goethe: 'growth', 'process', 'development' – these biological metaphors, from the poem's standpoint, prove to be just another construct.

The poem's persona builds onto the Robinson myth a further dimension by representing Steiner's own experiences in terms of culture circles ethnology and marrying this with the more structural sociology of 'circles' developed by Simmel. Echoing out from Steiner's Bohemian homeland in the opening poem, the *Conquests* evoke various regions as if they could be understood as a single whole, one culture circle. Dalmatia and Palestine feature in the fourth poem, connected by the mediterranean habitat of vines and olives. The specifics of the culture circle are denoted by distinct botanical species, e.g., 'the blue-eyed herb' in Bohemia (II, l. 63) and the biblical 'spikenards' in Palestine (IV, 4, l. 40), yet the regions are brought together by the experience of the subject.

It is into this synchronically conceived geography that the poem maps its diachronic schema, by which it links the speaker to biblical time:

> This hurrying man in an evening mood
> And with a heaving breast believes:
> That long ago he stood before the Holy City:
> That he paced around the walls
> And saw in the shade of the olive trees
> The Kidron ... (IV, l.1ff.)

The imagery recalls the past via detailed associations that accrue to this biblical landscape in modern German poetry: Trakl, in his own cyclical poem, *Helian*, similarly imagines himself looking back to the river Kidron (Lindenberger 1971: 79), allowing his lyrical persona to merge its identity with Rimbaud, Hölderlin, and Christ (Sharp 1981: 89). In contrast to Trakl's Helian, however, Steiner's persona seems to envisage a reincarnation – though less endemic in Judaism, the doctrine is as familiar in the teachings of the Kabbalah as it is in Hinduism (Scholem 1956). By such small ambiguities, Steiner's poem merges Jewish doctrines with other Eastern religions. The cited passage has about it such a ring of truth that we may well imagine that it captures Steiner's self-discovery in Jerusalem. The mythical quality gains resonance both from the poem's facticity, and from the conceptual grounding given to myth. Notions like 'ritual' and 'sacrifice' inform the whole discourse, even when the terms themselves are not uttered.

Besides the culture circles ethnology, therefore, there appears to be a new dimension to Steiner's thought here, that cannnot be explained in terms of myth and Central European ethnology alone. This is most apparent in his treatment of the human subject. Goethe and Wordsworth bequeathed to modern poetry its sense of the subjective self which is celebrated in Romantic music and verse as the individual's defining feature. Modernism has rent this subjectivity asunder, and in particular German poetry since the turn of the century increasingly contended with Ernst Mach's dictum, that 'the subject cannot be saved' – *das Ich ist unrettbar* (Mach 1900: 17); Gottfried Benn, who in an early poem writes of the decaying subject in terms of *Ich-Zerfall* (self-dissolution) and the *Zersprengtes Ich* (exploded self; Benn 1966: 52) recalls Mach's *unrettbares Ich* in his 'lost I', the *verlorenes Ich* (lost self; 1966: 215); and Malinowski, too, wrestles with this problem in his diary, posthumously published as *A Diary in the Strict Sense of the Term* (1967), which in the place of a coherent 'subject' represents the 'self' as a fluid bundle of seemingly unconnected impulses. When Steiner deconstructs traditional notions of the 'subject', he develops Mach's ideas which, in their anti-subjectivism, fit extremely well with Steiner's Eastern sources. Not even the body in the *Conquests* is regarded as a single coherent whole. This is clear from the start:

> The step swings away,
> The body hurries through the evening,
> The stretched breast does not heed the arms,
> The arms are loosely attached and helpless. ... (I, l.1ff.)

Likewise the inner self seems to consist of compartmentalised elements overseen by the 'heart' as the poem's unifying organ:

> The heart, the created interior being
> In a body, that hurried through evenings

(the breast never heeded
The arms, lightly and helplessly attached).
Which preserves the fleeting person. ...(III, l.1ff)

Bodily detachment, as an extension of Mach's loss of the 'subject', provides a concrete correlative to the psychological compartmentalisation which the poem enacts. One recalls Mach's dictum that the distinction between 'I' and 'body' is arbitrary (1900: 15), and that 'It is not the "I" which is primary, but its elements (feelings). The elements form the "I"'. Along with Mach's concept of the 'I', Steiner's understanding also shares Mach's concomitant anti-subjectivity, his collectivism, his respect for otherness, and his stoic acceptance of death as a mere rearrangement of elements (1900: 66ff). Steiner's divisible self may be localised intellectually between Mach and Simmel.

In *Conquests*, Steiner's 'self' is seen in various roles. Typically distinguished expressions of selfhood include the lover, 'the lonely man', and 'the dying man' – these last being introduced as two of the *Conquests*' key types in the second poem. The view which becomes apparent here is no longer internalist, lyrical or subjective, but is, we believe, cognate with Steiner's growing sociological awareness. We sense that the poem's 'self' is a social being as understood by Simmel in his *Soziologie*, and is perhaps indebted to Simmel's notions of 'concentric' and 'overlapping' circles which meet in any given subject. As Simmel writes: 'The number of the different circles in which an individual is situated is the measure of a culture. ...'; the greater the number of 'circles' a given individual occupies, the more unique his individuality will be, as the point of intersection of several quite distinct circles (1923: 311-13). As in Simmel, the circles in which the *Conquests*' subject participates are not just cultural, but social. This can be seen for instance in the sixth poem. In 'With a sleeping woman at his back', the speaker as lover remains in a bedroom on a Sunday morning, whilst others go to church. His mistress still lies asleep in bed after their night of abandon. While she sleeps, he assumes the role of *homo religiosus* and glimpses the 'Way' that passes through the bedroom. In looking at the woman's body as 'neatly sculpted' (VI, l.39), he betrays his familiarity with Goethe's celebrated fifth *Roman Elegy* in which Goethe compares his mistress to a classical sculpture, and in commenting on the girl's 'stockings' and 'gown with silken fringes, rosy tinsel' (VI, l.23ff.), he alludes to modern luxury goods and modern forms of entertainment – this is a dancer's dress – and indeed to the whole modern *Kulturindustrie* typified by fashion-wear, consumption, and display. His self is thus intersected by several distinct social circles in Simmel's sense: he belongs to modern industrial society characterised by a conspicuous display of consumer goods which also define the female body; within this frame, we see him as a (possibly dissolute) lover; and he is also marked by being a non-churchgoer. He is, therefore, a social outsider. Yet at the same time he is intimate with German literary culture (Goethe) and scientific thought (Mach) as well as with Eastern teachings, both Hebrew and Taoist. And finally – though the list could be extended – he is the upholder of a personal myth of Robinson Crusoe (note the reference to the 'feathered tree', VI, l.91), i.e., a mental voyager, an anthropologist of the spirit. The poetic subject at this moment in the poem is therefore the point of intersection between the divergent and indeed conflicting social circles represented by primitivism, Eastern teaching, the Christian Church, and modern Western manners.

The view of the self that here emerges is, then, only in part to be associated with Ernst Mach's *unrettbares Ich*. It is also a sociologically informed, early structuralist view: the subject is defined by his social role, by his participation in different institutionalised fields of activity. We are close here to Simmel's notion that the subject encompasses conflicting circles and is actually enriched and strengthened by the dualisms it has to bear: 'the more manifold the group interests that meet and issue within us, the more decisively the I becomes aware of its unity' (1923: 313). Crucially, Steiner's 'I' in the poem thinks together the very circles which, according to Simmel, have created the greatest conflicts in the past – different religions (1923: 322). The constructed 'I' of the poem, by syncretising Judaism and the Tao in the context of an adjoining Christian 'circle', exercises a harmonising, ecumenical function. In distinction to the normal lyrical self of romantic poetry still propagated by Rilke, there is nothing remotely 'private' or 'inward' about Steiner's notion of self. There is also another oddity about it. His 'self' appears to have no kinship ties: it is a kindred spirit of his enslaved people and of the subject of his dissertation. His 'self' is defined by its partibility, its ethnographic reach, and its capacity to encompass alterity. Here we return to the observation with which we opened this essay: Steiner was not a fieldworker – in the accepted sense of anthropologists of his time – but the range of his interests, cultural capacities (both in language and knowledge) and the range and emotional depth of his experience, allowed him to internalise the ethnographic attitude. Steiner discovered within himself the wonder, the terror and puzzlement that he sees as the source of ethnographic curiosity.

The definition of the 'I' in sociological terms is inseparable from both the religious and the mythic tenor of the *Conquests*. This can be seen from the definition the poem lends to the 'lonely man', who is 'the firmament', and the 'guardian' of 'home' and of 'time' (V, l.142 and 182). As a figure, the 'lonely man' recalls the Jewish Zaddik, one of the 36 just souls whose existence guarantees the continued maintenance of the universe (Scholem 1963: 216ff.). As a 'guardian' of time, he also acts as the steward of human memory. Paradoxically, therefore, Steiner's 'lonely man' is a fully integrated human being – the ambiguity being suggested by the German *der Einsame* (etymologically: 'one-same', as in English 'alone' or 'all-one'); integrated by virtue both of his social function towards other people, and towards the cosmos itself. As 'steward', though, the 'lonely man' also approximates closely to the figure of the poet in Steiner and Canetti (Volume I, pp. 78-79), who is – depending on whose formulation one chooses – 'the guardian of metamorphoses' (Canetti) or 'the guardian of the myths of every people' (Steiner). Poetry, religion, myth, sociology, and psychology meet as an amalgam in the 'self' of the *Conquests*. This distinguishes the poem from its English and German parallels, and places it, perhaps, in the ambit of Chinese philosophy.

How Steiner sees a religion of this kind emerges in the following remark: 'The maximum in religion: to be order *and* way' (Steiner 1988: 315). The categorical, structuring role in religion as Steiner understands it provides the conceptual basis for the linkage between religion as teaching ('way') and sociology ('order'). It is somewhat ironic that the intepreter is left to unpack the poem's densely allusive texture by means of such cross-cultural excursions, whereas its very success depends on its melding of diversity. The *Conquests* sternly rejects any kind of colonialism, whether military, cultural or epistemological. In so doing, the poem adds a surprising urgency to the ancient doctrine of *nirvana*.

Another poetic project of Steiner's has a strong link to his anthropology. This is his translation of what would in an earlier age have been called folksongs, his *Variations* of the 1940s. Collections of folksongs have had a foundational role in modern German poetry (Gillies 1945: 39-52; Kaiser 1996: 73-78; von Bormann 1983: 245 f.). Herder's great eighteenth-century collection, *Stimmen der Völker*, went beyond Bishop Percey's *Reliques* (1765) in gathering materials from all over the world, and in so doing gave a major impulse to the comparative study of folksong. In the Romantic age, Arnim and Brentano's *Des Knaben Wunderhorn* did a similar service for German song in gathering a garland of national verse. The Grimm's collection of fairytales, *Kinder- und Hausmärchen*, also needs to be seen in this connexion (Tully 1997: 136-69). A problem with these anthologies is their emphasis on nationhood. Herder, at the outset of this tradition, sees the *Volkslied* as a focal point for the *Volk*. Steiner's much smaller collection of *Variations* sets itself in Herder's tradition, but overtly dissociates itself from this and other traditional features.

Steiner's *Variations* may be understood as both linked and as opposed to Herder's ideas. Like Herder, Steiner introduces alien cultures to his reader, and like Herder, he does so as a comparativist. How-

ever, whereas Herder and his successors aimed to heighten national
– e.g., German – self-consciousness, Steiner opposed the roots and consequences of nationalism by including only poems by noncombatant
nations or peoples in his war-time collection. When he heard that a
people had entered the war, he removed their poems from the *Variations* (H.G. Adler: PC). A further way in which his *Variations* take issue
with the Herderian tradition is in Steiner's rejection of the notion that
folk poetry is a 'natural', 'spontaneous', 'healthy' and immediate
expression of the best qualities in a *Volk*: for Steiner, folk materials are
capable of expressing the very 'dissonances' typical of modernism (J.
Adler 1994a: 143). This can be clearly seen in his 'Lied von der Ruhe
und sonst nichts mehr', which varies a song of the Papago Indians.

> *Song about rest and nothing more*
> (Variation on a Song of the Papago Indians)
>
> Much time passes when the sun takes his leave.
> But the bat streaks; otherwise nothing more.
> The souls underneath: how nimble their play in the fluff.
> Play in the fluff and nothing more.
>
> The sun's leave-taking is slow,
> Still slower his going down.
> When the sun is down, the bat streaks
> And there's nothing more.
> The soul infants are underneath.
> They move to and fro,
> Drop in the fluff of white eagle down
> And otherwise nothing more.
>
> Long the leave-taking was, the going down seemed endless.
> Long the bat streaks, eagle's flight seems endless.
> When the sun is gone, only the bat streaks.
> Souls play in the white eagle down;
> Underneath are the souls ... and nothing more.
>   (Steiner 1992: 58 f.)

This haunting poem captures, presumably, both the alterity of the
original, with its mythology of the soul, and evokes the spiritual empti-
ness typical of the modern sensibility. The statements and repetitions
could seamlessly be accommodated into the stanza forms and refrains
that typify English and German folksongs, but Steiner resists this west-
ernisation of the material, instead using a controlled free-verse form
that recalls Malinowski's rendition of Trobriand charms and spells.
Nonetheless, the repeated line-end 'nothing more' at the end of each
stanza sufficiently recalls such folksong refrains as the German *nim-*

mermehr and Poe's 'Never more' in *The Raven* to evoke an affinity between the Papago song and European counterparts. Yet against the auratic aestheticisation so typical of the first wave of post-Herderian folk-worship that was, at the time Steiner was writing, experiencing its direst consequence in Nazi *völkisch* ideology, Steiner sets an anti-auratic abruptness which enshrines a wholly non-Western view of soul, death, after-life and nothingness.

Steiner's attitude to myth in his poetry does not preclude rationality, nor mortgage his thought to an irrational, inchoate realm but, rather, enables him to place ideas derived from apparently contradictory localities – from science, religion, or anthropology – into a single conceptual space, and thereby create a new cosmos (to use his word). He is quite clear that 'myth' and 'the book' represent different epistemes (1988: 530); it follows that using myths in books cannot reinstate a mythological age. Correlatively, he knows that the very notion of a 'public' which defines modernity is inimical to myth (p. 236, below). This distinguishes his approach from Romanticism and its 'new mythology'.

Yet Steiner's poetry provides him with a place where he can harmonise the distanced, sociological perspective of an anthropologist with an acceptance of mythic reality. This can be observed in his poem, 'Kafka in England', one of what he called his 'exemplary poems' – a mode that became his aesthetic ideal after he abandoned *Conquests*.

> *Kafka in England*
> Neither via Belsen, nor as a maid of all work
> The stranger came, by no means a refugee.
> And yet the case was a sad one:
> His nationality was in doubt,
> His religion occasioned lisping embarrassment.
>
> "Have you read Kafka?" asks Mrs Brittle at breakfast.
> "He's rather inescapable and quite fundamental, I feel."
> "Have you read Kafka?" asks Mr Tooslick at tea,
> Then you'll understand the world much better –
> Though nothing in him is real."
> Miss Diggs says: "Is that so?
> I thought that was reactionary. Don't you?"
> Only little Geoffrey Piltzman
> Dreams "Who?"
>
> "I mean, who does well out of this,
> They must be dead, after all,
>
> I mean those people in Prague – well, no matter what name ..."
> Yet the glory of him shines through the gateway all the same.
> (Steiner 1992: 61)

The poem delightfully and plangently builds on the German-Jewish refugees' characteristic irritation with English 'small-talk and sherry' (Berghahn 1988: 179) and recalls the social satire of Heine and T.S. Eliot; yet it differs from both in its handling of multiple viewpoints – the English natives', the foreigner's, Kafka's – which, in line with the complex ethnicities here observed, are treated as intersecting observational systems. The poem has several distinct strands, presented in terms of different, societal circles: it telescopes the fate of Kafka's work upon its reception in Britain with that of an unnamed, anonymous figure also arriving there – the 'stranger', who is 'by no means a refugee', who also evokes Steiner himself; it then juxtaposes these two figures with the annihilation of their brethren ('they must be dead, after all'); at the same time, the poem satirically represents Kafka's cultural appropriation by the uncomprehending English characters, Mrs Brittle, Mr Toooslick and Miss Diggs, whose titles (Mr, Mrs and Miss) stand in for the social range of the English middle class; it simultaneously ironises the Jewish assimilation of local values (the German Jewish boy Piltzman has the English forename Geoffrey, which is fairly common among British Jewry); and yet, at the end, it concludes by reasserting the value-system which might be detected in Kafka's work.

For the English, the name 'Kafka' has become a formula, to be invoked during their daily, self-defining rituals (breakfast and tea being the specifically English meals which distinguish the island race from continentals). The triteness of the English views ironises the speakers – and does so all the more strongly, paradoxically, because of their statements' strong truth-content: 'inescapable', 'fundamental', 'you'll understand the world much better' are all apposite if shallow responses to Kafka's texts; and yet the comical names (Brittle, Tooslick) imbue the irony with a genuine (if slightly condescending) warmth. By contrast, the German Jewish boy Geoffrey Piltzman appears to deserve our sympathy, and he, at least, ponders the fate of the Jews in Prague: his connectedness to a group linked to Kafka presumably gives him the insight to associate the Prague writer with the death camps – a horrific but accurate link (members of Kafka's surviving family in Prague were in fact deported and slain). This validates Kafka's terrible authenticity, but is wholly lost on the members of the English host-nation. Yet irony enters our sympathy for Geoffrey Piltzman, too. He has assimilated into English society, and conforms to the stereotype of the Jew: when he reflects on Prague and the dead, he thinks of the royalties for Kafka's works ('I mean, who does well out of this ...'). For the English, Kafka has become a commodity for exchange in conversation, the boy treats him as a genuine commodity. His sadness is that he has lost the religious horizon to formulate an adequate response to the fate of his own people, and remains trapped within the host nation's institutions, manners, and speech acts. Neither the English, nor the Jews, are capable of absorbing contemporary reality. Each group is tied to its own observational frame, which in its turn is anchored in a specific social universe. No-one establishes a translational frame by which genuine communication could occur. Finally, the poem's speaker recalls the conclusion to Kafka's highly ambiguous parable 'Before the Law' in *Der Proceß* (*The Trial*). Notwithstanding the ambiguities of the novel, the tragedy of the Jewish people, and the sordidness of England and exile, the poem implies – offering only *one* of the possible views on the novel – that an obscure metaphysical realm remains intact. The poem's ironies and cultural relativism (the heirs of Steiner's anthropological method) serve to demonstrate the inadequacies and limitations of the individual human perspectives against the absolute horizon of a divinity via a negative theology, the unnamed power appears in the very inability of humankind to glimpse the transcendental world. Thus Steiner's poem both represents the differing value-systems of his subjects, based respectively on ritual exchange, circulating money, and suffering; the poem thereby intimates the values of the Nazis as destroyers (anti-values might be a better term) and also validates an authentic religious experience discernable in Kafka's text, framing knowledge ('light') as a quotation. The conclusion, accordingly, embeds a mythical dimension – religious truth – into modern social reality.

An aphorism of Steiner's on Kafka also sums up the procedure in Steiner's poem. Kafka, Steiner writes:

> constantly shifted from a mythical to a historical level, because in the end, notwithstanding all the mystical elements and notwithstanding everything that is said about him, he was not a mystic (and hence not even a 'disguised kabbalist'), but a Jewish mythical thinker. (J. Adler 1992: 153)

Steiner, as he claims Kafka does, includes both a historical and a mystical level in his text: this linkage, on Steiner's reading, anchors the statement in the natural (as against the transcendental) world, and therefore handles reality as 'myth', not as metaphysical. Such intersections between Steiner's thinking on Kafka – in aphoristic and poetic form provide a vital guide to his own thought-processes.

The Joseph story provides Steiner with another seminal point of intersection, linking poetry, aphorisms, and scholarship. His paper 'Enslavement and the Early Hebrew Lineage System' grew out of his thesis, and applies anthropological categories to a biblical story. The relation between the Hebrew Bible and sociology mattered to Steiner. He has no time for 'the sociology of religion', which he calls 'the oddest product of our age' (1988: 62) – it is little more than evidence of

the fact that modern society has lost contact with its 'inner life' and
'rootedness in cult' (p. 62f.). Conversely, 'sociology' is the discipline
that can be learned 'most immediately from the Pentateuch' (1988:
74). The figure of Joseph, on whom the article centres, earlier appears
in *Conquests* V, which treats him as the 'Increaser', 'the first one among
us, who lost his home' (V, l.152ff.). Joseph is the mythical antecedent
for the later Hebrew people, even anticipating Jesus in that he is 'sold
and betrayed': 'we still mirror ourselves' in him, i.e., he is the founder
by virtue of whose sacrifice life continues. An aphorism on Joseph elsewhere provides Steiner with the opportunity to demarcate modernity
and myth, in the following scathing remark relating to psychoanalysis:
'It's good that Pharoah told his dream about the the seven fat cows and
the seven lean cows to Joseph and not to a psychiatrist, who would
have interpreted the dream as a symbol of a manic-depressive cycle'
(Steiner 1988: 90): modern introjection by symbols displaces the
physical world with mental constructs, destroying the basis for an act,
whereas myth and sacrifice operate at the level of action, as appears in
this remark: 'We are still living from Abraham's preparedness to sacrifice his son' (Steiner 1988: 85). What counts for Steiner is not intro-
jecting action as symbol, but externalising the mind in a deed: the
reality of Abraham's psychological preparedness frees later generations, talking to an analyst leads nowhere. Sacrifice provides a pivot of
change, and the Bible provides a model of such change. Another point
about 'sacrifice' that Steiner asserts is that 'Relation and being are not
different or opposed in sacrifice' (1988: 89). Hence in sacrifice there
can be no difference between 'meaning' and 'being' (no symbolisa-
tion), and the sacrifice can be both wholly existential and relational.

Where the *Conquests* reenact the Joseph myth, and an aphorism
can provide an incisive light on it, the learned paper on 'Enslavement
and the Early Hebrew Lineage System' establishes a conceptual frame
with which to relocate and reinterpret the Joseph story. The interlocking, overlapping modes of utterance provide alternative, but
interconnected heuristic tools, for approaching a single set of events.
The article, in the view of Bernhard Lang, had a foundational role in
the anthropology of the Bible. Alongside Shapera's 'The Sin of Cain'
(1955), Lang claims that the 'Enslavement' paper marked the turn
away from Frazer (1984: 163f.), towards later work such as that by
Lienhardt and Mary Douglas. Steiner brings to the Bible an anthropologist's understanding of African kinship systems (particularly that
he derived from Laura Bohannan's analysis of partible rights in persons and applied to his thesis on slavery, see above pp. 35-36). We
may recall that Steiner defined kinship as the most social of human
possessions and slavery as its antithesis. Despite being father/genitor
and son, Jacob and Joseph cease to have the kin relation father/pater

and son once Joseph has been sold into slavery. Freed in Egypt, Joseph's new status derives from his position at court: it does not restore his earlier kin ties. Steiner looks to the Indians of the Northwest coast of America for an even more striking example of a severance of kinship ties. He closes by suggesting that in focusing on family units, previous commentators have overlooked the existence of a lineage system among Semites which sub-Saharan African parallels make highly plausible. The Joseph story suggests evidence of transition from one type of slave law to another in the biblical sources. Steiner's article uses the comparative method to examine two contexts in which we know him to have been interested: the interrelations between kinship and slavery (the predominant subject of his thesis) and the practices that accompany oaths (treated in the paper on the Chagga). It is thanks to Steiner's formal, sociological framing of the situation that he is able to elucidate the Israelite situation in terms of more contemporary sub-Saharan African analyses. In the parlance of the lectures on taboo, classification is related to social institutions.

Steiner also recalls Joseph in his poem, 'The Overseer'. This hermetic text poses several problems of interpretation. It begins by introducing the Hebrews' bitter life in slavery: 'Joyless are the awakening and the brittle bread. ...' (Steiner 1992: 37), and slavery provides a constant theme: 'Joyless are the forced labour and sleep. ...'; but towards the end, the speaker appears to focus on Moses's killing of the Egyptian overseer (Exodus 2, 11ff.), after which he fled to Midian, the place repeatedly invoked in positive imagery in the poem: 'O Midian. / Midian, there the waters sing and and women sing by the water'. The slaying of the Egyptian is introduced in the final stanza:

> Two voices cut into each other:
> O master and slave. O master and slave.
> Hard loam bursts under the prince's rod;
> Dominion's painstaking drudgery falls apart, into the master's vault
> The blood of life trickles. O Midian!
> The dun rears up; sparks welcome: to Midian, Midian
> Where without effort the wellsprings sing
> Sweet water.
>
>   (Steiner 1992: 37)

There was no argument between Moses and the Egyptian in the Bible, but perhaps the debate between Moses and the slave on the day after the slaying (Exodus, 2, 14) is here being projected back into an altercation between Moses and the Overseer. Onto the biblical material, Steiner projects a series of different perspectives to crystallise the meaning of the episode. This becomes clear from an explanatory note to the text which he wrote, and is included in the German printing, but which is not published with the translation (Steiner 1954d: 106). In this note, Steiner shows how the poem adds an understanding of Egyptian mythology to the biblical perspective. He comments that the poem treats the overseer 'as Ushapti, as part of the order of the dead, so that Moses's blow does not just kill the overseer but the whole order of the kingdom of the dead, from which the people is then led forth into life.' This appears to be glossing the words 'Hard loam bursts under the prince's rod' which, the note informs us, refers to the 'clay images' of Pharoah's 'servants and soldiers' buried with the dead king (Steiner 1954d: 106). Thus Steiner appears to locate the end of the Egyptian domination over the Israelites long before their exodus, at the moment of the killing. The killing seems to be seen as a kind of sacrifice. The poem pointedly refers to the relation between Moses and the Egyptian in terms of Hegel's master-slave dialectic, indicating the role reversal which Moses's act brings about. This is also suggested by the title, 'Overseer', which is ambiguous in referring explicitly to the Egyptian but also to Moses's role among the Hebrews. Indeed, the use of the term 'Overseer' in the poem may itself recall the episode when Joseph became an 'overseer' in Egypt (Genesis 39,40). The use of the biblical term for Joseph thus sets up a typological chain linking Genesis and Exodus: Joseph – Pharoah – Moses. The poem, highly allusively, appears to invite the reader to interpret the changing power relations between the Hebrews and the Egyptians in terms of a master-slave dialectic revolving around focal episodes. Just as the oath forms a focal point in the learned paper on the lineage system, the killing forms another in the poem. And even in the poem, historical change appears to be interpreted in terms of institutional change – the Egyptian's death means not just the end of a person, a myth, and a set of power-relations, but of the institution associated with that myth and with those relations. In his poetry as in his anthropology, Steiner absorbs contemporary issues – the killing of the Egyptian may be reworking Steiner's views on the inevitability of violence as expressed e.g., in the 'Letter to Mr Gandhi' – and places them into a different contextual frame. Just as he brings social thought to bear on the Bible in his scholarship, so he includes an awareness of social thinking in his most hermetic representations of biblical themes.

We turn again to the notion of a 'mathesis' lying at the centre of Steiner's work, which we can now begin to demarcate with greater clarity. In his poetry, Steiner developed an aesthetic of the palimpsest, by which he embedded allusions, references and quotations into his verse. He does this in methodological terms, too, and some of his most remarkable aphorisms simultaneously allude to a whole cluster of different ideas. This is the case in the following, late remark, which reintroduces a recurrent motif in Steiner's method that we have isolated in

different contexts, namely the 'circle', whether in the 'culture circles'
ethnology of Central Europe, or in the formal sense that the term has
in Simmel. This late remarks on method reintroduces the concept of a
'circle' as a heuristic tool, and may perhaps be an attempt to figure
what was involved in the 'circles' of Simmel's sociology:

> The chief sociological principle is probably this: that no indvidual can
> occupy a position without identifying themselves with something, and that
> there is no identification without transformation. The need for identifica-
> tion is primary. This is the chief difference between human and animal
> forms of association. The 'I' of human association is at the apex of a trian-
> gle, the other points of which are called 'communication' and 'identifica-
> tion'. The sides adjacent to the angle at the I-point are called 'language' and
> 'transformation'. The circle described around the triangle is a point in
> another triangle, whose other points are called communication and trans-
> formation. The circle which describes this is 'society' – in a metaphysical
> sense. (p. 241, below)

Steiner's reflection conducts a dialogue with several thinkers – both
living and dead – simultaneously. If the 'circle' of society recalls Simmel, Steiner's concern with what is 'primary' in sociology continues
his debate with Malinowski, and his critique of Malinowski's 'needs'
(pp. 238-39, below); focusing on 'transformation' introduces Canetti's
key category of *Verwandlung* (Steiner uses the same German term),
which Canetti treats as primary in *Masse und Macht* (1960: 385ff.);
Steiner's own category, 'identification' – from his perspective – goes to
a more important layer than either Malinowski or Canetti by mediating the individual *sociologically*. Unlike Malinowski's 'needs' and
Canetti's 'transformation', Steiner's 'identification' is a specifically
human category, i.e., it differentiates human from animal society: the
individual can only occupy a 'position' in society, i.e., be a human,
social being, by 'identifying' with something outside him- or herself.
From this notion, Steiner advances to an understanding of a primary,
human social mechanism, distinct from categories like sexuality and
the family. To do this, he introduces the 'circles' model, which seems to
recall several earlier layers of methodology. Firstly, his image of the
individual in a circle that parallels society turns the traditional
imagery of macrocosm and microcosm into a sociological model; secondly, the triangulated man in the circle, whose 'limbs' – Steiner's German word, *Schenkel*, means both 'the sides of a triangle' and 'thighs' –
suggests Leonardo's drawing of a human figure spread out in a circle,
or such kabbalistic symbols as were used by the hermetic philosopher,
Robert Fludd (Godwin 1979: 68-72): Steiner's model reactivates the
mystical imagery as a scientific tool. And thirdly, the actual use of the
model as a heuristic device recalls Ramon Lull's *ars combinatoria*,

which operates with concentric circles that the investigator rotates in order to create new knowledge (Yates 1982: 9-77). Steiner's acquaintance with this influential system seems beyond doubt – in his Prague days, he began a play with Ramon Lull as the somewhat unlikely hero, the first act of which was presented at a public reading (Fleischli 1970: 16). It is conceivable that the play was to stand in the German tradition marked by Goethe's *Torquato Tasso* and Hölderlin's *Empedokles* – dramas which represent their central figures in terms of their own philosophy. Steiner presumably knew the principles of Lull's 'art', which his own reflections vary in a highly fruitful manner. One can observe him engaging almost formalistically with the *ars combinatoria* in aphorisms like that on 'Education and Illusion' (p. 234, below), which produce their deductions by means of a series of permutations. 'Cityscapes' similarly has a distinctly permutational quality to its argument (pp. 232-33, below), as does 'Last Things but One' (pp. 233-34, below), which treats the 'combination' of 'dream, service' and 'adventure'. The humourous, playful side to Steiner's nature also finds expression in this method, as in the following combinatorial reflection – a typically exile squib – on the English weather:

> The English climate is characterised by the fact every season has its spring and autumn days, summer days are most common in spring and autumn, and winter is distinguished from summer above all by the fact that it has more spring days and fewer autumn days than the latter ... (Sundry Essays and Discoveries Ms 1947a: II,80)

Such playfulness is an essential feature of the *ars combinatoria*, as Novalis – among others – has recognised. Writing of the art, he commented: 'Language is a musical instrument of ideas. The poet, the rhetor, and the philosopher *play* with ideas' (cited by Neubauer 1978: 9). Steiner's playfulness – attested in Iris Murdoch transforming him into the figure of Ludens in her novel *The Message to the Planet* (1989) – appears to find a serious outlet in this method, echoes of which can perhaps be heard in such diverse procedures as his systematically questioning the whole chorus of existing scholarship in *Taboo* and in the cyclical repetition and variation of key lines in *Conquests*.

Yet Steiner does not simply rehearse Lull's method in aphorisms like that on the 'circle'. Whereas Lull works with a model of *concentric* circles, Steiner's triangulation also envisages *overlapping* ones: the 'circle' which he imagines becoming the 'point' in another circle is not necessarily the centre; and the new 'circle', 'society', will link *other* individuals and connect to *other* societies in the same way. Steiner's earlier reflection on social units in terms of 'culture circles' and Simmel's 'circles' now correlates directly to Steiner's method; and his preoccupation with overlapping geographical borders appears to match a concern with a new variant of the *ars combinatoria*: Steiner's method privileges *overlapping* areas as a means for generating and structuring knowledge. The shift from Lull's centred circle to a multi-centred universe follows directly from two principles: Mach's observational relativity; and Simmel's formal sociology which enabled Steiner to embed Mach's theoretical insight into a social context.

One of the most remarkable fruits of Steiner's epistemology is 'Chagga Law and Chagga Truth', in which the method for discovering knowledge is reapplied to the problem of structuring truth, whereby Steiner is able to demonstrate the social viability (and, indeed, equal validity) of different truth concepts. This far-reaching analysis has since been taken up by Godfrey Lienhardt and Mary Douglas (Douglas [1975] 1978: 128), but warrants rereading in the interpretative context provided by Steiner's other work. Notwithstanding the paper's own concern with 'truth', it must be said that Steiner's own handling of his source in this instance is open to question. Basing his comments on the hitherto unpublished complete version of Steiner's seminar presentation on Gutmann, J.C.Winter – one of the few commentators to recognise Steiner's importance in the Oxford School (Winter 1979: 27) – commends Steiner's explication of Gutmann's ideas while cautioning that his use of examples from Chagga ethnography may be 'careless, to say the least' (1979: 25-27 and footnote 80). Winter's detailed study helpfully shows how Steiner's Gutmann reception not only in his paper on 'Chagga Law and Chagga Truth' but also in 'Towards a Classification of Labour' played a part in the development of early structuralism (1979: 25f.).

During the course of our Introductions, we have traced Steiner's views on Western and Eastern values to several sources: to literary precedents in books like *Robinson Crusoe* and *Moby Dick*, in which the observer's values are confronted with an alternative, 'native' position, and to Steiner's own experience of multi-ethnic communities in Prague and Jerusalem; and we can infer his awareness of different currents in modern thought which overturned established notions of truth: Nietzsche's 'perspectivism', Ernst Mach's variety of relativity, and Einstein's special and general theories – we know of his friend Canetti's interest in Einstein in the 1950s (PC). We have also followed the early working-out of his ideas on linked concepts in the paper on 'Superstition'. If Steiner's paper on 'Chagga Law and Chagga Truth' is in some way the culmination of his own thinking on these various currents, we may add to them a personal experience which he reports in one of his few autobiographically styled aphorisms, 'Memory of a Turning Point' (*Erinnerung an einen Wendepunkt*). The title may echo Rilke's poem 'Wendung' (Turning Point) which signals the major 'turn' between his middle phase and his late poetry. Steiner's aphorism purports to record an epiphany in which he recognised the identity of separate spheres: intelligence (*Klugheit*), piety (*Frömmigkeit*) and scepticism (*Skeptizismus*). The insight strikes him after watching a quarrel in the street in an unnamed town – presumably Prague or Jerusalem. Two men argue so fiercely that they attract a crowd of onlookers which Steiner joins, eager to know who is in the right:

> Suddenly I said to myself: why are you entering into this [quarrel] so deeply? Are there so many people, who are 'in the right' in any way whatever? You know that there are only very few. And if you wished to seek them out, you would not be looking for them among these angry disputants. How could either of these men screaming in the street be 'in the right' in any way at all? (Ms [?1944]: fol.1)

He then describes his own insight apropos of this event:

> People often speak of collapsing illusions. It was not an illusion that collapsed, it was an entire piece of reality which had collapsed by the evening. ... I felt like someone who had always carefully avoided an abyss and suddenly discovered that it had been filled in without doing anything about it himself, and that there was a path where before there had only been detours.
>
> On this day, a new life began for me insofar as I was no longer able to distinguish between [three previously distinct] abilities: being deeply moved, exactitude in thinking and the strength of doubt could no longer be regarded separately. The separation had lost its meaning. ... (Ms [?1944]: fol.1-2)

The experience reverses Steiner's attitude to truth. From implicitly presupposing a positive quest for truth via assertions in the outside world where others commonly seek it (the quarrellers in the street here assume a wider, symbolic function), Steiner reverts to an alternative position. He redefines the subject and the faculties engaged in the search for truth: aspects of the self commonly regarded as mutually exclusive, notably 'being moved' or 'faith' – Steiner, using his *Kombinatorik,* now substitutes *Ergriffenheit* for 'piety' – and 'doubt' – Steiner now calls this *die Stärke des Zweifels* – come together in a new combination. In linking these qualities, Steiner thinks together the modern West's chief opposed universes, religious experience (*Ergriffenheit*) and science (*Zweifel*) conjoining them with the capacity to 'think exactly' (*Denkgenauigkeit*). The epiphany entails, on the one hand, holism in Steiner's grasp of the subject, here understood as integrating the opposite qualities of intellect and emotion; and correlatively produces an integral notion of 'truth', which now encompasses both science and religion in a single vision. Steiner's aphorism reconstitutes the subject as a being with two valencies, a negative and a positive – doubt and faith – the latter contributing an addition in value (*Ergriffenheit*), the former a parallel subtraction (*Stärke des Zweifels*), the two poles being mediated by exactitude of thought (*Denkgenauigkeit*).

Steiner thus exhibits a preparedness to entertain a complex 'truth' that may be at odds with conventional method. His aphorism is also a parable about truth. It attacks the notion of a supposedly objective epistemology – dialectics, symbolised by the arguing men – and its putative findings, putting under severe strain the notion of a pure 'method' which can be used in a quasi-objective form to arrive at a truth independently of its users: 'dialectic method' in itself may be objective (the men are watched by the crowd) and yet totally useless (both men may be wrong). We will encounter a similar juxtaposition of two truth-worlds in the 'Chagga' paper. The strength in Steiner's position is that whilst attacking a central tool of rationality (we can read the parable as an attack on Socratic method in the wake of Nietzsche's assault on 'theoretical man'), it refuses to countenance irrationalism as an alternative.

Mary Douglas has drawn attention to the fact that Evans-Pritchard develops a framework similar to Wittgenstein's idea of 'language games' (Douglas 1980: 36). Writing on the 'Chagga', Steiner comes to related conclusions. Douglas finds it extraordinary that E.-P. wrote in terms so reminiscent of Wittgenstein while having not read him by the early 1930s; for his part, Steiner had read the early Wittgenstein, and could conceivably have encountered the later idea of 'language games' through *The Blue and Brown Books* (1933-34; 1934-35; in [1958] 1969: 17; 172). However, both Evans-Pritchard and Steiner may have reached this convergence with Wittgenstein via Malinowski's contribution to Ogden and Richards's *The Meaning of Meaning* (1923), in which Malinowski stresses the importance of what he calls 'the context of situation' for determining the meaning of linguistic statements. In the 'Chagga' paper, Steiner thinks this further by way of his analysis of Gutmann. He argues somewhat tantalisingly that 'Gutmann ... leads us a long way towards an analysis of truth concepts and their relation to structural situations', but that he 'stops at the threshold' (vol. I, p. 248 above). Ironically, Steiner, like Gutmann, does not fully develop his thoughts here, but his idea of finding truth in the external world (as opposed to his holistic take on the subject) is much contained in this phrase: he entertains different 'truth concepts', which may be so thoroughly divergent in constitution as to be contradictory in logic, and wishes to relate these to 'structural situations' – one notes the echo of Malinowski's 'context of situation'; but Steiner's 'structural situation' replaces Malinowski's pleonastic phrase by a more sociological term: Steiner's 'structural situation' to which the 'truth concept' relates presupposes not just a general situation or social relations, but a framework of kinship, legality and other institutions (the 'context') within which a specific form of 'truth' assumes meaning.

In the convergence between Wittgenstein and the anthropologists, the movement was not entirely one-way. In his postumously published remarks on Frazer's *The Golden Bough* dating to 1930, Wittgenstein brings a central European critique to bear on Frazer which often coincides with Steiner, and which indicate how anthropological materials fed into Wittgenstein's own understanding of truth. As Steiner sees in Frazer's views of his subjects no more than a narrowly English perspective, Wittgenstein finds Frazer's limitations are his 'narrowness' and the England of his day (1967: 241); as Steiner adopts the mask of a 'primitive' in *Taboo*, Wittgenstein – here using the English word 'savage' in his German remarks – turns the tables on Frazer and calls him and his explanations more 'savage' than most of his 'savages' (1967: 241). Wittgenstein criticises Frazer's treatment of 'magical and religious views' as 'errors' (*Irrtümer*), observing that one should preserve the 'depth' of magical thought ('Von der Magie müßte die Tiefe behalten werden.') (1967: 234), indicating that an explanation of magic should not lose its essential truth – a view compatible with Steiner's 'Memory of a Turning Point'. On one occasion, Wittgenstein also notes how where Frazer discerns 'superstitition' (*Aberglaube*) we are probably dealing with 'truth' (*Wahrheit*) (1967: 253). However, by this Wittgenstein means a truth which can be grounded within our own values (here illustrated by *The Brothers Karamazov*). Steiner's reading of Gutmann goes beyond Wittgenstein's 1930 Frazer analysis to the extent that he reconstitutes differing 'truth concepts' on their own terms within their own 'structural situations'; this strategy more radically than Wittgenstein's accepting stance towards otherness avoids weighing up or balancing Western and non-Western models.

We can now approach the arguments in 'Chagga Law and Chagga Truth' in ways that illuminate the paper's long preamble, which Laura Bohannan wisely excised from the first printing, since they would have been regarded as 'digressive' within their first printed context, a scholarly journal devoted to Africa, whereas within the context of Steiner's research and his Oxford seminar they provided an essential 'structural situation'. Steiner begins by addressing the subject of the Oxford seminar series and then singles out Gutmann's *Das Recht der Dschagga* as 'the only major contribution in German to descriptive social anthropology' – not absolutely, but – 'as we understand it, in its classical stage' (Volume I, p. 235). It is a 'classic', by which Steiner means a book 'which, even when outdated, would set standards for knowledge, research and its presentation' (p. 235). In making this judgement, Steiner is following the British view of this book which variously regarded it as 'the best monograph ... on an East African tribe' and as 'Gutmann's *magnum opus*' (Winter 1979: 10). Gutmann's account is serving Steiner as the prime, indeed the only, successful example of German social anthropology, and he embeds it precisely into the German social and intellectual context. According to Steiner, Gutmann's book takes 'a rational, scientific approach'; this Steiner contrasts with both the philosophical approach to society, which produced Simmel and von Wiese, and 'another approach ... more typical of the German situation', for which the 'chaos of mysterious society', i.e., irrationalism, provided the parameters for social enquiry (p. 236). Scholars focused on 'nuclei and clusters of consistent behaviour' based on 'religious movements of the past' – a method that became fruitful only thanks to 'the genius of Max Weber'. Steiner presumably has in mind thinkers like Ferdinand Tönnies, with his fundamental distinction between a mystical 'Gemeinschaft' and modern 'Gesellschaft' (1963; see Liebersohn 1988: 11-38), Werner Sombart (1902), Ernst Troeltsch on *The Social Teachings of the Christian Churches* (1912; Liebersohn 1988: 40-77), Lujo Brentano, Alfred Weber and others. Common to this line of thought was a belief in a romanticised ideal of a pre-capitalist community based on barter. Having thus distinguished two traditions in German social thought Steiner launches an assault on the entire German intellectual class: 'the actual structure of his own society remained mysterious for the German intellectual ... his awareness of his own society lacked important rational elements. Nothing can be explained by reference to mysteries' (Volume I, p. 236, above). One need only compare the worlds portrayed in George Eliot's *Middlemarch* with that in Thomas Mann's *Der Zauberberg* (*The Magic Mountain*) to understand the drift of Steiner's contrast. The mind-set which Steiner attributes to German-speaking intellectuals also conditioned the method of historical ethnology. German-speaking scholars engaged in 'busily and skilfully collecting those observable items which seemed to need least contextual reference'. The critique also seems to apply to Steiner's own early foray into 'culture circles' ethnology, which produced a paper on dog sacrifice bristling with data, but wholly lacking in a sense of social context (Ms 1938). 'Standards of relevance and significance were destroyed' and scholarship created an 'all-embracing jigsaw puzzle' (p. 236). According to Steiner, the approach represents a form of 'escape', an irrational avoidance of social reality. The result was epistemic meltdown – and ultimately (though Steiner does not say so here, but see our comments on translation and value, p. 51, above) social breakdown. Scholars whose society 'remained mysterious' to them were unable to arrange their 'experiences' in what Steiner calls a 'translation pattern' (Volume I, p. 236), and hence lacked the basis for understanding a different society. One recalls the problems German society faced with 'otherness' in the 1930s. The implication is that such a society lives under an illusion, incapable of recognising 'truth' in any form. Steiner then comes close to naming the actual context for his paper – he is writing in 1949, four years after the end of a European war which marked a climax in the 'irrationalist' tendency of the German school – but makes the point with extreme restraint, demarcating the moment at which he crosses from a scholarly to an ethical argument:

> Thus the fiction was preserved that people who had the whole equipment of modern thought and science at their beck and call, were facing the multi-form social universe with all the active interest that befits civilised man. This I feel to be a moral issue and I wish it to be regarded as something apart from the scholarly merit and faults of diffusionist schools. (Vol. I, p. 236, above)

Steiner then contrasts Gutmann's position as a missionary with that of the ethnologists, without further elaborating why this provided him with special access to a better method, but does stress how Gutmann's interest in legal systems enables him to focus productively on 'social mechanisms' (p. 237). Steiner then continues to delineate a series of further contextual factors for Gutmann's account: his book's place in a series on developmental psychology, the book's epilogue, Gutmann's twenty years among the Chagga, his other works, his curious translations of Chagga words, his attitude to women, and Kierkegaard's influence on him which led Gutmann to understand the Chagga not as 'superstititious' but actually as existentialist 'afraid of the nothingness of his isolation' (p. 239). Balancing both positive and negative judgements in his assessment, Steiner recreates Gutmann's 'structural situation' as a starting point for his own analysis, and sufficiently reveals his own methodological presuppositions to locate his argument within the Oxford School: its hallmarks include the sociological approach, rationality in method, self-reflexivity with respect to social mechanisms, and an acceptance of both alterity and the profundity of non-Western thought styles. Steiner's exegesis, and his knowledge of existentialism, may have fallen on fruitful ground. According to Mary Douglas, he may have been 'influential in opening paths to European currents of philosophy' at Oxford (Ms 1994: 3), and his remark on Gutmann's use of existentialism has an echo in *Purity and Danger* when she refers to the Lele meditating on the inner rites of the pangolin cult being most like 'primitive existentialists' (1984: 170).

Having set up the contextual frame for the Gutmann analysis, Steiner presents his own critical analysis of Gutmann's Chagga society which establishes the social structure of the Chagga – which we pass over here – before turning to his account of Chagga 'truth'. Here, too, Steiner introduces the argument by explaining his own premises (p. 244), developing an analysis of Western truth concepts before advancing to a synthethis of Chagga ideas. He carefully distinguishes 'the logician's concept of truth' from 'any concept of truth to which observable behaviour relates': he thereby severs the observer's logical frame from the social applications of truth which can be made the 'object' of sociological study. He is rigorous on this point: 'I do *not* mean by this that the Westerner, holding the logician's concept of truth, finds among the Chagga another and incompatible sort' (p. 244). Western logic does not constitute the observer's structural frame. The reason is contained in Steiner's next point, which continues the analytic heralded by the earlier claim: logic is not the sole arbiter of 'truth' in *any* society. Steiner then proceeds to distinguish different ideas of truth that operate in Western society, ranging from the (then) contemporary modern logical positivist's account back to Hebrew, Greek, Roman, Celtic and Teutonic ideas: the historical line merges in the early modern idea of a timeless, 'Absolute Truth' (p. 246), to which the logical positivism of Steiner's day is the response. In the course of this survey, Steiner makes several seminal distinctions, notably that between 'witnessing' and 'oaths', which correspond to what he calls 'two groups of truth concepts: the one relating to a change in the social reality of a statement, the other to the degree of applicability of a myth to one or more situations of life' (p. 245). Having outlined this binary opposition and established the plural contexts for 'truth concepts', he turns to the Chagga.

Steiner characteristically begins with the Chagga language, and then relates this to 'certain signals or signs ... certain ejaculations and to the use of the Dracaena leaf' (p. 217): by treating language within *practice* he approaches Wittgenstein's parallel development from his earlier position: 'I suggest ... that the use of this leaf is complementary to the *lohi* words and that one cannot be discussed without the other' (p. 248). This closely corresponds to the proposal at the outset of the *Philosophical Investigations* to call 'the language and the activity with which it is interwoven' a 'language game' (Wittgenstein 1960: 292f.). In making his case about the Chagga language game, Steiner can thus separate out the Chagga from Western procedures, and from Gutmann's psychological interpretation, thereby demonstrating how the Chagga may validly call 'truth' what a Westerner would call 'lying' (p. 248). Where the later Wittgenstein focuses on 'rules', Steiner's analysis enumerates each aspect of the 'structural situations' pertaining to Chagga truth: social structure, lineage system, language, ejaculations, signals, the Dracaena leaf, the clan copses containing the ancestor shrines, the rules pertaining to clan members' activities there, the procedure engaged in by an aggrieved man, the acts of a man with a grudge, the court action, and the role of witness and eyewitness. He thereby attempts to recreate in their entirety the 'structural situations' of Chagga truth, and analyse the manner in which different principles may be placed into a 'structural arrangement' (p. 248) by which the internal coherence of Chagga concepts becomes apparent. The structuralism here envisaged does not mean mapping trans-cultural patterns – quite the opposite: it entails grasping the internal organisation of 'truth' within a unique culture. Accepting variant frames of reference with respect to 'structural situations' is crucial to Steiner's methodology. It is this situatedness of each unit of observation that permits Steiner both to accept different accounts in 'Chagga Truth' and subscribe to a religious idea of 'truth' in a poem such as 'Gebet im Garten' (Prayer in the Garden).

Steiner's deeply moving – Hugo Bergman calls it *ergreifend* (Ms 1952) – meditation on the Shoah, 'Prayer in the Garden', was begun on the birthday of Steiner's father in 1947, and bears this date in the subtitle (1992: 75). As a long elegy on the death of a father, the poem also distantly recalls the Spanish world of Steiner's forbears by echoing Manrique's *Coplas por la muerte de su padre*. Written in the cyclical free verse form developed in his *Conquests*, 'Prayer in the Garden', represents the *summa* of Steiner's poetic and religious thought, completing the spiritual journey left unended in the earlier work. In contrast to Paul Celan's better-known *Todesfuge* (Death Fugue), his poem removes the catastrophe from its historical frame by avoiding the words 'Germans' and 'Jews'. It similarly avoids the imagery of the camps. Terms of national and religious difference could merely perpetuate the original sense of difference that led to disaster. Instead, Steiner's poem centres on a shipwreck. As in Gerard Manley Hopkins's *The Wreck of the Deutschland*, the sinking serves as the terrible object for spiritual analysis. This imagery recalls an earlier poem that Steiner wrote in the depth of the war during his crucial middle years, 'In den Werften' (In the Wharfs), which is dated November 1943. In this poem, the speaker imagines himself reading the names of ill-fated vessels that contained Jewish refugees, listing the names: '*Dumera, Struma, Arandora Star*' (see Steiner 2000). The sea imagery translates the cataclysm into a timeless frame and points beyond a specific national guilt towards shared human responsibility, as can be seen by considering one example. Thus, the *Struma* sank on 24 February 1942, carrying 767 Jewish refugeees fleeing from Romania (Wasserstein 1994: 4; Ziegler Ms 1994). Responsibility for this loss lay not just with the German persecutors, but with the British and Turkish governments too (the latter would not admit the Jews) as well as with Russia (it was probably a Russian submarine which torpedoed the vessel). The sinking was widely reported and caused public outrage in Britain. There were other, similarly ugly episodes. In November 1940, the *Patria* was blown up by Haganah to prevent the deportation of immigrants, but the plan backfired causing the boat to sink and 250 refugees to drown (Gilbert 1998: 105). It seems probable that these earlier losses came to mind again in 1947 with the wave of 'illegal' migrants aboard ships like the *Galata, Trade Winds, Orletta* and *Anal* which brought several thousand persons to Palestine between mid-April and the end of May

1947 (Gilbert 1998: 145). This was the time of the notorious case of the *Exodus*, which reached the coast of Palestine from Genoa with German and Polish camp survivors on board: the ship was ordered back to Europe again by Bevin, and eventually landed in Hamburg (Gilbert 1998: 145, 209). Steiner's poem condenses these events into a single, mythical shipwreck, that serves as a symbol for the Shoah. The speaker hears the voices of the survivors at sea – we may imagine the migrants on the *Exodus* – who are a 'part' of the 'part' which has survived the war, and seems to recall the earlier drowned voices:

> One part alone has survived,
> And what a part:
> That mercy might have mercy;
> And has lived to see the hour,
> O what an hour:
> And now there is this crying out at sea,
> Once more distress and anyone's sport at sea.

In the mythical mode we can now recognise as habitual for Steiner's thought, at the point of the sinking, recounted later in the poem, the allusive imagery connects key moments in Jewish history, including the fall of the tower of Babel, the flood, and the Babylonian exile, with contemporary events, a single word, 'gas', once used when recounting the wreck, serving to evoke the recent horror:

> Seven thrusts of the ram into splintering wood:
> Beaks made of steel, the pride of Babel.
> Broken the clasp and the plank, the chair and the table,
> Burst the reservoir, dried up the flood.
> Beaks made of steel, the pride of Babel:
> Seven thrusts of the ram into splintering wood.
> Not a drop with which to cool the eyes,
> The eyes of children which gases cauterise,
> Eyes of the mothers, hard in the midst of horror.
> > (Steiner 1992: 85)

The speaker finds a way of relating to the events by mediating between the whole Jewish people, the suffering of the dead, and his own fellow-feeling, somewhat unusually – in a poem – incorporating the idea of the limited perspective suggested by Mach's term, 'the part' (*Teil*), for the human subject in relation to the 'whole' (Steiner 1992: 79): 'I am only one part', and extending the same term to all life: 'Whatever lives is only a part' and 'Whatever died is a part', as are all the survivors: 'One part only has survived' (1992: 79-83). Indeed, in true Machian terms, even the *inner* self, the 'inwardness' of the speaker, is also understood as a 'part'.

Steiner's poem manages to utter the unspeakable by negating the will and the identity of the speaker. The end of the self, envisioned as a *nirvana* with which life concludes at the end of *Conquests*, is here internalised to the point of complete self-abasement – the only posture from which the poet can utter the dead:

> The prayer of the will is not fitting for me
> For the words I utter turn against myself ....
> The prayer of wishing is not fitting for me,
> The prayer of the will I am not able to say,
> For the will is only a part
> And it prays for only a part:
> But what the will destroyed
> Became the cornerstone of peaceful glory,
> And what the will has wounded
> Turned to the glow of inwardness within me.
> (1992: 75-7)

The meditation leads the speaker to turn what has been 'wounded' into his own 'inwardness': meditation also involves a mythic transformation of value, whereby pain assumes a positive value as an inward 'glow'. In a manner that perhaps echoes Steiner's stress on biblical witness in 'Chagga Law and Chagga Truth', the speaker invokes his parents as witnesses to truth. The poem's 'now' encapsulates the fruits of Steiner's religious thinking since the middle years of the war, when, as we have seen, his life and work began their spiritual deepening. He offers a heart-rending picture of his mother and father:

> O both of you
> The sufferings you went through.
>
> My light and grief are that you were
> What you have been in me was horribly perverted
> Darkness more than grief extinguishing I must bear
> Because from you, so pale already and so frail,
> The monster's clutches could not be averted.
> For your sake I recovered from your death,
> And now this darkness, now this light
> And other light
> At the time of my ripeness
> Together merged into my inwardness.
> Witnessess, witnesses,
> Join me in what I speak, be near me now.
> Let me speak truthfully.
> (Steiner 1992:83)

'My light and grief ... the truth let me speak. ...' (1992: 83) he affirms. The 'truth' that the poet here wishes to utter is that of those who have perished, the 'creatures out at sea'. The term serves to denote the absolute of honesty, but the 'truth' is also 'God' – this is the only occurrence of the word in all Steiner's poetry. The concept of truth here gains such intensity because the poem reverts to the ancient biblical sense of 'witnessing' as defined in 'Chagga Truth', yet implants the witness into a modern, subjective sensibility, a person who must also testify to the most terrible defilement of the sacred. Thus the speaker introjects the external 'truth' into the inner subject, where it affords a revelation. As a witness, he recognises both the divine presence ('light') *and* also His absence in the form of 'darkness'. Nor is it only the 'truth' of God before man to which he testifies, but the 'truth' of man – the creatures at sea become 'true' (p. 83) – before God (p. 85). In these paradoxes, one senses the speaker's anguish, as he wrests meaning from suffering:

> For all the suffering out at sea
> Is a pain for glory's sake,
> Itself into glory turning,
> Transforming everything.
> (1992: 85)

These words, that echo the idea from the *Kaddish* that the souls of the righteous are written in the Book of Life, and which might here conceivably be regarded as blasphemous, become sayable because the poet denies himself, and, in witnessing the transformation of pain, accepts his own spiritual death as a consequence of his witness: 'A great, a mighty frost has entered my heart. / In the dark I stand alone, see nothing any more' (1992: 87). The *Conquests*' 'lonely man' who acted as the world's 'guardian' here becomes a martyr, taking upon himself the world's pain, in order that God's glory may be seen. Read as autobiography, the lines indicate that Steiner's early death should be read not just as a consequence of the war, but as the result of self-imposed penance. His poem displays an idea of a truth that is grounded in loss and pain: 'On pain I stand and firmly plant my feet, / It is my rock, a rock I did not form' (p. 85). Whereas the poet 'stands on pain', those at sea 'suffer' (p. 87).

And so the 'Prayer in the Garden' reverts to the theme of Steiner's much earlier 'Letter to Georg Rapp' (pp. 115-22, below), which elaborates on the role of pain and suffering in his thought. Suffering, Steiner here argues, differs from pain in that pain has a definite relation to time. Suffering, on the other hand, is the medium of time. He continues:

> A life without suffering is valueless. A world without suffering is valueless.
> What the religions of mankind have to offer – and when I say religions, I

mean religions, not myths, not mystical absorption, not rituals, but the symbolic systems which result from all of these and are accepted as religion, which is binding – what the religions of mankind have to offer, then, is in the end nothing other than the ground upon which, and the language in which, people can communicate about the possibility of ending their various sufferings and our own, common age of suffering. (p. 116, below)

For Franz Steiner, suffering provided a ground for value; and religions as social institutions created the means for communicating about such suffering. At this point, where all his concerns and forms of writing meet, Steiner locks into a debate central to modern German thought, to which Nietzsche gave his characteristically deconstructive stamp in 'Die Geburt der Tragödie' (The Birth of Tragedy), where he first unmasks the 'Untergrund des Leidens' (ground of suffering) that lies beneath the Apolline i.e., also Socratic, modern, theoretical worldview ([1873] 1954: 34). Nietzsche hereby discovers what he calls 'die Weisheit des Leidens' (the wisdom of suffering; 1954: 32). In Nietzsche's wake, Steiner's own poetic model, Rainer Maria Rilke, returns to the same original ground in his own poetic testimony, the *Duino Elegies*. Using a characteristically Nietzschean term formed with *Ur-*, Rilke speaks of *Ur-Leid*, the original suffering that lies behind and validates all existence, in the grand, concluding *Elegy* (1955: 733). In this poem, as later with Steiner, suffering provides the genuine measure of value, which is contrasted with modernity's pleasure-seeking economy represented by the so-called *Leid-Stadt* – the city of suffering (1955: 721) in which pleasure masks pain. Steiner echoes this contrast between existence and inauthenticity in *Conquests* (pp. 263-65, below). Elsewhere, he takes the question concerning the place of suffering to a characteristic extreme. In an unpublished aphorism, headed *Der Mensch und das Leid* (Man and Suffering) he develops the ideas about suffering which may date back to the time of the letter to Georg Rapp. Drawing a new corollory from Lessing's famous Enlightenment definition of the morally best human being – 'Der mitleidigste Mensch ist der beste Mensch' (The human being who feels the most sympathy is the best human being) (Lessing [1756] 1973: 163) – Steiner asserts: 'Der leidende Mensch ist das wichtigste Geschöpf der Welt' (The suffering human being is the most important creature in the world). Upon this characteristic perspectival reversal, Steiner continues by arguing that suffering is that which makes man human:

> What distinguishes man from the animals? What more does he have? What more does he know? Many say he is cleverer, more intelligent. Others say that we have no criteria and means of measuring a comparison like this. We certainly do not. Nor for the question of whether the animal is happier.

But who has enquired about the criteria of suffering? There just are no criteria here because the sufferings of all creatures appear to be the most real thing that we are capable of perceiving. It is the intensity of our pains and sufferings and feelings of happiness, not our thoughts and decisions which distinguishes dream and reality. ...

Having combinatorially slipped from the man/beast contrast into the dream/reality divide, Steiner turns to 'reason' as another definitorial trait for disposal, before reaching a conclusion which takes Lessing's statement of human value to a new logical conclusion: 'Der Mensch leidet, weil er Mensch ist. Je mehr er leidet, umsomehr ist er Mensch' (The human being suffers because he is a human being. The more he suffers, the more human he is.) By this route, Steiner sets himself against the whole line in Western thought which sees 'happiness' as the goal, and regards value as grounded in the pursuit of happiness, a view also widespread in the human sciences running up through Bentham and still held by Freud, for whom it appears certain that 'human value judgements are categorically guided by their wishes for happiness' (Freud 1930: 135).

According to the letter to Georg Rapp, two possibilities present themselves: either to seek the opposite of pain in timelessness which renders suffering an illusion, the option embraced in some Eastern religions, or:

to live boundlessly in suffering, to allow oneself to be filled with suffering, trusting in the strength that comes only from suffering. There is no other human deepening. We weigh only the weight of our sufferings, we can never be found too light, but at the same time we have to know that all of this is so, so that we become lighter, like feather-down. (p. 117 below)

From this stem attitudes towards one's own suffering and towards others as fellow sufferers whose time also passes irrevocably. In Steiner's own case, Judaism offered him the 'riches' to transvalue his suffering – a distinctly Talmudic idea, stated e.g., in Rabbi Joshua's words that 'suffering redeems the world' (Mayer 1963: 533: *Taanit* 8a), which feeds into both the rationalist strain in Judaism, represented by Maimonides, and the mystical Kabbalah. The other-than-personal ramifications of Steiner's philosophy inform the delicacy of his anthropology through a recognition that all religion seeks to transvalue human suffering. In this, Steiner clearly shared the religious aesthetic of many of the Oxford School of anthropology, notably the Evans-Pritchard of *Nuer Religion*, Godfrey Lienhardt of *Divinity and Experience* or Mary Douglas in her celebratory final chapter of *Purity and Danger*. Here we rejoin the lectures on 'Tabu', for each social system in Steiner's terms is established in relation to regimes of classification defined and supported by an allocation of danger. These both mediate human suffering and transvalue that suffering in order to establish the ultimate truth and values of the society. It is a vision at once sociological, religious and aesthetic.

Conclusion

Art and science: I have two irons in my own hellfire: instruments of torture.
                                    Essays and Discoveries (Ms 1948)

All the possibilities that make my life impossible....
                                    Essays and Discoveries (Ms 1948)

A conclusion compels us towards some resolution of the strands of Steiner's writings that, given his suspicion of the ambitions of stable syntheses, he would surely have disowned. We offer such only to suggest a (almost mnemonic) device to make the diversity of his work thinkable.

Steiner's writings – to adopt a model he himself introduced – are triangulated by the three disciplines to which he submitted them: anthropology, poetry and political activism. Each of these corresponded to a genre: his anthropology was represented by the academic papers and lectures he composed, and the medium of his expression changed from German to English almost as soon as he relocated from the German- to the English-speaking world; his poetry continued to be written in German throughout his life; while his political writings were composed in both languages almost from the outset, but increasingly in English as time wore on. Steiner's aphorisms sit in the middle of these triangulated disciplines and genres: composed in German to the last (Steiner translated none of them into English), and with complex generic relations to his anthropological, poetic and political writings. Arriving late on the scene of his intellectual production, the aphorisms were located as three-way mediators of his diverse projects and even began to displace one of them (poetry).

Steiner's submission to three disciplines of thought each had a temporal trajectory. The anthropological is the most explicit: we have seen how, over time, the dominance of his ethnological interests in 'culture circles' theory began to yield, without ever being entirely submerged, to the force of structural analysis in terms of institutions and formal, first Radcliffe-Brownian then Simmelian, sociology. His sense of Jewish identity, which informed his political writings, transformed from self-discovery and self-exploration, as a young man in Jerusalem, of himself as an 'Oriental in the West', through his later poetic evocation of the hostility of the West to alien presence, and his last depiction of his poetic 'I' in terms of the repetitions through recollection of the aspects of himself, and his previous experiences. Politically, the same trajectory leads from the validation of a modernising Jewish community to the need for a theocratic state in Israel which would recuperate all that was Oriental (in several senses) within the communities in exile.

All this suggests formal similarities between the trajectories of Steiner's three disciplines: from the charting of diffusion to an appreciation of the simultaneous co-presence of the diverse aspects of complex individual and collective entities. Person and society come to be figured in similar ways, as the structured (to some degree compartmentalised) expressions of diversity mediated through the practice of institutionalised social life. The ways in which complex entities are structured are diverse, but in reading *Conquests* we drew particular attention to the idea of repetition. Each repetition establishes the occasion of its recollection as the grounds for further repetition. What goes for individual recollection also applies to social recollection; memory is the result of repetition and recollection. In his aphorisms, Steiner remarked the slippage by which theorists accept that remembering is culturally diverse but assume that forgetting is a common human process (p. 233, below). Societies and individuals forget differently, in their relation to repetition and recollection, myths are carriers of a particular order of not-to-be-forgotten truth (a lesson both for individual and collective subjects).

Each of the poles of his disciplinary imagination bordered on danger. For anthropologists, the danger lay in erecting upon the logical groundings of knowledge edifices of prejudice which fed directly into domination. In the history of the West and its others, this tendency nourished a secular drive to expel or destroy alterity, driving it deeper within the individual person (as evidenced by the appeal of psychoanalysis) or into the systematic character of social connexions (as in economic collapses, like that of the Weimar Republic, which presaged the collapse of values more generally). To this, Steiner contrasted the society, with strong classifications undergirding collectively held values, which held danger at bay outside the social body, or incorporated it within through respecting the essential character, not just of common humanity, but of human difference. On these grounds, the Jewish people were, historically and properly, an Oriental people and their State should cherish the collective values of a theocratic order. Like Mary Douglas after him, Steiner found himself defending a hierarchical conception of society in terms of social theories devised within a Western individualist setting. Applied to the person (especially his own person through the medium of poetry), the same intellectual trajectory and concern for danger resulted in a depiction of what we might describe, in more contemporary parlance, as a multiple subjectivity conditioned by recollection of the past and the need to occupy multiple-subject positions in the structured social life of the present. Eventually, the conquests represented by individual striving and achievement must yield to the renunciation of the individual's will to domination, and the recognition (at least by a person of faith) of the certainties of death and of a higher power.

In the close-to-inexpressible space, as it were, between these syntheses of religious, political and sociological ideas, lay the intimation of what H.G. Adler called Steiner's 'universal mathesis', only partly coterminous with Lull's 'art', because it is itself a shifting promise of what his complete immersion in so many forms of knowledge (both of himself and others) and of expression boded. We are not suggesting that a longer life would have rendered this space more lucid, such was not its nature, but through his early death we were denied Steiner's further triangulation of what he intimated.

PART II:
ORIENTPOLITIK AND THE CIVILISING PROCESS

ORIENTPOLITIK[1]

In recent days, since the troubles are making even people who understand the situation uneasy about the rationale of our Palestine policy,
different voices are making themselves felt, saying things like: 'We
ought rather to have done so-and-so... ' and 'in those days we should
have done such-and-such... '. It is typical for our present situation that,
even when we recognise the silliness of admonitions of this kind, we
cannot actually control ourselves by recognising how silly they are.
Secretly, we carry on asking: 'Perhaps we did make some fundamental
mistake after all ... ?' Yet after a brief pause for thought to consider our
foundational work in Palestine and all our efforts and the sequence of
the events themselves, we must reject any such self-recrimination.

It is time to change the fateful question. Was there anything else
that might have been done? Something that should not now be overlooked? If what we did was not actually wrong, but we only did too little, when we change the question, certain things become clear. Given
that we acted with all our strength, to ask us to do more is a very considerable demand indeed.

'We should not have accepted Arab terror passively.' That is the passionate objection now being made. But the way it is raised and discussed is most unfortunate. The problem of *Realpolitik* is immediately
turned into one of *Weltanschauung*. It is surely obvious that a violent
response to the Arab terrorists would have had very different chances,
depending on the exact timing (in the second or third week of the troubles, in the days of the Dizengoff letter,[2] or now). But let us not now
waste time talking about the past. It is clear that a violent response in
the face of Britain's increased activity and the strengthening of the
British military presence in Palestine would be a mistake. The voices of
the *galut*,[3] who demanded violent action, must be met critically. Many
of us, who have no choice but to remain completely passive in the
midst of the hostile chaos in Europe, would have enjoyed the spiritual
release of identifying with heroic fighters (which would have fitted in

with the heroic ethos of our own surroundings!), even if this had been a completely pointless battle, against all reason. The 'debate' we conducted was a dispute between reason and our own irrational wishes. It rarely had any real-political content. That, as I have said, is a pity.

It is to be hoped that the demand for increased action (not action at any price) will be the lasting positive outcome of these terrible days. Action – in the present circumstances – means *Orientpolitik*. A politics based on our 400,000 people in Palestine. In the last few weeks, no-one said anything about the 400,000 in this connexion, but only spoke about our few thousand armed men. In future, it would be better to speak of the 400,000, without forgetting the others. If it really comes to a temporary ban on immigration, our *Orientpolitik* will have more meaning. It will be a means to increase Jewish power. That is what we should concentrate on, and not give way to self-destructive despair.

Three things stand in the way of a well-thought-out politics of this kind to be directed from Jerusalem. The first is the phantasm that English policy is 'opaque'. The past year has revealed that the opacity of English policy is nothing other than a consquence of England's extreme indecisiveness and the complete absence of any plans. This weakness in the English Empire will hardly diminish in the forseeable future. On the contrary. The decisive factor in dealing with clueless, changeable England – that is the lesson of the events – must be nothing other than our own *Orientpolitik*.

The second obstacle is the phantom of the pan-Arabic front. The idea of a pan-Arabic front was first dreamed up and consistently nurtured in England. Isn't it enough that we Jews are viewed through English spectacles and are allotted our place accordingly? Must we look at our own Arabic environment through their glasses, too? *Istiklal*,[4] the radical Arab movement for independence and unity, has positions in Syria and Iraq. Do we wish to completely disregard how weak these positions actually are and how insignificant they have been in supporting the Palestinian strikes? After all, they have contributed no more than a mere £1,200. What have Egypt and Saudi-Arabia to do with *Istiklal*? The Egyptian *Wafd*[5] Party has wisely distanced itself from the *Istiklal* movement. If the *Wafd* has not yet built on an alliance with *Istiklal* in its struggle against England, then it is impossible to see when it actually will.

Istiklal and *Wahhabis*[6] only have in common the fact that they are both Arabic and are both uncompromising movements. However, you can hardly treat them as sharing the same 'national banner' without doing violence to the modern political meaning of the word 'national'. What have the State that the *Istiklal* people want and the State created by Ibn Saud got in common?

On the one hand, you have a national movement which would gladly do in its own country what Turkey and Egypt have done: achieve independence or near-independence, build a modern life of which one need not feel ashamed in comparison to European superiority, enact countless reforms, and bring about enlightened autonomy; on the other hand, you have nothing but the despotic realisation of the prophet's commandments, harshly puritanical obedience to religious prescriptions, and the Koran as the sole basis for political goals. Among the former you find intellectuals thirsting for enlightenment, among the latter the men of the desert, roaming around with their herds, cultivators of oases lost in the sands, guardians of the sacred places, for ever saying 'Mohammed's teaching is the sword', forever living in an aggressive State as a reaction to overpopulation in the desert. *Istiklal* and Saudi Arabia are two different worlds. It may well be that in the near future, the Wahhabi will collaborate a little with the *Istiklal* in order to expand his own position, and tiny *Istiklal* will boast with its army in the desert. But this should not hide the fact that these movements are separated by the very greatest sociological, ideological and political differences that can be found anywhere in the Arabian Orient.

The third obstacle for a normal, well-planned *Orientpolitik* is us – the ones who come from Europe. If you had to express our own, unconscious view, it could be formulated as follows: 'We have now reached the Orient because of our desire for a homeland. We are now surrounded by Orientals. But what good can they do us? If only we could force the English to keep their promises!' If this is not the way we think, how else can it be explained that we do not even publish an Arabic newspaper to keep our neighbours up-to-date about our goals and achievements?

Let us be clear: *Orientpolitik* is the second stage of our journey, only *Orientpolitik* can finally release us from the passivity of the *galut*.

So how should we start? What do we mean to the Orient? Let me single out just one set of issues. The task we face is to show the Egyptian public living in the towns that there are 400,000 people in Palestine, among them the most progressive people in the whole Orient, who are infinitely more interesting to them, the modernising Orientals, than all the Bedouin and Fellaheen put together. The task we face is to show the Orient that, insofar as Palestine has any interest for them, we actually represent the Orient as regards Palestine.

I therefore think it would be appropriate to open an Egyptian Institute in Tel Aviv, just as France and Italy do in European countries. By exploiting every connexion (such as Egyptian Jews) we will surely find Egyptian intellectuals who are prepared to represent Egyptian culture in a fashionable town, near to home, and to hold Egyptian language courses and lectures. At the same time, we must launch a propaganda committee in Cairo that will supply Egyptian newspapers with articles and organise excursions to Jewish Palestine with Jewish guides. All to be done at reduced rates and so on. That does not in itself constitute

Kulturpropaganda, but it will be a start. Next, under the heading of 'Arts and Sciences', we have to create opportunities for debate. In all of this, we have to avoid two dangers. First, we must not argue for Zionism. We must not appeal to justice. We must not discuss the Jewish suffering which forces us to head for Palestine. We must not aver that we will not harm the Arabs in Palestine. All of this, however important it may seem to us, must take second place. No, in view of the constant agricultural crises in Egypt, we have to point out the advantage that a study of our *kevuzot*[7] and *moshavim*[8] can provide for Egyptian Wafd students. Secondly, in these endeavours we must not exploit a standpoint towards England that is superficially self-justificatory. We cannot force our neighbours to adopt a particular view of us. We can only act according to the image they ought to have of us. And people will have to notice us soon, when England takes action which disadvantages us. Of course, the English suppress the most progressive elements in the land in favour of the least difficult ones.

Why begin with Egypt? Because she is our strongest neighbour. Because in this very developed country, the Jews still have an important, stable position.

All of this indicates that our university will be allotted an important new role. Where, if not on Mount Scopus,[9] should our people acquire knowledge of their neighbours' situation? Hitherto, our University has been a meeting place of Jewish learning, scholarship and science (*Jüdische Wissenschaft*), which was condemned to death in the *galut*. What has been achieved under these circumstances and in the face of other difficulties is marvellous. We know it. We know that the names of the men to whom we owe this achievement already belong to Jewish history. However, as long as our students merely acquire profound learning in linguistics, cultural history and the history of religion, which are subjects whose importance derives primarily from their value as pure knowledge and from their place in the sciences as a whole, but learn very little about Oriental agrarian problems, the laws of Ibn Saud, and Egyptian exports, there will be an imbalance. It is hard to see how this can be redressed in the short-term. Yet as long as this imbalance persists, our University will remain the refuge of a noble Jewish spirit, a jewel of the nation, but will not represent its scientific vanguard.

Here lies a way forward for our national effort. A way which demands the involvement of every able person. A way of twofold timeliness. It is timely, first, because by taking it we can overcome everything which England has inflicted on us. If we are forced to pause in our other efforts, we can still press ahead to concentrate on this goal. But, second, it is also timely because the chance might soon disappear. If we only begin after the Orient has been so overtaken by the

Schacht[10]-Goebbels propaganda as the Balkans are today, there will not be much hope for us.

NOTES

1. This article first appeared on 15 Tishri 5697/1 October 1936, in *Selbstwehr. Jüdisches Volksblatt* (Prague) XXX (41): 6-7. It is published in English here for the first time.
2. Meier Dizengoff (1861-1937): Author of the *Report on Urban Colonization* (1927); founder, and first mayor of Tel-Aviv at the time Steiner writes; instrumental in Tel Aviv becoming seat of Israeli government. [Eds]
3. *Galut*: 'exile'; condition of the Jews between the destruction of the Second Temple and the foundation of the State of Israel; the time when the homeland and the political and cultural centre of the people was lost. [Eds]
4. *Istiklal*: Moroccan modernising and independence party; cf. *Wafd* in Egypt. [Eds]
5. *Wafd*: 'delegation', nationalist party formed in Egypt in 1918. [Eds]
6. *Wahhabism*: Islamic reformist movement founded by Syrian jurist Abd el-Wahhab (1903-92). Particularly strong presence in Saudi Arabia. [Eds]
7. *Kevuzot* (pl.): small collective agricultural communities. Later virtually synonymous with *kibbutz*. [Eds]
8. *Moshavim* (pl.): villages of cooperative smallholders also practising private farming. [Eds]
9. Mount Scopus: Hebrew University in East Jerusalem founded in 1918 and officially opened on Mt Scopus in 1925. [Eds]
10. H.H.G. Schacht (1887-1970): as economics minister and President of Reichsbank revived German economy in preparation for World War II. [Eds]

GYPSIES IN CARPATHIAN RUSSIA[1]

Of the 32,857 Gypsies living in Czechoslovakia the census of 1930 recorded 32,630 as domiciled in the eastern parts of the Republic. Of that number, Slovakia accounts for 31,188, and Carpathian Russia for only 1,442. Thus the great majority of Czechoslovak Gypsies live in territory formerly belonging to Hungary, and the conditions under which they live must be explained with respect to the area as a whole in which they used to live.

In the eastern areas of central and in south-east Europe the Gypsies form a substantial proportion of the population. The reason for this is to be sought, among other things, in the following circumstances: the characteristic occupations of the Gypsies are those of coppersmiths and tinkers, and musicians, both of which doubtless provided them with a living in the days when they were settled in India. The musician life of the Gypsies and the continued practice of the not directly productive craft of an outcast race is linked up with a feudal system of rural life or with an orientally influenced form of amusements and amusement establishments in the towns. The practice of the metal-working craft just mentioned was encouraged by the agricultural character of the regions where the Gypsies lived, by a shortage of industrial products, and by the lack in particular of an adequate craft of this kind in the towns.

While Slovakia includes some of the corn area of the Danubian Valley and has taken over its Gypsies as heir of the former Hungarian economic system, the case is quite different as regards Carpathian Russia. This one-time frontier region of Hungary – consisting chiefly of forests and mountains, economically neglected by the former Hungarian rule, and only of interest by reason of its wealth of timber – receives its characteristic impress in the matter of population from the Ruthenian peasants, herdsmen and woodmen. The East-Slavonic peasant is by reason of his poverty, and his self-sufficing life on his own plot of land, a hindrance to the spread of the gypsy element.

Only in the lowlands of Carpathian Russia, in the surroundings of the larger towns such as Mukačevo, Užhorod and Berehovo are there gypsy settlements. An exception is to be seen in the case of Rachov which, as the largest self-contained mountain settlement, also has its Gypsies.

The returns of the year 1930 relating to the occupations of the Gypsies give the following figures: only 142 recorded themselves as following a free calling (these were mostly musicians), 314 were agricultural workers, 171 were metalworkers including tinker's work, while 216 were workers in quarries, on the roads, and navvies. These figures must be accepted with caution as they are based solely on the statements of the Gypsies themselves. Only 37 Gypsies declared themselves as beggars. The figures from the social angle show that 349 were independent earners, 100 employees, 289 proletarians and 661 labourers.

As regards the language spoken by the Gypsies of Carpathian Russia, the Magyar language plays the main role alongside the gypsy language itself, Romany. Only in the surrounding of Užhorod, where the Slovak lingual area pushes forward over the political frontier has the Magyar tongue been compelled to give way among the Gypsies to the Slovak. On their own request Slovak has been fixed as the language of instruction in the gypsy school at Užhorod. Small groups of Gypsies in the Perecîn district speak Ukrainian; they live pretty much isolated from other Gypsies, their knowledge of Romany is insignificant, and signs of degeneration, such as dwarfish growth, indicate inbreeding and thus permanent isolation.

In view of the small numbers of the Gypsies of Carpathian Russia, serious cultural problems such as the question of emancipation are not broached, and it is impossible to speak of a planwise cultural policy in that connexion. The only points to be noted are the measures taken by the parish and education authorities, which of course are of considerable importance.

Carpathian Russia possesses two gypsy schools: one at Mukačevo started this year, and an older one at Užhorod. This latter has become quite famous. Visitors from many different lands request permission to be present during lessons, and, to judge by the entries in the Visitors' Book and in the school archives, these seem to rank among the most important sights that Carpathian Russia has to show.

The small school is attended by 64 children. The difficulties attending such an enterprise are not to be under-estimated. The teacher has to deal with children whose talents are so different from the ordinary, and he has to change the curriculum accordingly. Moreover – and this is one of the great drawbacks of gypsy life – the children cannot be allowed to take either book or copybook home, so that everything has to be learnt in school. In arithmetic the children, says the teacher, are above the average, but they find reading difficult. Their lack of imagination in drawing is most noticeable. Special attention is devoted to singing and music; an endeavour is made not only to acquaint the children with Slavonic folksongs and to maintain their knowledge of the domestic gypsy songs, but also to introduce Romanian gypsy songs to them, and this gives the children very special pleasure. They learn with great zeal the songs, so similar to their own, that 'have come in a letter'. More frequently than in other schools the lessons are interrupted, and the children taken out into the schoolyard and taught gymnastic drill. In this way, and by means of games to which the children devote themselves with uproarious vivacity, the drooping attention of the class is re-won.

This school came into being in the following way: a large number of gypsy children attended a Slovak school. As the teaching was very much hindered by the presence of these children a special gypsy class was formed. In this way the difficult material could be dealt with successfully, and the results proved very satisfactory. The children, too, felt at home. With this class as a foundation a State gypsy school was established. On its model the second school at Mukačevo has now been inaugurated.

The gypsy school is designed not only to impart elementary education but also to combat the worst evils in gypsy life – gross uncleanliness and child prostitution. In so far as the children are secured while very young for the school, the success achieved in these directions is a very notable one. The teacher is, of course, not yet quite satisfied with results. He has become a personage much looked up to in the village, is called in to settle disputes, and can use his authority with the children, if necessary, outside school. In his opinion, however, the influence of the parental house is still too strong to enable the school to play the role which it should play in gypsy life.

From time to time theatricals are given by the school. But they are not mere performances by the schoolchildren alone. The whole youth of the village participate intensively, and a performance is a great event for the Gypsies of the whole district far and wide. The pieces chosen are connected with gypsy life, or have some gypsy roles.

NOTES

1. This article first appeared, in English, as 'Gypsies in Carpathian Russia' on 4 March 1938 in *The Central European Observer* (Prague) 16 (5):70-71.

LETTER TO GEORG RAPP[1]

In your last letter but one, you wrote about something very important: the distinction between pain and suffering. The search for an exactly corresponding pair of opposites cannot be pursued assiduously enough.

At first, language itself assists us. We notice that we give pain a name, just as we do other emotions, and we connect it with expressions of feeling. We always ask about the cause of pain, too. After all, in future we want to avoid exposing ourselves to circumstances which cause painful sensations. When a pain lasts for a long time, we normally speak of suffering. We automatically reject the word 'pain' since it seems to lack one decisive aspect, namely a relation to time. Alternatively, we lessen the inaccuracy by saying that someone is suffering from a pain. Pain in itself seems to have nothing to do with the passing of time, but in the case of suffering time seems to be the medium for the very essence of the emotion.

We do not ask to explain the cause of pain in terms of pain itself. We look behind the pain. We do not enquire about the cause of suffering at all, but only about the time when it started and the time when it will end; although we do, of course, enquire about the cause of suffering when we believe we are dealing with a series of pains – or, more precisely: insofar as we represent the sufferers as creatures experiencing a succession of pains. For when we suffer, the suffering and the time in which we suffer are one and the same. If we ask as sufferers, it is only within the time of suffering. But these are all tautologies. It is clear that as sufferers we do not know when our suffering began. We can say: that is when I felt the first pang of pain. But even in expressions like that, we are saying that we are unclear as to whether the suffering began with a particular pain which can be located exactly. Why, I wonder? Above all because for us as sufferers, suffering and time are so very much the same that enquiring about the time when our suffering began seems to lead beyond time itself. None the less, we pose these questions. They seem important to us, like all questions whose answers seem so questionable that we can treat them as expressing the questionability of existence as a whole.

If we seriously consider whatever could be called 'value', it must be this: everything that contributes to the alleviation of suffering, everything which gives us the strength to overcome suffering, everything which can make suffering cease.

A life without suffering is valueless. A world without suffering is valueless. What the religions of mankind have to offer – and when I say religions, I mean religions, not myths, not mystical absorption, not rituals, but the symbolic systems which result from all of these and are accepted as religion, which is binding – what the religions of mankind have to offer, then, is in the end nothing other than the ground upon which, and the language in which, people can communicate about the possibility of ending their various sufferings and our own, common age of suffering.

Suffering as such is not a value. There may be other opinions about this, which have been called forth by the decline of Christianity and for which that religion itself bears no direct responsibility. None the less, these opinions are false, this use of the concept of 'value' is meaningless. To treat suffering as a value is simply coquetting with a denial of life for which Europeans lack the strength.

But the power to overcome suffering only comes out of suffering itself. And that is why there is no value outside suffering. This is the contradictory dialectic of suffering. It is the sum of all wisdom – or could be regarded as such if we really wished to invoke metaphysics to explain this first, inadequate step towards knowledge.

Since you will unfortunately have to deal with that other religion, perhaps I may add that the myth of Christ's death is the most beautiful, transfigured expression of what I call that inadequate, first step towards knowledge. The life and death of Christ represents everything that could be said about the contradictions of suffering: this life seems to aim at nothing other than the end of all suffering, in a climax of suffering and sacrificial death; and this is supposed to have produced a power so great that people dare to believe that everyone was redeemed by it. Thus, if Christians today maintain that suffering is a value, they show that even those simple parables are too difficult for them to understand.

A legitimate procedure – in contrast to that semi-denial of life – is that well-known Eastern one, according to which no suffering exists, no suffering in reality. All suffering must be seen through to grasp its unreality. Hence there are no values either. Values are just as illusory for Buddha as suffering.

The opposite of pain is simply a contrary feeling. The opposite of suffering has always been described as a condition of timelessness. By this means, words such as timeless, eternal, gain richness of meaning. Eternity is not only that absolute concept which is opposed to finite life, but something thoroughly relative, too, about which it can be said that it reaches into life. Its inadequate embodiment in language hangs together with the relativity and questionability of the length of suffering. But this leads to meditations which are already removed from that 'inadequate first step towards knowledge'.

A knowledge about all that is demonstrable in language. The very persistence with which pain is always connected with the so-called bodily suffering, and sufferings with the so-called spiritual. This goes so far that people speak expressly of spiritual pain, that is to say they add the spirit to indicate that they are not speaking of normal pain or feelings of a 'bodily kind'.

I don't want to write on endlessly. Nothing essential could be added. And if this is not clear enough for you, I'll add some practical advice.

It is clear that there is no other possibility apart from either living in an Eastern-monastic manner by turning all suffering into an illusion, or to live boundlessly in suffering, to allow oneself to be filled with suffering, trusting in the strength which comes only from suffering. There is no other human deepening. We weigh only the weight of our sufferings, we can never be found to be too light, but at the same time we have to know that all of this is so, so that we become lighter, like feather-down. What is called value in art is this coming-to-terms with the weight of suffering. The representation of suffering is not enough. I've finally reached the stage now that one or two of my poems can be taken up by other people as objects of comfort. That is the only small justification for my life, useless journeys, endless dreaming, chewed-through libraries, solitary sophistries.

The relationship to suffering, the complete experience of suffering, can be seen in the most trivial everyday things, even in formalities. What is politeness in the end? An exact consideration for other people's time. That is the most primitive of all. Consideration for other people's time: not, say, because it is worth money. But consideration out of understanding the suffering of other people, out of understanding the unity of suffering, time, personality. If you respect other people's time so little that you invite them to visit you and then do something in their presence which makes them completely superfluous, if you therefore absolutely do not wish to understand that the chief thing people have in common is that their time passes irrevocably, if you do not see in a human being that pile of irrevocable losses and scattered possibilities, which are exactly the things at which one should direct one's love ... if you do not do all this, but perhaps begin writing a letter, there is a lack here which neither true loveableness in other contexts, nor affectionate sympathy, willingness to help and the adornment of devotions can make good.

This is getting nearer home, as the English say. Reluctantly I come to the central part of my letter, the part which I find the most difficult.

It is quite natural that we wish every person we appreciate a valuable life, and every artist the greatest validity of his art. If however we know how much such results are connected to the fulfilment of suffering, we hesitate with our well-wishing. If psychology were any good, we could enquire disinterestedly by observation how much a person can suffer, how strong to bear it. We can very quickly form a judgement about a person's receptivity for pain, almost never about his strength to suffer – and even if we can, we cannot attach any demands to it. If I think about you, I am conscious above all else how receptive you are to pain. You can feel subtle pains and, what fills me with anxiety, is that you can be confused by pain. Compared to you I have a thick skin which can bear a considerable amount. And yet I know that I would not have withstood much of what my friends had to suffer before they were murdered. Two years in Prague under Nazi rule would certainly have driven me into madness or suicide. That is how relative everything is that can be said about the receptivity towards pain. The fact that the preparedness of a person to take on suffering depends on the degree of his receptivity towards pain needs no explanation. You simply never know how much another person is capable of in this respect, and for that reason religious life is not founded on presumptions and corrections of this kind. But you never know either how much suffering another person takes on. You can only resort to guessing, which is better left alone. I remember friends violently criticising me and saying that it was unbearable to see how little the whole war and all its misery really meant to me. This was said to me at a time at which I could hardly think of anything apart from all its senseless destruction, all its meaningful evil. Perhaps my participation was really limited in comparison with those who reproached me. Perhaps … that's just what no-one can decide.

It was out of considerations like these that I accepted almost everything which I experienced at your hands almost without objection. I nodded at many a word which horrified me, nodded and forced myself to think how differently most people express themselves. But I cannot let you believe that I agree with you and if I do not now warn you about this misunderstanding, I fear that I will never again be in a position to do so.

I have never moaned in your presence or complained about what the Germans are doing to my people. I have not, as is usually the case, condemned even the most brutal events, and never twisted what oppresses us into a realm in which political machines could be 'accused' or 'justified'. Don't think that I have discovered some special comfort which enables me to keep silent when others complain. It is much rather the case that, for me, every horror which people perpetrate (against whomsoever) defines the nature of man. That man am I. If I refused to recognise that every, but really every abomination which so-called Germans, so-called English, Romanians, Poles perpetrate is simply the precise extension of obscure thoughts and feelings which I have had at one time or another, then everything that I believe about man, about creation, about sin, would become meaningless. Nothing is made easier for me by it. I am not permitted any accusation of that which 'takes place outside myself', of a sin, 'which has nothing to do with me'. Nor am I permitted that which Christians apparently love so much: forgiveness. For me it is not a question of accusing or forgiving so-called 'other' people. What does that mean: other? Here, humanity as a single whole is committing a crime, and the longer that continues, the less it can be seen how you, YOU, WE can be forgiven. The fact that the greater part of the Jewish people is undergoing destruction can only intensify our suffering into boundlessness.

Like some old woman I now have to dig up something that you once said. Don't think my remonstrances are petty because of that. You once said that if only 10% of everything were true that the newspapers are writing about the persecution of the Jews, that would be ... And a painful shrugging of the shoulders ended your sentence. But how do you come to assume only 10%? Are you a cold English simpleton who blows the cigarette ash away from his newspaper and says 'It can't be as bad as all that?' Remember with me. You said that on the evening when I was your guest. First we sat with your parents. Then your mother showed me the *Jewish Chronicle* which printed a report of the Belgian Government, which hardly has cause to exaggerate, unlike the suddenly very philo-Semitic Poles. Then we went to your room, you announced your 10% horror, and as we went on you told me you had decided to marry L., and, if you were living in an age when the persecution of the Jews were more limited, you would have nothing against marrying her in a Christian church. We discussed the changing extent of the persecution of the Jews, then we went to sleep, or rather I wrote that poem about my parents, my proportion of the 10%.

But how on earth can you assume that 10%? Don't you see in that a rejection of intended suffering? Or do you have some special news? And if you won't carry this suffering, what will you carry? What will you arm yourself against? What will you live for? What will you make good? Oh, what other questions shall I still ask you?

Last Summer at Oxford you showed me your Donne translations. There was a poem among them which, if I am not mistaken, spoke derogatorily about the Jews, the Christians' betrayers, and I said that I could not appprove of that translation. I was surprised why you had picked just that poem. And you replied that it was simply a beautiful poem for you, a piece of language, lovely words without a relation to the Jewish fate which we were suffering. You indicated that it was my particular gift that one thing always occurred to me in connexion with another, that made me connect words, connect everything, and that did not permit anything to exist in my consciousness in isolation .... But you are very much mistaken. That is not a gift. That is our suffering. Suffering makes connexions. Suffering opens the poet's capacity for the human lot. There are no gifts which do not subordinate themselves to suffering.[2]

You repeatedly said in my presence that you longed to travel to Germany after the war to hear the language again, as it is impossible to write without the living experience of the German language. Well, I can't argue about that. But you *always* said when speaking of this longed-for visit how much you wished to cross the road and hear someone who had accidentally stepped on your foot say 'I'm sorry'. Apparently, at the moment when experiencing this wish, you don't consider what terrible kicks that same harmless foot must have been distributing not too long ago. Please don't think that I consider all Germans to be criminals. Please don't disprove me in your mind by thinking of me as a spiteful little emigré buffoon artiste. You must not have your thoughts so easily. This is neither about how 'all' Germans are, nor have I ever presumed to have an opinion about that. This is about something else. It's simply that at the thought of that gentle kick, you don't think of others: that you can cheerfully disregard suffering. As with that passage in Donne, you 'don't think of anything'. I must have explained to you by now that this does not demonstrate a very serious attitude to life. Here I only want to point out a small contradiction. One needs real closeness to the mother-tongue in order to write poetry. But if anyone thinks that one needs this 'thinking' about weightier and unpleasant things any the less, that is a great error. I don't expect you to write war and disaster poems. On the contrary. If you follow me, you understand that one must not keep suffering, and especially collective suffering, locked up in a little room. And those 'relevant' poems come from the fact that some people have little rooms like that and now want to empty them for some reason or other. This is just as pointless as keeping them locked. It does not show an intense, full manner of experiencing, no deeper humanity, and does not produce great poetry. After all, these things are connected. The fact that poetry is a moral matter is not an invention of the Philistines. True, here and there a pretty poem can succeed.... But to be a poet by calling, my God! But where does one take all the necessary insights, you will ask. What should guide us? You more or less grew up in England and it's clear that no imitation of the English way of life can help you. Whether we admire it or not, it's clear that people like us can't make much of that: that strange equilibrium somewhere between a cold-blooded performance of duties and securing personal advantages, with the nonchalance of the ruling classes here. You do not belong to the one universal church, the Catholic one, nor will you ever belong to it. You have never joined any party which wants to change society by every means and demands sacrifice and subordination from its members. From Germany and your childhood you have brought hardly anything other than the wish to be a poet. Wishes are no equipment. And I am speaking of the very thing which is missing for you to achieve your wishes. You have not even found it necessary to join one of those little groups that somehow wishes to contribute to the rebirth of Judaism on national soil. So, in its most critical moment, Judaism cannot even expect the most modest contribution from you. Don't let yourself be misled by that egoistic composure of the English intellectuals. These people only have to open a few old books by their people to find themselves in the deepest nexus of their own most peculiar tradition. At any moment they can switch from their pale insolence into a prayer and everyone will approve. To imitate these people is like the behaviour of an insomniac who, instead of seeking a cure, imitates the daily behaviour of well-slept people, as if he didn't know that they were prancing about so freely because of the nightly peace that eluded him.

What kind of support, what kind of guidance is open to you? I don't know how you explain my attitude to Judaism. If you think that it was given to me at home by my parents, you are mistaken. My surroundings were much less Jewish than yours. And my knowledge of Jewish things, of the Hebrew language is shamingly limited. And yet ... And yet ... Or did you ever think I was a petty Jewish nationalist? Did you think – you must surely have thought about me a little – did you think I was so enthusiastic about the idea of nationalism that just at the moment at which those bloated ghosts, the opinions which peoples have of themselves, that float around like disgusting corpses in the ocean of blood and sin, did you think that at just that moment I found it necessary to add Jewish nationalism to all the other nationalisms floating around?

If you only halfway treat me justly in your thoughts, you *must* see that I was just as empty and despairing as people of this age can only be. The fact that I found a support in Judaism does not mean that I had long and aesthetically searched around for a suitable support. There is no other way for me to be a complete person. That is all. I recognised that in this 'confession of poverty' lay my only riches. And what riches! If only you knew!

What other support, what other way do you know? This has to be asked with some emphasis since you are about to turn to the only possible support, in that you are preparing for a marriage with L.

Every mixed marriage is a tragedy in this age. In this epoch of the destruction of Jewish life it is simply a monstrosity. I hope you don't think I wish to dissuade you from your happiness. I only want you to see what a tragedy it is, I only want you to *experience* this, not to push it away, like 10%, like German kicks, or like anti-semitic remarks in 'otherwise beautiful' poems. If you do not wish to see what you are losing if you do not suffer *because of this,* I don't know what can deepen you.

It's easy for me to speak of mixed marriages and mixed loves as I do now, without being suspected of prejudiced arrogance. This is the problem which has destroyed my own life from the very root.

NOTES

1. This paper represents the substance of a letter to Steiner's young friend Georg Rapp, dated 29 October 1943. The translation is based on a transcript made by H.G. Adler which is preserved in Steiner's *Nachlaß* in the Deutsches Literaturarchiv, Marbach am Neckar. We have omitted the material contained in an opening paragraph (eleven lines) and the conclusion (three pages) which frame the general argument with personal references to Georg Rapp and the problems surrounding the translation of Steiner's poems for *Poetry London.* First publication.
2. The relative clause is ungrammatical in the original. 'There are no gifts, which do not suffering to make subordinate themselves'. Our emendation follows H.G. Adler. [Eds]

ON THE PROCESS OF CIVILISATION[1]

I

There have been many attempts to define the process of civilisation or the civilising process, i.e., to explain what is called a civilised state and what is an uncivilised one, as well as that which lies between the two, where the two states merge so closely into one another that this could be described in terms of a continuous process.

Normally, European culture is rightly defined as the culture characterised by the greatest and most extensive control over nature that is known to us; so-called natural peoples include those which exhibit the least amount of control. The degree of control over nature seems to be a very important criterion. This is purely a question of power. What determines this criterion is purely a power potential. The more control over nature *per capita* – so one might put it, absurdly – the more powerful the people.

What does this power concern? After all, there is no consciousness of power without an object. Does it concern nature when nature is 'controlled'? This can be refuted empirically and historically. In the lives of those peoples whom we are thinking of there is only one variety of power: power over other groups of people, that is to say military, political, economic power, power which guarantees the exploitation of other groups or permits their annihilation. In the head of a scholar it may well be that a new technological advance (including the sociological adaptations which this enforces) means an increase in the power of 'Man'. In the life of the planet and at the present moment, it simply means an increase in power over other people. Is there then only such a thing as power over people and not over nature?

We have arrived at a false impression. Before correcting it, let me interpose a question.

Let us for a moment drop the idea of control over nature and speak exclusively of technical achievements. What is the difference between the technical achievements of the Europeans and those of the natural peoples? Is it only a matter of degree?

Let us think of a people which is particularly simple in sociological terms, which has proven itself particularly well adapted technologically and has done so under the most severe climatic conditions – a people which has not just kept alive, but which has bravely fashioned its way of life. As to technical specialisation, the Eskimos have no equal among the natural peoples. But it is not their harpoons with their ball-and-socket-joints nor their arrow-heads with spiralled threads which fill us with such respect, it is their acts of adaptation. Who can build little houses in those winter nights when the snowstorms cover everything? The Eskimo builds houses of snow. Lo and behold, snow provides a warm place to dwell. Who can sail through the cliffs and dales of the ice-grey sea in a rowing-boat? The tiny kayak of the Eskimo is built and made water-tight in such a way that it can capsize and turn on its horizontal axis without damage to boat or occupant. These are certainly great achievements. What distinguishes them from European ones? We are looking for a criterion. In so doing let us exclude the quantitative element as well as the issue of (non-technical, but socio-psychological) adaptation to nature and control. The only difference then proves to be as follows: the Eskimo has no scientific system from which the applied sciences could be derived, of which ship building would be one branch and house building another. For this reason these Eskimo achievements strike *us* as accidental. But they are not. They presuppose a rational (albeit always purely empirical) research method. Anyone familiar with Arctic ethnology will confirm that this method is rational and not magical. (The Eskimo's magical practices concern other spheres.)

Accordingly, we find unsystematic empiricism on the one hand, and system and theory on the other. And, since we have excluded such questions, we cannot ascribe any importance to the world picture and cannot enquire how it came to this or that world picture. We cannot even cry 'aha!' and prove that the essential element about primitive world pictures, namely that which excludes modern civilisation, can be explained in terms of strange individual rituals and individual magical concepts.

Even if we concede all this and admit that our purely technical questions have been irrelevant and wrong, where have we got? We end up sharing the viewpoint of contemporary science. That is to say, on the one hand we have one of the frequently described magical world pictures of the primitives, and on the other we have European civilisation, which, we admit, does not ground itself on a scientific world picture, but honours the people who hold such a world picture, because it confirms their control over nature. From this scientific viewpoint, no magical world picture is 'complementary', or lies hidden, preserved in its entirety in some mysterious depths. The only religions, on this view, are fragmentary. They do not possess the authority to establish any kind of relationship between the human and the extra-human spheres or to determine the nature of the extra-human. Religions are merely fragments and can only provide archaic protection for ethical maxims, a home for lone enthusiasts, and a crass justification for endangered privilege, as well as holding out the cup of comfort in all crises when reason proves too weak.

We do not understand the transition from one type of culture to another. A world picture cannot transform itself into another world picture. There is no such thing as development in these matters. One world picture is smashed, and if the relevant people survives the catastrophe, another is adopted. If anyone enquires after the origins of the scientific world picture he is, on the one hand, directed towards a number of scientific insights obtained by the ancient mediterranean cultures, which fitted curiously well into magico-religious world pictures, and, on the other, he is directed to the history of the Renaissance, where he learns sociological details about the emergence of capitalism, and to this belongs the awakening, as it is called, of the scientific spirit.

But what is the *process* involved here? What sort of gradient is there? What direction is the stream flowing in which Europe is swimming? In the end, we are only told sociological or historical details or are fed visions which see cultures as organisms, whether in the pride of youth, in their masculine prime, or in senile decay. But what is this stream into which civilisations like Europe are torn?

And if we ask the historian of religion about religion, they tell us something about primitive magic and then move on to the great world religions, which allegedly owe their existence to a number of isolated, elevated priest-like men.

II

We obtain more essential information from the Eskimo example. Let us disregard the technological criteria and compare the so-called adaptation to nature with its control.

We have dropped the idea of measuring our powers with nature, as this is simply an allegory with the help of which predatory social elites transfigure the beliefs appropriate to their own technology. There is no such thing as the powers of nature on the one hand, those of 'the human being' on the other, an ensuing struggle, a growth of human powers, and finally a defeat of nature. That is simply the trite myth of capitalism.

It is pointless to imagine the individual European and the individual Eskimo existing in nature with the means which have been placed at his disposal. They can both exist before nature or within it. The conceptual shift which we undertake in order to move from the picture of the Eskimo to that of the European is purely a shift within a technological series of ideas. What really distinguishes them is not the power potential of the individuals compared but the boundaries of the two societies.

A society borders on danger. The Eskimo may employ his kayak and, thanks to his clever technique, he may travel unharmed through storms and between icebergs – none the less, he is travelling through the realm of danger. This realm exists prior to the birth of the individual, after death, and outside the structure created and constantly renewed by human relations ... The spirits, however wild and wicked they may be, do not dare to enter the meeting house. The fact that these spirits exist outside human society and that they are evil is a tautology, which rehearses the same idea in different words: 'outside society/danger'. The Eskimo treats those magicians or 'sorcerers' as dangerous persons who know how to cast a spell on the spirits from the danger zone which are willing to do their bidding and can be controlled within the sphere of social relations.

Let us compare this to modern civilisation. Clearly there are dangers outside the sphere of human relations, but these dangers are not organised. They arise diffusely, and do not necessarily reside within an area which surrounds the human sphere as a dangerous, demonic zone. There is no such thing as danger as such, but – insofar as we consider the extra-human sphere – there are only causal-models of disasters, which in reality exhibit an irregular diffusion.

In the course of a process, the boundaries of a society are increasingly extended; the alterations in this displacement are the changes upon which everything else depends. We cannot say anything more exact about the process of civilisation than to identify it with precisely this displacement.

It would be helpful to treat Christo-European society in the Middle Ages as a society which constantly felt itself threatened by the non-Christian peoples surrounding it. In so doing they equated heathendom with the demonic danger sphere to such an extent that the heroic deeds performed on the crusades were considered to represent a legitimate, unbroken continuation of those mythical heroic deeds which had to be performed in heathen or semi-heathen days against dragons and demons. Anyone who believes that views like the one that Mohammed's religion was the work of the devil or that the Turk was the Antichrist are merely politico-religious clichés or 'superstitions', and cannot accept our insight into this form of political demonology and cosmology, would be better advised to leave the study of cultural history to those who possess not more imagination (no! certainly not!), but a greater sense of reality.

It is only through modern technical achievements that it has become possible to control the politico-demonic sphere. Thanks to technology, we can misguidedly interpret the devilish horrors of the politico-demonic sphere as but a foolish charade by means of which that weakness can be hidden that must endure every form of exploitation.

In modern civilisation there are only a minimum of external dangers, the demons, which still survive outside society. They are few in number and very weak. By contrast, the maximum danger resides in society itself.

III

Let us disregard wars – however difficult that may be – and let us consider normal social catastrophes, for example those of a healthy economic body like the United States. Let us compare the waves of unemployment or the consequences of a stock-market crash with the floods and crop failures in the same region. The question as to which is more dreadful needs no reply. The individual is stricken and helpless when confronted by the forces of society. He has no rational weapon. No means to defend himself – let alone 'control' anything.

How much more does this apply in the wars of this civilisation, which in character so closely resemble civil wars. I will never forget how comfortable and comic a thunderstorm appeared to me which I experienced shortly after a bombing raid. How childish and touching those forces seemed to be before which humanity had trembled for millenia! Competent scientists are already thinking about how to direct thunderstorms to wherever there happens to be a 'need'. Yet the same clear-thinking men believe that the wish to abolish wars and bombs is pure fantasy. They *know* it. Here we are confronted by the incalculable and busily churn out illusions, more helpless than a Tasmanian in a thunderstorm.

The demonic sphere lies within our own society. Would anyone who has been in a concentration camp believe that wild animals are worse than a human torturer? This form of torment is new: trapping human masses in close-knit nets, building gigantic cages past which 'healthy' life floods by. This is more demonic than the torments of slavery, more horrible than the worst that ever happened before: the religious wars of European Christendom. For the captive does not know why he is captured, the guard does not know why he should torment him – and the people outside – alas, what do they know? The human beings fall victim. Stricken, they stagger. As if affected by a stock-market crash, by the fall of political units or of particular party cliques or other clubs.

Yes, indeed, human society has expanded. It has flooded the demonic sphere. What should we call the power that drove it onwards, impelling it to swallow danger and to gorge itself on horror? The result, however, the extending of the boundaries, the constant process of extension is the progress of civilisation. Let them speak of development! Let them speak of controlling nature! Let them turn volcanoes into servants and then wonder why their servants have become volcanoes! ...

IV

Of course it is possible to control the organisational activities of the demons within society just as the demons in the outer sphere have been pacified, and so to create a peaceful society. After all, the forces are already at work. What they can achieve is this: the exclusion of the demons from intra-personal relations, and their removal more deeply into the interior ... What was once outside society, what was later inside society will, when this society triumphs, one day be within the individual. That is the process. The process of civilisation is the conquest of man by the natural forces, the demons. It is the march of danger into the heart of creation.

Whoever recognises this lives in the black night of despair, illuminated by but a single star, the star of a dual discipline:

regarding man, who was created in His image;

regarding society, whose boundaries are immutably set forth in the covenant.

NOTES

1. This essay, dated Oxford, March 1944, is included among the first of Steiner's aphoristic *Allerlei Feststellungen und Versuche* (Sundry Essays and Discoveries) in Esther Frank's three-volumed typescript. It was first published in 1995 in *Akzente* (3): 213-19. The present version is translated by Michael Mack and Jeremy Adler. The text appears here in English for the first time.

LETTER TO MR GANDHI[1]

Dear Mr Gandhi[2],

The *Jewish Chronicle*, London, the 27th of Tammuz, 5706, prints an extract from an article you wrote in *Harijan* on 20th July.[3] I do not know whether the rendering of the *Jewish Chronicle* is correct. Therefore I shall repeat first the points you have made, then I will take the liberty of explaining my reason in commenting on them, and finally, I shall have to ask your patience for the comments I am going to make.

The first point of those I am going to quote is this:

'The Jews have erred grievously in seeking to impose themselves on Palestine with the aid of America and Great Britain, and now with the aid of naked force.'

The second:

'Their citizenship of the world should have and would have made them the honoured guests of any country.'

The third:

'Their thrift, their varied talent, their great industry should have made them welcome anywhere.'

The fourth:

'It is a blot on the Christian world that they have been singled out owing to a wrong reading of the New Testament.'

The fifth:

'No wonder my sympathy goes out to the Jews in their inevitable sad plight. But one would have thought adversity should teach them lessons of peace. Why should they depend on American money or British arms to force themselves on an unwelcome land?'

The sixth:

'Why should they resort to terrorism to make good their forcible landing in Palestine? If they were to adopt... nonviolence, whose use their best prophets have taught...their case would be the world's, and I have no doubt that among many things the Jews have given the world this would be the best and brightest.'

II

On these points I wish to comment. May I state now briefly my reason for doing so?

I am not representing a body of public opinion, nor have I any personal merits which would give me the right to demand your attention. I am simply one of the Jewish people, I regard my people as an Oriental nation and the Zionist effort (however critical I may be of some of its phases) as part of the resurrection of Asiatic civilisation.

Therefore, in this dreadful crisis, there is nothing I could desire more than speaking to the man whom I regard as the greatest leader Asia has produced in my time, and whose life, thought and leadership I profoundly respect.

At present I am living as a refugee in England. I am a student of sociology and social anthropology. When I grew up at Prague, I had to miss the advantages of an orthodox Jewish education, I had to walk a roundabout way to find my place. Next to the Hebrew Bible the Gita gave me guidance; it was the Gita which opened my eyes for many things of my own heritage, and some parts of the Bible which now are most dear to me I would not have understood properly without the help of the Gita. I have taken a deep interest in India ever since, I have sought Indian friends wherever I found myself. I am making these personal remarks so that you may not think I intend to parade as an attitude shared by many a conviction the individual conditioning of which is obvious; nor am I going to show that my thoughts are that which all Jews 'really' think. There is no 'really' or 'unreally' in my approach.

I hardly ever think of you as a politician; much more as your people does, I think of you as a father of millions. I have told my parents of you, and we talked about you at home as one talks about a father. My parents are not here. They have been murdered. But I am convinced that they would have wanted me to write to you in this situation. So I have asked for guidance in prayer and set out to write. I say this to assure you that I will not dwell on political catchwords.

III

Before commenting on these six points, I wish to tell you the meaning which they have for me.

That you regard the Jews as an European people is clear from your attitude. About this I will write later on, discussing the alternative. But a different matter it is, and one that for me is unspeakably painful: that you regard the Jews as a European does. Some of these sentences could be said by an English Protestant.

The third point which I take to be intended as a compliment, shows this attitude. You enumerate commendable qualities of individuals. That is how the Europeans talk when they mean to be 'nice' about us. At the highest pitch of their hatred, the English would not have talked in that manner about the Germans, nor the Germans about the English. When one of these nations talks about the other, they mention, however distorted or abridged, the history of the people, their collective achievements. They refer to ethnical units which have a definite place in their picture of the world and their conception of history. To tolerate a group because of merits some of its individuals may have, is another matter. It may imply one of two things: either a denial of views to the contrary (which is one of the many forms of anti-Semitism), or it may be a sort of testimonial given to individuals of no fixed abode who will do well wherever they turn, whatever land or house they may enter. In ordinary life we talk about servants in that way. Now, such an attitude towards the Jews must originate where its function can be explained. It is in Europe where the national life of the Jews has been frustrated. When the Europeans after centuries of religious persecution gave freedom to our religion it was not because they had come to respect religions, or our religion, or us – it was simply because religions to them had ceased to be of paramount importance, and nationhood had taken the place of religion. The same edict of Napoleon that gave us full citizenship compelled us to resign our nationhood. Thus the war against our religion (a war of nearly seventeen centuries) was followed by attempts to disrupt and discredit our unity. Therefore, a kind European conditioned, however, by this attitude may have spoken as you did. But why should an Asiatic speak like that? Obviously, it has nothing to do with Zionism: the refusal to regard the Jews as a collective and to judge their situation against the background of their national history – this refusal concerns Jews regardless of their location, and their intention concerning Palestine. Whether Jews in Europe are or are not a nation, this question as such does not involve Asiatic interests. Therefore the possible prejudice involved in your attitude originates in your European informant. I do not believe that other information was accessible to you. You have to regard us as the people do who have been hostile to us for 2200 years. Their point of view is consistent with their history; in sharing their view, you are sharing a consistent view, and it is not my intention to say that you ought not do so. I only want to make it clear that I regard your attitude as European. The same meaning has for me a passage in the sixth point. You say that our 'best prophets' have taught nonviolence. Now, apart from the profound significance of nonviolence, apart from the question whether any Hebrew prophet in the strict sense of the word has spoken about nonviolence in the strict sense – there remains the fact that you are telling us who of our prophets are the best. There is nothing wrong or unkind in this, and we are used to such expressions – from Europeans. They know our Bible chiefly through some translations which they have spread abroad, and they know it better than we do, and they are telling us. That is the European way toward the Jew. I suppose you are familiar with this European 'approach' in other contexts.

In your fifth point you are saying that Christianity has singled us out, that this happened according to a wrong reading of the New Testament and this treatment of us is a blot on Christianity. I do not want to comment in the least on a conjectural passage of that book which you believe has been misunderstood by the Christians, nor does any of us want to know what the right meaning of it may be. More important to me is that you seem to regard this as something irregular, inconsistent with Christian civilisation. About this many Europeans, in particular Protestants, will agree with you. They are convinced of the superiority of their civilisation, and when a disgusting trait is pointed out to them, they say it is inconsistent with the rest.

Reading the history of the Europeans and of my people, I have come to a contrary conclusion; and for this reason I attach importance to the notions of the Europeans about themselves and us, notions which you seem to share. My conclusion has been that the fact of anti-Semit- ism is essential for the understanding of Christian Europe, it is a main thread in that fabric. No non-European power has ever built a colonial empire. Do you regard the ceaseless encroachment on the life and lands of other races, that of Asia in particular as inconsistent with European civilisation? Has there been one single year since the expan- sion of the Roman – the first European – Empire when no European country exercised some kind of control over another of Asia or Africa? Would you not say that European civilisation that does no more hold other cultures in tutelage or suppression ceases to be the Europe we know? And if they do so to Asiatic countries what they have done to yours, how must they treat an Oriental people which lives among them and is always at their mercy?

You speak of the New Testament; can you not see how there already starts the vituperation of the older religion? In that famous sentence attributed to Christ it says: you have been told of old to hate your enemies. Have you ever heard of a religion in Europe, Asia, Africa, America or Australia which tells people that it is necessary to hate their enemies? If a civilisation imbibed with hostility towards Asia builds itself on a religion confessing hostile opposition to a religion of

an Oriental people, and this people lives among them, and the persecution of this people goes through all the centuries of that civilisation:
then I do not regard it as an inconsistency, and remarks that the Gospel
of Christ is this and that and perfect and on a different level, simply do
not meet my point.

It is natural for me, holding these views, to look to the other Oriental nations for understanding. And what I find is your belief that the
Europeans occasionally ill-treat a kind of thrifty and skilful Paria
group of their own, and that this is inconsistent with their civilisation.
Forgive me, if I have misunderstood your words or overstated their
meaning. I wanted to make clear, why they have this meaning for me,
and why this is important.

IV

You are saying (point 1) that we are or were seeking to impose ourselves on Palestine 'with the help of America and Great Britain'. The
meaning I attribute to this passage is completely at variance with
responsible Jewish opinion; because of this difference, I have to explain
it very clearly. It is this: while we hold that an international obligation
exists to facilitate the return of those of our people desiring to do so to
Palestine, you are of the opinion that our champions are these two
Western powers; that whatever they do in our favour, is done of their
free will or under our pressure and more or less in their own interests.
This must commit you to the assumption that, when these Western
powers fail to do so, when they adopt contrary views in favour of the
Arabs, they further Asiatic aims which, in the last analysis, must prove
detrimental to their own interests.

May I confront the two views more fully? I do not hold that we have
no claim to Palestine before the Balfour Declaration. We have never
renounced our right to Palestine, ever since early European Imperialism, in its first brutal shape, has driven us from our land, we are bound
to ask in our instituted prayers for the return. I do not hold that the
Balfour Declaration has established a claim. When the British
'promised' us – as they call it – a country not their own, this promise
does no more establish a claim, than would a promise of the Spanish
Government to the Turks concerning England. However, the Balfour
Declaration was embodied in the League of Nations Mandate, this
Mandate is the only vestige of a legal right the British have in their
occupation of Palestine, and it is therefore that we concern ourselves
with the Balfour Declaration. Britain has been committed to facilitate
our aims, not because they have given promises, or, to use their pet
phrase, because they have made themselves responsible. We are not

their father confessors, we do not care how they discharge their responsibilities to themselves. It matters to us how they discharge international obligations. When we say e.g., that they have failed to fulfil the Mandate, we are not merely prompted by our feeling to say so, but we are repeating the findings of the Mandatory Commission of the League of Nations.[4] Now, the League does no more exist, but the British still occupy the country, they occupy it as Mandatory Power without fulfilling the terms of the Mandate. Their hold on the country is non-legal, we have told them that. We have called on all righteous people in Britain and America to force the British Government to fulfil their obligations. It is a different matter, whether or not one thinks that there is a grievous error in this attitude. Later on, I shall unfortunately have no difficulties in agreeing with you about that. The attitude of our people – whatever is right in it or wrong – is a stand for law and order, for violence against the lawless oppressor. It may be said that what we regard as lawful obligations came about against the wish of the Arabs, and therefore the righteousness of our stand is doubtful. To this we can only answer:

At the time of the Balfour Declaration no responsible Arab statesman, party, or ruler objected to the Zionist programme. The British and their friends have obscured facts which are accessible to those interested. There are, after all, the Minutes of the Peace Conference (*vide* David Hunter Miller, *My Diary at the Conference of Paris*, vols. 14-16[5]). There is extant the great and most carefully worded plea of King (then Emir) Feisal, brought before the meeting of the Supreme Council, 6 February 1919, the plea for 'the independence of all the Arab-speaking peoples of Asia' (Miller 1924 vol. 14: 227) which explicitly excepts Palestine from his request. He left 'Palestine... on one side... for the mutual consideration of all parties interested. With this exception he asked for the independence of the Arabic areas enumerated in his memorandum' (Miller 1924 vol. 14: 230). We are not advancing a case built on the assumption that the Emir or any other Arab from Hejaz,[6] or delegation from another Arab-speaking country had been entitled to deal with Palestine as stated; but we regard it as significant that, when we look for protests against our planned intrusion at a time they were really called for, we find utterances and documents as the quoted.

Preserved, too, is the wording of the treaty, signed by Feisal and the Zionist Organisation, represented by Weizmann. This treaty never came into operation (England being what it is), but we feel that it is important that this document concerning 'the Arab State and Palestine' provides in its first article for 'Arab and Jewish duly accredited agents... (to be)... established and maintained in the respective territories'.

Can there be anything more straightforward than Feisal's letter to the Zionist delegation at the Peace Conference (1 March 1919)? 'The

Arabs, especially the educated among us, look with the deepest sympathy on the Zionist Movement. Our delegation here in Paris is fully acquainted with the proposals submitted by the Zionist Organisation to the Peace Conference, and *we regard them as moderate and proper.'* (The Zionist proposals at the meeting of 27 February 1919; *vide* Miller 1924 vol. 15: 106. These 'moderate and proper' proposals went much further than the Mandate; like the original Mandate, not to mention the Balfour Declaration, it concerned the whole of Palestine, on both sides of its river, not merely the Cis-Jordanic area which the British are calling Palestine now.)

Neither the Hejaz, nor the Syrian delegation demanded Palestine; the Arabs did not protest. Four years almost elapsed (since the Balfour Declaration) before they deemed it necessary to call us intruders, etc.

Now, whatever are the merits of our attitude to obligations, treaties, and laws, I am telling you about it, because it is a reality of which not enough is known in India. It is possible to say with the Europeans that we are formalists, that we believe in the letters of the law, that we make laws and obligations our fetishes and forget reality. All this has been said by the European who derides a conception of law and justice not his own. There is nothing to be said against this derision. We cannot expect anything else from Europeans, it is consistent.

You, on the other hand, believe – I fear I am right in saying that – that the Jews came to Palestine, as tools of and being tolerated by Western Imperialism, having formed an alliance with it. The reluctance of the Westerners to comply further you must regard as the awakening of their conscience, or as their withdrawal before the growing might of Asia in general or of the Arabs in particular.

I am not saying that this view is ill-informed, I have merely to point out to you that to some extent it is shared by many Englishmen, in and out of Government: viz. that there is no obligation towards the Jews, beyond the voluntary effort, the desire to give them a good turn, of the English and/or Americans; and that this programme has to be scrapped because the Jews are after all not entitled to Palestine, or because the Arabs have 'awakened'. (You may or may not be aware that a case has been made by Jews, showing up the part Britain played in the coming about of this 'awakening' which was their pet child at a time when they dreaded the awakening of other Oriental nations. As this is not relevant to my approach, I will not dwell on it.)

In your fifth point you mention, among other things, that we 'depend ... (in Palestine) ... on British arms... '

This is the general view of the British public. This is always asserted by English politicians and their journalists when they 'explain' to their people the difficulties in which we have landed them. It is of great importance that you share this view.

Our firm conviction on the other hand, is quite the reverse. In telling you about it, I am not committing myself to any views about the value of armed force – of which later. We know that our defence militia of 80,000 well-trained and well-equipped men is not only superior in organised strength to the Arabs of Cis-Jordanic Palestine, but that this force is capable of defending the country against any Arab-speaking country, or any combination of such powers; though it is not realistic to consider the major military performance of crossing the Syrian or Sinai deserts as feats which Arab armies could perform now or during the next ten years. This latter possibility is quite out of the question, as any student of the British Sinai-South Palestine Campaign of the 1914 war, and of their Syrian Campaign in their 1939 war can testify. But if the Arabs should come in irregular Bedouin detachments upon a Palestine un-'protected' by the British, I shudder to think of the terrible defeat of the Arabs by large armed bodies skilled in modern warfare. This tragedy must be avoided, and talk about our relying on British arms, is not a means to prevent it.

As to the strength and capacity of our militia compare the recent articles in the *New Statesman* by Mr Crossman, M.P., member of the Anglo-American Palestine commission.[7]

But those who do not believe our facts may consider the reality of Palestine, however repugnant to them bloodshed may be. It is a fact that many actions of violent resistance and aggressive acts are planned and carried out by Jews against the British army in Palestine. You yourself are protesting against it. Is there in history a parallel, of a population attacking and damaging an armed force on whose protecting power it depends? I do not know of any such case. Surely, we cannot be as exceptional as all that, whether you care to explain the exception we form in terms of fanaticism or stupidity.

V

I feel that I have made clear the meaning which rightly or wrongly I attribute to the points I believe you to have raised. My comments shall concern two things: the application of nonviolence to Jewish situations, and the general aspect of the Jewish renaissance.

As you yourself have forged the most powerful weapon of your nation, nonviolence, in your humility and venerable identification of your person with your cause, you cannot evaluate, even with the most thorough knowledge of its discussion abroad, the profound impression it has made on us; you have heard words only, and words can never reproduce profound shocks, or describe the thoughts which relate to changes in the fundaments of human existence. It was not even the possibility of applying nonviolence outside India – the sole fact that a people of hundreds of millions had the strength, cohesion, and discipline of a moral society, of a religious movement: that changed the whole picture of the world for many of us. It was a complete alternative to everything we saw around us, it restated the values of fortitude, courage, strength, conviction, and discipline which after this experience seemed to have been only mock words; it is not right to say that it gave us hope, for it had changed the very meaning of the word hope.

Such a profound enrichment puts the recipient under obligations, there is no doubt about that. At least, that ought to be the Jewish attitude, as I see it, while the European one has been exemplified by their treatment of the Jews: to take a people's teaching and tradition, then sneer at them and claim that you understand it better than they, the unworthy bearers ever did. No, surely, both my tradition and the obligation I feel to you and your people makes it impossible for me to take such a line. If I should fail in making myself clear, please, do not believe for a moment that I am trying to improve your knowledge of nonviolence. It is the very obligation mentioned which prompts me to say what I have to say, my interest in nonviolence makes me guard it against the least and unintentional cheapening and blunting of the great weapon.

When, at the eve or outbreak of the Second European War, you said that the English ought to resort to nonviolence, that through nonviolence was leading their victorious road, let the Germans occupy the country and make passive resistance, I heard many disrespectful comments. Even people who believed in your wisdom and sincerity said that you simply do not know what a German concentration camp means, and how a ferocious terror, more cruel and devastating than anything you have experienced, can torment and break a nation. Some people said that you had hit upon one method, and wanted its application everywhere, in short, that you could merely repeat yourself, and had to do it regardless of the occasion.

It was due to my illusions that I too was confused for a little while. But when I considered matters more carefully, I found myself in agreement with you, though it was not easy for me. I saw that such a policy would be the ultimate test of England, of all for which this much boasted Christian civilisation stands; I saw that such a policy would show whether England's people could materialise not only as a powerful state, but as a moral society as well; and whether or not such a choice is likely to be made, people must be told of this choice that is before them. And you did that. I recognised in it your detachment and your moral force, and again I was deeply moved.

Nothing can shake my conviction that nonviolence is the most powerful weapon of any social body which by a foreign body is being forced to serve as means to ends the society deprecates, or which wants the people to live in a way they detest. Even in the very acts of passive resistance the social bonds of the threatened society are being reinforced, while the application of force loosens with necessity social cohesion.

But a social body which is not threatened by others who want to use its people to their own detestable ends, a social body threatened merely by ejection and death? What use can it make of nonviolence? If India had been overrun by an English majority who persecuted Hindu religion on the scale you experienced at the hands of the early Muslim invaders – what then? If this majority was determined to kill you, what about nonviolent resistance? Can you threaten those who want to exterminate you by famine (mark you, exterminate, not *reduce* your members!) with your decision not to eat? Can you impress those who do not want to employ you by your decision not to work for them? Can you move those who want your death anyhow with the words 'even if I die'?

This has been our position. You cannot say it has not occurred. I am not merely thinking of the recent murder of over a third of Jewry (according to the official figures of the Europeans, 6 millions); I am not thinking of the huge pogroms of Poland, the Ukraine, Romania, not of the expulsion from Spain, the martyrdom that was Portugal; of all these things about which you may or may not have heard I am not thinking; I do not know how much you have been told by your trustworthy, noble, unbiased, and well-meaning European informants – whom neither you nor I can control – of the horrors of the Middle Ages when the Jews so often had to kill their women and children to prevent their falling into the hands of the loving Christians; however, I am not thinking of them; all these events which beat the rhythm of our history are represented as anomalies by the Europeans – but I am not thinking of them so much as of the intervals.

One, only one of these intervals, the period of Jewish life in the West between 1780 and 1931 has been represented by the Westerners (and certainly to you as well) as THE Jewish life. What is this life in the breathing spaces like, surrounded by merciless terror? Nonviolence has no sense of meaning during the 'anomalous' persecutions. What sense has it in the times of mercy, which every Jew who knows history (and those are the people who matter to their community) knows to be short-lived? Can any concerted action, violent or nonviolent, but contract the breathing space? Concerted actions are actions of social bodies, not of the aloof, asocial, secure, and rich individuals.

Our social body is a diver who now and then comes to the surface to breathe. Under the water, he cannot breathe, and therefore not sing. Do you want him to sing a hymn while he is emerging? This means not to breathe. Continuation of breathlessness means not to have stuck out the head from under the water. Surely, you cannot mean that we ought to have tried passive resistance during the Middle Ages, or in modern times in the West, or in Poland or Russia?

We have been passive, we went to the pyres of Spain, to the gas chambers of the Germans, as we were ordered. But this never was resistance. Sometimes we resisted, in Poland, in Russia. Then our resistance was violent. It was of the violence of the drowning man who drags to the bottom as many of his enemies as he can. That was the violence of the rising of the Warsaw Ghetto during the 1939 war.

In these situations there is only possible passiveness without resistance or resistance without passiveness, the resistance of the doomed. I challenge any friend of nonviolence and of my people, to look through these twenty centuries, to name a place and a date and say: here was nonviolence an alternative for the Jews! I mean an alternative, as you suggested it to the English, in the place of the last war, an alternative of greatest sacrifice, but of *victorious* martyrdom. I know, to some extent, my people's history and I am certain in my challenge as a man can be. I am certain too that this would mean a disservice to the idea of nonviolent resistance!

Let us turn now to the post-war situation. Our survival is threatened and survival means children. There are about 10,000 Jewish children who have been 'saved' from the Nazis and hidden by Christian families and institutions in France, Holland, and Belgium. The Christians refuse to hand us back our children. I do not know whether your European news service has deemed it necessary to tell you about that, or about the humiliating mission of Dr Herzog, the Chief Rabbi of Palestine, who had to go to the Pope and beg for the release of our children.[8] We have not got them back yet. Can you suggest any actions of passive resistance that would either bring about the return of our children or make possible the survival of childless communities. I have studied the medical reports of the child tuberculosis section of our national institution in Switzerland. According to this report (early this year) the largest amount of surviving Jewish children is in Poland. With the arrival of more children from Russia our children in Poland will number 100,000. It is these children on whom our future depends. The report says that over 50% of these children are in different stages of tubercular diseases. The infections continue. Can you say what we can do passively or otherwise to bring these children into medical supervision of Swiss-Jewish experts of Davos? Or can you tell me of a campaign of nonviolence, however self-sacrificial and strenuous which could compensate us for the loss of these children? I am not speaking of the suffering of the children – there is no need to dwell on that. I am interested in the survival of my people. Or is it a little thing? You know terrible things in India, you have heard of European tragedies, suffering certainly is not confined to us. But can you give me another instance of a child population more than half of which is tubercular, and on whom the survival of a people depends?

What about the internment camps in Germany, our 'displaced' persons? Which passive actions can make the 'displaced' 'placed', and return to them their houses the Christians have stolen?

I feel that you are thinking of Palestine only when you speak of nonviolence. There are thousands of refugees in ships outside the Palestinian harbours. They cannot land. What passive measures can be adopted by those who want their landing? But then, this is the Palestine issue, and in your fifth point you speak of our 'inevitable sad plight'. It seems to me that you regard our presence in Palestine as a wrong situation and I fail to see how a wrong, if it is a wrong, could be changed into a rightful and unassailable position by ethical means as those of nonviolent resistance. If it is a wrong that we are in Palestine, we have to atone for it. Do you advise nonviolent resistance to a thief so that he may be able to get away with his swag? And contrary: if our position in Palestine is one in which we ought to adopt nonviolence, our presence in that country must be a rightful one, as that of the English in England or the Indians in India.

To repeat: (1) in the dispersion, as we call it, outside our homeland, we fight for *mere* survival, if we fight at all. Nonviolence does not ensure survival, it serves different, if not less important ends; (2) in Palestine you regard us as wrongfully intruding people and the best means, as those of nonviolence cannot improve vicious ends. On this point I feel that your argument is inconsistent, and I cannot see it to be a good thing for the idea of nonviolence to be involved in inconsistent arguments.

VI

There remains the issue whether we are entitled to be in Palestine. I am not going into the Jewish claims which have been set out over and over again for whose who desire to read them; nor am I going to refute the Arabs' claims, however foolish some of them may seem to me. All this has been done too often, is a waste of time. No, I am not going to present a 'Jewish case'. I want to explain to you my conception of the Jewish renaissance and its place in history; I want to compare this with what I believe are your views, and I want to point out the consequence of either view for the people we are interested in.

It is really unfair when I believe of you that you regard the Jews as a kind of European pariah group, with an important, but very distant Oriental past, and a not enviable present, of which they have to make the best, as Europeans. You may be puzzled by the fact that in your countries the outcasts and the low castes, however badly treated, were always part of your civilisation and were never murdered; this you may explain by the differences between the two civilisations. The Jews then, as a European group, have no more right to an Asiatic country, as any other European people. The attitude is thoroughly consistent, it offers advantages.

First, you need not bother to investigate whether all you know about the Jews, their culture, their tradition comes from Christian European sources. If the Jews are Europeans, these sources may be unfair to them, they may be influenced by that constant discord, bickering, and warring which is so typical of Europe, but no reason to assume that they are completely misleading.

Second, to you as a Hindu leader, the opportunity is offered to know the Muslims of India that you can go with them and support them in all general issues of the common Asiatic heritage. You stand with them against the non-Asiatic intruder of Palestine, the Jew.

Third, in criticising Jewish violence, you can criticise at the same time the principle of violence, so disastrous, wherever it materialises, and a great danger for your own country.

Considering these points, I cannot see any reason for you to alter your views.

Now, returning to my conceptions of the Jewish people. When I ask myself whether they are Europeans or Asiatics, I am not considering criteria of race. There are many races, both in Europe and Asia. And I think that through Nazi propaganda, the whole conception of race as something conditioning the culture and structure of a people, has become disgusting to both of us. For me, the decisive point in assessing a people, are the observable relations between individuals and the value attached to *them*, as differing from the value attached to the achievements of the individuals. It is the social structure which I consider as decisive. And never, never I have found in all the literature the opinion that the Jews, prior to their emancipation were a European people. Their contributions to civilisation, their medieval philosophy and science, their share in the development of scholasticism, have been claimed as European contributions. But through the ages the Jewish communities and Ghettos of Europe have been regarded as foreign bodies. Their very confusion – confusion from a European point of view – of the political and religious community marked them as foreign to European civilisation. Their strictness in their dietical prescriptions which amounted to the impossibility of interdining, their severity against intermarriage were disgusting to the European. Had we come to your country instead of to Europe, surely, all this would not have been extraordinary. We would have settled down as one of the many castes of India, we would have worshipped the God of all mankind, and as your castes do, we would have strictly preserved our ways of wor-

ship, our seclusion and tradition. If there are two ways of life, there is
no question to my mind for which of them the Jews are fitted.

All the claims, Jewish or European, that the Jews are Europeans refer
to the period beginning with the emancipation, the opening of the Ghettos, the conferring of equal rights. This is a period of five generations, of
150 years, and it took place only in Eastern Europe and America. These
five generations have seen many changes, much can happen during 150
years, but I refuse to believe that they can change a people into its opposite. Considering our history as that of an Oriental people, we ought to
acknowledge to have made – not one, as you think – but two grave mis-
takes, errors the interconnexion of which you will easily understand.

Our first error was the emancipation itself. I do not want to go into
historical details, or assess the responsibilities that must be assigned to
European pressure. I am satisfied that there was a dominant 'progressive' party among us, clamouring for the release from the Ghetto. It cannot be denied. But there are more and more of us, particularly among
my orthodox friends, who deplore it now and wish that we had never left
the Ghettos. With the Ghettos we left a world that 'belonged to the past'
– as many of us imagined. Such delusions we shared with many of our
brethren of the other Oriental nations, in Turkey, in Syria, in Egypt, and
in your own country. Like they did (though later) we thought of loosen-
ing the burden of our tradition, of opening up to 'modern' life; but while
they, with the new misconceptions stood after all on their own ground,
in their own social reality which sooner or later must call them to order
and to a creative compromise – we stood naked, unprotected in foreign,
in European societies which we tried to imitate.

Connected with our first error, our second came: the desire to build
in Palestine a national state on European lines and possibly with European support. We conceived our revival in European terms. This was
the real consummation of our first error, of emancipation. Again, we
are not alone in this situation. Is there any Oriental nationalism which
has not been influenced decisively by Europe? How long will it take for
all of us to shake off this alien fanaticism!

All this is born out by the history of the Zionist movement. It had a
twofold origin. There are two teachers, two teachings to consider. Let
me say a few words of Dr Theodor Herzl and Ahad Ha-Am, the Jew
from the emancipated West and the son of Russian Jewry.

Herzl published his *The Jewish State* in 1896. He, a Viennese journalist, a completely westernised product of emancipation who knew
about his own people only what the European schools taught him in
his childhood; he saw that in order to be really like Europeans, really
emancipated, we must have our own state as well. Otherwise our existence as Westerners is threatened. This Jewish State he described: the
book is obtainable and still much read. My friends and I, we feel

ashamed whenever we open it. There is nothing in it but the desire to imitate the European State, its offices, armies, schools, decorations. We can do just as well as they! This is the burden of the song; and in our century, we heard the same song in Syria, Anatolia, Egypt, Turkey and not unfrequently in your own country. It is significant that Herzl did not stop to think which language the Jews ought to speak in this state. Anything would do as long as we had a European state and European institutions. And the Europeans became interested. England offered us a vast territory in East Africa, Herzl was delighted to have found a land for his state. Then the shock came. The Zionist Congress, the congress of the movement he had founded, stood against the leader, an overwhelming majority turned down the offer.

Why did this happen? There had been formed, almost coinciding with Herzl's beginning, another movement in the East of Europe. It called itself 'Hobebeh Zion' – lovers of Zion. It was led by a man who shed his name in order to take a Hebrew one which is the most humble possible: one of the people, Ahad Ha-Am. He stood for the revival of our old culture, our language. This we really owe to him. And from the point of his revival Ahad Ha-Am judged political devices and institutions as means to an end. His personality in many respects resembles some of the most venerable Hindu reformers of the last century.

The most important event in our recent history is the merging of the two movements. The lovers of Zion entered the organisation for the creation of a state; thus Herzl was defeated. Few Jewish nationalists do realise how opposed the two streams are which unite in them. One, an affirmation of emancipation and of European civilisation, culminating in the desire for a European state of our own. The other, a negation of European civilisation and withdrawal from it. Which of the two views will be victorious in the long run? It depends on us, the Jews, on the composition of the influential Jewries. It is therefore important to know that the greatest loss in the recent massacres was the Jewry of Eastern Europe, that therefore American Jewry is the most numerous, and it is significant that the American Jews want the Jewish State.

There are two other factors to consider. One is our conflict over Palestine with Europe. In spite of all machinations of the English our conflict with England has overshadowed the Jewish-Arab strife. The deeper our national conflict with Europe becomes, the more precarious will be the asylum we have given to European ideologies. War with England means to become less European. Another factor will be the attitude of the other Oriental nations, India and China. When they understand us, they will understand our common heritage, and thus strengthen it, as against the European ideology in us.

What sense is there in this Jewish revival when we see it against the background of the history of the world's great civilisation?

The Jewish Temple was destroyed, the Jewish State abolished by the Romans. The Roman expansion was the first European expansion, conditioning all the others that followed it. The Jews were the only Asiatic people thoroughly to resist. We resisted with our religion, our arms, our naked hands, our women and children. It was not merely a fight of princes against foreign armies. The uprisings were numerous, the Jewish wars shook the Empire. It took 200 years to suppress us. To achieve this they had to devastate our places of worship, they had to prescribe the death penalty for the circumcision of children, they had to massacre over a million people, they had to disperse us. European might is built up on the ruins of our temple. When Europe's civilisation declines – who can doubt that this time has come – and shares the fate of all great epochs, the temple will emerge again where it once stood. In what shape the temple must materialise in our time, we do not know. (Though I am positive that, if there is any sense in history, it cannot take the form of European institutions.)

The fact that we are emerging again in Palestine is a verdict on European history, on the present European situation. The Europeans dread it. Though we are no threat to them, they want to prevent our renaissance, while compromising with potentially much more powerful Oriental nations. They know that if our Hebrew voices are heard again, the world has turned round once more and Europe has had her say.

It is because of this universal aspect, that I had the courage to write to you about our small people while over you is India's fateful hour.

May I say, lastly, which advantages and disadvantages I would connect with your sharing my view?

You would be in a position to criticise our movement in a manner different from your article in *Harijan*. While now you criticise us because you do not regard us as a nation, or as an Oriental nation, you would then tell us your disapproval and approval, because we belong to you, because you feel a desire to protect that part of Asia's population which has suffered the longest and most cruelly under the Europeans. When you cease denying us Asia, you immediately will assume the right to tell us that we are entering, as it were, Asia through the wrong door. The fact that a great nation of the East stands up for us as for their brethren, would promote a change in Zionism and strengthen the people – it cannot be otherwise.

These would be our advantages. But for you I can see only disadvantages. Every well-intentioned word you say will be regarded as insult by some Indian Muslims. While now you are believing comfortably what people whom history proves our enemies, tell you about us, you would have to learn and seek facts for your independent judgement.

But these disadvantages exist only for you in your capacity as a Hindu leader. The leadership of India – whoever her leaders will be – involves more. It involves obligations towards other Asiatic nations, irrespective of your internal Muslim problem. These new responsibilities and obligations will be of dimensions undreamed of before. The more you feel responsible for the fate of the weaker peoples of Asia, the more protection and advice you can give them, the more free, too, will be India and Asia.

Once the tutelage of England is thrown overboard, India will have to seek independent information about many a thing; when dealing with the South Americans, information offered by the English and the U.S.A. will be dismissed as not sufficient or misleading. And thus it will be in any case, for the position of sovereign nations implies it. There is no reason why this new attitude must be delayed till your freedom is complete. But there I leave my suggestions, it would not be pertinent for me to pursue this here. However this must be said: whenever you and your people want information, some of us are ready to come to India and devote our life to the task of mutual understanding. And – be it soon! – when your young and gifted students should venture on their journeys between Europe and their land, to stop at Palestine, we shall show them all that is to be seen: first of all our new village communities, our varied experiments in collective settlements and non-competitive economic units. These are our present achievements. Let your students study and then let them make up their minds whether these are European or Asiatic achievements!

I thank you deeply for your patient reading. If I went on writing it would be a book and not a letter. I have therefore left out many things just as important as those I mentioned. I have not said a word about the real problems (as I see them) of the Arab people, a people to whom I am greatly attached. When in Palestine, I lived among them, till the English police made it impossible for me to lodge with them. But the problems of their renaissance, the abuse to which the Europeans have put them, the crisis of the Islam which has made no recent contribution to any issue, but claims to unite them – these matters are near to my heart and I wish I could talk about them.

This letter I have sent to you through a friend, because I cannot afford my identity to be known outside the small circle. I am a refugee in England.

Once more, Mr Gandhi, I thank you warmly for your attention. I greet you with the most sincere wishes for your people and yourself, with the Hebrew word Shalom which is the same as the Arabic Salam, and means what you and I love most: peace.

Yours

      Franz Baermann Steiner

NOTES

1. Steiner composed this letter in English in 1946. The original is preserved in a carbon copy in Steiner's *Nachlaß* at the Deutsches Literaturarchiv, Marbach am Neckar.It is published here for the first time. Because of the almost confessional character of this letter, we have refrained from modifying its syntax. [Eds]
2. Minor discrepancies between FBS's annotations and Gandhi's original are due to inaccuracies in the *Jewish Chronicle* report. [Eds]
3. In fact, 21 July 1946. [Eds]
4. The Commission reported in 1939. [Eds]
5. David Hunter Miller, *My Diary at the Conference of Paris*, 21 vols. New York, printed for the author by the Appeal Printing Company, 1924. [Eds]
6. Saudi Arabia: from Ḥijaaz – Mecca, Medina and adjacent territories. [Eds]
7. Richard Crossman, Labour Member of Parliament, recalled his membership of this committee in *Palestine Mission: A Personal Record*, Hamish Hamilton, London, 1946. [Eds]
8. Pope Pius XII (1949-58) had promulgated *Quemadmodum*, 'A plea for the care of the world's destitute children' in January 1946. [Eds]

MEMORANDUM[1]

Throughout its existence Zionist policy has had this remarkable feature: that the maximum of our attention was directed toward European powers and civilisation while the nations of the East have been neglected. Herzl's approach of the Turkish sultan, the first step of this kind, has remained almost the last; since England's occupation of Palestine, since her various solemn promises concerning the fate of our land, and since the odious bargaining between Britain and the United States concerning our national survival, Zionist foreign policy has meant negotiations with and protestations against Western Powers. We had come to recognise as indisputable fact that the obstacles for our movement lay in the West, and future generations will understand that because of this our attention was riveted on the statesmen of the West, and what we considered adequate propaganda, had been trying to appeal to the public opinion of these countries. We shall have no difficulties in defending our policy. But this will not suffice as an apology for our complete neglect of Eastern countries, political movements, minority groups.

This neglect has resulted in a number of deficiencies which without attempting completeness we would thus enumerate:

1. No permanent relations have been established between the *Yishuv*[2] and the non-Arabic or non-Muslim minority groups of the Middle East whose life is threatened by Pan-Arabism or Islam. Our contacts with such groups have been casual. The favourable attitude of the Maronites at the time of the Anglo-American commission has come as a surprise to many.

2. The American and British pro-Zionist protagonists and pressure groups were left uninformed about the position and plight of other Middle Eastern communities than the Jews. Pro-Zionist views had to be anti-Arab, and not weighing a supranational issue, which puts against the claims of an English-made Arab League the claims of all

minority groups, that is to say, the claims for a democratic federation of the Middle East which would assure the national and religious status and survival of Jews, Kurds, Maronites, Druses, etc. alike.

3. The *Yishuv* has failed to show sympathy to any violated and struggling community of Asia. There were several opportunities to do so. We did not avail ourselves of them because, having no foreign policy concerning the affairs of our own continent, we saw the issues isolated relating each of them to our own urgent need and short-lived convenience. Thus when the Indians proclaimed a strike in sympathy with the Indonesians we failed to join in. Had we done so we would have justified in Indian eyes a claim to Asiatic solidarity, a claim that must be strong enough to rival that of the Palestinian Arabs.

4. Far too long have we believed the English statements about the Arab front which is built against us. Negotiations with Egypt and other 'Arab States' were begun too late. Our surprise about the almost immediate success of these negotiations speaks for itself – and against our political common sense.

5. India's and China's knowledge or rather ignorance of the Jew has not been affected by the fact that during the last thirty years Jews have re-established their political and cultural life on the Asiatic continent. The Hindu's knowledge of our Palestinian achievement is based on Arab propaganda. The explanation to the Chinese and Indian intelligentsia of the nature of our religious heritage is left to the European Christians, who believe that we have ceased to have a religious life after the birth of the Saviour, and for whom we represent an initial stage of a religion the fullness of which they are offering to the world, bestowing on our unique tradition, if not malevolent vituperation, an equally misleading and nauseating benevolence. The influence of that kind of information can be seen in every Chinese and Indian book dealing with the variety of philosophic views or religious systems; people who have never read a genuine Jewish book, Asiatics who are not Christians write about the "Old" Testament, about Phariseeism, about Jewish legalism. As we have failed in informing the Indian Socialist of our trade unions, labour movement, kibbutzim, so have we failed to acquaint the man of Confucian tradition with our moral teachings, the Indian who tends to mysticism with a representative selection from our mystics.

This would not matter so much but for the fact that by all the rising nations of Asia our right to Palestine is being discussed in these terms: are the Jews Asiatics or European intruders or tools of European Imperialism? Gandhi's and Nehru's statements have left no doubt that these great leaders regard us as European intruders. What success can there be for our denial, however indignant, however often repeated? And even a cleverly devised propaganda campaign which were to claim for us all supposedly Asiatic features would deceive no one, as we have failed absurdly in the easiest task: to explain to the East that in the clash between Europe and Asia the oppression of Asia was twofold: an oppression of those Asiatic races whose countries the Europeans had seized, and an oppression of the one who had the worst fortune of them all and had come to live among the Europeans after the Europeans had destroyed their state and were therefore completely at the mercy of Asia's enemies. This would have been more convincing than all our talk about Fascism, Democracy and anti-Semitism. Is it thinkable that after an authoritative proclamation of such views a Gandhi or a Nehru could have advised us to migrate to another country of the same anti-Asiatic civilisation, rather than to return to Asia?

It is necessary to acquaint, as far as it is in our power, the intelligentsia of India and China, with the basic facts of Jewish life. It must be left to them to decide whether they can regard us as their kin and whether they are willing to compare the European features of our present make-up to their own borrowings from Europe; the result cannot be doubtful to anyone who has lived with Eastern people and knows their attitude to Europe.

6. This entails a great number of activities, both political, and cultural, and makes necessary the founding of an office, an Asiatic Department as it were, to coordinate these activities. Though this task is urgent, we could approach it now in a comparatively leisurely fashion, were it not for two political facts of recent date and unexpected to those of Western orientation, which facts are of the greatest importance for our national existence and call for immediate action.

These two facts are the Chinese membership of the UNO Trusteeship Council and Pandit Nehru's invitation extended to the *Yishuv* to participate in the Panasiatic Conference in two months' time.

That we must win Chinese support and sympathies is clear; it is equally clear that our delegate to the Panasiatic Conference must avoid as far as possible the Jewish-Arab conflict. He must have two chief aims: to establish contacts with the Middle Eastern minority groups present at New Delhi, and he must make a constructive contribution to all discussions on *general* Asiatic affairs. Moreover: these general issues touch Jewish interests: thus a formulation of an Asiatic Monroe Doctrine not merely involves, because of the Dardanelles, our attitude to Russia, it also involves American Pro-Zionist intervention in Palestine; therefore our delegate must come with definite views about our foreign policy and with well-prepared contributions to the discussions about the setting up of international Asiatic organisations and their legal aspects.

The Constitution of the Asiatic Department

It is perhaps unnecessary to make a case for the centralisation of all these obviously interdependent activities. It is equally clear, that this department or office cannot be built up in Palestine where many opportunities and contacts are lacking which are offered in London, and that such an office, if situated in London, must be responsible to Jerusalem only.

At the start the work would have to be done by two people: by an organiser and his technical assistant who could draw on the information service of the Z.O.[3] To this nucleus at a later stage would have to be added a contact supervisor, i.e., a person who keeps in touch with and reports on all Jews who are in contact with Oriental persons and groups staying in England. The possibilities of further additions and the extent of funds necessary will be seen from a brief description of the activities.

The Activities of the Asiatic Department

These activities, as indicated, will range over a wide field. The first issue, viz. the preparation for the New Delhi Conference, will not be discussed before the attitude of the Jewish Agency to the wider issues implied have been asserted. As to the rest, it is useful to distinguish between a short-term programme and one for a longer period of time. The activities of the first kind, all of which must be well under way within six months from our start, are the following.

Translations of Texts

Translations of various groups of texts in various languages are necessary. It must be decided which texts are to be translated, perhaps experts asked to submit manuscripts for translation, and the translators must be paid if necessary.

The following books ought to be published in *Chinese*:

A short account of and selection from our post-biblical moral teachings.

A book 'Moral Law and Politics' being an anthology drawing chiefly on Ahad Ha-Am.

A brief history of the Zionist movement, neglecting the Jewish-English-Arab controversy, chiefly concerned with the various degrees of our political emancipation.

International Law and Politics in the Middle East, a general book summarising the Arab Awakening, Modern Turkey, Zionism, Western and Russian interests stressing the various treaties.

As to books for *India* we have to bear these points in mind: special attention has to be given to the Indian women's movement who will be chiefly interested in the lives of our women pioneers, and to the linguistic situation of India. The latter makes it possible that a book in Bengali, the new literary language, well translated, becomes a literary event and is much read regardless of its contents.

It is proposed to bring out a series of booklets, descriptions of various features of the life in our kibbutzim. The existence of non-competitive communities founded by peaceful means is so intensely interesting for Hindu thought, that this can bring us millions of friends, irrespective to our attitude to Islam, and other political issues. Further is recommendable:

> A book 'Jewish Women of Palestine' bringing a selection from the well-known Hebrew book.
> The religion of *Awodah*: a brief and careful selection from Gordon's[4] work.
> A symposium 'Judaism and the East' bringing essays such as the following: The collectivism of the Pentateuch, Jewish and Hindu mysticism, Jewish religion and socialism, Jewry a vehicle of Asiatic influences in Europe, The religious significance of the Jewish return to Asia, The kibbutz and the Asiatic pattern of life.

Contact Activities in England

As soon as feasible we have to found a very exclusive club for Hindus and carefully selected Jews; the club will arrange for series of lectures on Indian and Jewish subjects. The Jews in the committee will be responsible to the Asiatic Department. The Club should serve as a nucleus for similar groups in the university towns for which we shall have to train contact men.

The Long-Range Activities

These will be scheduled for a two-year period, and for this purpose invaluable will be the experience and the contacts collected inside the short-term programme. These activities will have to take place outside England. They comprise:

Indian-Palestinian cultural relations

a. It is advisable to establish in the course of 1947 an 'Institute for Indian Culture' in Tel-Aviv; it ought to be a popular not an academic institution (therefore not directly connected with the Hebrew University) and Hindu lecturers should be asked for.
b. A group of Hindu students should be invited to study our kibbutzim.

c. Companies of Indian actors and dancers should be invited officially to come to Palestine and it ought to be arranged for *Habima*[5] to play in India.

d. Contacts with Middle Eastern minorities. It is hoped that in New Delhi these contacts will be put on a firm basis. We must try to find a non-political platform for the non-Arab and Muslim groups of the Middle East. This ought to be a journal, published preferably in the U.S.A., the chief contributors to which would be Palestinian Jews and American Armenians.

NOTES

1. This 'Memorandum' was composed in English by Steiner, possibly in collaboration with fellow Zionists such as Chaim Rabin, in 1947. A typewritten copy is preserved in his *Nachlaß* in the Deutsches Literaturarchiv, Marbach am Neckar. The text is printed here for the first time.
2. *Yishuv*: Jewish community in Palestine prior to the foundation of the State of Israel. [Eds]
3. Z.O.: Zionist Organisation. [Eds]
4. Aharon David Gordon (1865-1922). Kibbutz pioneer, ideologist and promoter of Arab-Jewish understanding. His Philosophy emphasised the importance of identification with nature and physical labour as supreme human values. [Eds]
5. *Habima*: Collective theatre ensemble founded in Moscow by Naum Zemach in 1916. Its productions were taken on many international tours. A permanent theatre was founded in Tel Aviv in 1935. [Eds]

PART III:
SLAVERY, ECONOMICS, AND LABOUR

SLAVERY[1]

I. Slave: A Term of Inter-Structural Reference

What use can the comparative sociologist make of a word like *slavery*? Surely, the word's ambiguity does not warrant disapproval from his point of view. On the contrary, he will find it belonging to a group of terms which we conveniently may call terms of inter-structural reference. The English words *husband*, *wife*, *king*, when used in a certain way, belong to the same group of terms. They do not merely mean husband, wife and king of contemporary English society; they point also to institutions of far-away societies and ages. These words are pointers, and as such they defy definition, which would be necessary if they were descriptive or analytical terms. Unless we adopt an abstruse algebraic vocabulary, we have to use such words. What we call ambiguity is the logical aspect of their very function.

But we must note a difference which we make in our use of such terms. When a student sets out to describe marriage in an African tribe, he uses of course the words *marriage*, *husband*, *wife*, etc. The meaning of these words is clarified by the subsequent unfolding of social contexts. The writer may even define marriage in that particular society by saying: *husband* and *wife* 'mean' in this society this and that. Whatever he says, it cannot be put under the heading 'What do we really mean by *marriage*?' This we may explain as a conscious use of terms of inter-structural reference. It is as if *marriage* implied two groups of facts, the person using the term being conscious of that grouping. The first group, however small, would include certain facts which can be enumerated, while the second group would consist of facts infinitely numerous. Thus, when we say that a Chinese princess or a Siberian chieftain is or was married, only facts of the first group, the minimum group, are being alluded to. But when we say: 'The Smiths are married', we have said much more, because we have attached to these two persons an almost infinite number of data which are due to our social training. We use *marriage* as a term of inter-structural reference consciously, being aware of the minimum and the maximum range of allusiveness.

Or, when a writer refers to a man as King of Dahomey or Tahiti, he will later set down the relations existing between such a king and his subjects, thus clarifying his terms. The use of *king* as a term of inter-structural reference is a highly conscious one. The positions and persons of English monarchs are surrounded with images, associations and values which are regarded as so far specialised and unique, that to call an African *king* does not at all make his image conform to the images and connotations of English kingship. Hence we shall not find in contemporary books questions which come under the heading 'What does *kingship* really mean?'

Terms of inter-structural reference have different histories which are part of our social conditioning, and which precede the scientific use we may make of them. The reason for the fact that we are using with so little consciousness *slavery* as a term of inter-structural reference, is indeed a simple one: there are no slaves in our society at present, no persons have taken part in our social training who would be implied by the full range of the allusiveness of *slave*; and, psychologically speaking, the place of 'the slave' of our immediate social experience has been occupied by the Roman servus or the negro slave of America's past. These figures are familiar to us because of our education, but not because of our immediate social training: we know of them but little. Nevertheless we do use *slave* as a pointer term like *husband* and *king*; hence the uncertainty and the question 'What does *slavery* really mean?'

Moreover, while we know in every instance with certainty whether *husband* or *king* are used simply for reference or as a metaphor, we have to exercise conscious care in order to detect the metaphorical use of a word like *slave*. The phrase: 'The proletariat are the slaves of modern civilisation' is a case in point.

II. The Slavery-Serfdom Dichotomy and European Experience

A more confusing difficulty is this: while *slave* amassed the allusiveness above described, European societies know servile institutions of a different kind, the serfdom of the feudal order. Parallel with *slavery*, *serfdom* accumulated allusiveness, in such a way that the conception of servitude worked with a dichotomy. Any servile institution came to be regarded either as one of serfdom or as one of slavery. Under the heading *serfdom* came anything that differed from *slavery*, such as the institutions of villainage, peonage, etc., while the meaning of *slavery* was constantly being widened in order to embrace every servile institution to which the label *serfdom* could not be attached. The peculiar dualism continues into our day.

Medieval studies provide us with different definitions of forms of serfdom, definitions based on legal documents and illustrated with such items of human behaviour as can be gleaned from contemporary literature. This lucidity may be said to continue when European writers discuss Japanese feudalism, or the legal documents representing the feudal period of ancient South Arabia. But outside these and similar provinces of research, terminology becomes vague. Were the people of the agricultural servile class in ancient Mexico or Peru slaves or serfs? This question has been asked several times. But no such classification can give more meaning to the scanty data in our possession.

Often, when authors describe servile groups in African or Indonesian tribes, they state that the institution under discussion ought to be called *serfdom* rather than *slavery*. Various reasons are given for such a decision. It may be that the institution is involved in a pattern of land tenure, or that people of that inferior status enjoy a freedom of economic enterprise not suggested by American negro slavery, or that they are not being treated harshly.

Opinions about harshness or mildness refer either to pre-conceived ideas as to how slaves are "generally" treated, or they reflect the attitude of the observer who, putting himself into a slave's place, distinguishes between a treatment which, being a slave, he would resent, and another which he would be able to bear for some time.

Social anthropologists fashioning generalisations about institutions seem particularly helpless when approaching this nebulous dichotomy. To quote one instance, Thurnwald says that it is difficult to draw a hard-and-fast line between slavery and serfdom. But, if pressed for criteria for differentiating the two, he would suggest that there always seem to be more serfs in a society than slaves (Thurnwald 1924-32).

Pre-scientific sociological inquiry is not limited to Europeans. But this dichotomy does not seem to influence non-European minds; at least it has not occurred to Ibn Khaldun, or to the writers of Chinese chronicles or Japanese jurisprudence. It is our historical conditioning which makes us look back to the slavery of antiquity, to medieval serfdom and to that unpleasant prank of 'evolution', American and colonial Negro slavery. To realise the peculiarities of this conditioning may help us to distrust generalisations which are in agreement with it. The chronology just mentioned is part and parcel of this conditioning.

It is not the contention of these remarks to blame scholars for something that belongs rather to the history-lore of this civilisation than to their work. No historian accepts, e.g., that Christianity has abolished Roman slavery. But the very way in which historians describe its gradual eclipse and survival into the Middle Ages (Langer 1891; Sombart 1921: I 689f.), that air of discovery and contradiction certainly presupposes ideas which, much better than any historical research show what European civilisation would like to regard as its past.[2] The same air of discovery and contradiction surrounds investigations into the system of colonial slavery in the medieval Levant (Langer 1891) or into the slavery of Renaissance Italy.

Today it is only a popular belief that types of organisation which show the greatest economic complexity and in their regulation the greatest efficiency, represent the highest stages of moral evolution, whatever 'stages' and 'moral evolution' may mean; it is unlikely that an educated person would regard the economic life of medieval feudalism as 'more advanced' than that of the Roman Empire; nevertheless, it seems difficult to discard the notion that serfdom developed out of slavery, as a further step taken by evolution. Spencer is not the first thinker to try to dispel this misconception (Spencer 1876-96: II, 295), and the *Encyclopedia of Social Sciences* will not be the last work of its kind to include a similar admonishment (Knight 1935).

If we accept the continuity of slavery from Mediterranean antiquity down to the colonial slavery of modern times, if we recognise that slavery played an important rôle in Mediterranean economies through the ages, and was tied to money economy in all parts to which Mediterranean capitalism (Roman, medieval or modern) spread, we have to regard modern colonial slavery as the culmination of this tendency and as the consummation of a European economic inheritance; and that it developed in the wake of the cultural Renaissance of Europe, is hardly surprising.

To sum up: *slavery* and *serfdom* are terms of inter-structural reference. For historical reasons they are used with a small degree of consciousness and interdependently. This interdependence appears as alternative. But we ought not to relate this dichotomy to the wealth of sociological data relevant to theories of servility.

NOTES

1. Franz Steiner worked on his doctoral dissertation for ten years, from 1939-49, and submitted it to the University of Oxford as *A Comparative Study of the Forms of Slavery* in 1949. He was awarded his D.Phil. the following year. Paul Bohannan prepared an edited version for publication after Steiner's death, more accurately called *A Prolegomena to a Comparative Study of Slavery*. This, like Steiner's thesis, was never published. Typescripts of both texts are preserved in Steiner's *Nachlaß* at the Deutsches Literaturarchiv, Marbach am Neckar. The extracts we print constitute the third and fourth chapters of Steiner's original dissertation (29-36). First printing.

2. The following passage from Professor Toynbee's ambitious historical work, may be quoted in illustration of these very popular ideas: 'Since the institution of slavery

has been recognised to be intrinsically evil by a consensus of all men in all times and places who have been in a position to study it at first hand objectively, it must be regarded as *one of the merits*, or at least as one of the advantages of *Western Civilisation* that in its history down to the advent of the democratic and industrial regime, *this pernicious institution had never played at all a dominant part'* (my emphasis) (Toynbee 1939: 137f.). [F.B.S.]

BIBLIOGRAPHY

Knight, Melvin M., 1935 'Slavery. Medieval', in *Encyclopedia of the Social Sciences*, 1st edn, Vol. XIV, New York: Macmillan, pp. 77-80.

Langer, O., 1891 *Sklaverei in Europa während der letzten Jahrhunderte des Mittelalters*, Wissenschaftlicher Beitrag zu dem Programm des Gymnasiums zu Bautzen. Bautzen: Gymnasium.

Sombart, Werner, 1921 *Der moderne Kapitalismus*, 4th edn, 4 vols, Munich and Leipzig: Duncker und Humblot.

Spencer, Herbert, 1876-1896 *Principles of Sociology*, 3 vols, London: Williams and Norgate.

Toynbee, Arnold 1939 *A Study in History*, Vol. IV, London and Oxford: OUP.

Thurnwald, Richard, 1924-32 'Sklave' in Max Ebert ed. *Reallexikon der Vorgeschichte*, Vol. 12, Berlin: W. de Gruyter, pp. 209-28.

NOTES ON COMPARATIVE ECONOMICS[1]

Anthropologists have for some time known that wherever livestock is herded in large units, whether the animals be cattle, horses, camels or reindeer, the attitude of the owners to the value of the animals cannot be expressed merely in terms of utilisation or exchange. A dialogue between a rich herdsman of the Yurak-Samoyede and a stranger poses the problem:

Stranger: Sell me a reindeer!
Yurak: There is none for sale.
Stranger: Why don't you take money ? You may buy brandy with it.
Yurak: I have got brandy enough.
Stranger: You may buy something for your womenfolk; or you may get furs of the arctic fox to use as bridewealth and get yourself another wife.
Yurak: I have got two sledges full of fox already.
Stranger: You own 3,000 reindeer. What are you keeping them for?
Yurak: The reindeer wander about and I look at them. Money I have to hide, I cannot see it. (Lehtisalo 1932: 156)

Similar sayings of Lapplanders have been noted. Hatt points out that this 'lust for ownership' stands in the way of a more intensive care for and utilisation of animals ([1919]: 114). Herds become too big to be useful as far as labour and subsistence are concerned; they are an impediment to the owner. The same sentiments have been attributed to many a cattle-owning tribe in Africa.

It is the purpose of this article to investigate attitudes such as are here displayed with a view to discovering their implications for (1) the general interchangeability of goods (which underlies all trade), (2) the process of increasing the utility of goods (which is the essence of all production as understood by Western economists), and (3) the classification of economies dependent primarily on exchange without the use of coin or paper money.

By an economy here is meant a system of production and distribution of units of value.[2] This is a very broad usage of the word.

Two Categories of Non-monetary Economic Types

Leaving aside the economy based on the extensive use of money and related to complex class structures, two widely representative types of economy may be distinguished. The first is characterised by the existence of three groups or categories of goods, always kept separate and distinct: raw materials, implements, and personal treasure. In the second type of economy, raw materials are not kept separate from the implements, and there is no class of goods which has value solely as personal treasure.

In the first type, with its three groups of goods (1) foodstuffs and other raw materials, (2) implements, including everyday clothing, and (3) personal treasure, it is possible to make subdivisions according to the various relations which may be thought to exist between the items belonging to these various groups. For example, the objects of the second and third groups – implements and personal treasures – may or may not be exchanged for one another, depending on the ideas of the people involved, hence leading to different sub-types. By personal treasure we mean things valued by their owners, either because of their rarity or because of the memorably intensive attention given to them during their production. Examples of objects of this kind are the boomerangs made by some Australian aborigines, which are carved so beautifully that they are not used in hunting, or the magnificent 'luxury bows' of the Andamans which are precious but are also not used, or the carvings of the Eskimoids – objects executed in hours of leisure and not related to religious life. These things are treasured by their owners, but no universal value attaches to them. Parallel cases are found in the animal kingdom, and in the human child.

But all these sub-types have one decisive feature in common: the social unit, based on cooperation in the task of preserving the lives of the constituent members, is concerned in its organisation only with the first group of goods. In so far as we can speak of the circulation of goods in these societies, it must be with regard to goods of the first group: foodstuffs and other raw materials. These goods may be gained in a common enterprise and then distributed, or they may be gained by the various sub-units (households, families) who distribute their surplus. The members of the society respond to the distribution by actions of solidarity enabling further production.

Whatever arrangements are made for the distribution of the raw materials once they are gained, two conditions are preserved: (1) no object belonging to the first group is exchanged for objects belonging to either of the other groups – in fact, there is no value relation, no common value standard, between these groups. It follows, then, that (2) any object into which raw material has been transformed – be it a piece of meat cooked by the members of a household, or a tool or clothing – *ipso facto* is disengaged from what we may call the primary economic cycle. Thus, additional human labour, far from adding 'value' to the thing, removes it from the economic sphere. This does not mean, of course, that these objects are not desired (that is, they have not lost 'utility' in the terminology of Western economists): as presents they function in the creation of alliances, as loot they function in war.

No wealth is accumulated in such societies, no markets are held. It is only within the sphere of the primary economic cycle – that is, exchange of foodstuffs and raw materials – that market-like situations arise, if by that we mean that demand conditions the distribution.

In the economies of the second type, on the other hand, exchange of objects differentiated into different categories from raw materials are not so detached from the primary economic cycle. Subdivisions of this type are constituted by the various modes by which people integrate, classify and interrelate the different groups or categories of objects. The feature which is common to all economies of this second type is that they do not recognise merely personal treasures: treasures have either a generally recognised value bestowed upon them by ritual, or else they have a limited exchange value. Thus, broadly speaking, there are two kinds of objects present in economies of this type: those whose value is generally recognised and founded on usage, and those whose value is ritual, or at least non-utilitarian.

The value of those objects which is generally recognised and founded on their usage is called utilitarian value. Some of these objects may be used in exchanges as standard units of value – pots, iron bars, and salt in Africa are examples. Such exchange goods are not only valued because of their prominent utilitarian function, but wherever they are used in this manner, they are not produced within the society. Their exchange character is based on steady supplies from alien centres of production. Such external monopolies function in the same way as does limited and controlled production within a society, perhaps by a privileged group.

The whole group of objects may be expressed in symbolic terminology[3] as $U \pm E^u$, if we let U stand for 'useful objects', $\pm$ for 'value' and E for 'exchange'. Thus, E^u comes to denote such useful objects (U's) as have standardised exchange properties. Thus in the same language we may distinguish *barter*, or the exchange of one useful object direct for another [U $\rightleftarrows$ U], from *trade*, which is exchange of a useful object for the exchangeability-of-a-useful-object [U $\rightleftarrows$ E^u], or the exchange of a useful object for the exchangeability-of-a-useful-object which is in turn exchanged for a different useful object [U $\rightleftarrows$ E^u $\rightleftarrows$ U].

The second group of objects comprises, among others, units of ritual value and such treasures as may be used in exchanges. No utilitarian value is attached to either. Thus 'shell money' or 'money' consisting of strips of plaited feathers differ from salt and iron 'money'. This second group of objects can be described as R$\pm$ E^t, because there are units which have ritual [R] value [$\pm$] or are exchangeable [E] treasures [t].

Taking both groups U$\pm$ E^u and R$\pm$ E^t into consideration, further exchanges are possible: a useful object for exchangeability-of-treasure [U $\rightleftarrows$ E^t], or a useful object exchanged for exchangeability-of-treasure which is in turn exchanged for another useful object [U $\rightleftarrows$ E^t $\rightleftarrows$ U]. Both mean trade, whereas the exchange of the exchangeability-of-useful-objects for exchangeability-of-treasure [E^u $\rightleftarrows$ E^t] is a financial transaction akin to trade.

Translation

We must be very careful to distinguish from all these transactions of barter or trade, another exchange – that of a useful object for a ritual object [U $\rightleftarrows$ R], a process which I shall call 'translation'.[4] The two main logical models describing the activities to be discussed will be called negative and positive translations.

Negative translations

The general form of a negative translation is [U $\rightarrow$ R], the translation of a useful object into a ritual object, where useful objects [U] may or may not include exchangeability-of-useful-objects [E^u] or exchangeability-of-treasure [E^t]. The ownership of these objects, and thus their utilitarian or exchange values to the owner, are all relinquished by the transaction which related the former owner to units of ritual value. Thereby these units of ritual value become pure, or isolated. They are detached from the economic cycle. In all these contexts the units of value do not occur grouped logically, according to their relation to usage, as U$\pm$ E^u : R$\pm$ E^t, objects of utilitarian value and exchangeability-of-useful-objects set against objects of ritual value and exchangeability-of-treasure. Rather, we find such forms as objects of utilitarian value, exchangeability-of-useful-objects and exchangeability-of-treasure set against ritual objects [U$\pm$ E^{u}E^t : R]. In such cases the relations E$\pm$ E^u E^t can be called 'empirical values' [U^i].

Negative translations occur among the Yap Islanders when goods which have been accumulated for several years are exchanged for circular plates of stone broken in a distant quarry (Furness 1910; Müller 1917: 129-32). The stones are so huge that many days' labour of groups of people is required for their transport. At their destination they are buried under the huts, after a ritual has been held to acknowledge their value. These stones do not function in any further transaction. They are left in the ground and not 'used' in daily life. Their value, rather, attaches to the status of the owner and to the ground on which the hut stands; it increases the respect shown to the hut's inhabitants, the family. Thus, the translation of empirical values into ritual values [$U^i \to R$] has various phases: some useful objects are converted into exchangeability-of-useful-objects, while others are converted into exchangeability-of-treasure, then finally all are translated into ritual objects:

$$\left[\left(U \begin{array}{c} \nearrow E^u \\ \searrow E^t \end{array} \right) \to R \right]$$

This instance may suffice to illustrate one of the modes of negative translation.

Another mode of negative translation can be seen in that type of gift exchange in which the presents given do not merely establish or confirm an alliance between the exchanging persons, but the amount *given away* (not received) under ritual circumstances affects a person's rank.

The instance of this mode of negative translation most often referred to is the potlatch which obtained among the various Northwest American societies. There at more or less regular intervals, or on important occasions like the birth of a child or the building of a new house, families and larger competitive kinship units invited the other members of the society in order to give them a feast and to present them, under ritual circumstances, with goods which had been accumulated over long periods. Whenever it suited their disposition, the invited parties reciprocated invitation and gifts. The value of the distributed gifts attaches either to the kinship unit who called the potlatch, or to the person in whose honour the potlatch was given, and each potlatch modified the status of those concerned. The value of the goods disposed of in this manner is the social *agens*, while no public recognition attaches to their value contexts. This recognition is implicit only in the public transfer of ownership. In such a transfer the values of the object are split: (1) the units of empirical value (which are not social *agens* in these societies) are at the receiver's disposal, while (2) units of ritual value in quantity correlated with the empirical values can become overt in terms approximating those of ownership, and are related to the giver.

A variation of the custom obtaining in the same area is one to which ethnographers have given much attention: in the course of potlatches goods may be not given away, but burned or destroyed, which approaches still closer the model of sacrifice, which is the paramount model for all activities designed to disengage units of value from the economic cycle. Through annihilation of the goods the empirical values are completely eliminated, and the ritual values 'owned' by the promoters of the potlatch are certain, pure, and unambiguous. The competitive element in the ownership of these ritual values is strengthened by discarding the cooperative one which is, however, a negligible concomitant of this gift exchange.

Before the Administration interfered with these customs, it had been known that competitive sacrificial potlatches were becoming ruinous to the communities concerned. From this it was inferred that the whole potlatch custom is an economic anomaly. But in answer to such a contention two points have to be made.

It can be shown that procedures such as those creating the giant stone 'money' of Yap can be related to the same logical model as those creating gift and sacrificial potlatches. While the Yap example can be symbolised as $(U^i \rightarrow) \rightarrow R$ [translation of empirical values becomes of ritual value], the gift exchange of the potlatch must include two occasions: on one occasion A gives objects of empirical value to B; the empirical value of the objects goes to B, but the ritual value of the giving remains with A; in the second transaction, we get the exact reverse: B gives A objects of empirical value, whose empirical value goes to A, but whose ritual value remains with B. This can be symbolised as:

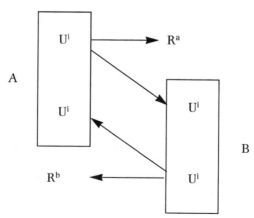

The sacrifice potlatch, on the other hand, approaches the Yap formula more closely, since there is no splitting of values, but rather a direct translation of empirical to ritual values:

$$U^i \rightarrow R^a$$
$$R^b \leftarrow U^i$$

A transaction conforming to so general a pattern cannot be dismissed as an anomaly. Certain features of the 'ruinous potlatch', however, must be considered abnormal, reflecting a disnomic state of the communities where they occur. These features I would explain as modification of the potlatch in two ways as a result of culture contact. First, a reaction against the disintegration of tribal society would throw into relief the major features of social cohesion. In the societies in question the structural basis is indicated by the competition of rigid sub-units and respect shown to rank. Thus, before complete disintegration sets in, we should have to expect the solidarity within the sub-units to become exaggerated, and greater emphasis to be laid on their competition at the same time that rank consciousness is becoming more vulnerable. Second, the introduction of money economy made more things exchangeable, thus the range of objects eligible for translation into ritual value increased. Boas's comparative lists testify to this. Thus potlatch economy, far from being an anomaly, is so much a consistent pattern that it is incompatible with other economies. Alien elements made the system ruinous to the respective societies; integration was impossible.

Positive translations

In positive translations, we find a different basic arrangement of values: $[U : (\pm E^u E^t) R]$, that is, exchangeability-of-useful-objects and exchangeability-of-treasure are here associated with ritual objects and excluded from useful objects (instead of, as with negative translation, associated with useful objects and excluded from ritual objects), where useful objects are seen in opposition to objects or treasures with exchange value or ritual value. Accumulation of wealth, trading and marketing are, in varying degrees, characteristic of societies which stress positive translation.

Intertribal exchanges of the following types take place: (1) Useful objects from society A traded for useful objects from society B $[U_a \rightleftarrows U_b]$, (2) useful objects of society A are exchanged for exchangeability-of-useful-objects from society B $[U_a \rightleftarrows E^u_b]$, (3) exchangeability-of-useful-objects from society A exchanged for exchangeability-of-treasure of society B $[E^u_a \rightleftarrows E^t_b]$, and (4) treasures with an exchange value of society A being traded for treasures with an exchange value from society B $[E^t_a \rightleftarrows E^t_b]$. When such exchanges between areas of productive units occur, with or without professional negotiation, at regular intervals, at fixed prices, we speak of 'markets'.

Neither on sociological nor on purely economic lines has a classification of market types yet been attempted – treatments classifying markets as to their time intervals (yearly, monthly or weekly) can be discarded as not relevant.

It may be felt by many that if one extends the range of the term 'market' to include, at one end, regular meetings at which barter exchange takes place between the members of two or more villages, and, at the other end, a regular disposal of surplus produced solely for this purpose (while professional traders compete and calculate their profits), it has no claim to be used in scientific contexts. The chief disadvantage, however, is that the term 'market' suggests to most of us the operation of laws of supply and demand, while clearly such laws can relate only to exchanges of certain types.

When, for example, New Guinea tribal groups exchange regularly useful objects of society A for treasures with an exchange value from society B [$U_a \rightleftarrows E^t_b$], it certainly does not mean that a surplus of useful objects [U] has been produced by society A for the exclusive purpose of purchasing society B's exchangeable useful objects or exchangeable treasure; nor does it mean that society B's exchangeable treasure is produced in order to be exchanged for the useful objects from society A. Therefore, the exchange rate equating quantities of the two kinds is more or less stable and does not depend primarily on laws of supply and demand.

Market situations can arise from the relations of two social groups under only two conditions, or in a combination of the two. One possible condition is that a common denominator of value applies to the exchangeable useful objects, exchange value of a useful object, or exchange value of a treasure [U, E^u and E^t] of societies A and B. The other condition is that the two social (and perhaps political) units are functioning as parts of *one* economy.

Social units integrated into one economy will be found to exchange primarily useful objects [U]. A most fascinating instance has been recorded from the Manus people of the southern part of the Admiralty Archipelago (Mead 1937: 210-39). There groups of 'sea people', the true Manus, are allied to groups of 'land people', the Usiai (inland) and Matankor ('eye of the land'). They depend on daily exchange to such a degree that we must regard every economic unit as being composed of groups of both populations. Political life has been adapted to this symbiosis, and in warfare a settlement of Manus would keep truce and entertain exchange with its Usiai partner, while attacking another Usiai group which enjoys the partnership of another Manus settlement. This symbiosis is based on carefully balanced cession of economic sovereignty, and goes to the extreme of barring the sea people from direct use of the land and its products, and the land people from any use of the sea. Nevertheless, the sea people who live out in the lagoons in pillar dwellings, need boats, the wood for which grows on the land; the land people eat the fish of the sea. Intentional restrictions make possible a regular exchange, in which boats and vegetable produce are given for sea products.

Throughout this arrangement, which retains many features of barter (as Margaret Mead points out) a market situation obtains; the policy in dealing with these situations is made possible by the absence of a common denominator of value:

> There is [writes Margaret Mead] one quaint example of this tendency outside the realm of food proper. While the land people grow the betelnut and the pepper leaf, the sea people burn and refine the coral lime with which the betel and pepper leaf are chewed. In the market the same sized fish will command ten taro or forty betelnuts. But a cup of lime commands eighty betelnuts, but only four taro. Betel chewing need is matched against betel chewing need, to coerce the sea people into providing enough lime for the land people. (1930: 130)

Here we see the laws of supply and demand functioning without a common denominator expressing the values of the exchanged goods. In such cases, there is a tendency to group exchangeable goods in pairs.[5]

This standardised and business-like bartering in Manus goes on side by side with more elaborate exchanges such as $E^t_a \rightleftarrows E^t_b$ and $U_a \rightleftarrows E^u_a \rightleftarrows E^t_b$, etc., and with the accumulation of exchangeable treasure $[E^t]$ within one group. This latter value-hoarding of the exchangeability-of-treasure goes with the rank system within the social group, but not with the sea–land intergroup exchange. Thus, two different economic processes, involving different social relationships, interlock. These junctures are very different from negative translations, in which two spheres of value are brought together. In these two types of transfer, for which I am suggesting the term 'positive translation' no units of value become completely detached from economic life, in spite of accumulation.

The difference between the two processes cannot be overemphasised. Dealing with the *kula* system of the Trobriand Islanders, a system of intertribal exchanges of treasure $[E^t]$ of very wide circulation, Malinowski remarks on the generosity and decorum displayed in the (ritually relevant) *kula* transactions:

> The natives sharply distinguish it from barter, which they practise extensively, of which they have a clear idea, and for which they have a settled term – in Kiriwinian: *gim wali*. Often, when criticising an incorrect, too hasty, or indecorous procedure of *kula*, they will say, 'he conducts his *kula* as if it were *gim wali*.'(1922: 95-6)

Comparisons and Conclusions

These facts have hitherto received very little systematic treatment. No classification of exchanges and markets in simpler societies has been essayed, and nobody has worked on a comparative sociology of trading groups. The position of specialists in simpler societies (e.g., that of the smiths in Africa) has not been brought under comparative survey, although concomitant ideologies (the smith's magic power or inferiority) have been noted. It is perhaps no exaggeration to say that the comparative method has not yet been extended to economics.

Of late this deficiency is more noticeable, since we have become possessed of precise monographs detailing the economies of South African and Oceanic communities. But so far as the rest is concerned, we are left with the pioneer work of men like Schurtz, a type of research which has been discontinued and which is outdated by far more accurate material and more pertinent problems.

Generalising on a large body of facts which have not been systematically treated, and making surmises in a field in which the little which is known is obscured by worse than meaningless terminologies, does not allow the formation of valid theories. The few remarks that one can make are either stressing the obvious or must be made subject to constant correction.

To the reader of ethnographic accounts, it is clear that many economies cannot be classified exclusively in accordance with a single type of economic process which is accompanied by many activities. Several types of economic process may together build up the economy of a society. To call one of them dominant is premature in many cases, as even criteria of such predominance have not been discussed.

Thus, Mead has shown in the case of the Admiralty Islanders a function of asymmetrical equations of quantities in barter exchanges between social groups $[U_a \rightleftarrows U_b]$. The same, however, cannot be said of either group's internal exchanges of useful objects or treasure $[E^u$ and $E^t]$.

On the other hand, on Rossel Island, as described by Armstrong, different kinds of exchangeability-of-treasure $[E^t]$ build up a monetary system in such a way that there are several species of 'money', and in every species several kinds of units (coin). The intricacy of the system is due to the existence of asymmetrical equations between currency units. Because of the fact that we associate asymmetrical properties least of all with monetary systems – indeed, they are thought to prevent asymmetry – Armstrong calls the Rossel economy anomalous (1928: 59-75).

Wherever we find the establishment of prices and the fluctuation of exchange rates between two economies, it must be caused by changes in the internal evaluation of exchangeable treasure connected with conditions of its production. There is no exchangeable treasure which a society produces for 'export only'. Seligman records from the Koita of British New Guinea that at a marriage, after the appropriate gift exchange, the woman's parents received as bridewealth a number of armrings. In 1876 this number was ten, but as iron tools made the manufacture of the rings easier, the number had risen by 1909 to forty or forty-three rings given on the same occasion (1910: 77). Thurnwald concludes quite rightly that this change in evaluation can be explained in terms of supply and demand (1932: 179). But it must be insisted that, however a change in the internal evaluation of exchangeable treasure may affect external change in the long run, no supply-demand relations inherent in the external exchange can be made responsible for the change.

One can find a great variety of economies in which negative translations do not seem to function predominantly (using this qualification with the above reservations) – that is true, in fact, of the economies of most known societies. One such type is of particular interest. In this type we find instead of (or coexisting with) the situation 'useful objects opposed to objects associated with ritual value' $[U : (E\pm E^t E^u) R]$, an arrangement whereby the *quantity* of the useful objects becomes decisive. Useful objects are being hoarded and treasured, but the units thus treated are not dealt with in conformity to any mode of exchange or translation: they are not excluded from use by the owners. Yet the great quantity of these units is not related to the needs of usage; the stores have a value transcending the empirical value of the units. The empirical values are merely a component potential.

We find the non-empirical aspect of sheer quantity acting in the same way as $U : (E\pm E^t E^u) R$. In storage assembly of units it is not particular qualities of particular units which matter, but the quality of the organised whole. To make this clear, we may *assume* value units 1-100 which relate to the objects' usefulness as nutrition or clothing. We see then, that under certain conditions a storage assembly of $100n$ (U) exceeds the evaluation of $n(100 \; U)$, non-empirical assembly value overruling the empirical values contained in the units.

The greater the quantity of units in an organised assembly, the more numerous are the possibilities of arranging these units and the greater is the owner's power when expressed in terms of control of the assembly. In this context, it does not matter whether this assembly is a store of vegetable produce or a herd of animals.

Among the Trobriand Islanders the houses for the storage of yams are built so that the quantity of the food can be gauged and its quality ascertained through the wide interstices between the beams. The yams are so arranged that the best specimens come to the outside and are well visible. Special varieties of yams, which grow up to two meters in length and weigh as much as several kilograms each, are framed in wood and decorated with paint, and hung on the outside of the yam houses. That the right to display food is highly valued can be seen from the fact that in villages where a chief of high rank resides, the commoners' storehouses have to be closed up with coconut leaves, so as not to compete with his. (Malinowksi 1922: 168-69)

These assemblies, says Malinowski, serve to enhance social prestige:

Magic is intended to make the food last longer.... [It] will make food plentiful in the village and will make the supplies last long. But, and this is the important point for us, this magic is conceived to act not on the food, but on the inhabitants of the village. It makes their appetites poor, it makes them, as the natives put it, inclined to eat wild fruit of the bush, and mango and bread fruit of the village grove [not individually owned]; refuse to eat yams, or at least to be satisfied with very little. They will boast that when this magic is performed well, half of the yams will rot away in the storehouses and be thrown on . . . the rubbish heap at the back of the houses to make room for the new harvests. (1922: 169)

It is important to recognise that the value transcending the utilitarian properties of the stored yams are confirmed by something that is nearly a resolution not to use it. The magical rites are rites of thrift and not of fertility. Only the fact that these objects are perishable makes the wastefulness of the procedure so obvious. This aspect of the attitude to value may be weaker, or may escape us altogether, when we consider, instead of yams, objects with properties which remain unchanged over longer periods – or better still, objects which reproduce or even multiply themselves.

The similarities between negative translations and assembly values of the Trobriand kind are striking. On the other hand, there is a similarity between Trobriand assembly values and those of people who apply such notions to their herded animals, where 'wastefulness' is less prominent. Two features are common to negative translations and assembly values: the existence of values transcending the empirical ones, and the connexion between the non-empirical value and the attitudes negating the empirical values. As the differences have already been stressed, the similarities can be summed up in the following manner: affirmation of non-empirical values is accompanied by and made possible by destruction or rejection of empirical values. These affirmations may be strengthened by ritual functions of the units of transcending value, as in the case of African cattle economies.

The principle stated above is general; it applies not only to simpler economies. After all, the conquest of Western civilisation by a total money economy meant the bestowing of transcending values on money. The holding of money, the position in which a person's money is 'working' for him and does not lie 'idle', are aims the evaluation of which transcends the evaluation of the goods which can be purchased with this money and used. The rise of capitalist economy came in the guise of a gospel of saving and ascetic rejection of the use of goods. No reader of the works of Max Weber and Tawney can doubt the fact that this ascetic rejection was postulated in a religious terminology.

It is for the psychologist to state the ultimate affinities, or rejections, in favour of transcending values and of sacrifice; it cannot be the concern of the anthropologist. For the student of social anthropology who can see thrift and Protestant ethics in connexion with potlatches and Trobriand yam stores, a much discussed controversy loses its significance: whether Puritanism has made capitalism or vice versa (Weber-Tawney). Moreover, if science were ever in need of an experiment to test the thesis of the relation between the transcending nature of economic values in modern civilisation and a society's religious life, an experiment can be pointed out which took place on the hugest scale history can provide. After the first European war an inflation caused the loss of property of the German middle classes. This was followed in Protestant Germany by a complete disintegration of not merely what Weber called *Wirtschaftsethik* (itself a Protestant departmentalisation) but by the disintegration of the whole ideals and codes of the middle classes. No short-lived hardship, however severe, can account for a loss of confidence on such a scale.

For the most general aspect it is irrelevant which side – whether abstention from usage or glorification of transcending values – is reinforced by religion, or expressed in religious terminology. The inevitable is common to all forms: the acceptance of ownership of units of value as a virtuous state, and the disparaging of tendencies contrary to that virtue.

Glossary of Symbols

±	Value	E	Exchangeability
U	Useful object	U^i	Empirical value: $U + E^u + E^t = U^i$
R	Ritual object	E^u	Exchangeability-of-useful-objects
T	Treasure	E^t	Exchangeability-of-treasures

Though the last two symbols [E^u and E^t] are sometimes transcribed 'exchangeable useful objects' or 'exchangeable treasure' for purposes of convenience, the primary sense is always the exchangeability itself.

NOTES

1. This paper derives from a project which, according to Franz Steiner's letter to Paul Bruell (cited in our Introduction, p. 46, above) and to Paul Bohannan, who first edited the text, 'was eventually to be turned into a book on the economics of primitive peoples' (1954: 118 fn1). A typed fair copy of the paper, almost identical to the

published version, survives in the bound volume, *Franz Baermann Steiner, Lectures and Papers Oxford 1949-52* in the Library of the Institute of Social and Cultural Anthropology of the University of Oxford. The paper first appeared in June 1954 in *The British Journal of Sociology* 5 (2): 118-29. A German translation was published as 'Notiz zur vergleiechenden Ökonomie' in Fritz Kramer and Christian Sigrist (eds) 1978 *Gesellschaft ohne Staat*, Frankfurt: Syndikat.

2. In the terminology of economics, this word 'value' should probably read 'utility'; the wording of the original has been retained. [P.B.] Against P.B.'s note, the present editors would point out that 'value' is the term F.B.S. invariably employs when relating questions of economics and religion, and that in this essay F.B.S. contrasts 'value' and 'utility'. [Eds]

3. A glossary of symbols is appended at the end of the article. [F.B.S.]

4. In order to get the full meaning of this word in this context, it should be thought of with reference to its Latin original, or even better, with reference to its German equivalent, *Übersetzung*. [P.B.]

5. In a very general manner such asymmetrical equations can be thus symbolised, the small letters referring to quantities, the capitals to kinds: $aM = bN$; $aM = cO$; $bN = dO$. I would, instead of referring to an economic system as 'rational' or 'logical' merely say that the equations, though manifold, are symmetrical. [F.B.S.]

BIBLIOGRAPHY

Armstrong, W. E., 1928 *Rossel Island*, Cambridge: C.U.P.

Furness, W. H., 1910 *The Island of Stone Money*, Philadelphia and London: J.B. Lippincott and Co.

Hatt, G., 1919 'Notes on Reindeer Nomadism', *American Anthropological Association Memoirs* 6: 73-133.

Lehtisalo, T., 1932 'Beiträge zur Kenntnis der Renntierzucht bei den Juraksamoyeden' *Institut für Sammendignende Kulturforschung* series B, vol. 16.

Mead, M., 1930 'Melanesian Middlemen', *Natural History* vol. 30, no.2.

———— ed., 1937 *Cooperation and Competition among Primitive Peoples*, New York: McGraw-Hill.

Malinowski, B., 1922 *Argonauts of the Western Pacific*, London: Routledge.

Müller, W., 1917 *Yap. Ergebnisse der Südsee Expedition 1908-1910*, Hamburg: L. Friedrichsen and Co.

Seligman, C. G., 1910 *The Melanesians of British New Guinea*, Cambridge: C.U.P.

Thurnwald, R., 1932 *Werden, Wandel und Gestaltung der Wirtschaft*, Berlin: Walter de Gruyter.

TOWARDS A CLASSIFICATION
OF LABOUR[1]

Labour, in the broadest sense possible, is associated with or conceived as a kind of subdivision of a still broader category concerning which the sociologist often exhibits signs of uneasiness, and towards which the social anthropologist has developed an attitude which resembles now a joking relationship, now pure avoidance. I am thinking of what is usually called 'economics'. The typical attitudes of anthropological uneasiness concerning economics can be summed up in two questions: (1) Can I give a true picture of a simple society when I leave out economics? (2) How far can I apply the economic concepts of contemporary industrial society to the life of a primitive group? The second was Malinowski's question. As to the first, since we know that we are not neglecting large bodies of fieldwork data, what we are leaving out must be rather a systematic approach than the facts. In both questions, economics stands for an approach and a terminology, not for facts.

For the sociologist or anthropologist, there are no economic facts. We can define economic relations as those relationships existing between human individuals and groups which can be best described in terms of values and non-human quantities. But these economic relationships are social ones. Both the values and quantities reflect cultural norms. From the sociologist's point of view, every economic statement is a shorthand account of human behaviour and relationships between individuals and groups. This statement applies to the law of supply and demand, to inflation, and to all the rest.

A whole complex of very complicated and misleading questions is simplified when we reduce it to one reasonable question: have those social relationships which we single out as economic relationships nothing more in common than the fact that they are amenable to description and treatment by one particular terminology? The position of the classical economist has been to answer in the affirmative and to seek the factual similarity in the supposed subsistence nexus of all economic 'facts'. My position is that when we deal with economic relationships we speak of social relationships which can be described in a certain way. The usefulness of a descriptive terminology varies with the society of discourse. After these terminological reminders, let us consider what is meant by labour.

Labour and its Historical Meanings

The story of the definition of labour, particularly in the eighteenth and nineteenth centuries, is such a tangled and weary one, the thoughts put forward are so unattractive and contradictory, that to acquaint you with this part of the history of ideas would involve twenty times more space than we can spare and the building of a whole historical-critical apparatus which would be useful for no other purposes. Reading through that literature, one cannot suppress the suspicion that the people who tried to use the concept of labour were after several quite different things.

In the main, labour has been used in four different contexts. In each of these contexts, admirable use has been made of the word. But difficulties began when scholars tried to define labour in such a way as to account for more than one context – perhaps for three or even all four. I maintain that nothing connects the four contexts except the use of the same important and misleading word. As the resulting confusion has bedevilled anthropological discussion, I shall deal with the contexts briefly.

The first context (1) can be called that of the relation between occupational activities and status. In a society with a certain amount of social mobility and with a developing middle class (of course, the discussion in which all four contexts occur presupposes the existence of a middle class) there is bound to arise a situation in which the relative merits or demerits of occupations cannot be discussed in terms of an inherited status. Thus other terms must be sought. They comprise the supposed intrinsic qualities of those activities which constitute an occupation. In such a system of valued activities one might, as Cicero did, distinguish between the trading classes by placing the great merchant above the retail trader, not because he is richer, not because he has inherited a higher status, but because, in the course of his activities, he is less likely to cheat than the retailer. Since his activities are more moral, they confer a greater dignity on the person. Cicero influenced Augustine; thence the idea served as a model throughout the Middle Ages, whenever the relative merits of professions were discussed. The last of the important books using such arguments is *The Perfect Housewife*, the work of the sixteenth-century Spanish humanist,

Fray L. de León. This book is, I believe, still given to girls in Latin America before they marry, as an introduction to their duties. We learn from it that the farmer is superior to the trader because in his toil he takes his gains from nature and not from man. León takes care to employ two sets of terms: one for the professions or occupations themselves, the other for the activities. Without this terminological separation the consistent value judgement would be impossible.

Quite a different context (2) is that of the so-called division of labour. This refers to the system of terms in which observations are made concerning social changes during which occupations and institutions become more specialised, tasks increasingly shared and subdivided. I will deal more fully with the concept later on; I pass it here, observing only that Aristotle has written very lucidly on the subject without finding it necessary to evolve a labour concept.

A third context (3) is that in which productive labour was distinguished from unproductive labour. Adam Smith is only partly responsible for this most enormous red herring of economics. It is the result of the discussion between the representatives of eighteenth-century state capitalism and mercantilism on the one hand, and those of growing industrial capitalism on the other. For the former, productivity referred to the return in state revenue in an overall estimate. Undertakings that did not fit into the scheme of wealth production were termed unproductive. Smith, however, applied this notion to the microcosm of economic activities rather than to taxation policy, thus creating a concept of an activity which can be either productive or unproductive. For an account of some of Smith's considerations, and at the same time for a muddled attempt to use this productivity notion in a modern context, I refer you to Marshall's well-known textbook (1949).

The fourth main context (4) is that in which we relate labour to nature on the one hand and to capital on the other. This is a use of the word which is quite necessarily (like the foregoing one) limited to societies of a certain type. There are innumerable occasions on which we make lists carefully under three separate headings: the resources which are given and can be used; the equipment, its value; and what has to be done. To define, revalue or re-examine an item means moving it from one to another of the three interdependent columns.

To sum up: we find labour used in theoretical contexts of four main kinds. In the first, labour relates to an activity, the moral perfection of which is supposed to indicate the status of the respective occupation or profession. In the second, a social process in the course of which human beings perform more and more specialised activities is discussed in terms of the division of something which, as a category, is called labour. In the third, economic processes are made relevant to political theory, and the smallest unit of such an economic process is called labour. In the fourth, attempts are made to analyse industrial production as economic processes (that is, transformation of one kind of value into another), and labour is called something of calculable value, which is distinguished from investments, commodities, profits, and from resources, but is related to them as something valuable.

There is no reason for being critical in the use of the word in any of the four contexts. Our criticism must begin, however, when definitions of labour are sought which intend doing justice to the use of the word in two, three, or all four of the contexts, especially when difficulties created by such a confusion begin to masquerade as genuine problems. There has been a tendency to fill the gaps between these contexts by noxious paddings and links, common sense reasoning of the worst kind, ideological fragments of secularised Puritanism, psychological constructions such as the distinction between efforts concerning an aim in the future and others which are their own end (and therefore cannot be labour), or such as the theory of pain which is inflicted on every person who works, and which must be balanced somehow by the enjoyment occasioned by the fruits of this labour to make it – of all things – rational![2]

A Sociological Definition of Labour

Do we want to use the term 'labour' as a sociological concept? If we do, we must not try to define several meanings of the word at the same time. Rather, we must relate – even contrast – the sociological meaning to others. With this idea in mind, we have a second list of contexts for the term 'labour', which is of a different sort from the first list.

First, there is labour as an *ecological* concept: we may say that a colony of beavers does a measurable amount of labour or work, referring to the change of the environment of the colony's activities. Here the use of the word is legitimate because it is necessary. In the same ecological sense we talk about the labour of a human group.

Second, labour is also used in the *bio-physical,* or as some German schools had it, ergological sense, meaning a certain type of bodily function described in terms of that organism's nutrition and expenditure of energy.

Third, labour is used in *psychological* contexts where the use of the term presupposes knowledge of the drives of the respective individual, not mere surmise about conjectural 'motives' behind a population's activities.

If we intend to use the term labour in a fourth sense, we must mean something not alluded to by the other meanings of the word. If that concept is to be a *sociological* one, we must mean something characteristic of social relationships and social groups. It is the purpose of the rest of this section and of the next to examine this context and to clarify this fourth sense of 'labour'.

There is no activity as such which could not be labour at one time and something quite different at another. We may make a distinction on the basis of the cash nexus and translate the latter into more economic terms. But even that does not cover such instances as the fishing and hunting performed as sport, the yield of which activities is nevertheless sold – a not uncommon occurrence. Or we may think of the often discussed distinction between the amateur and the professional sportsman, and go on distinguishing degrees of gainfulness among the so-called amateurs. Or we may think of the case of the priest celebrating a family ritual in his own house. The activities under varying circumstances of wet nurses and prostitutes could also be made the food for much profound thought. But not only is the cash nexus, where it occurs, insufficient for such distinctions – we have to deal with societies in which services are reciprocated and gifts exchanged, and where people are indemnified rather than remunerated. Moreover, the cases in which it is difficult to distinguish labour from sport and play are in those societies not, as they are in our own, restricted in the main to solitary activities. Quite the contrary. As one example for many, we can cite Firth's quotation from R. H. Mathews about a Maori fishing festival held in 1855 (1929: 216-18).

It seems to me to be impossible to distinguish, either with the help of Sombart's 'objective' criteria, or with those of Firth, the labour element from the sport element in that instance. In general, I cannot see what purpose is served by classifying activities in terms of attitudes and supposed motives of the people who perform these activities. Looking beyond the social function and immediate social gratification seems particularly out of place in a primitive economy. In the long run, to distinguish labour from play and from sports is to be left with a riddle: how does labour, something so disagreeable, happen to be done at all? The historian of ideas recognises the old argument: a natural existence of man without labour, hence labour as an unnatural element to be explained, an activity to which man must be forced if he is not to idle away his time in the most pleasant way he can think of. And perhaps the historian will agree with me in my preference for the original story of the Fall to this unpleasantly garbled secularisation.

Labour as an Integrating Activity

When, in a sociological context, we say that an Eskimo watching an ice hole is performing labour, we do not mean that his motives for doing so are different from his motives in performing other activities, as this presupposes a choice having been made by the man, which is begging the question. Nor do we mean that in the tribe's language there is a formulated concept of labour which is used to differentiate that kind of activities from others. Nor do we allude to the fact that man needs food. When we single out this activity and call it labour, we mean that the Eskimo is doing something his household expects him to do; on his return home his wife will clean and unfreeze his gear and deal with the catch; the activities of the man and the woman are interdependent in a way which cannot be altered without affecting the social structure.

Thus, sociologically speaking, it is impossible to define labour and to discuss afterwards the way in which it is apportioned and divided. Contrarily, we have to describe labour as part of an activity which is divided and apportioned in a certain way. No psychological surmises can veil the tautology. Labour is an activity, interdependent with other activities of other people, which other activities in some cases belong to the same category as the first, in others they do not. The rules of apportionment of these activities are part of the given social system. Thus, when a man performs activities which are in accord with the laws of his society, and does so in order to gain his livelihood, we regard it as labour not merely because this is necessary to the man's physical survival, but because his society expects him to do something towards gaining his livelihood, and certain activities of others are performed under the condition that he behaves in the way described.

The difference between labour on the one hand and other activities on the other hand, including games or ritual activities of laymen, consists in the fact that the apportionment of the roles and functions in the latter activities is regulated by other kinds of authorities or offices and connotes other sets of values. This is, as it were, the organisational aspect of labour.

Of labour itself, we can say – and this is the sum total of the preceding – that it is a socially integrative activity. It is a general feature of simpler society (and not only of the very simple ones) that we cannot discern inducements, incentives, motives, apart from the integrative function. The notion that, apart from the promise to make the labouring person a part of a whole to define his place among his fellows, society must hold out carrots or sticks in order to make its members work at all: this is a notion which, fortunately, makes sense only in a limited number of societies. Nor must we forget that, wherever European and other more complex societies have encountered primitive man, the carrot has been a bribe (and a pitiful indemnity) for those who must willingly neglect the performance of what are to them socially important functions so that they can perform during that time activities which are not integrative in their own society. To talk in terms of a more complex society: when a man makes a choice between a paid job and playing football (not as a professional) he is choosing between an activity which assures him of his role in his family group, among other things, and an activity which is irrelevant to this group, and his place in this group.

We have to assume that we can study, when dealing with an integrating activity, all its socially situational aspects, and can endeavour to relate them to some structural ramification. This, then, would be part of the sociology of labour in a narrower sense, and such a study could be distinguished from the economics of labour, again in a narrower sense. And this, finally, is my subject.

Division of Labour

The sociology of labour has been discussed in the past in terms of two concepts which sometimes accidentally, sometimes intentionally, are made to overlap: the division and organisation of labour.

The idea of division of labour is familiar to most sociologists from the title of that misnomer, Durkheim's *Division du travail social*, a book which does not deal with labour at all. Durkheim, looking back on a long tradition of the use of this expression, hardly bothers to explain it. He speaks of the function of what he calls division of labour and, characteristically, thinks it necessary immediately to explain what he means by 'function' but not what he means by 'division of labour'. From what he says later on, it becomes clear that by labour he means all social activities.

Durkheim himself cites Aristotle's *Nicomachean Ethics* (EN 1133a 16) to illustrate the antiquity of the idea, though he does not mention the relevant passages from the *Politics*. Moreover, he makes no reference to the long and learned discussion in Adam Ferguson's *Essay on the History of Civil Society*, where the phenomenon is called 'separation of arts'.

The two main influences on Durkheim and other nineteenth-century writers on the subject were Comte and J.S. Mill, dissimilar as they were in many ways. Both these thinkers, because of their notions of progress and because of the function of economic speculation in these notions, derived not a small degree of precision from using economic processes with which they were familiar as prototypes of all social developments. (After all, nineteenth-century economic determinism was only one of the ways, and perhaps the most reasonable one, of recognising the prominence of some economic phenomena of the new industrial society.)

So, when the descendants of Mill and Comte talk about division of labour, a statement about industrial division of labour covers the division of all social activities, just as a statement about the proportions of a skeleton applies to the proportions of the body inside which the skeleton is found.

Another feature of the division of labour problem is already obvious at the fountainhead: it is impossible to decide when these authors are thinking of principles of social organisation and when of principles of social grouping. This confusion is more fully developed by Adam Smith himself: 'The greatest improvements in the productive powers of labour, and the greater part of the skill, dexterity, and judgement with which it is anywhere directed or applied, seem to have been the effects of the division of labour' ([1776] 1904).

Three factors were overlooked which refute this point of view. First, the so-called sexual division of labour is a primary example of integrating activities. It conforms to the most general principle of complementary activities without ever giving rise to occupational specialisation, either directly or indirectly.

Secondly, the value system of a people may lead to specialisations which affect social organisation, but be downright contrary to what the classicists meant by social growth. In a famous passage Adam Smith says that: 'In a tribe of hunters and shepherds, a particular person makes bows and arrows, for example, with more readiness and dexterity than any other. He frequently exchanges them for cattle or for venison, with his companions and he finds at last that he can, in this manner, get more cattle and venison than if he himself went to the field to catch them. From a regard of his own interest, therefore, the making of bows and arrows grows to be his chief business and he becomes a sort of armourer' (ibid: 19).

Smith was wrong on this point. Obviously, the modern anthropologist cannot fathom a man dextrous in manufacturing bows giving up cattle in a cattle society, one where ritual values and status are connected with cattle, merely in order to make bows.

Finally, where primitive man invokes the help of his fellows he asks not for a complementary effort but rather for a quantity of energy which he cannot supply himself. The labour group of neighbours who work in unison, marked by the absence of dividing devices, is organisationally the most primitive form of labour, and the very negation of specialisation. So the tendencies toward specialisation and institutionalisation do not coincide.

Smith's theory can be briefly summarised: man, not the 'political man' of Aristotle, but the bartering animal, exchanges services; the unit of worthwhile exchange is also the basis of socially recognised occupational specialisation. The basic assumption is that of the commodity character of services – it is this notion which creates the distinction between feudal and capitalistic concepts of labour. Smith projected this notion back into the childhood of man. Very ingeniously his theory ties up with all major issues of eighteenth-century trade-mindedness. But, of course, it does not fit primitive life as we know it.

The major critic of the classical theory was Karl Bücher. He pointed out in *Die Entstehung der Volkswirtschaft* (*Industrial Evolution*, 284-86) that Adam Smith failed to distinguish between production which is separated into various departments in a single factory, and a tradelike situation in which a good undergoes one or several changes in proprietorship before it reaches the point at which it is ready to go to the consumer. Smith, in short, has two criteria: (1) a process of production, and (2) ownership. Bücher separated them.

Bücher's idea is, today, as dated as Adam Smith's. When Bücher says 'economic process' he invariably means 'industrial processes'. He thinks, not in terms of social relationships, but in terms of the actual changes taking place in the raw material, in the commodity, and in terms of disposition of working power. His analysis, which was at the time he did it enlightening and simplifying, now seems merely to get in our way. We are, however, permanently indebted to him for the separation of 'division of production' (*Produktionsteilung*) from 'subdivision of labour' (*Arbeitszerlegung*). In an altogether different context and with a fully developed industrial society as his frame of reference, Max Weber has dealt with these points in the *Grundriss der Sozialökonomik*. As in all his general writings on the sociology of labour, Weber bases his treatment on Bücher. I cannot, however, regard Weber's distinction between economic and technical division of labour as sound; this would give to his phrase (division of labour) too many functions.

Sexual Division of Labour

We are indebted to Bücher on another point: he was the first non-ethnographer to give attention to the sexual division of labour. However, since this phenomenon does not fit into what he described as division of labour – 'increase of the number of labourers necessary for the accomplishment of a definite economic end, and at the same time ... differentiation of work' – of course he cannot call it division of labour. And he does not. It is to him simply one of the phenomena of the sexual dichotomy. He relates it to other features of that dichotomy and regards it as something peculiarly primitive (Bücher 1918: 30-31).

This is a mistake we find in the whole earlier literature on the subject, and very understandable it is. The simpler a society is (that is, the fewer differentiating features there are) the more attention is given to the few. Hence, in societies without professional grouping, without class or caste formation, without specialisation of any kind, the allocation of different tasks to the different sexes seems a very prominent feature. And so it is. But the notion that the more primitive a society the more rigid its sexual division of labour does not follow from it.

The only English monograph on the subject is Dudley Buxton's *Primitive Labour*. He – like all who share his commonsense approach – tries to establish classes of activities in terms of ends, finished products, categories of ecological entities or commodities, and then to centre each class of activities around one sex. He then tries to account for the exceptions in this classification by differences in the so-called cultural stages, which when examined closely turn out to be ecological types scarcely related to degrees of social or cultural complexity. With a few exceptions which we shall discuss later, no such permanent categories can be shown to exist. To cite one example for many: sexual division of labour in pastoral pursuits varies widely. It is possible to find, in Africa alone, (1) societies in which only men have to do with herds and women are excluded completely; (2) both sexes have duties with regard to cattle, but only men milk; (3) the same, but only women milk. These differences cannot be accounted for by any ecological theory or by any *one* principle.

If one reviews the relevant passages of a good many ethnographic monographs, one comes to the conclusion that there are several bases on which we might classify facts concerning the sexual division of labour. The first is what I have called integrative directives: what ideological factors lead to the integration? By and large, there are two: one is a space-sex reference, and the other is a tool-sex reference.

The space-sex directive is the more general. Perception of space is sharpened by associating some areas with one sex or the other. In the case of the Lele, reported by Mary Douglas, the spatial arrangement is into three spheres: village, scrubland, and forest. Social space is made to coincide with the sexual spheres of activities (women work in the villages; men in the forest; both in the scrub). A similar element is apparent in Tepoztlan, described by Redfield: men's work is done in the fields, and hence is subject to one rhythm; women's work, done in the house, is subject to a completely different rhythm (Redfield 1930: 84).

Secondly, we can classify by the organisation of activities: whether the tasks of women and those of men are interlocking, parallel or separate. In the case of Eskimo division of labour, when the women unfreeze and repair the men's hunting gear on their return from the chase, the tasks are interlocking. Gutmann describes instances among the Chagga in which men and women do parallel work at the same time, but do not perform it together. And finally, one can find many examples of tasks which are performed solely by women, which do not interlock with those of men, and vice versa.

These two sets of criteria can be placed on a single chart for ease of characterisation.

Sexual Division of Labour

Integrative Directives	ACTIVITIES		
	(1) *Interlocking*	(2) *Parallel*	(3) *Separate*
(a) Pragmatic (space-sex reference)	1 a	2 a	3 a
(b) Contextual (tool-sex reference)	1 b	2 b	3 b

[N.B.: 1 b and 3 a seem not to exist.]

It is useless to talk about the causes or origins of sexual division of labour. Although it is a complex matter, we can discern a few main principles which seem to rule it – but there may be more:

1. Biological. The female is excluded from a number of acts because of biological limits. This does not mean that women are 'the weaker sex'. This point has been greatly overemphasised: there is a difference between biological conditions and the rationalisation of an existing mode of division. Professor Radcliffe-Brown was fond of pointing out that sexual division of labour related to the social personalities of men and women, and not to their bodily characteristics.
2. Psychological. There are groups of activities which are regarded as extensions of motherly functions, such as feeding the family. Therefore, they are woman's work in all societies. In all societies, women are excluded from killing (as labour) and activities derived from it.
3. In all societies there is a male sphere and a female sphere which are mutually exclusive but not strictly so (though the concomitant ideology may claim that they are). There are rules for sharing the work, which tend to be stricter. Sexual division of labour connoted the two, supplied the terms in all societies for the two.

We have to assume that work cannot be done without minimum differentiation, and the sexual lines of cleavage make it possible for whole classes of activities to be added to those primarily identified with a sex. The result is a network of activities with polarity as organising principle.

I have introduced into this discussion the concept of integrating directives: I noticed a pragmatic directive and a contextual one. The first referred to a linking of space and sex, the second of tools and sex. These integrating directives of the sexual division of labour relate to the social personalities of men and women of a society. I would be inclined to argue that we can, in regard to labour, discuss in terms of such directives, that is, the distribution of kinds of tasks within a group of human beings, division of labour in a narrow sense.

There is one last factor concerned in the sexual division of labour which must be mentioned here, although it will enter into the classification proposed in the next section: the prevailing division of labour does not apply to menial tasks or to persons in a servile status. An example from our own society will illustrate the point: however unwomanlike and 'strenuous' a task which ought not to be performed by the housewife, it can be done by another female – the servant girl. A male servant finds it within his province to do some of the most extremely 'womanish' work.

So far as the servant is concerned, the sexual division of labour of his master's group is a privilege from which he is excluded. This exclusion, making the servant into a sort of 'sexless' person who ranks with the children, is a mark of servility easy to recognise.[3]

Organisation of Labour

Only in the most primitive organisational types is it easy to distinguish division of labour from what is customarily called organisation of labour. The difference is a conceptual one: organisation of labour does not refer primarily to the apportionment of types of tasks to types of people, but to the way the allotted tasks are performed, either singly or in cooperation with other persons; the nature of the cooperation may lead to further qualifications. If we distinguish single work from group work, the first can be meaningfully subdivided in reference to control or supervision or their absence. The latter, group work, is more complex. Malinowski made a distinction between *communal* and *organised* labour, which led to valuable observations in his fieldwork.

Organised labour, says Malinowski, 'implies the cooperation of several socially and economically different elements'. However, 'when a number of people are engaged side by side, performing the same work, without technical division of labour, or social differentiation of functions', Malinowski terms it communal labour (1922: 159).

I find Malinowski's terminology cumbersome and definitely misleading, for where a group of people engages in labour this performance can be called both organised and communal. I will use instead of Malinowski's communal, the word 'uniform'. Instead, of organised, I will speak of 'composite' labour. Both kinds are group labour. Group labour implies that the total of all the activities performed lies in one undivided social field of its own. This social field is conditioned by the other social fields in such a way that allotment of rôles and supervising activities which are part of the process do not exist independent of status relationships within the total structure. That is to say, we generally have to subdivide the forms of group labour first as to the uniformity or multiformity of the component individual tasks, and secondly as to the nature of control.

The distinction between series of interdependent tasks performed by several people, and the kind of labour which I have called composite, cannot be drawn by a hard and fast line. This is a case of gradual transition. It is these transitions which we are talking about when we discuss the technological developments of mankind, or the increasing 'division of labour'.

However the difference between these two forms of labour on the one hand, and uniform labour on the other, seems so clear-cut as to deserve theoretical comment. The main difference lies in the authority structures latent in the forms of group labour. In uniform labour processes, we commonly find a particularly loose and 'unorganised' authority structure. The classic case is individuals performing together, for the sake of group stimulus, tasks which they may and do perform independently as well. To this class belong many female activities, particularly food-gathering, not only in simpler societies but also, e.g., berry picking in country districts. The rota system of women spinning together was fairly widespread in Europe. Similar arrangements are resorted to in emergencies (mending or knitting in groups for soldiers). But even in the spinning meetings, at least in parts of eighteenth-century Germany, particularly in the Slav minority areas, a modification of the voluntary association is noticeable: it becomes the custom for the assembled girls to nominate one to be in charge of the procedure. This overseer had to warn slackers who were talking too much, and she had to use determination with male visitors who kept the girls from working properly.

On the whole, free-working associations of this kind are appreciated for the semi-recreational character of the group activity (hop picking in England). Bücher was the first student to draw attention to the semi-recreational aspect of unison work. In his book, *Arbeit und Rhythmus*, he treated the whole range of phenomena from this point of view. He was the first to realise that uniform labour was a worldwide feature of human society, the more dominant the simpler the social organisation of that society, and that all the world over this uniform work is very often unison work. He made the mistake of arguing that unison work of this type was the more primitive kind of work (which is wrong), that therefore it is the earliest kind of labour and represented the origin of labour (the more wrong), and that therefore labour can be proved to have originated in play.

This theory, the obvious errors of which must not blind us in our estimate of this pioneer work, of course angered the Puritan sociologists who, for religious reasons they had long forgotten, preferred to see labour as a pain, the self-infliction of which had to be explained by hard necessity if not by the Fall. I would only point out what we all know: that Bücher's theory can be refuted out of hand by anthropological and ethnological evidence, especially from groups like the Pygmies and Bushmen.

The transition is gradual from this type to cases in which the labour group is performing work which, though consisting of many uniform individual tasks, could not be achieved by a single individual. The greater the discrepancy between the achievement which is within one individual's working capacity, and that of the group, the more permanent is the structure given to the work association.

In a later essay, Bücher made a further discovery, of what he called *Bittarbeit*, a term which Firth translates as 'invitation labour'. The invitation technique, the combination of labour with a feast, in which the man who needs the work done turns into a host, are archaic features found all the world over. They do not always disappear when a new evaluation of labour is introduced. Majumdar tells us that the Ho, a Munda tribe, having been thoroughly assimilated to wage labour, still practise agricultural assistance for which they insist on being 'paid' with a goat, even though it is of much less value than they could receive for the same work at prevailing wage rates (1937: 44). The preference for the goat payment seems absurd on economic grounds alone. We must realise that the goat is offered on the basis of reciprocal obligation, a sphere into which wage payment has not intruded.

'Invitation labour' must also be seen from the standpoint of the authority structures of the labouring group. Basically there are two major contexts for this sort of work: (1) reciprocal obligations (neighbours; kinsmen; age-sets and other associations may always act as uniform labour teams). (2) Chiefship. Malinowski, like Bücher before him, has stressed the great similarity between invitation labour (for in-laws) and tribute labour (for a chief). The difference between the two is that tribute labour is not on a basis of reciprocity, but the feast character of invitation labour is preserved in tribute labour. The chief may act as overseer or appoint one to act on his behalf or officially acknowledge foremen elected by the teams. This makes some difference in the authority structure of the teams, but does not constitute a different type of labour. Firth and Malinowski have confused the organisational (managerial) element contained in such supervision with the terminologically unsatisfactory distinction between communal and organised. This is the only difficult part in the functionalist theory – a difficulty, I maintain, which is merely verbal.

Firth gives an instance which illustrates very well how the chief, apart from being the recipient of tribute labour, may also be the work leader in other tasks, simply because of the association of political leadership with groupings connected with uniform activities: every unison group is a potential army (Firth 1939: 223-24). We may find this mode of work generally associated with the bidding of the chief or the claim of kinsmen or neighbours, performed by a corporate group with exclusively ritual functions (Spicer 1940: 52-53ff.). Of the limits of the use of invitation labour we became aware when examining a case of a society where almost anybody can get invitation labour teams, with hardly any trouble. This is the case with the Tarahumara Indians of Northern Mexico (Bennett and Zing 1935).

Uniform teams are often combined, and in some parts of Africa are combined on the basis of sexual division. The case of the Chagga was mentioned above.

Let us now turn to servile labour, and define it by our organisational approach. Here the difference between single uncontrolled work and single work which is controlled or supervised in various manners is of little importance. However a further subdivision of the latter (controlled) form matters greatly: this is the kind of labour which is usually called *menial*. The word is used chiefly in reference to work done in the household, implying despicable work or drudgery. But the same work when done by the housewife according to the prevailing division of labour, is not regarded as menial. To understand the degradation, we must realise the servile implications of the absence of sexual division of labour.

Finally, there is the type of labour organisation which we called composite labour. Examples are to be found when men combine to form a small boat's crew. They may divide carefully their functions in the fishing team, but they are held together by their organisation only during a particular activity or a particular kind of activity. This does not mean that they are necessarily unrelated while not engaged in this activity – they may form a closed group or a kinship group, but the kinship unit is not identical with the fishing group. A very full description is given in Firth on making a canoe (1939: 118 ff.).

Another example of composite labour is found in Japanese villages in which a specialist carpenter is called in to oversee composite labour in house building (Embree 1939: 125-26).

The distinctions we have made are summarised in the chart opposite.[4]

Thus, to sum up, and giving the only possible sociological definition of labour, we may say: labour is any socially integrating activity which is connected with human subsistence. By 'integrating activity' is meant a sanctioned activity which thus presupposes, creates and recreates social relationships. Only thus have we isolated a group of social phenomena which it is reasonable to treat separately. And if the nineteenth-century economist and would-be philosopher, or his offspring, were to approach us with some of their profounder questions such as

Classification of Labour Types

I. Single individual task or group tasks
    1.1 Independent of other tasks
        1.11 Uncontrolled
        1.12 Controlled
    1.2 Interdependent with other tasks
        1.21 Uncontrolled
            1.211 Working pair alternating functions
        1.22 Controlled
            1.221 Complementary days on seniority basis (junior help-mate)
            1.222 Menial

II. Uniform group labour
    2.1 Non-accumulative effort
        2.11 Free association 'bee'
    2.2 Accumulative effort
        2.21 Free association
            2.211 Without leadership
            2.212 Foreman pattern
        2.22 Closed group
            2.221 Composed of sub-groups based on tasks differentiation (sex and age groups, etc.)
            2.222 One group only
                2.2221 Team with foreman
                2.2222 Team with overseer
                2.2223 Labour gang

III. Composite labour
    3.1 Navigational type
    3.2 House-building type

'What about Robinson Crusoe, is he not working in his solitude? Is it not labour? What distinguishes this from the isolated farmer?' etc., etc., – we can afford not to be amused, and to say that we are interested only in social phenomena.

NOTES

1. This paper was edited by Paul Bohannan and derives from the series of eight lectures Steiner delivered under the title 'Division and Organisation of Labour' (Hilary 1950-51, Michaelmas 1951-52, Michaelmas 1952-53). The bound volume *Franz Baermann Steiner, Lectures and Papers Oxford 1949-52* in the library of the Institute of Social and Cultural Anthropology at Oxford contains a typed fair copy. This is divided into seven lectures, A-G (the eighth lecture of the series was based on pp. 88-104 of

Steiner's dissertation). These amount to 102 pages. Paul Bohannan's abridgement is about one third of the original. Bohannan makes some changes to the text, on stylistic grounds, and excludes most of Steiner's extended examples. The paper was first published in October 1957 in *Sociologus* New series 7 (2): 112-30. It was subsequently anthologised as a foundational text in Cliften Bryant (ed.) 1972 *The Social Dimension of Work*, New Jersey: Prentice Hall, pp. 18-34.

2. Dr Steiner here cited examples from Sombart 1920: 72, Malinowski 1925: 927, Firth 1929: 128. [P.B.]

3. For a further discussion of this point see Steiner 1949. [P.B.]

4. Like most of Dr Steiner's manuscripts, this one becomes more cryptic as one approaches the end. Composite labour was dealt with only very superficially and needs a more thorough analysis, as Dr Steiner would have been the first to insist. [P.B.]

BIBLIOGRAPHY

Bennett, W.C., and Zing, R.M., 1935 *The Tarahumara Indians of Northern Mexico*, Chicago: University of Chicago Publications in Anthropology.

Bücher, K., 1893 *Die Entstehung der Volkswirtschaft*, Tübingen: Laupp. English translation *Industrial Evolution*.

————, 1918 *Die Entstehung der Volkswirtschaft. Zweite Sammlung*, Tübingen: Laupp.

Embree, J., 1939 *Suye Mura*, Chicago: University of Chicago Publications in Anthropology.

Firth, R., 1929 *Primitive Economics of the New Zealand Maoris*, London: Routledge.

————, 1939 *Primitive Polynesian Economy*, London: Routledge.

Majumadar, D. N., 1937 *A Tribe in Transition*, London: Longman.

Malinowski, B., 1925 'Labour and Primitive Economics', *Nature*, 25: 926-30.

————, 1922 *Argonauts of the Western Pacific*, London: London School of Economics Studies in Economic and Political Science, no. 65.

Marshall, A., 1949 *Principles of Economics*, 8th edn, London: Macmillan.

Redfield, R., 1930 *Tepoztlan*, Chicago: University of Chicago Publications in Anthropology.

Smith, A., [1776] 1904 *Wealth of Nations*, London: World Classics Edition.

Sombart, W. 1916-27 *Der moderne Kapitalismus*, 2nd edn, 3 vols., Leipzig: Duncker and Humblot.

Spicer, E., 1940 *Pascua*, Chicago: University of Chicago Publications in Anthropology.

Steiner, F.B., 1949 *A Comparative Study of the Forms of Slavery*, D.Phil. thesis, Magdalen College, Oxford.

PART IV:
KINSHIP, CLASSIFICATION,
AND SOCIAL STRUCTURE

LANGUAGE, SOCIETY,
AND SOCIAL ANTHROPOLOGY[1]

I do not want to start with explanation and complicated definitions and, defying a well-established convention, I will take for granted that you know what language is and how one might define society if one wanted to do so; I simply take for granted that we agree about all that. 'Social Anthropology', however, a phrase which occurs in the title of this brief talk of mine, is another matter, for this expression keeps changing its meaning. At first it used to suggest some kind of elaboration of ethnology or ethnography, that is, studies of the significance of the distribution in time and space of human groups, institutions, customs. Now it implies a branch of sociology, a very independent and energetic branch which tends to destroy the sound proportions of the tree. Let us see now what the relation of this branch to the rest of sociology is, so that we can understand better why there is talk of the anthropologist's attitude to language problems as being different from the sociologist's.

Most people, and these include some of[2] my elders and betters, when trying to distinguish between sociological and social anthropological research, do it in terms of research techniques, or special problems, or the setting of problems. The dichotomies they postulate accordingly are of three types: questionnaire interview versus 'living with a people and observing it', quantitative problems versus structural ones, complex societies versus simpler ones, etc. I believe these distinctions to be rationalisations *ex post* of the turn our divided interests take, and for people who study professionally the causes and conditioning of rationalisations, this is a sorry performance. Let us state in the simplest terms possible the story of the division of our interests.

We do not take a systematic interest in social phenomena as we do in all the others. There is not, steadily growing through the centuries, some body of secure knowledge. We take interest in social phenomena in fits and starts, we observe society systematically and philosophise thoughtfully about it when we are worried, or irritated, or frightened, or shocked, or intrigued or puzzled by social phenomena. Most of the situations which affect us in this way, the situations, that is to say, in which we formulate our social problems, can be summed up under two different headings. One is 'social change'. We may be made uneasy by an impending social change and think about what may hasten, what retard, what survive it: we may be describing with curiosity or glee the changed or changing scene, the new rich and the new poor; or we may fancy ourselves installing a new social order while we are already its product, and so on. Interests and names – as diverse as those of Aristotle, Marx, Ibn Khaldun, Montesquieu, Daniel Defoe, Saint Simon, Beatrice Webb, Spencer and Vico – can be put under this heading.

The other group of situations I'd label 'confrontations'. There are several kinds of them; let us consider the two most important – for informing research – and most widely different ones. One is the American situation, that of a country (or rather its observers) which is entered by individuals from other lands, people grown up with other customs, a different system of values, each one of them, before he is digested, an obstacle to the smooth running of American society, each one of them coming as an isolated creature or a very small group, their social bonds severed, no longer a matter for observation, but their otherness still intact, referring back to those relationships which they left. There is not much difference between these newcomers and the remnants of the aboriginal populations whose independence and political institutions had been destroyed by the white man a long time ago. Both these types present a problem of otherness, this otherness is personal, the persons have absorbed certain qualities of a body social which for most purposes does not exist. They are people with a foreign culture, and this culture is seen as part of the personality. It is no accident that 'culture', 'personality', 'culture and personality', 'culture in personality', etc. are the most important catch-words of our American colleagues. It is not very wise to put as an abstract question why the Americans investigate 'culture' and not really society, and whether they ought to do so; let us rather recognise the urgency behind such endeavours.

Now a quite different confrontation, and the only fruitful one for our subject matter, is that in which the observer intrudes the group, and where the stimulating otherness is that of a complete, life society which curiously differs from his own. To experience fully this confrontation, the observer who uses modern methods comes alone, dispenses with an interpreter as quickly as possible and learns. He makes the acquaintance of language and people at the same time. When he 'knows' the language he can make himself understood and understands; when he 'knows' the society he can predict the behaviour of people in typical situations. He studies the society through the medium of the language, and he studies the language as an important or (when he is wise) the most important social phenomenon. To be understood and not to be surprised become one.

Now, while this fieldworker will share all his interests with the sociologist of language – the division of language into various sub-languages, e.g., which are related to special activities, or social spheres, or groups (like the professional language of the hunters, the ritual language of the priests, the language of the ruling group); and when, or under what condition, a word or other part of speech can be moved from one sphere to another; which expressions are multivalent and what may be the social significance in each case; further, what correlations may exist between a traceable extension of meaning and a social change remembered by the people or (even better) observed – while all these interests are shared, the overriding one of the social anthropologist, as you will readily understand it, is in translatability. It is a problem of meaning, or rather several problems of meaning, put again and again into the most precise empirical and sociological terms.

It is because of all this, that when visiting our discussions you would hear sentences like these, 'It is better not to know too much of a people's language before going into the field. If you know the language, you take too much for granted', or, 'One cannot really study one's own society, because anthropology is translating one culture into another', or, 'If a person has successfully studied a group in his own society, this means that it was really a strange group, speaking a – however little distinct – dialect which he had to learn'. Thus, language and society, for us, is much more more one thing than it is for other people; and while for the theorist of language it is a laborious task to prove that that there is no meaning in speech parts outside the situations in which they are used, this is the tacit assumption of every young anthropologist going out to study.

This is the tacit assumption in all cases nowadays, but twenty-five years ago all this was very forcibly and vocally maintained by Malinowski.[3]

Now this notion of translatability is affected in various ways by the 'social context'. Rather, there are many meanings of being translatable and being untranslatable, and these meanings have different sociological significance. At school, translation difficulty may take the form: a Latin word in one context cannot be reproduced by an English word in an English rendering of the context.[4] But here we are dealing with other contexts; not with the part of speech in which a word is found, but with the different significance of the complete situations of the utterance of which the word forms a part. And here misunderstanding and translatability are connected. Examples: 'All change.' 'I should call the doctor if I were you.'[5] Are these misunderstood expressions translatable into the language of the misunderstanding person? Example: 'Are you sitting outside?' Does this correspond to an English remark on the weather? It is not, because the social situation cannot be the same.[6]

NOTES

1. This lecture is preserved as an untitled typescript of slightly more than four pages in Steiner's *Nachlaß* in the Deutsches Literaturarchiv, Marbach am Neckar. The content suggests that the title contained the words: language, society, and social anthropology. Elsewhere, Steiner references Malinowski's chapter in *The Meaning of Meaning* (Ogden and Nash 1923) as his major contribution to this topic. Thus, if Steiner's reference to Malinowski writing twenty-five years previously is precise, then this lecture dates from 1948. With a couple of years latitude, it may be the basis for Steiner's contribution to the seminar on 'Social Anthropology and Language' (run with Peristiany, Michaelmas (first) term 1950) and 'Language and Society' (run with Dumont, Hilary (second) term 1952). First publication.
2. 'All' is altered to 'some of' by hand. [Eds]
3. At this point, F.B.S.'s typescript contains the following bracketed *aide memoire*: '(A few words about Malinowski's research conditions; his two versions; his tilting against windmills; language not 'thought' but 'action'; study of language in context of other actions; total and topical social situation. No meaning otherwise, but this no special problem of the primitive. Gardiner's example of 'This side up'.)' [Eds]
4. F.B.S.'s dots here indicate that he may have elaborated this example. [Eds]
5. F.B.S.'s dots indicate verbal elaboration. [Eds]
6. There follow cryptic notes that suggest F.B.S. went on to look at the relation between use of diminutives and attitudes of familiarity and respect in Slavonic, German, Spanish, and Arabic languages. He seems to have suggested Slavonic languages conjoined the features of 'familiarity' and 'respect' elsewhere separated, concluding: 'Separation of attitudes and spheres of life by linguistic means. Metaphors – this is one function of metaphors – make it possible to use the same speech parts (no other "language") by reassembling them and mark other attitudes.' [Eds]

THE STUDY OF KINSHIP[1]

Lecture A

Introduction: Kinship and the nuclear family

Our problems are shaped by the situations which gave rise to our enquiries. And when asked where to draw the line between social anthropology and a sociology which is not social anthropology, I would not point to the difference between empirical and non-empirical pursuits, nor distinguish techniques of research, but I'd rather be inclined to separate two groups of situations each of which have urged men to put searching questions concerning the nature of the social phenomenon. One group of these situations are those brought about by social change; how many studies and theories and schools of thought can we safely pigeonhole by correlating them to either the French Revolution or the industrial revolution? But these are not the only social changes which have engendered sociological ratiocination. The other kind of situation is that of confrontation: a human being, by his social training integrated as a member of one society, finds himself vis à vis another, and is made to think, to give reasons for the apparent variability of fundamental things which before seemed to allow of only one kind of procedure, and to translate value concepts of the strange society into the idiom of his own.

I think that both kinds of situation can give rise to either abstract theorising or empirical investigation. Let us recall only the level of abstraction and the perpetual generalisation that accompanied the Greek Herodotus when confronting the highest cultures or the barbarians of the East; or, on the other hand, the very empirical and detailed procedures of that most brilliant and penetrating journalist of social change and stratification, Daniel Defoe. In both kinds of situation (change in one's own society, or confronting another society) detachment and involvement is possible. And both situations are pro-

found: the one can make one realise the basic insecurity of social existence, the other is apt to infuse all observation of social phenomena
with that questioning bewilderment, *taumazein* as the Greeks called it
who believed it to be the mainspring of all our more important knowledge. Thus both kinds of situation are 'existential', at least potentially.
These two kinds of situations make us formulate different problems,
make us describe things in different languages; but the object of investigation, the social phenomenon, is the same. Thus the overlapping of
the two interests produced by the two different situations becomes
more and more apparent, the closer we get to the centre of the social
phenomenon, the normative bio-social nucleus.

Sociologists in every sense of the word, and created by any conceivable situation of enquiry converge on the family: be it in its aspect
as domestic group, as cooperative or ritual unit, as smallest part of
consanguineal associations – and this converging indicates clearly
how conscious we all are of the fact that the family, the centre of consanguineal association, not only patterns wider kin relations, but all
other relationship – in Hegel's words the family provides the formal
element for social reality.

Once we realise that kinship is the essence of the social phenomenon – something that has to be described and explained and translated from the terms of one society into those of another, but cannot
be broken up into particles which are not kinship – once we realise that
fully, the family as a social institution becomes a thing of paramount
importance. That is why Aristotle starts his analysis of society with the
domestic group, that is why Herodotus develops his most charming
theory of sibling incest, that is why Le Play returns to the study of the
family. With our empirical research into the life of other societies, the
concern with the family was intensified.

A quite reasonable claim can be made for social anthropology's
deserving a special place in the mansion of sociology because of the
immediate insight it gives into the life of the family; moreover, social
anthropology in its modern sense, became what it is by virtue of its
detailed and painstaking examination of kinship relationships. This
we owe to Morgan's inquiry into the kinship behaviour of the Iroquois.
The interest in kinship has dominated social anthropology ever since,
and the belief was general that primitive societies were more or less
elaborate kin groups and possessed no other structural principles of
importance. This was changed, chiefly, by two discoveries: that of H.
Schurtz who realised the importance of age sets – they were the first
non-consanguineal principle recognised – and by Evans-Pritchard,
who discovered a type of political organisation which exists – one is
tempted to say under the disguise of kinship terminology. All this has
not rendered kinship problems less important.

I called kinship the essence of the social phenomenon; it is not only a human phenomenon. In his systematic sociology of animals, Alverdes distinguishes solitary from social animals.[2] These he further subdivides according to whether their mateship is seasonal or permanent, which yields four types: solitary seasonal mateships, seasonal mateships within the herd, solitary permanent mateships, permanent mateships within the herd. Promiscuity is not found within the herd.

Every theorist of animal society has remarked that two factors condition the family formation of mammals: whether their rutting season is fixed or not, whether children need the care of grown-ups for a long period (of years). Periods of intercourse that are not fixed and long-term needs for care on the part of the child lead to permanent mateships within the herd. These were the conditions for the development of the human family, which makes it unlikely that it developed from a state of human promiscuity.[3]

Lecture B

When we talk about the family, we usually mean one or both of two things: family and household. This is most confusing, because both family and household have jural and spatial aspects.[4]

The household or domestic group can be formed by: the nuclear family, a married woman and her child(ren), these people and inmates (attached people, like servants), parts of – or whole – extended families (to be discussed later), or groups of people who behave like any of the aforementioned. These are typical domestic groups; others – like a man with many servants – can be disregarded here.

The family in the narrowest sense (as something different from the household), can be talked of as a socially recognised procreatory group; the children ensure the family's place is ensured in the total social structure; and only through the family is the individual's place in terms of descent ensured within society. It is a general social institution found in all societies that all persons ought to be 'legitimate' (all free; [at least] that is all those whose status means they are regarded as forming society), and that they are 'legitimised' through the family. To say that and to say that in all kinds of societies we find some institution of family and wedlock is the same thing. The jurally recognised interests of the household concern not procreation directly but shelter and the distribution and preparation of food. The household appears as a unit of consumption in the economy of the society but not necessarily as a unit of production.

Marriage confers and fixes both procreative and domestic duties. The domestic group combines the authority structure of the family and the institutionalised regulations concerning the division of labour, and a discrepancy between the two is impossible. Thus when people are added (as inmates) to the household, this is done in terms of the existing authority structure of the family group dominant in that household (whether as co-familiar, honoured guest or servant). Established servants may be 'treated as members of the family'.

The most important features of familial existence include:

1. ('Laws') a person is a member of two families in the course of his life; this is relevant to processes of adaptation and jural position.
2. Inside-outside.
3. Nobody's activities and social intercourse are restricted to the family or household (every individual is in several social scales – Simmel – this is not to be confused with activities on different social levels).

Although the family confers status on its members (legitimises them), and although in many jural, even legal, contexts the family is seen together as a unit, as a persona (juridically), the family does not observe joint rights of ownership. Nothing is held in common by father, mother and children; joint ownership is found only in the form of joint rights of siblings in extended family types. It needs to be realised that this universal feature of familial existence, viz. the impossibility of holding property rights jointly, is a negative statement describing the family as the vehicle of inheritance. The principle of inheritance is that goods are handed on, in descent lines, from one generation to another. In the family persons combine in the usufruct of goods and titles, from the ownership of which they exclude each other. Thus it is that within the human family we find the not always successful attempt to harmonise the maximum tension between generations.

Legitimacy is a subject about which there exist many misconceptions. Illegitimacy does not necessarily involve a person's total status; the Tswana are an example of a society in which 'illegitimacy does not matter'. Other examples include: poor peasants, the former slave populations of the West Indies, Seychelles, Cape Verde.[5]

NOTES

1. These two lectures were presumably held as part of the course, 'The Study of Kinship', which Steiner (according to the University Calendar) gave together with E.E. Evans-Pritchard and Godfrey Lienhardt at the Institute of Social Anthropology, University of Oxford, Hilary (second) term 1950-51, and again with unspecified 'others' in 1951-52. This version is based on handwritten and typed notes preserved in Steiner's *Nachlaß* in the Deutsches Literaturarchiv, Marbach am Neckar for what appear to be the first two lectures in the series. First publication.

2. Two of Friedrich Alverdes' books were translated into English as 1927 *Social Life in the Animal World* (transl. K.C. Creasy) and 1932 *The Psychology of Animals in Relation to Human Psychology* (transl. H. Stafford Hatfield). It is probable that F.B.S. had the first of these in mind. Alverdes, a professor of zoology in the University of Marburg, was particularly interested in the degree to which humans and animals shared their social, psychological and bodily processes. [Eds]

3. The ensuing remarks (on animal and insect societies, ecology, ritual and psychology) are too cryptic to interpret confidently.

> [The] animal state as different from the herd: permanent relationships between groups or types. Insects: here too, the immature have to be cared for and have specific functions; the 'classes' which are related arise from age groups, then special fixation of type.
>
> [increasingly cryptic notes with illegible annotations]
>
> Human kinship: Fortes' definition; discuss monogamy versus thesis of promiscuity. Pygmies. Functions of family ecology – economic unit or 'domestic group'. [illegible hand-written annotations 'primary ....']
>
> Ritual unit is not identical with ecological unit or 'domestic group'.
>
> Psychological matrix: pat[-riarchal, -ernal] deity, Oedipal situation, brothers as alliance, Paris situation ... types of affection, apart from sexual, is according to family pattern. There is husband/wife relationship – via children, via household with all the conflict implied thereby and all the techniques for smoothing out conflicts. Apart from this man loves his spouse as his mother, sister or daughter. [Eds]

4. The latter expression, spatial, is different from talking simply of a territorial unit. All spatial terms – like spatial distance and so forth – derive from one kind of observation: just as two bodies cannot be in the same place at the same time, so it is impossible for two institutions or groups or corporate groups to be distanced in the same way. This is an aspect of social phenomena, part of the relationships between groups, which cannot be described in jural terms. [F.B.S.]

5. Steiner's lecture ends with some increasingly cryptic remarks on 'examples for generalisations on the family and household structure' of 'authority'. [Eds]

ARISTOTLE'S SOCIOLOGY[1]

It is possible to appreciate Aristotle's sociological thought much better now than during the last few centuries, and this is very significant, not only for the stage reached in the development of sociological reasoning but generally for our cultural situation. Between us and a revaluation of Aristotle, the sociologist, there intervened a large body of theories and theorems, associated with the rise and subsequent fortunes of the European middle classes. None of these theories preceded the Renaissance; none was elaborated further after the First World War.

All these theories and doctrines – and in the course of these seminars you will hear more about them – assumed a knowledge of the human individual and explained society as something designed to satisfy certain needs of the individual; or they assumed a knowledge of so-called social forces and explained individual human activities in terms of social forces acting upon the individual. From both these points of view an approach must seem very much lacking in interest which concerns not the individual versus society, but relationships and institutions. And this seems to have been Aristotle's concern: to distinguish kinds of social relationships and to explain social units and institutions as combinations of relationships. The isolating of kinds of relationships is the work of abstract reasoning which, however, does not involve motives or other psychological constructs; the interrelating of various kinds of social units is a straightforward affair of everyday observation and commonsensical generalisations. The existence of various levels of social organisation is taken for granted and nowhere explained. All this must have sounded rather uninspiring to the eighteenth century, but to the nineteenth century it was utterly childish and unworthy of the father of science. Thus Jowett, in his Introduction to his translation of Aristotle's *Politics* (1885) says:

> ... we are struck ... by the different mode in which the thoughts of ancient and modern man are expressed. To go no further than the first book of the *Politics*, the method of Aristotle in his inquiry into the origin of the state is

analytical rather than historical; that is to say, he builds up the state out of its elements, but does not enquire what history or prehistoric monuments tell about primitive man.

Moreover, Aristotle does not take much interest in human progress. His outlook has the pessimism that befits a wise man, and he tends to assume a cyclic movement in the change of social types. This he has worked out only in reference to political organisation, or rather, as he would have called it, the kinds of government. The application of the cyclic principle to the social phenomenon generally was left to Aristotle's great if indirect disciples: Ibn Khaldun and Vico.

So distinctive is Aristotle's contribution to sociology that it is possible to grade European sociologists of later times according to their similarities in interests, outlook and approach with the master; and all the thinkers who will receive good marks in these seminars can be regarded as being more or less in the Aristotelian tradition.

What is the most characteristic feature of this approach? Like all things of genius it is something very simple. It is the refusal to regard the human being and human society as two separable things, or, in the philosophical idiom, they are not 'given' separately: they may belong to different levels of reality, but within every human being, society is given. The human individual himself is a social phenomenon, and human beings cannot be abstracted from society, just as for us it is nonsensical to separate word-language from thought, as if there was something in our thought that is not words but can be thought and eventually expressed in words. Aristotle refuses to regard man as anything but a societal creature, a *zoon politikon*. A contractual society was just as unthinkable to him as a contractual biologic. That does not mean that Aristotle indulged in organismic theorising or that he anywhere pressed an analogy between social and biological phenomena. His pragmatism is remarkably free from all such trends. He does not explain social units by analogies, but only relationships in the case of which he is aware of his dealing with abstractions he created. Thus he will elucidate the relationship between master and slave by applying the analogy of soul and body. This, however, concerns only the abstract relationship, not slavery as a social phenomenon.

Whence comes this sound realism in a man famous for his abstract reasoning, his overpedantic classifications? One reason is a purely personal one. I think that the impact of social, just as biological, reality perturbed and excited this scholar much more than it would have affected a really practical person. Take, for example, his biological interest after marriage. What he wrote about slavery came not from an ivory tower: he had married into the family of a freed slave. All indications point to Aristotle having had a difficult career; he must have come up the hard way, without Plato's security. This makes for social realism. Talking against writers who, with the exception of Plato, are lost to us, he utilised this realism.

Aristotle's most important sociological writing, an essay on the foundations of society, has been cruelly mutilated by the author in order to serve as 'Introduction' to his *Politics*. At least that is the opinion of contemporary research. W. Jäger writes, in his 'Introduction' to *Nicomachean Ethics*, that:

> [Aristotle] intended to develop in the introduction the fundamental natural conditions of all political existence, in order to construct the state from nature, out of his simplest propositions. These presuppositions are the three fundamental elements of all social life, master and slave, man and wife, parent and child. The way in which he carries out, or rather fails to carry out, the resulting threefold division of his material shows that there were certain difficulties in his path. The first book discusses only the first of these fundamental relations, the question of slaves and its connection with the economy of social life. As to the two other subjects proposed, marriage and children, Aristotle consoles his readers by remarking at the end that these had better be discussed in connection with the problem of the family, 'when we speak of the different forms of government'. At first sight this looks like an incomprehensible failure in consistency and lucidity, and it makes the close of this book very unsatisfactory. The explanation is that he was in a very awkward position, and only violent means could help him out of it. Marriage and the family had already been liberally discussed in the earlier version of the *Politics*, on the occasion of the criticism of Plato's demand that wives and children should be in common. He was therefore obliged either to delete this earlier treatment, thereby destroying the main attraction of his criticism of Plato's *Republic*, or to abandon the account of it in Book I, and content himself with a reference to that in II. He chose the latter. The mutilated structure of the first book is thus a consequence of its adaptation to the older version .... (Jäger 1948) [2]

Let us now start with the celebrated and misleading opening.

> Observation shows us, first, that every polis [or state] is a species of association, and, secondly, that all associations are instituted for the purpose of attaining some good – for all men do all their acts with a view to achieving something which is, in their view, a good. We may therefore hold [on the basis of what we actually observe] that all associations aim at some good; and we may also hold that the particular association which is the most sovereign of all, and includes all the rest, will pursue this aim most, and will thus be directed to the most sovereign of all goods. This most sovereign and inclusive association is the polis, as it is called, or the political association. (Barker 1948: 1; square brackets original)

I said this opening is misleading, for we might easily misunderstand Aristotle to mean that he knows what the good is for which social organisation exists, and that he will continue to classify kinds of institutions according to the kinds of good for the attainment of which they are instituted. But this is not the case. What Aristotle really tells us is that, because of its associational character, the polis can be regarded as belonging to the class of associations and, moreover, can be discussed as a social activity. Insofar as all such activities are purposeful, it can be said of the polis that it has a purpose. The levels of social organisation can be understood in terms of the grading of purpose.

First of all, there must necessarily be a union or pairing of those who cannot exist without one another. Male and female must unite for the reproduction of the species – not from deliberate intention, but from the natural impulse .... Next, there must necessarily be a union of the natural ruling element with the elements which is naturally ruled, for the preservation of both.

The female and the slave [we may pause to note] are naturally distinguished from one another. Nature makes nothing in a spirit of stint, as smiths do when they make the Delphic knife to serve a number of purposes: she makes each separate thing for a separate end; and she does so because each instrument has the finest finish when it serves a single purpose and not a variety of purposes. Among the barbarians, however, the female and the slave occupy the same position – the reason being that the naturally ruling element exists among them, and conjugal union thus comes to be a union of a female who is a slave with a man who is also a slave. ... The first result of these two elementary associations [of male and female, and of master and slave] is the household or family. (Barker 1948: 3, 4; square brackets are original)[3]

Let us postpone a discussion of the three Aristotelian 'ideal types' and return to his discussion of the levels of social organisation. We shall find him discarding the grading of the good attained and very careful to distinguish between social growth as a causative principle and what our friends call the function of an institution. This important principle has been slurred over by the centuries that followed; he says:

The first form of association naturally instituted for the satisfaction of daily recurrent needs is thus the family .... The most natural form of the village appears to be that of a colony or offshoot from a family; and some have thus called the members of the village by the name of 'sucklings of the same milk', or, again, of 'sons and the sons of sons' .... This, it may be noted, is the reason why each Greek polis was originally ruled – as the peoples of the Barbarian world still – by kings. They were formed of persons who were already monarchically governed [i.e., they were formed from households and villages, and] households are always monarchically governed by the eldest of the kin, just as villages, when they are offshoots of the household, are similarly governed in virtue of the kinship between their members. [... of the polis] we may say that while it *grows* for the sake of mere life [and is so far, and at that stage, still short of full self-sufficiency], it *exists* [when once it is fully grown] for the sake of the good life [and is therefore fully self-sufficient]. (Barker 1948: 5-6; square brackets and italics original)

Thus, albeit without much purpose, the distinction is made between social growth, a part of nature, physis, and the relations between social phenomena, as far as these relations can provide functional, or pseudo-causal explanations. The conclusion is the famous passage:

> From these considerations it is evident that the polis belongs to the class of things that exist by nature, and that man is by nature an animal intended to live in a polis. He who is without a polis, by reason of his own nature and not of some accident, is either a poor sort of being, or a being higher than man. (Barker 1948: 6)

> We may now proceed to add that the polis is prior in the order of nature to the family and the individual. The reason for this is that the whole is necessarily prior [in nature] to the part. (Barker 1948: 7)

> We thus see that the polis exists by nature and that it is prior to the individual. ... [Man is thus intended by nature to be part of a political whole] (Barker 1948: 7-8)

With this social background the three relations – of master and slave, husband and wife, and parent and child – gain new significance:

> ... every subject of inquiry should first be examined in its simplest elements; and the primary and simplest elements of the household are the connection of master and slave, that of husband and wife, and that of parents and children.
>   The factors to be examined are therefore these – first, the association of master and slave; next what may be called the marital association (for there is no word in our language which exactly describes the union of husband and wife);[4] and lastly what may be called the parental association. (Barker 1948: 10)

To sum up, the theoretical achievement of Aristotle seems to me to be, distinctions between:

relationship and association (institution)
social growth and function
institutional and occupational differentiation.

NOTES

1. This paper may have been written for the Oxford University Classical Society, which invited Franz Steiner to speak at the suggestion of E.E. Evans-Pritchard. However, the opening reference to 'these seminars' (in paragraph two) suggests that it may have

been held as part of the series of Friday seminars at the Institute of Social Anthropology, some of which were devoted to individual thinkers and their work around 1950, such as that held by Laura Bohannan on Simmel and that attended by Mary Douglas, M.N. Srinivas, and Franz Steiner on Marcel Mauss (Mary Douglas: PC). Steiner examines Aristotle in his 'Discourse' on the Aristotelian theory of slavery appended to Chapter XVII of his doctoral dissertation, *A Comparative Study of the Forms of Slavery*, Oxford, 1949: 304-27. The typescript of this paper is preserved in Steiner's *Nachlaß* at the Deutsches Literaturarchiv, Marbach am Neckar. It is published here for the first time.

2. Steiner makes the same point in his dissertation by quoting Jäger (Steiner 1949: 323-24, footnote). We have assumed he used an identical quotation here. In his dissertation, Steiner comments, 'Thus, the essay has suffered from the use the author [i.e., Aristotle] made of it by turning it into an introduction to his *Politics*'. [Eds]

3. We assume that the quotation Steiner inserted included that he used in the 'Discourse'; this has been extended by reference to the full marginal annotation in his copy of *The Politics*. [Eds]

4. Steiner notes in his copy of this bracketed aside, 'The first place in history when a complaint is made about the lack of a scientific sociological vocabulary!' [Eds]

BIBLIOGRAPHY

Barker, E., 1948 *The Politics of Aristotle*. Oxford: Clarendon.

Jäger, W., 1948 *The Politics of Aristotle*. Translated with the author's corrections and additions by Richard Robinson. 2nd edn Oxford: Clarendon.

Jowett, A., 1885 *The Politics of Aristotle*. Oxford: Clarendon.

SOME PROBLEMS IN SIMMEL[1]

Lecture A

There are some authors who deserve an apology when we treat them selectively, talking of some of their problems: be it that time or space is too short to deal with their whole work, or that from a certain particular angle of view only some of their ideas seem to matter, or that some ideas of theirs are obviously more important than others, from whatever point of view we look at them. Simmel, however, is an author who cannot be treated otherwise. Had I six terms to do it in, had I an audience of sufficiently wide interest, and were I capable of the task of presenting the man's whole work, in the end I would have to realise that even then the fairest title of my course should have been 'Selected Problems in Simmel'. The man's whole work, I said, meaning his writings on epistemology, ethics, aesthetics, history of philosophy, theory of history, theory of money, sociology and those of his essays which belong properly to the class of *belles lettres*; but, had I a less ambitious scope and were I presenting only Simmel the sociologist, however much time at my disposal, I would still have to fall back on that restrictive and selective title. And I would have to adhere to 'problems' rather than saying 'ideas'. Not that the problems Simmel saw were more important than the answers he found to them – but the problem is the thing that remains in the mind of Simmel's readers, it is carefully constructed, grows, diminishes, disappears, to make place for a hydra of other problems. The problems are the lumps in a slowly moving river of arguing. We watch them dissolving. And Simmel has often been compared to a river, as by Professor Frischeisen-Köhler in his (1920) essay, the only full-length authoritative and academic appraisal of Simmel the philosopher. There Frischeisen-Köhler, recklessly mixing his metaphors, says, 'The unfootnoted river of presentation streams out of its own sources and does not enter a foreign sea'.[2]

Simmel was born in Berlin in 1858 and died as a professor of philosophy at Strasbourg. He came from a typical Berlin Jewish bourgeois family which, steeped in German middle-class culture, had gone as far as accepting the Lutheran creed. He was brought up a Protestant but left the Church in later life. His repudiation of one religion, however, was a purely negative act, and did not give him insight into another. We cannot assume that religious experience informed his life at any stage. Learned and stimulating as his excursions into the history of religion are, his statements about religious experience are curiously flat and pedantic, and can be compared to his references to polyandry.

Among his teachers at Berlin University were Mommsen, the historian, Bastian, the ethnologist, and Lazarus, a psychologist with wide interests in ethnology and linguistics. The influences in these formative years were threefold: the Kant-revival in Germany, the long drawn-out discussion about the place of the historico-sociological disciplines in relation to natural science, and the circle of polyhistors that had as its centre Lazarus's *Zeitschrift für Völkerpsychologie*. He must have known Hegel very well indeed, but there is no record of his growing acquaintance and changing attitudes to that thinker.

Heterogeneous as this mêlée seems to us, its dominant note was German philosophical idealism; and it was a whole when confronting the English influences: Darwin and Spencer. An odd confrontation, but Simmel seems to have owed to its stimulus his most searching sociological speculations.

At the age of twenty-seven he became *Privatdozent* at Berlin University, that is a gentleman honoured by permission to address academic audiences, without belonging to the paid staff of the University. Until recently, this was the first step in anybody's academic career in Germany, and those without independent means were in need of quick promotion or assistant librarianships. Simmel remained *Privatdozent* till he became Professor in the University of Strasbourg, at the age of 56; this appointment, and life in the war-overshadowed and war-congested city, was a painful anticlimax to his active teaching life, and he was a sick man already. He died a month before the end of the war which had destroyed all he stood for.

While he lived and taught in Berlin, he achieved a fame which is not associated with the position of *Privatdozent*. This lack of institutional academic success – on the part of a man who wielded a great influence among the intelligentsia, who had scores of books to his credit – is usually explained by University intrigues, and it is said that his Jewish descent was partly responsible. However that may be, and whether or not Simmel's parents miscalculated when thinking that a change of 'religion' would be a good protection for their offspring, it is clear that Simmel the writer of books on Kant, Goethe, Rembrandt, sociology, the philosophy of culture, the theory of money, would have been difficult to fit into the academic life even of a university much less conservative and pedantic than was that of Berlin at the time. And the more famous he became, the wider his writings branched out, the more he must have been felt as a cuckoo in the nest. What can you do with people who discuss with the same degree of seriousness and intensity the influence of Calvinism on Rembrandt's painting, the concept of matter in Kant, the social structure of mediaeval guilds, and, in one of his most charming essays called simply 'The Handle', the aesthetics of that part of vessels? He did not fit in.

But where did he fit? This man who was neither a really professional philosopher nor sociologist nor journalist? He was not a thinker, because the thinkers had died out before his generation: those peculiar nineteenth-century men, who were neither philosophers nor wise men, nor dons, nor poets, who lived in a terribly Germanic solitude, made all the world a witness to their internal struggles, disapproved of all established religions and, at the same time, castigated all collective forms of disbelief in their society. Simmel was most unlike these formidable creatures. He did not struggle – unless it was for clarification. Atheism was much too uncultured a form of creed for him – Yes, of course it is a creed, and a very interesting one, he said – and he was never a lonely man. He stimulated and needed discussion, surrounded himself with younger persons, teaching passionately. On the other hand, he was much too academic for a mere man of letters, all his books have a professiorial something. Nevertheless, you can lift out of his writings, his essays and even the *Soziologie*,[3] long, beautifully written, half descriptive, half generalising passages which clearly mark him as a contemporary, kindred mind of Thomas Mann, perhaps even of Proust.

Usually we single out one aspect of a person because this aspect may show us, more readily than the complex total, an undivided creature. But every aspect of Simmel will show us a man comfortably seated and eloquently at his ease between at least two stools. When we look more deeply, the ease disappears. He was in a profound and tragical sense both German and Jew. Thus we find among his posthumously published diary notes this entry:

> In toleration there is always arrogance. However aggressively you have said your 'no', you have taken your stand on the same level with the one who has said 'yes'. But when you tolerate him you are looking down and bestowing a favour.[4]

This makes sad reading, because it is not a defence of a dogmatic attitude, which was always far from Simmel. It simply expresses the lack of the most fundamental respect for divergent opinions. And how can you respect a man if you do not imply by your respect his right to form opinions differing from your own, whether you choose to challenge them or not? This leads, in the last analysis, to a state of affairs where people living on the same level – of status, of intellectual proximity or of social integration – are of one opinion and have either banned the chronic dissenters into a lower existence, or have invested them with the right to intellectual independence because of their exalted position.

This throws light on Simmel's peculiar hero-worship, for which he singled out the culture-heroes of the German middle class. He wrote much about Goethe, and expressed the belief that we have to concern ourselves with the life of that man which is significant beyond its affording explanations of his work; no, the life of Goethe is significant because it symbolises something, is itself a message. This message cannot, apparently, be carried by humbler beings: their life does not bear that kind of contemplation, it does not yield mythical significance. For they are the people who are one with you, or whom you contradict or whom you favour with sneering tolerance. It is not an accident that Simmel developed the concept of the charismatic leader, which occurs first in Bastian, and which Weber used freely and without acknowledgement, as he used many categories of Simmel's. But moral strictures apart – what of a sociologist, who is incapable of seeing one of the basic facts of human co-operation? For it is not only a desirable thing – it is very real. On the other hand, we come across passages like the famous opening of the discourse [i.e., *Excurs*] 'The Stranger', an often-quoted piece

> If wandering is the liberation from every given point in space, and thus the conceptional opposite to fixation at such a point, the sociological form of the 'stranger' presents the unity, as it were, of these characteristics. This phenomenon too, however, reveals that spatial relations are only the condition, on the one hand, and the symbol, on the other, of human relations. The stranger is thus being discussed here, not in the sense often touched upon in the past, as the wanderer who comes today and goes tomorrow, but rather as the person who comes today and stays tomorrow. He is, so to speak, the *potential* wanderer: although he has not moved on, he has not quite overcome the freedom of coming and going. He is fixed within a particular spatial group, or within a group whose boundaries are similar to spatial boundaries. But his position in this group is determined, essentially, by the fact that he has not belonged to it from the beginning, that he imports qualities into it, which do not and cannot stem from the group itself.[5]

It is unlikely that these extraordinarily remote and abstract sentences could have been written by anybody who had not himself had the experience of being a member of a society and confronting it from the outside. In stressing this I do not wish to provide arguments for those who in their childish way try to claim Simmel for this or that people, but it surely indicates the calibre of the man when he is capable of transforming the disabilities under which he labours into something that enriches others.

It is difficult to assign Simmel's sociological writings a place in his whole work. The connexion between his purely philosophical writings and his social thought is very tenuous. (He did not lecture on Hegel.) Nor is it easy to group his publications in a manner which would illustrate his shifting interest. Frischeisen-Köhler (1920) attempted this, by dividing Simmel's output and thought into three periods. The first period is one of 'reinstating sociology as an empirical science of society', the second the development of a 'philosophy of culture', the third one of metaphysical endeavour. But this does not hold water when we compare it to the titles of Simmel's more important publications in chronological order.[6]

1881   His dissertation on an early and rarely examined work *The Nature of Matter according to Kant's Physical Monadology*. This dissertation was printed with his three theses which he was going to defend.

1882   One year later, 'Psychological and ethnological studies of music', in *Zeitschrift für Völkerpsychologie* (13: 261-305).

1890   'On Social Differentiation'; *Über soziale Differenzierung. Soziologische und psychologische Untersuchungen*, Leipzig: Duncker und Humblot.

1892   'The problems of the Philosophy of History'; *Die Probleme der Geschichtsphilosophie*, Leipzig: Duncker und Humblot, and, an unGerman title, 'Introduction to the Moral Science' (2 vols; 1892-93); *Einleitung in die Moralwissenschaft. Eine Kritik der ethischen Grundbegriffe*, Berlin: Hertz.

1900   'The Philosophy of Money'; *Philosophie des Geldes*, Leipzig: Duncker und Humblot.

1904   'Lectures on Kant'; *Kant. Sechzehn Vorlesungen gehalten an der Berliner Universität*, Leipzig: Duncker und Humblot.

1907   *Schopenhauer und Nietzsche. Ein Vortragszyklus*, Leipzig: Duncker und Humblot.

1908   *Soziologie. Untersuchungen über die Formen der Gesellschaftung*, Leipzig: Duncker und Humblot.

1913   *Goethe*, Leipzig: Duncker und Humblot.

1916   *Rembrandt. Ein kunstphilosophischer Versuch*, Leipzig: Wolff.

1917   'War and spiritual decisions'; *Der Krieg und die geistigen Entscheidungen*, München and Leipzig: Duncker und Humblot.

1918   (posthumous) *Lebensanschauung. Vier metaphysiche Kapitel*, München and Leipzig: Duncker und Humblot.

1919   (posthumous) collected essays on culture and aesthetics: *Philosophische Kultur. Gesammelte Essais*, which was followed in 1922 and 1923 by two more collections of essays and lectures, and fragments.

It seems, from this list, that philosophy of culture was an early interest which accompanied him through life, associating itself now with aesthetics, now with the history of philosophy. The assumed sociological period is interrupted by books on individual philosophers (derived from lectures). His publications on sociology ceased abruptly but hardly his interests, for even his last notes bear vaguely on his sociological problems. And the metaphysical period, alas, if there ever was one, crystallised in only one book. His dissertation treated critically one aspect of a concept of matter and may be seen in conjunction with a later preoccupation, distinctions between form and content which appeared, however, only in sociological formulations – in respect of which Simmel influenced: Weber, Troeltsch, Ortega y Gasset and Radcliffe-Brown.

As far as our sphere of interests is concerned, his philosophy is remarkable for two things. One is the question concerning the nature and meaning of the historical fact. Here Simmel attacks the notion of, as it were, the two levels of the fact, the underneathness of the true meaning, and shows it to be an erroneous abstraction, oriented towards the familiar dichotomy which is exemplified in the body-soul concept. The historical fact is its own true nature, nothing factual can be abstracted from it. We can conceive it as a configuration of events and split this to obtain component parts, which, however, have no more true nature than the whole. The abstractions are due to our categories of thought and to value judgements. It is interesting to read Simmel doing away – in the case of an issue not very close to his heart – and doing away very astutely with a dichotomy.

In many other cases, especially in the problem of form versus content, he was himself guilty of elaborating dichotomies which bedevilled his work. This comes out clearly where he speaks of historical laws. Such laws are mere abstract correlations, and we can watch sociology, or sociology of history slowly emerging as a kind of natural history of society, holding the real laws (Spykman 1925: 64-67). Simmel's historical laws are straw men. He has pulled them down to show how different from them is exact knowledge. But we feel that this contrast makes our knowledge of society hardly more exact than it would otherwise be. What remains in the reader's mind is a device of accounting for an event in two different ways. The two explanations do not contradict each other. Radcliffe-Brown, too, maintained that every given event had two explanations, a historical and a scientific. One is an individual strain of causation, chronologically dissected; the other refers to real laws of science.

Radcliffe-Brown liked to give the example of a dropped glass. Why did it fall? (a) a girl dropped it; (b) gravitation. The former is an 'accident of history' – anybody else could have dropped the glass. But the law of gravity is a general proposition. And so we could go on asking – why did she drop it? (a) a black man entered and frightened her. This historical answer is merely the chronological connexion of events. But what is the scientific answer? All black men frighten girls into dropping glasses? All girls when frightened drop glasses? The appearance of an unusual thing like a black beard *may* frighten a girl of a certain nervous disposition and under certain conditions cause her to drop things? The last sounds the most sensible. This sense is bought both with the 'may' – and is bought dearly – and with the many individual features we are combining with general psychological and other statements. In fact, answers (a) and (b) of the first stage of our inquiry stand in a relation to each other different from answers (a) and (b) in the second stage. Radcliffe-Brown's tacit assumption is, however, that the relation remains unchanged, however far and into whatever stages we enquire, so that we can always pair off a historical and a scientific answer, one particular and chronological, the other general and not modified by the chronological arrangement of the case. This is obviously not so. All it amounts to is: the word 'why' has several meanings; we cannot think without using a plurality of concepts of causation. The combination of one kind of 'why' with the chronological order is arbitrary and facile. Simmel, who is responsible for this, related complexes, not events. But historically complex events are not structured so that they provide surfaces and deep-down material. What then is structured in this manner? The body of recorded events. The surface is either the more superficial statements of contemporaries or the coating provided by general statements of historians who have already digested and sorted the facts; either: the duke had a red coat – or: again the manorial system. No historian would be content to scratch this surface and leave the rest to exact knowledge. However – what is the nature of this exact knowledge?

In the essay under discussion[7] – from which Simmel travelled very far – it is a knowledge of laws. These laws concern hidden forces, they are statements about powers that move society hither and thither, and these forces have to be discovered by empirical investigation. At many points 'cause', 'law', 'force' become synonymous. Events are caused by a law, caused by a force, etc. The desire of sociologists to discover laws in order to be scientific, is well known. It is older than Simmel and survives into our time. In this the sociologist differs markedly from his idol. The scientist, like the physicist, aims at general statements concerning quantities and movements. He knows well that the expression force is only part of a descriptive vocabulary, a shorthand sign for relations between movements and quantities. Some physicists are none too happy about this, it is so unscientific (gravitation). The sociologist who is after the halo of real science desires the discovery of social forces. If he could only introduce this expression into a general proposition concerning social events so that it would make sense and could no longer be omitted – all would be well.

We shall not find social laws and forces in the later Simmel. Instead there is a careful sifting and comparing of abstract models of human relationships: the group of two, of three, conflict, subordination, etc. Weber has taken over these categories wholesale. He makes, not all too clearly, a distinction between ideal types and causal models. Ideal types may be: a few basic attitudes, causal models[8], abstractions, types of events, or structures. This terminology has been further complicated by the recent American usage of 'ideal type'. Inherent in Weber's system is a difficulty which is absent from Simmel who did not systematise to that extent; causal models are for Weber, as I remarked, both types of events and structural isolates. Hence, a sect, when at a certain stage of its development proclaiming the millenium, conforms to a causal model, while a certain type of chieftainship or trade union organisation can also be called by this name. The terminology and deeper contradictions thus generated do not interest us here. Very soon Simmel was to distinguish social from natural phenomena in the best way hitherto achieved. But at this stage he wanted the new science set apart from history. History, however, receded into a glorious distance (Spykman 1925: 70). A modification of these views is already found by 1900, in the *Philosophie des Geldes*. Here Simmel operates with the concept of different social sciences (Spykman 1925: 71). This he also abandoned for good reasons.

Lecture B

In my previous lecture I introduced you to Simmel's work and talked about his problem (sociology versus history), and his notion that there are several social sciences among which the theory of society should have a special place. These are ideas expressed in *The Philosophy of History* and *The Philosophy of Money*. In the work which I am beginning to examine today, the *Soziologie*, this theory of society becomes the sociology par excellence: sociology is no longer to be seen as a cluster of several social sciences. When we ask ourselves the question: what kind of system is contained in this theory of society? – there comes the first and fundamental difficulty. This is the lack of a system. Bohner, in his *Untersuchungen* (1930) says,

> It is extremely characteristic of Simmel's thought that it is built out of short pieces of analysis and quite discrete examinations. Thus, all his works have a loose structure, collecting aphorisms and fragments under common titles. Simmel was unsystematic entirely by intention, and this very characteristic of his philosophy, this lack of system (*Systemlosigkeit*) opens up the first approach to a deeper understanding.

Being a philosopher, Simmel has managed to weave an interesting theory round his anti-system complex. In his book on Kant, Simmel says that we can observe in all our cognition when it reaches its most satisfying form:

> ...two motives which are mutually exclusive, which run through the history of thought in manifold struggles, displacements, compromises: the choice between them, as in all ultimate decisions of an intellectual kind, originates in the instincts of the total personality which are beyond the intellectual existence (*Intellektualität*). One might call them (these motives) the systematic and the progressive drives. (1904: 22)[9]

And Simmel elaborates this idea, maintaining that every system falsifies our thinking. Apparently, this happens not only because we eliminate the exceptions to the rules – not just because the results of our thinking are modified to fit into the system – but also because the process of thinking itself cannot freely proceed from one observation to another. There are those, Simmel maintains, who cannot achieve the definite objectification of their thought without freezing it into a rigid system – while others cannot define and objectify their thought without subordinating everything to its progressive drive. The difficulty this raises is not contained in the question whether such a dichotomy really is at work in the minds of men, but rather in our readiness to concede this and associate systematisation with abstract thought, 'progressive drive' on the other hand with empirical procedure. But by the time Simmel wrote this, his whole interest in sociology as an empirical pursuit had vanished. He stated that the investigation he was describing was not one of those which leads to the discovery of new facts. This disposes of the necessity for any empirical enquiry.

Now, what we call Social Anthropology is empirical sociology par excellence: and the conundrum – what objectivity can there be in an enquiry where subject and object are identical: socially conditioned man and the social conditions of man? – that conundrum is solved by us as far as it can be solved at all: we are investigating kinds of social life quite different from the one which conditioned us. Our basic assumptions differ therefore from those of Simmel as much as sociological assumptions can differ; and it is ironical that when casting about for illumination by theoretical sociology we should find ourselves time and again attracted and enriched by Simmel.

What is the subject matter of an enquiry which is neither empirical nor aims at systematisation? What is the thing that all social science has in common and can be isolated? What does Simmel mean when he talks of social forms as something different from social content? These questions lead to the same point and we can therefore start asking wherever we wish. Tentatively Simmel suggests we are investigating social relationships; and he is at pains to tell us that societies are not the sum of their members. But social relationships can be observed;

they are not of the same level of abstraction as the 'units' with which he is going to deal, the synthetic units. He says:

> Let us grant for the moment that only individuals 'really' exist. Even then, only a false conception of science could infer from this 'fact' that any knowledge, which somehow aims at synthesising these individuals deals with merely speculative abstractions and unrealities. Quite on the contrary, human thought always and everywhere synthesises the given into units that serve as subject matters of the sciences. They have no counterparts whatever in the immediate reality. Nobody, for instance, hesitates to talk of the development of the Gothic style. Yet nowhere is there such a thing as 'Gothic style', whose existence could be shown. Instead, there are particular works of art which along with individual elements, also contain stylistic elements; and the two cannot be clearly separated. The Gothic style as a topic of historical knowledge is an *intellectual* phenomenon. It is abstracted from reality; it is not in itself a given reality. (1917; Wolff 1950: 4-5)

This is a rather trite exposition which, however, shows how much Simmel, when talking about forms, units, etc., was stimulated by the then current discussions about style in the developing German science of the history of art. At another point Simmel says (1923i: 8-9) that society as a concept has two meanings which we must distinguish carefully: one meaning is that of the whole complex of associated individuals, the 'human material societally formed'; the other meaning is the sum total of all those forms of relationship with the help of which the individuals become (or we would say: are) the society in the first sense. (cf. Radcliffe-Brown's definition of social structure – which has no 'forms'.) He uses the analogy of geometry, saying that a sphere too has two meanings: a part of matter shaped in a certain way – spherically – but also the shape itself, the mathematical concept which we abstract (or as Simmel, the idealistic philosopher says: through which mere matter becomes the sphere in the first sense). And Simmel maintains that legitimate enquiries are related to both these concepts of society, hence there are two different social pursuits. The first, attending to the 'human material societally formed' must yield a multiplicity of contiguous but otherwise independent disciplines, following the diversified nature of the subject matter, the social content. Here we find the cluster of social sciences again, ranging from economics to the sociology of religion. General sociology, however attends to forms only, it is formal, could not be general without being exclusively formal. Competition, for instance, is a type of relationship. We find it in the economic sphere, in competing religious communities, in the history of art (1923i: 10). The very question which is on our lips when we hear that catalogue of competition Simmel takes from us and utilises, a sure proof of his dialectical thinking, and says: the question how competition between groups differs from that between individuals is a search for formal criteria. Similarly, the types of hierarchies, the representation of corporate groups by individuals, the forms of imitation, the value which common hostility has for the internal cohesion of a group, the way circles form themselves round a 'secret', two-fold divisions and groups of threes – all these are formal elements which can be abstracted from the social content (1923i: 11).

There are several observations to be made here. That there is competition in various social spheres, economics, religion, etc., is no new thing. The new feature is that this common denominator is not explained in psychological terms, but that it is meant to constitute the societal phenomenon. Simmel would be the last person to deny the usefulness of a psychological interpretation of these forms, in fact he does some of this himself, but he discourages causal connexion between what we now call individual drive structures and societal forms. In this he differs slightly from Durkheim's anti-psychologism. Durkheim stipulates that one social fact can be explained only by another social fact, and not by reference outside this class of phenomena. Simmel justifies his isolating social forms not by the assumption that they are mutually explicable, but by the part-and-whole relation: all social forms of a given society are parts of a whole, the societal phenomenon of that human group. These parts are intelligible, that is why we deal with them, but no statement can be made about the entire societal phenomenon, the society in a formal sense. Thus, this is not a piece of anti-psychology but a closely reasoned sociological epistemology. Simmel even admits the psycho-social parallelism which seems to anger most sociologists, by saying bluntly, towards the end of the book, that it has been noticed very often that individuals or groups of one society are often related to each other like parts of the mind of one individual. But, he hopes, nobody will ask him to explain this fact.

Another observation is this: what Simmel calls 'forms' we are accustomed to call either patterns of behaviour or structural principles. When we translate from Simmel's terminology into a more modern one, we have to beware of this double value of the term 'forms'. And finally: we can better appreciate now the peculiar accident which creates an affinity between our empirical endeavours and this most abstract of all sociologists: we confront whole social entities and our analysis brings out the overall features of their institutional life. In this we differ from older ethnographers who came with ready categories modelled on the departmentalised investigation of our own society (departmentalised in the sense in which Simmel talks of differentiation through attention to social content) and tried to fit answers to their questionnaires into these preconceived categories. For us the elements, the social data, are, as a matter of course, unsorted, we do not e.g., put cattle under the heading 'economics', cattle fines under jural life, bridewealth under marriage custom, but once we realise that cattle are of paramount importance in a society, we try to see how cattle attitudes run through several of these categories. For any fact, any attitude, any principle we try to find all the social contexts in which they are operative. Simmel comes to a similar method as a result of abstraction.

And finally, a warning must be given concerning Simmel's primary process of abstraction, the distinction between content and form. When we say, as I have heard it said, we cannot confine ourselves to formal sociology, we have to study both form and content, this is like saying that Turkish is a wrong language because it has no gender. We can express criticism as to the terminology of abstraction but not concerning abstraction itself. Or we may find ourselves saying something like this: take the Nilotic ceremony of splitting a steer when the splitting of a corporate group has to be marked. Is Simmel maintaining that the ceremony is the form which expresses now-this-now-that content, or has this-now-that content which is irrelevant? [Then we would respond,] 'No, Simmel. For us this ceremonial form is of little importance, what matters are the lineages, the nature of the corporate group which you throw on the heap of social content.' Well, this is a misunderstanding. When we look more carefully at what Simmel means by social forms, the structural features of corporate groups have a priority in his attention. For him, the way a lineage may go through fission and fusion would not mark a chronological series but be the attribute of the form lineage. The difficulty which we encountered in the steer splitting was Simmel's aforementioned lack of distinction between structural principles and a pattern of behaviour. Both are 'forms', just as for Malinowski both would be 'institutions'.

Before dealing with some of Simmel's 'forms' let us revert to the tedious epistemological angle. He maintains that his concept of forms is directly related to the supposition that in any known society a multiplicity of these social or rather societal forms are active; and that, if one or other of these forms disappeared, the total phenomenon 'society' would still be there. Thus, the impression could be created that any given form is added to the sum total, could be seen as an accretion, or seen in causal relation, evolving from the rest. This cannot be so, Simmel maintains, because once we take away all the individual 'forms' no social phenomenon, no 'society', remains. And from this concept follows

> that a given number of individuals can be 'society' in a greater or lesser degree: with every rise of synthetic configurations, with every taking sides and forming parties, with every association for a common task of work, or common feeling and thinking, with every decisive distribution of serving and ruling, with every common meal, with every adorning oneself for others, such a group becomes more society than it was before. (1923i: 9)

This leads to the central sentence, which is most difficult to translate

> Nowhere does 'society' exist as such; that is to say: in such a way that it could
> form the premises under which special (discrete) phenomena of relationship
> could be formed. This is because mutual influence does not exist as such, but
> only special kinds of it; and when they occur, there *is* society; they are neither
> cause nor effect of society – they immediately are society. (1923i: 9)[10]

What does this mean? It means the avoidance of insecure tautologies, such as those with which every reader of Durkheim is familiar. When it is said that the function of an institution or social activity is to create social solidarity – and the implication of 'solidarity' is the cohesiveness of society – and when the cohesiveness of a social system cannot be imagined without social activities: what else is Durkheim then saying than 'Society is society'? Simmel's basic epistemological assumptions about whole-and-part relationships of forms and the overall societal phenomenon prevent such ruminations. The question, whether an absolute identity of forms is possible with varying content, is dismissed by Simmel, who says that approximations are quite sufficient to prove his point. To demand more, he says, would mean to confuse historical processes with geometry. Here you can again see Simmel's inability to think of social reality otherwise than as chronological sequences which, from our point of view, is a great handicap. But the great storehouse of social phenomena to him is history; to us it is the manifold and incredible variety of contemporary societies. Simmel's examples are taken from history, even when he, as is usually the case, is not dealing with processes in time but analysing static relationships.

Let us now examine some of these 'forms'. The main categories in the 'formal sociology' are: submission, opposition, numerical and spatial relationships between groups.

1. On submission (see Spykman 1925: 95-106, 109-10).
2. On opposition: Simmel is interesting in view of Radcliffe-Brown's ideas and the concept of structural oppositions and feud (Spykman 1925: 112-13).
3. Contest game, agon, artificial isolation of conflict, nothing but conflict (see Spykman 1925: 124).

Lecture C

Last time I ended by giving a quick survey of types of relationships which Simmel puts under the heading of 'subordination' or 'submission'. It is an interesting catalogue, no doubt, but what can we pin down as his problem? What puzzled the man who least of all was satisfied with pigeonholing types and dreaded the system? I will read out (from Wolff's translation) a lengthy passage in which this problem is contained. Any attempt to put it into other words would only lengthen what has to be said and make it less accurate.[11]

Superordination and subordination constitute, on the one hand, a form of the objective organisation of society. On the other hand, they are the expression of differences in personal qualities among men. How do these two characteristics compare with one another, and how is the form of sociation influenced by the differences in this relationship?

In the beginning of societal development, the superordination of one personality over others must have been the adequate expression and consequence of personal superiority. There is no reason why, at a social stage with no fixed organisation that would *a priori* allocate his place to the individual, anybody should subordinate himself to another, unless force, piety, bodily or spiritual or volitional superiority, suggestion – in brief, the relation of his personal being to that of the other – determined him to do so. Since the beginning of societal formation is historically inaccessible to us, we must, on methodological principles, make the simplest assumption, namely, that of approximate equilibrium. We thus proceed as we do in the case of the cosmological deductions. Since the beginning stage of the world process is unknown, it was necessary to try the deduction of the origin and progress of manifold and differentiated phenomena from what was as simple as possible – the homogeneity and equilibrium of the world elements. There is, of course, no doubt that, if these assumptions are made in an absolute sense, no world process could ever have begun, since there was no cause for movement and specialisation. We must, therefore, posit at the initial stage some differential behaviour of elements, however minimal, in order to make subsequent differentiations understandable on its basis. In a similar way, we are forced, in the development of social variations, to start with a fictitious simplest stage; and the minimum of variation, which is needed as the germ of all later differentiations, will probably have to be placed into the purely personal differences among individual dispositions. Among men, differences in reciprocal positions that are directed toward the outside, will initially, therefore, have to be derived from such qualitative individualisations.

Thus, in primitive times, the prince is required or assumed to have perfections which are extraordinary in their extent or combination. [Simmel gives examples.] This origin of superordination and subordination, of course, still operates constantly in society and continuously creates new situations. But out of it have developed, and are developing, fixed organisations of superordination and subordination. Individuals are either born into them or attain given positions in them on the basis of qualities quite different from those which originally founded the superordination in question.

This transition from the subjective relationship of domination to an objective formation and fixation, is effected by the purely quantitative expansion of the sphere of domination. The connection between the increased quantity of elements and the objectivity of the norms which are valid for them, can be observed everywhere. Two, actually contradictory motives are significant in it. The increase of elements entails an increase in the qualitative characteristics existing among them. This greatly increases the improbability that any one element with a strong subjective individuality has identical or even generally satisfactory relations to all the others. To the extent that there is an increase in the differences within the group over which domination or norm extend, the ruler or the norm must shed all individual character and adopt, instead, a general character, above subjective fluctuations.

On the other hand, this same expansion of the group leads to the division of labour and differentiation among its leading elements. ... The *a priori* elements of the relationship are no longer the individuals with their characteristics, out of which the social relation develops, but, rather, these relations themselves, as objective forms, as 'positions', empty spaces and contours (as it were) which must merely be 'filled' by individuals. (1917; Wolff 1950: 291ff.)

Let us now make our strictures, so that we can see what remains acceptable to us in this exposition, or perhaps even useful.

There is first of all the cold shower of the historical reconstruction; whether or not the problem has been put in such a way as to be answered only by such constructs, is a question we may leave for the end. That the construction is far from providing a true picture, is another matter. We do not know of any human group, however simple in its social organisation, which shows features of subordination and submission without having institutionalised any of it; whether we think of the relation between age groups or in a domestic group, in a labour team or a hunting expedition, institutionalised authority comes always to our mind. This need not be elaborated here, it is a trite observation. Institutionalised authority is an integral part of what Simmel calls the societal phenomenon. Nor have we the right to assume a stage of human life more primitive than those known to us that would be devoid of institutional authority. Zuckermann's study of the *Social Life of Apes and Monkeys* (1932) makes it clear that the more powerful baboon and other males not only succeed in having their will, but also that in response to their threat of force we can observe a stereotype behaviour of submission, token postures and gestures of hetero- and homosexual obligingness which are not, can never be, mere reflex actions of frightened animals: they are the result of social learning. And this learning is an integral part of that kind of social life. Whatever the future holds for theories of evolution, this at least is clear: we cannot credit a primeval human group with a behaviour less socially differentiated than that we find among apes and monkeys.

Again, when Simmel talks of a transition from the subjectivistic relationship of domination to an objective formation and fixation, the evolutionary time perspective is wrong. It is not only in societies he would consider instances of great complexity that we find objectified categories of rank into which individuals move to fill a place. The group of nobles among the Anuak and parallel institutions among

North American Indians come to mind. But a discussion of these points would be on uncertain grounds, because Simmel has nowhere distinguished authority structures from relations between privileged groups and groups lacking such privileges in one society. We can, however, free his statement from the causal-chronological argument and speak of correlations. Then we see instead our way towards a utilisation of Simmel's thought. We can postulate a correlation between the 'objective formation' and the 'quantitative expansion of the sphere of domination' [paragraph 4, above]. This correlation can be used not only in a comparative study of the authority structures of two or more societies – what is of greater interest to us, it can be used when we try to distinguish and analyse the social penetration, depth and normative character of various authorities in one society.

One important aspect of Simmel's 'objectification' is depersonalisation. One might cite as an example the development of monarchy in most Northern European countries, where in the course of the establishment of the constitutional monarchy of the kings who do reign but do not rule – a shrinking of the sphere of domination – the royal office has become increasingly personal.

With all this in mind, let us revert now to the initial statement and ask what parts of it lead to chronological speculations. ('Superordination and subordination constitute, on the one hand, a form of objective organisation of society. On the other hand, they are the expression of personal qualities among men' [paragraph 1, above].) 'Expression of personal qualities' is an awkward way of putting it. We must not be misled by it into thinking that Simmel conceived, for instance, poverty to be the immediate result of improvidence; that he, like some of the immoral dolts of the early nineteenth century, toyed with a justification of the existing distribution in society of worldly goods or 'stations in life' in terms of qualities of men which deserved a more, a less, or a nothing. There is no statement to be found in Simmel's writing in support of such an interpretation; moreover, he makes it quite clear that, for him, the objective function of the poor is to provide a foil to the rich; riches cannot be displayed without the poor, the rich need the poor and thus somebody has to be poor, improvident or not. Similarly, Simmel held that the criminal is necessary for the law to exist.

I mention these things to stress my point that in Simmel's mind there was never a connexion between the personality, the character as such of a person, and the allocation of roles; simply, because for Simmel – as for us – this as-such-ness does not exist. Behaviour is socially formed; behaviour enacts social relationships; and what we call society, social structure, social system, etc. are different types of abstractions made from the observed behaviour. There is nowhere (neither for Simmel nor for any twentieth-century sociology) a private individual that can be seen apart from society; there is nowhere the glove of social convention fitting the live and different and private flesh of a hand.

It is clear that when Simmel says 'personal qualities among men', and opposes them to the 'objective organisation of society', he is not thinking of the private-social dichotomy. What is it then? Two different aspects of society. Not two different things, nor two different statements about the same things. When I say: 'Chieftainship is to be found in tribe M; A is chief of M', these are statements describing a society, or, as Simmel would have it, a form of objective organisation of society. If I say, instead, that A partakes in a certain way of the socially patterned 'personal qualities among men', and that, in fact, this share constitutes the qualities of chiefship – then these are more than merely different statements, as has been shown in recent developments of American cultural anthropology: both Kardiner's basic personality concepts, as the 'personality in culture', are groping after similar things. The psychological answer – Is this a research into the genesis of socially conditioned individual traits? – will give us an explanation in terms of the relation between personal qualities and 'overall cultures' or structure. Simmel's approach to this connexion is also genetic: he thinks that the exploration of the genesis of the society will provide the answer. Hence his coupling the historical approach with that unfortunate word 'expression' which is misleading wherever it occurs, with the possible exception of Hegel's *Phenomenology of Mind*, from which Simmel's concept seems to derive. (About this later.)[12] But the phenomenological bias is unmistakeable. The question is: how is what appears to be, able, how does it manage to appear? Thus, the question: 'How is it possible that subordination and submission constitute, on the one hand, a form of objective organisation of society, and on the other, the expression of personal qualities among men?' is a specific manner of asking the Simmelian question: 'How is society possible?' We know a group of data, and the proof of our knowledge is our ability to frame in terms of that group of data the basic question concerning the societal phenomenon. That is really Simmel's way of discussing sociology. And, as we cannot ask in the same way (as 'How is society possible?'), how the physical is possible, sociology is not a natural science.

All this is complicated and abstract. For us it achieves importance when the whole field of conflict, strife, opposition comes under Simmel's scrutiny. There is, lingering on from the eighteenth century, a belief which equates sociology with the study of harmony. (Means-end-concord-reasonableness-institutional life.) Disruptive forces are nonsocial. Ibn Khaldun differed, but even for him the objective form was the institutional life, culture, etc., the destructive force a drive which kept the objective forms in balance but did not become institutionalised, reified; Simmel's famous opening however is:

That fight (conflict) has social relevance in causing groupings of interests, simplifications, organisations, or modifying them, has never been denied, as a matter of principle. But to the conventional point of view the question must seem paradoxical, whether or not the conflict itself, without regard to phenomena caused by it or accompanying it, is a social form. (1923iii: 186)

NOTES

1. Advertised as four lectures on 'Some Problems in Simmel' in the Faculty of Anthropology and Geography Lecture List for Michaelmas (first) term 1952-53 beginning Monday 3 November. Steiner died during the night of 26-27 November, three days after the day scheduled for the final lecture. Only three lectures survive in the *Nachlaß* at the Deutsches Literaturarchiv, Marbach am Neckar. Our transcription of Steiner's notes has expanded his shorthand omission of vowels, introduced paragraphs (Steiner's lecture notes had none), corrected a few obvious misspellings or typing errors, and occasionally emended a word or phrase to make the text more idiomatic. Additionally, we have attempted to identify the long quotations which were a feature of Steiner's lectures and added what bibliographic apparatus we can. In doing this we have referred in the first instance to Kurt H. Wolff, translator and editor, *The Sociology of Georg Simmel*, (New York: Macmillan, 1950). Steiner makes reference to Wolff's volume and evidently quoted from it during these lectures. One wonders whether the publication of Wolff's collection, which made a generous selection of Simmel's texts available to a readership in English, was in any way instrumental in persuading him to mount a course of lectures. However, if Steiner owned a copy of Wolff's collection – as seems likely – it was not found in his library after his death. This is unfortunate since Steiner was in the habit of marginally annotating copies of books he owned to indicate to himself the, often lengthy, quotations he used in his lectures. Some of Steiner's quotations from Simmel's *Soziologie* have been identified thanks to the annotations made in his copy (see note 3, below). The length of these quotations may also be a stopgap, as the following journal entry for 3 November, the day he gave Lecture A, indicates: 'Up at 6.00, after three hours sleep, to finish my lecture. It was tough. Inserted quotations to fill out the time, instead of explaining, and felt ashamed. The lecture was at 12.00. It was dreadful. Everyone loved it. Only Julian [Pitt-Rivers] said casually – with studied casualness – and nasally: "It was great fun, Franz"'. (MS 1952a: 39) First publication.
2. Steiner used this quotation for an image in his poem 'To Simmel', quoted in our introduction, p. 62 above. [Eds]
3. Franz Steiner's copy of Simmel's *Soziologie* (3rd rev edn, Munich and Leipzig, 1923) – incidentally the edition used by Kurt H. Wolff for his widely used translation of the selected works of Simmel – is dedicated: 'To Dr F.B. Steiner from A.R. Radcliffe-Brown 1946'. Cross-references to early translations of two sections of the work (by Albion W. Small in 1902 and 1910) appear to be in Radcliffe-Brown's hand. A handlist of works on Simmel in Steiner's hand carries shelf marks in the Bodleian and British Museum libraries. Steiner's journal notes have him working on the Simmel lectures from the second half of October 1952 onwards. [Eds]
4. One of seven excerpts, marked as p. 34, from Simmel's *Tagebücher* in Steiner's handwritten note in the *Nachlaß*. For details of the publication of Simmel's ephemera, see Wolff 1950: xliii, notes 11 and 13. [Eds]
5. A marginal annotation 'W, 402' suggests Steiner quoted the first paragraph of 'The Stranger' (1923iv) from Kurt H. Wolff's translation, *The Sociology of Georg Simmel*, Free Press, 1950: 402. [Eds]
6. Full titles and details have been added to Steiner's cryptic listing. [Eds]

7. Presumably 1892 *The Problems of the Philosophy of History*. [Eds]
8. Steiner's lecture typescript has K.M. which we interpret – both here and in the next but one sentence – as 'causal model' on the reasoning that he may have reproduced the German spelling, *kausal*. Another reading might be 'Karl Marx'. [Eds]
9. Steiner's copy of this work is dated: Oxford. IV. 1950. [Eds]
10. This single sentence in the German original is strongly – and unusually – marked in Steiner's copy of *Soziologie*. Steiner's English translation pluralises both 'premises' and 'phenomena of relationship' (*Verbindungsphänomene*). [Eds]
11. Here Steiner quoted from 'Super-subordination as a form of social organisation and as an expression of individual differences; person versus position', (Simmel 1923ii transl. Wolff 1950: 291ff.). We have had to guess how much to include from Steiner's ensuing comments. [Eds]
12. Steiner did not have the opportunity to return to the subject as he promised. A copy of G.W.F. Hegel *Phänomenologie des Geistes*, ed. J. Hoffmeister, Philosophische Bibliothek, vol. 114, 1949 Leipzig: Meiner, entered Steiner's library in its year of publication to judge by the annotation 'FBS 1949'. 'Expression' was a common butt of Steiner's criticism. His reference in this context is presumably to Section (C) (A) 'Reason' and 'Inner and Outer' (1949: 199) which defines 'the outer' as the 'expression' of the inner'. On Steiner's refusal 'to use the verb "to express"', see Mary Douglas (1975: 117). [Eds]

BIBLIOGRAPHY*

Bohner, H.F.A., 1930 *Untersuchungen zur Entwicklung der Philosophie Georg Simmels*, Dissertation, Freiburg im Breisgau.

Frischeisen-Köhler, M., 1920 'Georg Simmel', *Kantstudien* 24.

Simmel, G., 1904 *Kant. Sechszehn Vorlesungen gehalten an der Berliner Universität*. Leipzig: Duncker und Humblot.

———, 1917 *Grundfragen der Soziologie. Individuum und Gesellschaft*, Berlin and Leipzig: Walter de Gruyter. Transl. Kurt H. Wolff (1950) as 'Fundamental Problems of Sociology (Individual and Society)', as Part I of *The Sociology of Georg Simmel*, London and New York: Macmillan.

———, 1923 *Soziologie*. 3rd rev. edn, Munich and Leipzig: Duncker und Humbolt
  i. Chapter 1, 'Das Problem der Soziologie', quotations transl. Franz Steiner.
  ii. Chapter 3, 'Über- und Unterordnung', transl. Kurt H. Wolff as 'Superordination and Subordination', Part III of Wolff (1950).
  iii. Chapter 4, 'Der Streit' (Conflict) quotation transl. Franz Steiner.
  iv. Chapter 9, Note, 'Exkurz über den Fremden', transl. Kurt H. Wolff as 'The Stranger', Part V of Wolff (1950).

Spykman, N. J., 1925 *The Social Theory of Georg Simmel*. Chicago: Chicago University Press.

Wolff, Kurt H., 1950 (transl. and ed.) *The Sociology of Georg Simmel*, London and New York: Macmillan and Free Press.

Zuckermann, S., 1932 *The Social Life of Apes and Monkeys*, London: Kegan Paul.

BIBLIOGRAPHIC NOTE

* The handwritten list of references in Steiner's *Nachlaß* (see note 3, above) details over a dozen works on Simmel, with shelf marks at the Bodleian and the British Museum Library, including (apart from authors cited in his lectures) texts by Raymond Aaron, Max Adler, Krackauer, Frost, Fabian, Nobs, and Steinhoff. [Eds]

PART V:
ESSAYS AND DISCOVERIES

ESSAYS AND DISCOVERIES[1]

On the Margins of the Social Sciences

Progress and the West

Progress: instead of the dungeon walls which are much too high, the barred ones, which are very low. At last you are on first-name terms with freedom.

The principle of efficiency lies at the heart of the social doctrine of development (*Entwicklungslehre*). You come to terms with values by supposing a condition in which they did not exist. Indeed, a value only becomes bearable when you can think of the world without it. This is a fear of values.

Thus, the bourgeois scholars have invented a 'childhood' of the human era which lacked the institution of marriage. Even a few decades ago, the assertion that something like marriage had always existed would have created doubts about the value of marriage. True bourgeois respect for marriage shows itself in the assumption that there was once some incredibly swinish primal condition, in which everyone had their beastly sex with everyone else. A value with which you can't shout how far you've progressed simply isn't a value for these people.

The primal condition about which the European citizen who believes in development thinks with such pleasure, is the condition in which he would live if he let himself go. What he attributes to development is supposed to glorify his will.

When the bourgeois notices that he hasn't got very far, evolutionism falls into disrepute.

When we distinguish cultures which 'develop' more or less quickly, that is to say, those which change from those which are static, there is a strangely primitive error in play.

We compare those features of changeable cultures, which define that culture as changeable, with parallel features of 'static' cultures, which we then discover to be unchanging. That is all. In principle, after all, we know that everything changes, and that whatever changes and with whatever speed, some features remain unchanged. For there lies the identity, and with that the continuity, of living things.

Yet we have decided to declare that both what does not change fast enough among changeable peoples, and what changes among unchangeable peoples, is to be valued as unimportant, and to treat as important that which is the object of our changeability. That's the stupidity. For changes cannot be valued. Values are in being, or are thought about in relation to being, not in becoming, or thought about in relation to becoming. Thus, by relating an alien change to our being, we value it as being more or less important. But this has nothing at all to do with a scientific world picture, and even less with a religious one. It's just stupidity, vanity prancing around on an error of thought.

The Europeans have learned from the Bible that the sea was created. Otherwise they would have worked out that it had been filled by the rivers. For what purpose would the most restless of all activities have, if not to form the greatest store, the greatest known quantity?

The active European despises the contemplation of the Asiatic who observes his own navel. When the European interrupts his activity, he does something much more refined. There is nothing like European contemplation. It consists in observing the navel of the Asiatic.

The more intense and intimate the life of a community, the less human appear those enclosed within it who do not belong to it.

Many imitations are not a sign of subordination – on the contrary, they are a means of sympathising with something or participating in it which would be prohibited or prevented by subordination. If a child says 'I want to eat an apple like you' in many cases this is hardly different from its saying 'I want an apple too'. Why should the difference be so significant in the case of an adult?

The Public

The expression 'public' falsifies a great deal; traces of Roman barbarism still cling to it. A relation to a real artwork cannot be made valid within its framework; neither does a dream find a public in the person who dreams it. The public and a work of art (as opposed to gladiatorial wars and American films) cannot exist simultaneously. It belongs to the essence of an artwork, and is part of its limitation and its definition, that alongside and beside it there is also a non-artwork. But where the public existence of the non-artwork begins, a phenomenon's existence as an artwork ceases. The public receives into itself the phenomenon for which it is the public by exerting power over it. In a circus culture the stage –while it lasts – is exposed to the power of the people which it confronts; in a film culture, like the American one, power takes effect during the production of what is to be observed.

Don't tell me about '*the*' ideal society. There have to be at least two; otherwise all history and social science is nonsense.

Building up a culture also means, amongst other things: finding a standpoint from which to spread lies about death.

Cultural history is always the history of a homeless love and the architectural style which survived it.

The apostles of freedom were probably not very thorough people.

The more similar people become, the more they have to stress their differences. In those small groups of primitive hunters and fishers, where everyone displays different abilities in the same acquisition of nourishment and the differences between people and talents are obvious, say among eskimos and pygmies, not even social differences are necessary.

Without powers of command, social energies cannot be stored.

Whoever wishes to weed out society should reflect that institutions are neither decorative nor useful plants but the flower-bed itself.

Runaway slaves occasionally found new kingdoms. The masters who remain no longer appear capable of founding anything at all.

Some states proclaim their sacred right to parts of the earth's surface so emphatically that it is hard to believe that human beings have a home at all.

What saves a nation from its judge, and enables it to survive, are not its good deeds and noble achievements. Humanity has few such things to show for itself, and they seem to play no part in the history of different

peoples. What saves a people is the fact that, as a whole, and be it simply because its hands were tied, it did not take part in the greatest
crimes of the age.

Among the *Naturvölker* who engage in head-hunting, at least the tro-
phy head is a valuable object!

Did not perhaps the nineteenth-century's culture of the spa-town and
its ideas of paradise mutually influence each other? The complex
formed by the redeeming drink or bath, the spa-hotel and the musical
band is really very peculiar.

Cityscapes

What we call a cityscape is determined by three factors only. First the
dwelling unit is that of the family, which is so dominant an institution
that family housing is imitated even in order to fulfil quite different purposes. Secondly only certain workshops are excepted from the rule that
architecture should conform to the family housing. Thirdly all commodities can be purchased, and most of them are put on display as goods.

Basically there are now only three varieties of house:[2] the family
house, the house for a number of families and the as-if-family house,
and finally, the no-family house. The first two types of house are modest.
Their existence is self-evident and does not need to be explained by any
statement and needs no announcement. The no-family house (and by
this is meant not just the house which is not a dwelling house) has to
explain itself, because it is always distinct from the house as such. Its
subordinate types are interchangeable. I have seen stations, hotels, town
halls and universities designed as palaces, but also factories, universities,
museums and, exceptionally, hotels which try to look like churches.

Disowning its purpose as a family dwelling (a pension or an inn
does not need to deny its function, whereas it appears to be indis-
pensable for a larger hotel to do so) practically places the house
under an obligation: it has to resemble something which is connected to an institution which is opposed to the family: the church or
a ruler's palace.

What one understands by proper family housing, by a proper church
or a proper palace, may change from decade to decade. But these three
types will determine the housing of other activities, as long as power and
wealth on the one hand, and on the other religion, renunciation and
education (and sometimes education and power), go together.

So long as the capitalist basis has not been completely destroyed
there are no large workshops that cannot be interpreted ascetically.
Whatever can be interpreted thus can lay claim to being a church-like
building. Cold and striving, the modern factory stands there: achieve-

ment via renunciation and spiritual claims are unmistakable, and there is nothing profane about it.

It is not the workshop which is profane, but the place of sale. Shop windows are the profane as such. They are life – enticement and digestion, wakefulness, pleasure, desire of the flesh. Shop windows are unimaginable in an ancient, Oriental or medieval town. If they are covered at night, a void occurs. That is why people leave some of them brightly illuminated. They look like pictures, then, or advertisements removed from their billboards; the shop behind is dead; there is something cold about them, too, something ghostly; they look like quotations; like the representation of physical lust in an old miracle play. The electric advertisements and the prostitutes at different levels of commercial activity, who roam around like little shop windows and exemplify the profanity of consumption in the most perfect of ways, seem more natural and more alive.

These are the veterans of liberal capitalism, the permanently disavowed guardian angels of the free market. The same development which tossed other wares from the Oriental bazaars or the narrow streets of the guilds into the lights of the shop windows has driven them into the brightness of the boulevards. So they supplement the other wares in the profane category of consumption, and that is what creates the actual life of the city, its changing expression.

What in earlier ages were the intestines have now become the face, without which the city would be dead.

Remembering: An Activity

An obvious fallacy in everyday life: we say that people remember and in so doing think that they probably have very different ways of recalling an experience or retaining it. Anyone who maintained that everyone remembered in one and the same way would probably be considered stupid or rash. Remembering is thought of as an achievement, and we automatically assume that people differ in their achievements. The opposite has first to be proven to us. On the other hand we believe that we immediately understand what occurred in a person who forgot something. We automatically assume that in forgetting we are all the same. Why? Does forgetting strike us as something passive, and do we have an unconscious world picture according to which people only distinguish themselves by their achievements, but not in their passivity? That must be it. Are then our ideas of individuality defined by archaic concepts regarding the division of labour and achievements?

Last Things but One

The great things – or should we call them the last things but one – are: dream, service, adventure.

Only in combination are they readily available for constructing society. The dream combines with service or with adventure, and so on. The man who wishes only to serve and nothing else, the man who wishes only for adventure free from service, and does not wish to remain restricted within his own self, the man who wishes only to dream and nothing else: these are the men who cut loose from society.

The greatest enemies to one another in society are the men who wish to serve with their dreams and with their adventures. But woe to those who wish to serve the adventure of another man with their dreams, and those who wish to serve another man's dream with their adventure!

Education and Illusion

The kingdom of illusions belongs neither to adults nor to children. Children do not have illusions – they are our illusions.

Where the world of adults collides with that of children, adolescents are infected with illusions. This leads to two considerations:

Where children are mainly brought up by adults and not in more-or-less closed communities of their own kind (and both possibilities become characteristics of classes and cultures), they acquire illusions from which those of them capable of suffering must painfully free themselves later. Children 'brought up' by children grow up almost free from illusions; that is to say, in their case, educational maxims are only practical or magical.

People who grow up free from illusions in a society which loves illusions owe this to the difficulty of bringing them up in their youth. Is this much different from unbelief?

The kingdom of illusions is an educational maxim which has become emancipated and therefore assumes a pseudo-life of its own, a quasi-independence.

'Freedom from illusions' is the noblest form of infantilism.

Uniting a species into a society means, above all, that a sphere will be created in which enemies can live together without annihilating each other.

Institutions fall down according to their span.

The relations between sexes within the family – and not the beginnings of political, economic, or priestly power – are the nucleus of all striving after equality and inequality.

Capitalism: the consumer mentality cut loose from any cult, and a cult-bound savings mentality.

Money is a polyp whose suckers are humans. This – not that humans are being sucked – is the degradation of human beings.

It is characteristic of our civilisation that competition has no magical associations whatsoever.

The joy of work, too, like most other phenomena, can be described almost entirely in terms of symptoms and sickness.

The symbols of sovereignty and slavery remain almost unchanged. What lies between them changes.

The subjective role of poverty constantly changes with the kind of health care in a society.

The priesthood and the bourgeoisie: professional cleverness.

Decline and the Public

The decline of a culture may begin sooner or later than the decline of the affected society. Thus a society may function unchanged, the trades unions display solidarity, the judges be just and the actors alive, and yet the culture may already have dissolved.

How does this show? In the yearning for a public. In the end, a culture is a system of symbols, valued as a whole and for the obligations it imposes. It is in the nature of symbols that they relate to two spheres, a secret one and a public one. One, in which the symbols are single and constructed, and another in which they together possess a value. The one sphere cannot exist without the other. The meaning of justice, art, piety and adventure arises in the public sphere. This public realm does not have to be looked for; it is self-evident, given with the society and its symbols.

We see clearly in the Italian Renaissance or Elizabethan England what is meant by a culture suddenly coming into being. It is a question of being mature, of being opened up – in other words, a miracle. And looked at closely, culture depends on the existence of a public sphere the emergence of which is surprisingly abrupt, and which really exists: a public sphere in which actions are the measure, and people entirely unreflectingly experience the fact that they are nodal points in a set of relations. The public sphere creates an identity between being and value. It creates the certainty on the basis of which one can say that something is just nothing because it has no value.

The dissolution of a culture can be seen in the quest for a public sphere of this kind. People longingly seek it everywhere – in rarely visited parts of their own people, then among foreign peoples, outside their society; and they seek it with all the longing of people who, entangled in their own inner world of symbols and the secrecy of producing them, wish that what exists should possess value so that, united with everything of value and measured against it in the sphere where it is granted its value, they can validate their own selves completely.

Universal Comprehensibility

I have often heard it asked how it is possible that those difficult passages in Shakespeare, which on first reading we often have to work through, could have been understood by a theatre audience in Shakespeare's day. And, after this rhetorical question, people ask: how was it possible for an audience, the larger part of which was unable to follow these passages, to calmly allow themselves to endure such incomprehensible speeches?

Can we not pose the same question of attic tragedy? The ancient theatre was a matter for the people in the truest sense of the word, and yet we have no reason to suppose that the educated and the uneducated classes alike, people with no imagination, literati, the initiate and the dull all found the plays equally comprehensible. Yet today we consider that these plays exhibit the nobility of wisdom, audaciously concentrated knowledge, and an ethical interpretation of the myths which they so wonderfully preserve. Today, indeed, they are regarded as offering both the most general and the most particular definition of man's fate and place.

But why should this problem have been different before? The requirement for something declaimed in public to be universally comprehensible, the seemingly proper demand that a speech should address everyone, is not very old. It really seems to be the case that people once felt honoured by the possibility of being present at a speech whose intellectual flight they could not completely follow. They therefore waited patiently until something emerged for them, too. However, when a culture sinks to the lowest level, when everyone says that what he does not understand is rubbish, the demand for universal comprehensibility becomes decisive. There is a certain gruesome justice in this. It can be called both social and poetic justice. To a certain degree it is right, embarrassingly right ....

Terror and Revolt

One can exert force up to a certain point without terror. The happy phases in a tyranny are periods in which force is exerted without producing terror. The revolt against power is born from terror, not from dissatisfaction or from the desire for improvement. For whatever reason people rebel, they flock to the ones who are most profoundly shocked. Only someone who identifies a given power with his own death to such an extent that he finds the wonderful possibility of liberation in its destruction, that is to say the liberation from his own death, is really 'frightened to death'. Only a person of this kind is death to the power.

Mature Revolutionaries

It is often said that this or that group, class, or people is 'not yet ripe' to govern, by which it is meant that they are not capable of governing, but will acquire the ability at a later point in time.

History shows how ridiculous it is to speak of abilities as if they were acquired gradually, and as if not possessing an ability were the precondition for obtaining it at a subsequent point in time. One can indeed set up similar series in which abilities are lost. If we say that a group which has carried out a revolution is not yet ripe for government, as emerges from various subsequent misdeeds, we mean that the group was perfectly capable of achieving power by fighting, but subsequently proved incapable of exercising that power for the more general good. The evidence cited in such instances could equally allow us to infer that the group was capable of governing at the time of the revolution, but subsequently lost this ability.

Could there be any other reason for such a loss apart from the struggle for power itself? Is not every revolution a proof of the fact that a group exists which is capable of exercising power, and that it pictures a system of order? And what else does the ability to govern mean apart from power and possessing the image of a system of order?

Does it then follow that groups are 'ripest' for government while carrying out a revolution and that they lose this ability through the revolution? Certainly.

The exceptions are the very groups which are above all prepared for the power struggle. For them, the revolution does not result in an energy loss which might confuse their picture of a system of order. They are more secure afterwards. And they are the very ones who must appear most immature and 'unripe' both before and after the revolution.

The final revolution will be without theory.

Dangers of the All-too-Human

How peaceful, friendly, and full of love for mankind is the belief that all hearts, all systems of thought, all cultures and all peoples have something in common which we consider essential! Maintaining this commonality is meaningless without the consequent demand to strengthen it. What is 'common' can only be strengthened and enlarged at the expense of something that is not common. Hence this most humane of all reflections is contaminated by interference, persuasion, and everything that goes by the name of conversion. Persuasion and conversion are the mildest forms of a series of ways of suppressing one kind by another; political persecution, and the exertion of physical power, are the harshest. Now, the same,

strange thing always happens: that the people who desire a peaceful order
and an end to naked violence wish to bring this about through what they
regard as 'universally human', i.e., what is common to all and needs to be
strengthened. That way lies violence.

We have to do the opposite. Peace, satisfaction and order mean above
all that we respect each other's differences, treat *them* as essential. We
must treat encroachment upon the divergent character of even the smallest, most helpless group of human beings as an offence against ourselves
and against the whole of humanity. It is time to stop breaking down the
differences which supposedly divide us for the sake of some venerable
notion of 'common humanity' that will supposedly make us all happy.
Differences are endlessly valuable, almost sacred. Let us begin to honour
difference as something designed by creation itself. Only then will there be
everlasting peace. Do away with persuasion, meetings, congresses, common goals! They are the mild rain that feeds the rivers of war. Away with
false humanity! It's quite enough that we are all God's children.

Malinowski and Conrad

Now and again I have noticed a similarity between two phenomena
one would not normally compare: the way the ethnographer Bronislaw
Malinowski (whose often admiring pupil I have been) forms his sociological theories, and the way Joseph Conrad, master of the belated
dreams of adolescent boys, depicts characters.

Malinowski subscribed to an oddly rationalistic materialism, believing that you can explain an institution by describing its functions and
investigating these in terms of the aims they appear to fulfil, in terms of
the satisfaction of 'needs'. Primary among these needs are the desire
for nourishment, shelter, sexual relations. All this he assserted in an
age when the calculation of relations has been so greatly loosened by
debates surrounding causality and probability, and when determining
an 'aim' unequivocally had been rendered impossible by psychology! I
have often wondered whether this hectic rationalism, on the part of an
over-lively, deeply passionate person, did not mean something entirely
different to him than it did to us.

Did this Pole not yearn after the values of reason? His people did not
experience a particularly pronounced Age of Enlightenment of the
kind that would have forced him to regard it sceptically: is his thought
not a form of true eighteenth-century rationalism clothed in modern
garb? If not, whence its intensity? The almost hysterical dogmatism of
a hyper-sensitive, ironic human being?

Thinking of this it occurred to me to ask whether Conrad's Eastern[3]
yearning for enlightenment, freedom, and an autonomous life style

did not give birth to Conrad's Westerners, particularly his English characters. Englishmen, and Westerners of his kind, no longer exist; their time is over, just as it is for the rationalist explanation of social institutions. No, these driven men of action, these pointless individualists with their clear heads, no longer exist. Theirs is a Conradian wish-nation which he has placed in England, whose people sail the seven seas – and especially the warm ones – hard-boiled adventurers whose lust for cash, or for a fight, has no trace of the bourgeois about it, and who never even think of exploiting their entrepreneurial acumen to plan anything as petty as their own security. The English public scarcely recognises itself in Conrad's Englishmen. To the English reader, these figures are the creations of an enviable imagination. The English reader recognises himself in the most crotchety of Dickens's characters, but not in Conrad's adventurers.

Did Malinowksi, with all his ardent anachronisms, believe he was being a Western thinker in the same sense as Conrad believed he was describing Englishmen? I often heard Malinowski, speaking in jest to Englishmen, say, 'I'm much more of an Englishman than you! You are English by accident of birth. I chose it'. These words were more serious than either the speaker or his listeners realised. Conrad chose too, and his Englishmen are more English than real Britons ...

Remarks on Truth, Method, and the Sciences

More human effort lies behind the invention of the concept of 'truth' than behind any other abstraction. It is the first entirely un-biological concept, and the premise for many others.

A lie can slough off the truth just as the truth can slough off the lie....

Aristotle is the unluckiest of all philosophers. His minor themes have had more impact than his major problems: his system-building has created the model for European philosophy. His empiricism, his incredible curiosity have been buried by the centuries. It is as if people had used a big light as a source of warmth simply because they lived in a cold age.

Tacitus is the first modern ethnographer. His arsenal was above all historical, not geographical or concerned with myth as is the case with Herodotus and Strabo. His major innovation is the *monograph* on a people.

It is strange that Simmel, despite his great acuity, never got beyond distinguishing the form and content of social actions. Both terms are only the names for different abstractions and the same process. 'Form' is the name for every criterion considered with respect to the repeatability of an event; 'content' is that which I can only express in terms of intentions, drives, and needs. 'Content' does not say *what really* happens (as opposed to *how* it occurs), but only says 'why' or 'what for'. 'Form' cannot be explained by the 'why' or the 'what for'. Isolated in this manner, there is something esoteric about 'form'. This is what Simmel wants, since according to him we must assume the existence of 'content' and make 'form' into the object of sociology. Since an event can only be explained as a structural unit in relation to its repeatability, Simmel is right, at least insofar as sociology is the discipline of structures; none the less the distinction between form and content is misleading.

The concept of history is a function of the concept of causality and the concept of origins.

In ideal terms an individual is nothing other than the smallest unit of the obedience experienced by a group in answer to a law which the group experiences.

Time is power. No! It is a situation that is the aggregate of all the forces that overwhelm us.

'Why are you building a net?' someone asked the spider. 'To organise the flies,' he replied.

A society no more consists of individuals than a net consists of knots. The net is made with the help of knots. But no knot is a piece or a unit of some thing that in any sense or purpose could be called a 'net'.

The chief sociological principle is probably this: that no individual can occupy a position without identifying themselves with something, and that there is no identification without transformation (*Verwandlung*). The need for identification is primary. This is the chief difference between human and animal forms of association. The 'I' of human association is at the apex of a triangle, the other points of which are called 'communication' and 'identification'. The sides adjacent to the angle at the I-point are called 'language' and 'transformation'.[4] The circle described around the triangle is a point in another triangle, whose other points are called communication and transformation. The circle which describes this is 'society' – in a metaphysical sense.

The relation between chronological and morphological series (neither is a causal chain):

M1, M2, M3, M4, Mn

Chr1, Chr2, Chr3, Chr4

Chr and M are conditions considered as spatio-temporal units of observation (i.e., 'things' as well as 'states of affairs'); they are *elements* in the series. If both series are complete, what we postulate as adjacent elements in the M-series may appear as adjacent, near or distant in the Chr-series, and vice versa. If both series are incomplete, this reversability does not apply. Adjacent *ur*-'elements' can appear in the M-series only as adjacent or near to one another. The fact that this 'nearness' cannot be described in quantitative terms demonstrates the difference between the two logical structures.

The so-called 'culture element' of ethnology is a comparative unit; or, more precisely, an observational unit related to a comparison, which is meaningless outside that comparison. Its meaning does not arise from the functional analysis of observationally adjacent data: the culture element is not a sociological concept and cannot be supplied with sociological predicates. 'Culture' in the ethnological school of sociology is simply the largest observational unit related to comparison that features in any inventory of states of affairs, however that inventory may have been constituted. There is no point in asking in what relation this 'culture' stands to its 'carriers'. This 'culture' is the aggregate of individual details, which may be interpreted in spatio-temporal terms, but not causally or functionally.

The words 'structure' and 'system' should be used in sociology in such a way that one can speak of two *very similar* structures, but not of the *same* structure in two different societies. To the extent that a society is unique, its structure is also unique: the nature of the process – of generalisations, abbreviations, simplifications and abstraction – produces the structure of a social entity from the states of affairs prevailing within it. A structure never arises from comparison between phenomena. In 'structural sociology' we compare structures, not societies. The similarities may prove to be traits, or they may appear as systematically connected amongst themselves, so as to form a 'system'. Seen thus, various capitalist economies are particular instances of the capitalist system. A 'system' is at the same time a category (of structures) and the analytic symbol characteristic of that category, i.e., something which goes beyond the definition of the category itself.

It is misleading to treat herds and fields simply as 'possessions': they are, above all else, the extra-human sector of society, and the associated objects that lend society its permanence. Generations of herds and generations of human beings are intertwined. Sociologically (not biologically) regarded they are categories that reciprocally reproduce and constitute one another. Generations of tillers, the rules relating to fallow land, crop rotation, and the fields as units of inheritance are also intertwined.

This is why the system of genealogical series (and hence the cohesion of larger family groups) have mainly developed among herdsmen. Among farmers tilling the soil (in established villages of a unitary type) this system has developed to a somewhat lesser degree. In cases where groups wander through a forest, clear the land at will, and depart, or among gatherers, or especially among robbers, these genealogical series do not feature so markedly; among the so-called higher hunters, the continuity of political offices often achieves a parallel continuity with the biological unit. By and large it is correct to regard the system of genealogical series as a phenomenon of space-time, which is a throughly ecological function.

Soldiers make the enemy safe. Politicians make them dangerous.

For the French, 'order' is the most spiritual category; for the Germans, it is the most unspiritual.

Descriptive sociology treats societies. Analytic sociology treats structures. Comparative sociology treats systems.

Social structure:
    1. As an objective norm of typical social relations.
    2. As an organic principle of linking and layering situations.

A category can only be defined; an ordered group (network of relations, organisations) can only be represented symbolically.

The latter principle, which we may, with some reservation, call organic, is inexhaustible.

(A category is such not in itself, but only with respect to, in comparison with, an ordered group. Every ordered group may be a category in relation to a more highly ordered one – that is to say one more densely ordered – in relation to which it is 'unordered'; to that extent, symbols are a higher dimension of definitions.)

The genus 'real symbols' consists of disguised definitions. If, for example, I sketch a large stag beetle and say that it 'stands for' ['*vertritt*'] all stag beetles, the figure I have sketched can only fulfil its function insofar as, in a certain sense, it is itself a stag beetle.

This 'standing for' ['*Vertreten*'] *is* thus descriptive in relation to the individual members of the category. This kind of descriptivity is linked to the impossibility of simultaneously designating the (possibly) existing relations between individual stag beetles. The logician, who works only with categories, will say that the category designated here falls into the same category as that which is being designated. It is only someone who studies relations – this is the broadest, most profound defining purpose of sociology (and sociology is the discipline of relations within a group and between groups) – is in a position to, and interested in, distinguishing the actual symbol from what I have here called the 'real symbol', and from the hidden definition.

It can also be put thus: the genuine symbol is removed from the group of symbolised objects and its bindingness is a function of this selfsame differentiation. But the stag beetle that has been sketched is *primus inter pares.* Because it relates to particulars of the group, and not to generalities, the real symbol is rational.

In a consideration of this kind, the real symbol may be treated as a special case of definition. In the same way, a name is a special case of a symbol. Only a weakened name possesses a definitorial character and does nothing other than allocate an object to a group and name the object by means of the definition of the group.

A name may also declare an object to be the member of a group of which the object is the only member. In this case the name also clearly emphasises the individuality of that which is named (its name distinguishes it from all other names) and the structure of the group (which contains only one object). If these two functions completely coincide in a name, the naming identifies the object in a way which goes beyond demarcating and representating. It awakens forces in the sphere of naming which only relate to the representation of ordered groups: naming of this kind is called 'conjuration'.

The formation of spatial concepts in sociology is so difficult and contradictory because we speak of social places as if they were geometrical spaces, i.e., of entities which consist of the sum of all quantities, phenomena, and relations that correspond to a single definition. At the same time (i.e., secondly) the stratification of groups which relate to a hierarchy demands a similar expression. However (thirdly) this always becomes muddled up with (and here we are using that very same spatial concept!) the description of areas of influence, spheres, or put more exactly, the uniform traits of the limitations of coexistent functions. These (fourthly) obtain between social functions and parts of the real space which is allocated to a given society (transport networks, city districts, territorial areas of particular clans, the extent of a judicial circuit, etc., etc.).

Spatial concepts in sociology must therefore be ordered according to the following catch phrases:

1. Geometrical space.
2. Social 'above and below'.
3. Areas of influence.
4. Real space (physical space).

Concepts like 'the position of a class' and 'the stratification of groups in the social whole' lie between 2 and 3.

In Simmel, there is a tendency to reproduce 1 and 3 as planes and 4 in volumetric terms. There is no programme in that. It is practically unintentional. But it greatly adds to the clarity.

When Rasmussen, the Eskimo researcher, asked a native from the area of north-western Hudson Bay: 'Tell me something about your religion. What do you believe in?' the Eskimo replied: 'We don't believe anything, we simply fear, and above all we fear ... (name for a god)'. This is cited by more or less learned scholars as a proof of primitivism. Nobody notices that the Eskimo dealt the inquirer a splendid rebuke!

People have two possible magical mechanisms to protect themselves: taboo and talisman. It is striking that in some societies the majority of taboo prohibitions are observed by one category of people, whereas another category are essentially carriers of talismans.

This can probably be explained as follows: people exposed to acute danger carry talismans, the ones in the midst of latent dangers follow taboos. This is the case with the Eskimos, where the women follow more taboos than the men, and the men, who go off to hunt, are provided with amulets. In the case of the Arabic Bedouins, the opposite seems to be the case. Women are well provided with amulets, to catch men (overcoming the dangers of remaining unmarried and the bridal state), pregnancy, and confinement. The men, who are in the midst of latent dangers when guarding their flocks or when engaged in robbing, observe various rules regarding abstinence.

None of this seems absolutely decisive. What is important is the general feature: the talisman is a positive precaution (it often uses the logic of sympathetic magic and closely related forms), and abstinence is negative. This pair corresponds to that other binary pair: the positive joking relationship that prevails in tense and dangerous social relations (where the pretend joking relationship acts as a shield) and its negative counterpart, the complete avoidance relationship.

The secret of biology and that of sociology coincide!

Value is organised anxiety. It is also organised love. That is the mystery of value. And that mystery is the secret of sociology. It lies behind every sociological antinomy. (That is the difference, by the way, between sociological and political antinomies. The latter arise when opposites are posited as values.)

And is not the relation between death and love (or procreation) the biological secret?

Sociology is only meaningful for someone who treats the polarity of value between anxiety and love as a sociological polarity and not a psychological one. As soon as this polarity is regarded as lying outside the area of social regularities, social regularities simply cease to exist.

The foundations of sociology are far more connected to cosmology than, say, to biology. To that extent, cosmology and sociology together recreate the ancient and venerable unity of philosophy. The theologies of the world religions and the psychologies of the bourgeoisie have sundered this unity.

The sociology of children – the study of children's life in a group – has various tasks, the most important of which can be structured as follows:
1. The authority-structure of the group.
2. The learning technique within the group.
   a. (= 1 ↔ 2) The relation between authority-structure and the learning technique.
3. The group's boundary (how it differentiates itself from the adult world; self-imposed strategies of avoidance and values).
   b. (= 1 ↔ 3) The relation between the authority structure and the boundary.
4. The heteronomous surroundings of the group.
   c. (= 1 ↔ 4) The relation between the group's structure and its surroundings.
      α. Structural reciprocal relations and limitations.
      β. Group ideology (forming myths, acceptance of adult myths)
5. Absorption mechanism of society at large (e.g., group initiations).

NOTES

1. The aphorisms printed here have been selected and translated from typescripts that were edited from Franz Steiner's manuscripts by various hands. Steiner wrote the earliest group between 1943 and 1947. Esther Frank prepared a three-volumed, largely chronological selection under Steiner's direction, entitled *Allerlei Feststellungen und Versuche, 1944-1947* (literally 'various statements and experiments', or *Sundry Essays and Discoveries*). This is Steiner's own name for his remarks, and reflects their exploratory character in the manner of Renaissance collections like Ben Jonson's *Timber or Discoveries* (1616). Compare also Canetti's avoidance of the term 'aphorism' in his *Aufzeichnungen* (Observations). From this three-volumed selection,

Steiner prepared an undated collection in ca.1947, for which he pasted together remarks under 20 headings with thematic titles like 'On the Margins of the Social Sciences'. After Steiner's death, H.G. Adler edited several further selections, including nine chronological typescripts containing remarks from the period 1948-50. We reproduce (1) Steiner's own selection 'On the Margins of the Social Sciences' in its entirety, including the titles Steiner added, though these cannot be regarded as definitive. (2) From *Sundry Essays and Discoveries* (1944-47) we reprint 'On the Process of Civilisation' (pp. 123-28, above) and a further brief essay, which we call 'Conrad and Malinowski' (1947). (3) We print extracts from the later remarks dating from January 1948 to May 1950 transcribed by H.G. Adler under our own title as 'Remarks on Truth, Method, and the Sciences'. Some of these first appeared posthumously in journals (listed in J. Adler 1994b: 283-85), others in 1988 in Marion Hermann (ed.), *Franz Baermann Steiner, Fluchtvergnüglichkeit,Feststellungen und Versuche*, Stuttgart: Flugasche, and in 1995 in Jeremy Adler (ed.), Franz Baermann Steiner, 'Feststellungen und Versuche. Aufzeichnungen über Gesellschaft, Macht, Geschichte und verwandte Themen', *Akzente* (3): 213-27.

2. We have translated all occurrences of German '*Haus*' as 'house' to preserve the pattern of Steiner's thought here; the German word has a narrower sense of 'home' and a stronger sense of 'building' than the English. Cf. Scots 'house'. [Eds]

3. Steiner's word '*östlich*' seems to refer to a European East; both Malinowski and Conrad (as Poles) belonged to a society which Steiner argues did not 'experience a particularly pronounced Age of Enlightenment', and both therefore 'yearned' after Western values. [Eds]

4. Steiner's term '*Schenkel*' for the 'sides' of the triangle also means 'thighs'; the image recalls Leonardo's drawing of a human figure whose limbs are encompassed within a circle, and similar, kabbalistic schemata, e.g., those of Robert Fludd (see Godwin 1979: 68-72). [Eds]

PART VI:
CONQUESTS I-VII

CONQUESTS[1]

I. The Step Swings Away

How hopelessly the breast drinks its fill of the evening ...
Evening air between trees,
Evening air beneath clouds:
Between resting bodies the clarity, eternally prepared but also lost,
Spread over the full urns of black-edged valleys
With their little gardens, and bells,
With their columns of smoke.

The step swings away,
The body hurries through the evening,
The stretched breast does not heed the arms,
The arms are loosely attached and helpless ...

What the day gained, what did not die,
Must shiver now with a final note.
With dying smiles,
The striding man orders his treasures,
Worn-out remnants from the past,
That they, compressed,
May open their desired glory.
There can scarcely be any possessions other than such jewels,
Heaped up on the fading edge of the present,
Conquests,
The debris of formerly perfected bliss.

On some nights, the mountains lie quite naked beneath the sky,
A conquered height, no longer belonging to earth,

But enclosed into the ruling play
Of stars, storms, and darkest blue.
Conquests, shared by none,
Not the fruitful earth,
Not chance or substitutes between the towering heads.
A drunk in his misty labyrinth
May interpret the distances with a singing voice,
Call the heights that once he climbed
And the names that were familiar to his dreams.
This, once appropriate to life, is not objectionable,
It is appropriate to the cup, to the height of the summits,
And to the gait of man.

II. Memories

Memories: the gentle green of hills,
Coupled,
Pure colourlessness at rest.

There is a childhood, in pieces, sweetened by the cool sun.
Three meagre firs in the garden of a limping suburb.
Chimney stacks over the quarrelsome lust of blinded windows:
A slow sobbing captured the evening
The dusty red
Of the window flowers bordered anxiously
On the warm safety of whispering rooms
And the hungry soaring of the birds.

On either side of an open book
The hours of the day fell away.

Lashed to the mast, the captain
Stood with a pale, bleeding forehead,
And helplessly they brought before him the man, dethroned,
The foundling from the lonely shore.
He had a lot to tell:
How, many long years ago, he had been hurled
By black storms onto a land he feared
That then became his own.
How he grew together with the wilderness.
'that feathered tree, for example,
Is a proven friend,
We both love the raging monkey in the branches.'
And he sighed, the sufferer:

'I did not sail in vain.
You make me pious.'

On either side of an open book,
Away,
Fell the hours of the day ...

Then the hours by the pond:
Blue serenades, detached from the onset of their voices,
Enfolded the solitudes.
O solitudes, the first, the tempting ones!
Subdued voices came in slow boats,
Groped, demanded across the water -
Calls came.
Back into the abundant light
How swiftly the change occurred:
That was a 'glance here and then there' ... and gently the turn in
    the walk.

Wandering breathless along the scorched edge of the field:
The green butterfly net fluttering above his head.
And every butterfly carried on its outstretched wings
Coloured marks, the warm eyes of life.

The lovers, the shining and light ones,
They quietly soar, mouth bathed in mouth,
Entwined in dark walls -
Behind them the trees of the park.
And a drunk kneels sobbing
Before the house of the swans on the lake.
But the swans
Have long been bedded in their sleep.
Then words were spoken, o the many words of lovers.
Voices were cautious and pure.
A lad heard them all, lonely and sheer faint-hearted,
A lad, obedient, silent and faint-hearted.

Later, like legends from long ago,
A song that begins:
    'the white feet of my beloved
    Stood in the clear stream ...'
Lovely waves into the rushes,
Swelled the glimmer, blue-eyed herb.

... the feet of my beloved ... and who can say,
Whether she was mine, quite strange, whether sisterly
(fallen from pieces of the others, nameless,
Drawn in perhaps through the wide opening
Of a terrifying night ...)
And no-one participated ...

In silvery rooms grows the morning sun,
A white laughter removes from the dream.
O slow hours, slipping gently and without regret
Into a day without shadows.
Placed into proximity, that permits no further loss,
Lay the bridal visage.

Here is the end. wall of remembrance.
Sunken roads.

Is it an end?
Indeed the roads have sunk,
The tracks of an indolent man
Who raised himself up to harder solitudes:

The lonely man closed his heart to hope,
The dying man closed his heart to sorrow.

III. The Heart

The heart, the created interior being
In a body, that hurried through evenings
(the breast never heeded
The arms, lightly and helplessly attached).
Which preserves the fleeting person,
Who, awoken from darkness, is already falling
To the other edge of the light:
Hand and hearing submissively know the beat of the heart.
Thus the body perceives it: behold, here beats a heart.
The garments of time sometimes leave it uncovered:
Behold, here beats a heart, dwells a man.
Thus the world perceives it.
Beats a heart - and how far does its dominion extend?
For whom does it govern and for how much longer?

That it preserves the body, the dreams know,
For they experience it.

But too dependent in their density are the flickering beings.
The clarified figures, messengers, only arise
Between slow beatings.
Yes, the dreams know, most anxiously,
Do not interpret the closing of the heart.
They truly know the dying.
Like the petty relatives, they point at it closely and confusingly,
They know preparedness, death's heraldry,
They know precisely the customs of dying:
Expiration, rigidity, being a light in the vault of sorrow,
And how the arms of friendship are sawn apart.

Busily the dreams populate a vacationing stage,
Life covered with sleep from door to door,
Every figure slips away without lament,
And behind each a colourless wall grows together without a scar.

Yet the dreams very noisily apprehend our common death,
Bewail it with borrowed pain.
Death to them is but the destroyer of light.
Too sheltered, even in life covered with sleep,
The body for them is grounded immovably,
Its securely streaming blood does not become confused,
Its limbs are young in their trust of the brittle flesh,
And the flawless heart
Hammers in hiding.

Fruits of bitterness, fruits of beauty
Possess the time of plenitude and the time of origin
Upon the inner territories.
The crumb is arranged to receive and to nourish,
Its firmness prepared, the root of the crumb its loosened surface,
That there can be no hesitation, alien to the mode of ripening,
That there can be no detours and no evasion
Before the stratified light of the soul.
If they do not demand light, they grow dark.
Still restrained within what is encapsulated,
Still without lustre in secret,
They thrive irresistibly:
Thus the becoming of fruits in the times of the soul;
There ripen the times themselves, it is not
In generously fruitful nature, filled with winds,
Where the plants freely strive towards fruition,
Where times are merely their once,

Their later and their perhaps,
There ripen the times of the soul,
Appropriate to them, to the density of their fulfilment,
They rise and they ebb, break up, spray off
Fruit of bitterness, fruit of beauty.

The times do not close the heart in their ripening.

The lonely man has closed his heart to hope.
The dying man has closed his heart to sorrow.

IV. To Retain a Little

<1>

Even to retain a little
Of wandering journeys, countries,
Over which the perfect sun
Rises through fiery planes
To wander and sink again
Into a blue lullaby of limpid flutes,
Into a transfigured song of simple consolation:
Even to retain a little
Of the truly perceived objects of balance,
Ostentatious bodies;
Even to retain a little
Of the blinding and comfortably
Reposing towns, of the swarm of sailing boats,
Of the valleys filled with little
Shining stones, and of the shadows of long-necked,
Nodding, ringing caravans,
Cast onto the long walls of the *serajât*
By the edge of the town:
Even to retain a little
Of this and that feathered tree ...

Whoever retains it, is master of so little,
And how far
Does his dominion extend,
Master of so little –
And since when?
In whose name does he govern and for how much longer?
Who retains it?

<2>

Into the overgrowing
Memories are sown
The gentle faces of houses:
And the departing man himself,
A lad at that time,
Still marvelling
At the fate of beauty;
Someone to wander on the beach,
And surrounded by buzzing wasps
To lie in the sated vineyard on the hill,
When the imagery of the grape and its ponderous urgency
Were still a secret,
Earnest and half-known
To joyous eyes.

Nights unravelled,
Immaculately spangled,
And the booming song of the fishermen
Drifted and faded over the sea.

In a fragrant room, by the window,
In a cold bowl,
Blue figs lay,
Lithe and sweet,
Touched with sensible fingers and sultry joy,
And with parted lips.

And in the morning: was there ever again
Anything more noble than the moist coolness of the sand,
Reddish shells bedded into the grey, granular sheen.
Golden beneath the shading hat
Came the face of the woman.
Clothes billowing by the boat
And the brittle trace of the footprints
Blown away in the sand.

<3>

O the beloved mountains of Jelsa,
Of Hvar and Makarska ...

Olive-grey clouds over light walls;
How everything overhangs and stands
To the end in sharp effulgence

And warm air tastes good
To the creatures of the earth ...

The pine grove revels in the dusk,
The evening binds both word and song.
A little donkey strolls through the red glow,
Carrying its load of oil and brushwood,
A little donkey strolls on stony paths;
Small is the animal;
High is its load.
The land awaits the bells of evening.
There wait the walls of the vineyard;
The stones on the path
Are simple and lost in thought.

Bells of the valleys, bells of the hills.
A little donkey strolls through the red glow.
Over the cliffs a song slowly branches.
     'soul, o soul
     Beneath the stars,
     Hesitant and still:
     When will you finally
     Walk across to the other side?
     Behold, thus did
     Evening and day.
     Am i the threshold,
     Not yet low enough,
     That you stop and pause,
     Yet only offer yourself and linger,
     Look how open
     The murmuring night.'

<4>

This hurrying man in an evening mood
And with a heaving breast believes:
That long ago he stood before the Holy City;
That he paced around the walls
And saw in the shade of the olive trees
The Kidron, the valley before the town;
That he sat on the old wall in the spring
When the blue iris
Presses up through the cracks;
That he looked down on the town, the towery,
Blinding cubes, looked down into its narrow

Streets and heard the cries
Of the water-carrier and the melon-man ...

And hid him from the path
For the silvery peace of the olive trees,
Between which
Riders came, high up
On their camels
That ambled with a casual step
And ambled, satiated with their arrival.

Then he came to the black tents,
And often cooled
Hand and brow
On the marble columns of the prayer houses.
In black-green gardens,
Benumbed by the scent of the spikenards,
He heard
The falling of fountain jets, heard
The remoter voices, heard
The measured lute,
Heard the cries
Of the water carrier, of the melon man.

V. The Lonely Man

Whatever aspects of our thought looks upwards,
Helplessly, strengthened only by renunciation,
Finally admires the world because of its frailty,
And the body, too; then wonder remains
For the great tides of space, into which
The bodies' voyages are placed; objections crumble,
And unadulterated experiences flow
Faithfully into the constant sea of despair;
Another wonder, too, at how those tides
Lose themselves in minutiae
To accommodate more closely in a human being.

Memory, mirroring, sediments of the world
Do not seem regulated by the times of the soul;
As the oblique rain outside
Falls on differently remembered planes,
So plane upon plane symmetrically succumbs

To the times of the soul: of severed alterity
As of the nearer home.

Home, home of the heart ...

The entangled web of guilt
Is the home of life in which we grow.
Children are homeless.
How deep pure forgetting
Reaches into their guiltless being:
Rootlessly they flood
Into a nameless, unattested world,
They, who do not yet possess themselves,
And are filled with wonder:
Unrepented, time turns their pages,
In their world, alterity is undivided from home;
Birds soar through,
Pupae sleep through,
Shining beetles, girded armies,
Like among like migrate through the single space,
The narrow domain, where stillness grows
Mountainous, glassy, mossy.
In those days, things lay like coloured feathers
On the meadows of the world. Was it the breath from outside
That moved them, or was it your own? this was not asked:
The mild certainty of wonder
Was directed at the structure of the world
In those days, a unity of images pounded through the heart,
The hands were the life of life, a gate;
The faces of man were the procession of hills,
Grazing calves, a nodding tree, the beautiful one.
As they all shared the common fate of the world,
Once observed, the images
United, nourished by a single heart.
Yet then an individual fate emerged abruptly from the images,
Images fell from things,
Things grew persistent,
Measurable and strange, related to comparison and change.
The child breached the untouched world with a patient gaze,
But it gave him names
And now from year to year the world he covers diminishes.

How the heart closes, no-one can tell;
Dreams do not explain it; the times of the ripening soul

Do not announce it. hence no instruction.
And this is gradual – no-one knows when he began.
So the home is placed into worldly time.
It finds neither orientation nor enlargement.
It does not change in the ripening of the times of the soul.

O beginnings of home:
How intimate are the seeds of guilt
And those first, expansively uncertain boundaries of alterity,
Homely borders, into which the lonely man
Soon installs himself with his double-face.
He does not tolerate division.
He maintains both here and there in his loving eye, as long as he
    can,
But he is not able for long –
Just as a dying man, unaccustomed to times,
Is not able for long to see
The barely discoverable location of home.

And from year to year the world the name covers diminishes.
With a precious smile, the lonely man
Observes the shrinking of human beings; and his own.
'this you are
Among the others, among the fates.'
Name shrinking from year to year.
And how they wish to deceive, proffering possessions;
Was it grasped? it has already become
So many meagre hands, the powerless claws of shrinkage.
They say to the doctor, too: 'heal
This limb, this foot or tooth.'
The alienate body grows
In the mirrors of acquisition.
But the lonely man dwells at the borders of home,
The lost ones, the scapegoats, watches over their space
With loving eyes.
It is indeed so easy
Since he lost his double-face
And he sometimes believes that he stands with his back to the
    world.

Homes are built, new clothes tailored,
As people exchange friendships and furniture and little gardens
Asking: 'Is it nice?' - but whom do they ask?
Still doubting: 'Is it nice?' and they think: it's home,

The daughter's daughter of the ancient home,
And is the table or the tree by the window
Perhaps recognisable
In its origin? Is it 'nice'
(with a slightly open mouth), this new thing,
Will it grow together? and friendship?
Perhaps, as it once was,
With little steps, with many reconciliations
And with agreements, quite different ones,
As in the days ... and not the rigid
Agreement, which disguises
And fetters a pair of people?
But the guardian of home
Is not deceived by the deception of custom; he does not
Fondle things to give them
Friendly names, his heart
Closes to the images, refuses
The circulation of changing woes.
Yet, where the others
Utter words and little words
He utters the only Thou.
His little face is always directed
Against the sky, against the mountains of night,
Against the valleys filled with spring.
Alas, i am passing away, he sometimes says, but you
Are beyond, you do not pass away with me,
I gave you my home long ago.
The fountain before this gate is yours;
Because its water wets my hand
I could certainly have called it mine.
But the times for naming were over long ago.
What matters now is that you stay.
Thus i love.
I gave you my home long ago,
It has passed,
But everything past resides in you; don't i know
That i stand where i always stood, on the border,
Because that is how things are created?
My created heart says so with every beat:
Stay on the border.
For that is how everything is created: first the division
That became a firmament; it gave you a home,
Not its guardian, long ago, yours before his gifts;
Destroy him if you will, but before your inner space

The firmament is he.
For his stand he compared with the report of becoming.

The lonely man is the firmament of the world, he rarely knows it
And sometimes his own little face
And the ripening of the times of the soul remind him.
Fruits of bitterness, fruits of beauty
Break up, glitter away ...
This is the time in the firmament.
Thus time came into the world.

Is it the increase which oppresses you?
Do you ask, who now have no home, and are yet its guardian?
What did i give the eternal world? How have i increased it?
Oh do not be shy, remember that the Increaser,
The first one among us, who lost his home:
At the same time as his many-coloured coat of splendour.
And, we should not be loved ones, he fell
Into his first darkening, as one says
'sold and betrayed'.
The poorest, and yet, we call him Increaser,
Praise his body that has been disrobed.
And remember more urgently
That second darkening, after the woman
Tore off his second noble robe. Oh, how he fell:
It is you in every fall, in every recovery
His recovery: how coolly then and certainly
He spoke in the grief of his strengthening
With the lord of bread and wine ...
Yes, they took robe upon robe,
Threw him deeper and deeper.
But not the hope for return, invested life
Is possible for us: we still mirror ourselves,
Even the loneliest man has not destroyed his vanity.
With hope, the swarm of the despised creatures emerges
And hope destroys the firmament, the ripening of time.

The lonely man closed his heart to hope.

Every acceptance, every withdrawal
Occurs for the shining wholeness of the world.
If he did not push back, piece by piece,
Into the world, over his own, twitching edge –
How could he be saved, and smile?

Staring, he would mumble into the open:
You are my dream.
Then the times are lost.

The lonely man is the guardian of home, the guardian of time.
Bereft of that gracious authority, how could he exist and thank?
The deeds of love close the lonely heart.

Did he give all, not keeping the debris
Of formerly perfected bliss?
They are jewels, placed as often on the threshold
Like the goods of savages, those persistent tribes,
Who do not know the falsification of trade.
But the world left the shining ones untouched,
And so he often asked: for whom do i keep them?
Conquests, no-one participates in them,
And yet unrelinquished?

When they took off his coat,
Did the brothers leave the Increaser
This necklace, buckle and ring?
After all the turns of life
When they in turn sought protection, a hasty report,
Violent report of the grieving old man of their house,
The outcast did not enquire
(upon his summit - and now a son again):
'is my father still alive?'
Whence the preparedness? it had not yielded:
The preparedness to ask was never removed,
A son once again he was preparedness
Asking the answer.

The jewels of the guardian of time
Are placed on a ridge of twilight exuding the present.
It is his most precise laughter when, in the hours of weakness,
He whispers to address the world:
This is your own, thus you adorn me.
Oh, how lovely you are, and how rich.

VI. With a Sleeping Woman at His Back

It is perhaps inevitable to remember
Those mornings, imbued with otherness, dominical,
Which, spent in the cities of flight, still remain,
Fragments of time, brief, upright pillars;
Withering unwillingly on a blackish ground
A row of them arises,
Some sprinkled with lights,
Though most, already, resembling the blackish ground.

On a milky morning, misted beginning,
A single person sluggishly feels
His forehead with damp hands.
The worshippers' blissful bawling
Echoes from the craggy churches.
Dishevelled from the lusting night,
The cats are slinking cautiously
Through the grey gutters.

Milky morning, misty beginning,
A single person at the window:
Before him the street, craggy churches,
At his back the bedstead, a table and three chairs,
A pair of stockings, hanging,
A woman's things,
A gown with silken fringes, rosy tinsel,
Puffed out and crumpled.
And at his back the sleeping woman.
Sleeping woman, creature of sleep, indestructible body,
Visage hidden in sleep, breath upon breath.
Churchbells
Resound into the room.

Cats through the gutters,
Beneath his windows the hurdy-gurdy man
Plays and groans:
'soon she'll wake, breasts and flower-hair,
It could not be otherwise, she'll colour her mouth.'
In the dull dancehall, before the front door, on the street corner,
Cheaply extolled by mate and man,
Imploringly touched, kindled, and taken home,
She sleeps from bed to bed:
A creature of sleep, flower-hair and neatly sculpted body.

Sleeps her way through many beds,
Screams out of her dreams,
Her visage hidden in sleep,
Right leg, left leg,
A perfect pair.
To sleep away
Through the beds of others;
In a single bed,
No part in death.

Before him the street, gutters and steeple,
At his back the bed, the sleeping body.
But behind the bed
Already written on the wall:
With many
Lines,
Few colours,
Tangled,
Chequered,
The picture of the graveyard.
Gravestones, shop sign,
Raised up, knocked down,
Bare tree, full tree
And the autumnally rustling leaves on the cool, decaying way.
'here lies, o-god, o-god, beloved by all
A man, a beast, a toy without blemish.'

'soon she'll wake and colour her mouth.'

Having woken, she slowly walks the room
On her high legs, her head inclined,
A table and three chairs ... the decaying way.
Way without end, how unassumingly
It flows through the room,
Since she unsuspectingly awoke.
Does she not tread on its leaves?
If she walked on it longer,
Would she come closer to me?

'the world is beautiful, my little sleep. i stood
At the window for a long time.'
'the church bells are loud. What can you see
From your place at the window?' 'grey gutters,
The steeple, a bedstead, a graveyard hard by;

Behind it, a lonely land and the sea.'
'the graveyard is far, and lonely enough.'

Too near, too near ... every lover
Slides from bed to bed,
From the bedstead to the grave.
'even a wall of the room
Is its image
Even a step
Leads beyond the graveyard.
Distances fitted to distances,
Journeys do not empty them,
A feathered tree stands alone.'
'What kind of fruit does a feathered tree bear?'
'no fruit of any kind,
No seduction.' It stands
That someone may know it ...
And a mast on the sea. Is it far,
Is it near from one tree to the other?
Hardly further than
From the bed to the grave.
Always the same distance,
There is probably no other.

VII. The Leaf of the Ash

Consider the ash,
The tree with the black buds in spring.

When all the trees, sprinkled with the gentlest colours,
The big ones in wood and field become the most touching
In the common hope that breathes on the cheeks of the hills,
When here and there the quivering twigs climb
Into the air grown full of melted winters,
Shattered by the disconcerted sobbing
Of the blackbird,
And when even the houses of human beings,
The poorest among them, scattered on the meadows,
Seem comfortable when seen from a great distance
(alas, these indigent, bare,
Mossy homes, surrounded by trembling sprigs:
One supposes that they contain
Goodly beings,

And when a child steps out,
A woman with a red head-scarf,
It is immediately woven into the distinct colours of hope,
Into the dreamy recuperation of the land ...),
When single blossoms droop
By the stones, and the brownish bird's-nest
Rudely sways in the scanty thorn bush,
Then behold, and feel the pain, the black
Buds of the ash.
O do not walk on, but behold
How all the colours of hope
Are crammed into one, so strong and complete
In this bud of deadly
Dull blackness.

NOTES

1. The first seven of Franz Steiner's *Eroberungen* ('Conquests') are translated from the critical edition: Franz Baermann Steiner, *Eroberungen. Ein lyrischer Zyklus mit einem Nachwort*, H.G. Adler (ed.), 1964, Veröffentlichungen der Deutschen Akademie für Sprache und Dichtung, Darmstadt, Nr. 36, Heidelberg: Lambert Schneider 12-34. The translations of 'The Step Swings Away' and 'The Heart' first appeared in *Comparative Criticism* 16 (1994): 157-60. The other poems appear here in English for the first time.

BIBLIOGRAPHY AND REFERENCES
TO VOLUMES I AND II

Note

A bibliography of F.B.S.'s published writings to 1993 will be found in 'Special Bibliography: The Writings of Franz Baermann Steiner (1909-1952)', *Comparative Criticism*, 16 (1994): 281-92. A selection is listed here. In the absence of a catalogue of F.B.S.'s unpublished writings in his *Nachlaß*, they are here listed selectively in descriptive form. Our bibliography includes Ms drafts and all completed anthropological writings by F.B.S. and a check-list of the typescripts of his aphorisms, as well as selected letters by and to F.B.S., listed – according to the state of his papers – either individually by date, or globally as datable correspondences. The listings do not include notebooks, folders, excerpts, and notes, which can be identified by their description in our Introductions or by box numbers (S29, etc.). References in the main text preceded by 'Ms' and a date are to section I of the bibliography (unpublished sources), all others are to section II (published works).

Abbreviations

H.G.A. = H.G. Adler. F.B.S. = Franz Baermann Steiner. Ms = manuscript. PC = Personal Communication.
* = reprinted in this edition.

I. Manuscript Sources

i. *F.B.S.'s Unpublished Writings in the Schiller Nationalmuseum, Deutsches Literaturarchiv, Marbach am Neckar*

1934	'Studien zur arabischen Wurzelgeschichte'. Typescript. 1 + 33 pp.
1936	Diary I. Quarto exercise book. Blue cover. 56pp.
1936-37	Diary II. English quarto exercise book. Grey-green cover. 48pp.
1937a	'Einführung in die Kunstgeschichte der Naturvölker' (Introduction to the History of Art of Primitive Peoples). Three lectures. Delivered in Prague. Typescript. 30 pp.
?1937b	'Völkerkunde für Jugendliche' (Ethnology for Young People). Draft for a book. Typescript. 21 pp.
1937-38	Diary III. Quarto exercise book. Without cover. 48pp.
1938	('Hundeopfer und Wehengeständnis, ihre Beziehungen zum Nordeurasischen Wiedergeburtsglauben' [Dog sacrifice and parturition confession, their relations to North-Eurasian beliefs in reincarnation]). Paper delivered to the Congrès International des Sciences Anthropologiques et Ethnologiques, Deuxième Session, Copenhagen 1938. Typescript. 4 pp.
1939a	Diary IV. English quarto exercise book. Red cover. 48pp.
1939b	'Curriculum vitae'. Prepared by F.B.S. Typescript. 5 pp.
?1942	'Wir, die in der Oxforder Ortsgruppe der "Association of Jewish Refugees" ...'. (We, the Oxford Group of the 'Association of Jewish Refugees'...). Undated memoir. 2pp.
*1943	'Brief an Georg Rapp' (Letter to Georg Rapp). October. Typescript by H.G.A. 13 pp.
*1944a	'How to Define Superstition? Draft of a Lecture.' Being an Address to the Oxford Graduate Society. Typescript. 7 pp.
?1944b	'Der Mensch und das Leid' (Man and Suffering). Typescript. Prepared by H.G.A. 2 pp.
*1946	'A letter to Mr Gandhi'. Typescript. 25 pp.
1947a	'Allerlei Feststellungen und Versuche. 1944-47' (Sundry Essays and Discoveries. 1944-47). 3 vols. Typescript edited under F.B.S's direction by Esther Frank.
*1947b	'Malinowski und Conrad'. Oxford. April. In 1947a.
?1947c	'Erinnerung an einen Wendepunkt' (Memory of a Turning Point). Cycle of aphorisms, preceded by title aphorism, based on 1947a. Pasted Typescript. Ed. F.B.S. pp. 8.
?1947d	'Feststellungen und Versuche'. Cycle of aphorisms, arranged in 20 sections, mostly titled, based on 1947a. Pasted Typescript. Ed. F.B.S. 143 pp. Includes 3: *'An dem Rand der Gesellschaftswissenschaften' (On the Margins of the Social Sciences). 1 + 10pp.
1947e	Letter to Paul Bruell. 13 April. Typescript. Prepared by Paul Bruell.
*?1947f	'Memorandum'. Typescript. 7pp.
*?1948a	'Language, Society, and Social Anthropology'. Typescript. 5 pp.

?1948b   Curriculum vitae. Prepared by F.B.S. Request for stipend to study social structure of Jewish villages in the Atlas mountains. 1p.

1948c   'Feststellungen und Versuche'. January-June. A Selection. Ed. H.G.A. Typescript. 26 pp. Contains * 'All the possibilities', 'More human effort ...', 'The body is the time ...'.

1948d   'Feststellungen und Versuche'. July-October. A Selection. Ed. H.G.A. 12 pp. Contains * 'Art and science ...', 'A lie can slough off the truth ...', 'The concept of history ...'. 'In ideal terms ...', 'The chief sociological principle...', 'The relation between chronological and morphological series', 'The so-called "culture element"...'.

1948e   'Feststellungen und Versuche'. November-December. A Selection. Ed. H.G.A. 15 pp. Contains * 'Tacitus is the first...', 'It is strange that Simmel ...', 'A society no more consists ...'.

1949a   'A Comparative Study of the Forms of Slavery', D.Phil. Thesis, Magdalen College, University of Oxford. Typescript. 379pp.

*1949b   'On Gutmann's *Das Recht der Dschagga*. Seminar paper'. Oxford. February. Typescript. 1 + 23 pp.

1949c   'Some Remarks on Slavery. Notes for a Lecture'. Seminar. Oxford. 9 March. Typescript. 1 + 6 pp.

1949d   'Caste outside India. Notes [for] a Lecture'. Dr Srinivas's Seminar. Oxford. 6 June 1949. Typescript. 1 + 4 pp.

1950a   'Feststellungen und Versuche'. January-February. A Selection. Ed. H.G.A. Typescript. 14 pp. Contains *'Time is power ...'.

1950b   'Feststellungen und Versuche'. March-April. A Selection. Ed. H.G.A. Typescript. 29 pp. Contains *'Aristotle ...', 'The words "structure" and "system" ...', 'It is misleading to treat herds ...', 'For the French ...', 'Descriptive sociology', 'Social structure...', 'A category ...', 'The formation of spatial concepts ...', 'Someone asked the spider ...', 'When Rasmussen ...', 'People have two ...', 'The secret of biology ...', 'The foundations of sociology ...'.

1950c   'Feststellungen und Versuche'. June. A Selection. Ed. H.G.A. Typescript. 34 pp. Contains * 'The sociology of children ...'.

1950d   'Feststellungen und Versuche'. June (1). A Selection. Ed. H.G.A. Typescript. 10 pp.

1950e   'Feststellungen und Versuche'. June (2). A Selection. Ed. H.G.A. Typescript. 10 pp.

1950-52a   'Tabu'. Typescript. 12 Lectures. 1 + 44 + 1 pp.

*1950-52b   'Aristotle's Sociology'. A Lecture at Oxford University. Typescript. 2 + 1 pp.

?1951a   Theory of Classification. Fragmentary Chapter headed 'Introduction to the Problem and the Terminology used'. Typescript and handwritten notes. 10 + 11pp.

1951b   'Lectures on the Division and Organisation of Labour'. Oxford. Hilary. Lectures A-F + 1949a pp. 88-104 with handwritten annotations. Lecture G. Typescript. 38 pp.

*1951-52   'Two lectures on Kinship'. Delivered at the Institute of Social Anthropology, Oxford University. Typescript. 3 pp.

1952a   Diary V. Bound quarto volume.
*1952b   'Some problems in Simmel'. Three Lectures delivered at the
               Institute of Social Anthropology, Oxford University. Typescript.
               12 pp.
?1953   Anon. 'Book List. Franz Steiner'. Systematic catalogue of
               Steiner's books on Anthropology, Archaeology, Psychology,
               Social Theory, Sociology, etc. Over 600 items. Typescript. 38 pp.
1957   *A Prolegomena to a Comparative Study of the Forms of Slavery.*
               Prepared for publication by Paul Bohannan. Edited version of
               1949a. Typescript. 198pp.

ii. Unpublished Letters to and about F.B.S. and Memoirs Concerning him at the Schiller Nationalmuseum, Deutsches Literaturarchiv, Marbach am Neckar

Adler, H.G. 1953 'Brief an Dr [Chaim] Rabin'. (Letter to Dr [Chaim] Rabin).
     21 March. 18 double-sided pp.
Bergman, Shmuel Hugo 1952 Letters to F.B.S. 22 February and 4 June.
Bohannan, Laura and Paul 1949-51 Four letters from the field to F.B.S.
Bruell, Paul Letters to H.G.A 11 November, 28 December 1955; 28 March, 4
     April 1958. With Transcripts of F.B.S's letters to Bruell 3 February, 9
     August, 9 November 1936; 22 December 1937.
*Buchanan, Diana 1953 Letter to H.G.A. 20 June.
Canetti, Elias 26 Letters to F.B.S. 18 February 1939-5 July 1952.
Canetti, Veza 23 Letters to F.B.S. ca. 14 August 1939- ca. 14 March 1952.
Douglas [Tew], Mary Five letters to F.B.S., ca.1950-51.
Frank, Esther 1964 'Erinnerungen an F.B. Steiner'. (Memories of F.B.
     Steiner). Typescript. Prepared by H.G.A. 4-8 May. 9 pp.
Forde, Daryll, Seven Letters to F.B.S. written between 25 June 1947 and 15
     May 1950.
Marcus, Joseph, Four letters to F.B.S., 28 January 1942, 29 June 1942, 26
     December 1945, 29 March 1946.
Radcliffe-Brown, A.R. 1942 Testimonial for F.B.S. to the Czechoslovak Min-
     istry of the Interior. 6 January.

iii. F.B.S.'s Unpublished Writings and Other Sources in the Institute for Social and Cultural Anthropology, University of Oxford

Faculty of Anthropology and Geography *Lecture Lists: 1943-4* to *1952-3,*
     Oxford University Gazette.
Franz Baermann Steiner 'Lectures and Papers. Oxford 1949-1952'. Bound
     Volume. Typescript. Contains 'Lectures on Tabu' (229pp.), 'Division and
     Organisation of Labour' (102pp.), 'On Gutmann's *Das Recht der Dschagga*'
     (40pp.), 'Notes on Comparative Economics' (20pp.). Typescript prepared
     for publication by Laura and Paul Bohannan.

iv. F.B.S.'s Letters to Veza and Elias Canetti. Private Collection, Zürich

Ca. 115 letters written between ca. 11 July 1940 and ca. 14 August 1952.

v. F.B.S.'s Letters to Isabella von Miller-Aichholz, Private Collection, Vienna

20 letters written between 11 February 1951 and 2 June 1952. Manuscripts and typescripts.

vi. Letters and Other Written Communications to the Editors

The names of all sources who provided personal communications to us verbally and by fax, e-mail or letter are given in our acknowledgements. We here list additional writings, memoirs etc. in our possession.

Chandavarkar, Anand 1996 'Remembering Franz Steiner. Some random notes.' Typescript. 3pp.

Douglas, Mary 1994 Conversation. 14 January. Typescript. 4pp.

Murdoch, Iris 1952-3 References to F.B.S. in Journals. Edited and transcribed by Peter Conradi. 1997 Typescript. 5pp.

Pitt-Rivers, Julian 1997 Memoirs. Typescript. Extract. 4 pp. Numbered 36-40.

Wright, David 1993 Letter to the editors of 10 July. With copies of three undated letters from F.B.S.

Ziegler, Nicolas 1994 'Die Versenkung des Flüchtlingstransporters Struma' (On the Sinking of the Refugee Vessel *Struma*). Typescript with chart. 8pp.

———, 1996 'Zu Federbaum *iberis semperflorens*' (On the feathered tree *iberis semperflorens*). Typescript with drawing and xerox. 3pp.

II. Published Sources

i. A Selection of F.B.S.'s Published Writings

1935	Lešehrad, Emanuel *Die Planeten,* translated from the Czech by Franz B. Steiner, Prague: Orbis.
*1936	'Orientpolitik', *Selbstwehr. Jüdisches Volksblatt,* 30, 41, Prague, 1 October: 6-7.
*1938	'The Gypsies in Carpathian Russia', *Central European Observer,* 16, 5, Prague, 4 March: 70-71.
1939a	'Skinboats and the Yakut "xayik"', *Ethnos* 4(3-4): 177-83.
1939b	'Hundeopfer und Wehengeständnis, ihre Beziehungen zum Nordeurasischen Wiedergeburtsglauben' (Dog sacrifice and parturition confession, their relations to North-Eurasian beliefs in reincarnation). Abstract of a paper delivered to the Congrès International des Sciences Anthropologiques et Ethnologiques, Deuxième Session, Copenhagen 1938.
1941	'Some Parallel Developments of the Semilunar Knife', *Man* 41, January/February, Article No. 3: 10-13.
1950a	'Amharic Language', *Chamber's Encyclopaedia,* London, I, 371.
1950b	'Danakil' *Chamber's Encyclopaedia,* London, IV, 359.
1950c	'Galla' *Chamber's Encyclopaedia,* London, VI, 371.
1950d	'Somalis' *Chamber's Encyclopaedia,* London, XII, 705.
1951	Review of J.P. Murdock *Social Structure, British Journal of Sociology* 2(4): 366-68.

1952	Review of Sylvia Pankhurst *Ex-Italian Somaliland, British Journal of Sociology* 3(3): 280-81.
*1954a	'Enslavement and the Early Hebrew Lineage System: an Explanation of Genesis 47: 29-31, 48: 1-16', *Man* 54, No. 102: 73-75.
*1954b	'Notes on Comparative Economics', *British Journal of Sociology* 5(2): 118-29.
*1954c	'Chagga Truth. A Note on Gutmann's Account of the Chagga Concept of Truth in *Das Recht der Dschagga'*, *Africa* 24(4): 364-69.
1954d	*Unruhe ohne Uhr. Ausgewählte Gedichte,* (ed.) H.G. Adler, Veröffentlichungen der Deutschen Akademie für Sprache und Dichtung 3, Darmstadt: Lambert Schneider.
*1956a	*Taboo*, with a Preface by E.E. Evans-Pritchard, London: Cohen and West.
1956b	'Sätze und Fragen' (a selection of aphorisms), *Neue Deutsche Hefte* 29, September, pp. 356-58.
*1957	'Towards a Classification of Labour', *Sociologus* NS 7(2): 112-30.
1964	*Eroberungen. Ein lyrischer Zyklus,* (ed.) H.G. Adler, Veröffentlichungen der Deutschen Akademie für Sprache und Dichtung 33, Darmstadt: Lambert Schneider.
1967	*Taboo*, with a Preface by E.E. Evans-Pritchard, Harmondsworth: Pelican.
1983	'Notiz zur vergleichenden Ökonomie', translation of 1954b by Peter Bumke, in Fritz Kramer and Christian Sigrist (eds) *Gesellschaft ohne Staat. Gleichheit und Gegenseitigkeit*, Frankfurt am Main: Syndikat, pp.85-100.
1988	*Fluchtvergnüglichkeit.Feststellungen und Versuche* (ed.) Marion Hermann, Frankfurt: Flugasche.
1992	*Modern Poetry in Translation: Franz Baermann Steiner,* New Series No.2, with translations and an introduction by Michael Hamburger, London: King's College.
1995	'Feststellungen und Versuche. Aufzeichnungen über Gesellschaft, Macht, Geschichte und verwandte Themen' (ed.) Jeremy Adler, *Akzente* 42(3): 213-27. Includes 'Über den Prozess der Zivilisierung' (On the Process of Civilisation).
2000	*Gesammelte Gedichte,* (ed.) Jeremy Adler, Deutsche Akademie für Sprache und Dichtung, Darmstadt; Göttingen: Wallstein Verlag.

ii) Published Sources Cited in the Introductions to Volume I and Volume II

Adler, H.G., 1960 *Theresienstadt 1941-1945. Das Antlitz einer Zwangsgemeinschaft,* 2nd edn, Tübingen: J.C.B. Mohr (Paul Siebeck).

———, 1976 'Die Dichtung der Prager Schule', in *Im Brennpunkt ein Österreich,* Manfred Wagner (ed.), Beiträge zur österreichischen Kultur- und Geistesgeschichte Volume 1, Vienna: Europaverlag, pp. 67-98.

———, 1998 *Der Wahrheit verpflichtet. Interviews. Gedichte. Essays* (ed.) Jeremy Adler, Gerlingen: Bleicher Verlag.

Adler, Jeremy, 1992 'The Poet as Anthropologist: on the Aphorisms of Franz Baermann Steiner', in E. Timms and R. Robertson (eds) *Austrian Studies III: Psychoanalysis in its Cultural Context*, Edinburgh: Edinburgh University Press, pp.145-57.

———, 1994a '"The step swings away" and other poems by Franz Baermann Steiner' (translated and introduced), *Comparative Criticism* 16: 139-68.

———, 1994b 'Special bibliography: the writings of Franz Baermann Steiner (1909-52)', *Comparative Criticism* 16: 281-92.

———, 1994c 'An Oriental in the West: the originality of Franz Steiner as poet and anthropologist', *Times Literary Supplement* 7 October, pp. 16-17.

———, 1995a 'Die Freundschaft zwischen Elias Canetti und Franz Steiner', *Akzente* 42 (3): 213-27.

———, 1995b 'Erich Fried, F.B.Steiner and an Unknown Group of Exile Poets in London', in *Literatur und Kultur des Exils in Großbritanien*, Zwischenwelt 4 (ed.) Siglinde Bolbecher *et al.*, Vienna: Theodor Kramer Gesellschaft, pp.163-92.

———, 1996 'Franz Baermann Steiner: A Prague Poet in England', in *'England? Aber wo liegt es?' Deutsche und österreichische Emigranten in Großbritannien 1933-1945*, Charmian Brinson *et al.* (eds) Munich: iudicium, pp. 125-40.

———, 1998 'H.G.Adler is Deported to Theresienstadt ...', in Sander L. Gilman and Jack Zipes (eds) *Yale Companion to Jewish Writing and Thought in German Culture, 1096-1996*, New Haven and London: Yale University Press, pp. 599-605.

Adorno, Theodor and Horkheimer, Max, (1944) 1988 *Dialektik der Aufklärung. Philosophische Fragmente*, Frankfurt am Main: Fischer Taschenbuch.

———, (1972) 1979 *Dialectic of Enlightenment*, trans. John Cumming, London: Verso.

Adorno, Theodor W., 1992 'Um Benjamins Werk. Briefe an Gershom Scholem 1930-1955', *Frankfurter Adorno Blätter* V: 143-84.

Anderson, Perry, 1968 'Components of the National Culture', *New Left Review*, July-August 50: 3-57.

Anon, 1956 Review of *Taboo*, *The Listener* 23 August: 281.

Anon, 1957 Review of *Taboo*, *Times Literary Supplement* 18 January: 18.

Anon (Rodney Needham), 1967 'Dirt is disorder', Review of Mary Douglas 1966 *Purity and Danger*, *Times Literary Supplement*, 16 February, p. 131.

Anon, 1988 'The Oldest System-Program of German Idealism', in Thomas Pfau trans. and ed. *Friedrich Hölderlin: Essays and Letters on Theory*, Albany: State University of New York Press, pp. 154-56.

Atze, Marcel, 1998 *Ortlose Botschaft. H.G. Adler, Elias Canetti, Franz Baermann Steiner. Ein Freundeskreis im englischen Exil*, Marbach: *Marbacher Magazin* 84.

Banse, Ewald, 1929 *Frauenbilder des Morgenlands*, Schaubücher 5, Zürich und Leipzig: Orell Füssli Verlag.

Barnouw, Dagmar, 1979 *Elias Canetti*, Sammlung Metzler 180, Stuttgart: Metzler.

Bartolf, Christian, 1998 (ed.), *Wir wollen die Gewalt nicht. Die Buber-Gandhi-Kontroverse*, Berlin: Gandhi-Informations-Zentrum

Baur, John I. H., 1961 *Bernard Reder*, New York: Whitney Museum and Frederick A. Praeger.

Bayley, John, 1998 *Iris. A Memoir of Iris Murdoch*, London: Gerald Duckworth and Co.

Beattie, John, 1964 *Other Cultures*, London: Cohen and West.

Beidelman, T.O., 1966 Review of Mary Douglas 1966 *Purity and Danger*, *Anthropos* 61(3-6): 907-8.

Bell, Matthew, 1994 *Goethe's Naturalistic Anthropology. Man and Other Plants*, Oxford: Clarendon Press.

Benn, Gottfried, 1966 *Gedichte. Gesammelte Werke*, Vol. 3, Wiesbaden: Limes.

Berghahn, Marion, (1984) 1988 *German-Jewish Refugees from Nazi Germany*, Oxford and New York: Berg.

Bergman, Shmuel Hugo, 1950 'A Great Task', in Manka Spiegel (ed.), *The Hebrew University of Jerusalem. April 1950. Semi-Jubilee Volume*, Jerusalem: Goldberg's Press.

———, 1961 *Faith and Reason. An Introduction to Modern Jewish Thought*, trans. and ed. by Alfred Jospe, New York: Schocken Books.

———, 1969 'Erinnerungen an Franz Kafka', in *Exhibition. Franz Kafka*, ed. Reuben Klingsberg, Catalogue of an Exhibition at the Jewish National and University Library, Jerusalem: Daf Chen, pp. 2-12.

———, 1985 *Tagebücher und Briefe*, 2 vols, I: *1901-1948*, II: *1948-1975*, (ed.) Miriam Sambursky, Königstein/Taunus: Jüdischer Verlag bei Atheneum.

Bohannan, Laura, 1949 'Dahomean Marriage: a Revaluation', *Africa* 19(4): 273-87.

Bohannan, Paul, 1963 *Social Anthropology*, New York and London: Holt, Rhinehart and Winston.

von Bormann, Alexander, (1983) 'Romantik', in Walter Hinderer (ed.) *Geschichte der deutschen Lyrik vom Mittelalter bis zur Gegenwart*, Stuttgart: Reclam.

Branden, S.G.F.,1958 Review of *Taboo*, *British Journal of Sociology* 9(1) March: 104.

Brod, Max, 1966 *Der Prager Kreis*. Stuttgart and Berlin: Kohlhammer.

Brown, Judith M., 1989 *Gandhi: Prisoner of Hope*, New Haven and London: Yale University Press.

Bryant, Clifton D., (ed.), 1972 'Introduction', *The Social Dimension of Work*, Englewood Cliffs, New Jersey: Prentice Hall.

Bumke, Peter, 1983 'Vorbemerkung', 'Tausch und Wert in Stammesgesellschaften', in Fritz Kramer and Christian Sigrist (eds) *Gesellschaft ohne Staat. Gleichheit und Gegenseitigkeit*, Frankfurt am Main: Syndikat, pp. 47-51.

Bunzl, Matti, 1996 'Franz Boas and the Humboldtian Tradition. From *Volksgeist* and *Nationalcharakter* to an Antrhopological Concept of Culture', in George W. Stocking Jr. (ed.) *Volksgeist as Method and Ethic. Essays on Boasian Ethnography and the German Anthropological Tradition*, History of Anthropology 8, Madison: University of Wisconsin Press, pp. 17-78.

Burton, John W., 1992 *An Introduction to Evans-Pritchard*, Fribourg: University Press, Studia Instituti Anthropos vol. 45.

Buschan, Georg 1922-26 *Illustrierte Völkerkunde*, 3 vols, Stuttgart: Strecker und Schröder.

Canetti, Elias, 1960 *Masse und Macht*, Hamburg: Claassen.

———, 1962 *Crowds and Power*, transl. Carol Stewart, London: Gollancz.

———, 1966 *Aufzeichnungen 1942-1948*, Munich: Hanser.

———, 1978 *Das Gewissen der Worte. Essays*, Munich: Deutscher Taschenbuch Verlag.

———, (1979) 1987 *The Conscience of the Words* and *Earwitness* trans. Joachim Neugroschel, London: Picador.

———, 1985 *Das Augenspiel. Lebensgeschichte 1931-1937*, Munich: Hanser.

———, 1995 'Franz Steiner', in 'Aufzeichnungen 1992', *Akzente* 3 June 1995: 204-209; reprinted in 1996 *Aufzeichnungen 1992-1993*, Munich: Hanser, pp.17-24.

Chadha, Yogesh, 1997 *Rediscovering Gandhi*, London: Century.

Chandavarkar, Anand, 1994 'Franz Steiner', Letter to the Editor, *The Times Literary Supplement*, 25 November: 25.

Clifford, James, 1988 'On Ethnographic Self-Fashioning: Conrad and Malinowski', in James Clifford, *The Predicament of Culture. Twentieth-Century Ethnography, Literature, and Art*, Cambridge, MA, and London: Harvard University Press.

Cohn, W., 1957 Review of *Taboo*, *American Sociological Review* 22 (1) January: 132.

Collini, Stefan, 1996 'Outsiders and the "Reformer's Science"', *The Times Literary Supplement* 28 June: 4-5.

Conradi, Peter J., 1989 *Iris Murdoch: the Saint and the Artist*, 2nd edn, Basingstoke and London: Macmillan Studies in Twentieth-Century Literature.

———, 1997 'Preface', to Iris Murdoch *Existentialists and Mystics: Writings on Philosophy and Literature*, London: Chatto and Windus.

Cranstone, B.A.L. and Steven Seidenberg (eds), 1984 *The General's Gift: A Celebration of the Pitt Rivers Museum Centenary 1884-1984, Journal of the Anthropological Society of Oxford Occasional Papers*, No 3.

Dalton, Dennis, 1993 *Mahatma Gandhi: Nonviolent Power in Action*, New York: Columbia University Press.

Defoe, Daniel, (1719) 1994 *Robinson Crusoe*, Harmondsworth: Penguin Popular Classics.

Demetz, Peter, (ed.), 1982 *Alt-Prager Geschichten*, Frankfurt: Insel.

———, 1997 *Prague in Black and Gold. The History of a City*, London: Allen Lane. The Penguin Press.

Douglas, Mary, 1964 'Taboo', *New Society*, 12 March: 24-5.

———, (1966) 1984 *Purity and Danger: An Analysis of the Concepts of Pollution and Taboo*, London: Routledge and Kegan Paul.

———, 1975 *Implicit Meanings. Essays in Anthropology*, London and New York: Routledge.

———, 1980 *Evans-Pritchard*, Glasgow: Fontana Modern Masters.

Drehscheibe Prag. Deutsche Emigranten. Staging Point Prague. German Exiles 1933-1939 1989 Exhibition Catalogue (ed.) Peter Becher, Munich: Adalbert Stifter Verein.

Dubois, C., 1957 Review of *Taboo, American Anthropologist* 59 (2) April: 357-8.

Dumont, Louis, 1966 *Homo hierarchicus: le système des castes et ses implications*, Paris: Editions Gallimard.

Eichner, Hans, 1970 *Friedrich Schlegel*, New York: Twayne.

Evans-Pritchard, E.E., 1951a 'The Institute of Social Anthropology', *The Oxford Magazine*, 26 April: 354-60.

———, 1951b *Social Anthropology*, London: Cohen and West.

———, 1951c 'Some Features of Nuer Religion', R.A.I. Presidential Address, *Journal of the Royal Anthropological Institute* 81: 1-12.

———, 1952 'Obituary Franz Baermann Steiner: 1908-1952' [1909-1952], *Man* 52, No 264: 161.

———, 1956a *Nuer Religion*, Oxford: O.U.P.

———, 1956b 'Preface' to Franz Steiner, *Taboo*, London: Cohen and West, pp. 11-13.

———, 1959 'The Teaching of Social Anthropology at Oxford', *Man* 59, July, No. 180: 121-24.

———, 1962a 'Social Anthropology: Past and Present' (The Marrett Lecture, 1950), in E.-P., *Essays in Social Anthropology*, London: Faber and Faber, pp. 13-28.

———, 1962b 'Religion and the Anthropologists' (The Aquinas Lecture, 1960), in E.-P. *Essays in Social Anthropology*, London: Faber and Faber, pp. 29-45.

———, 1962c 'Anthropology and History' (Simon Lecture, University of Manchester, 1961), in E.-P. *Essays in Social Anthropology*, London: Faber and Faber, pp. 46-65.

———, 1965a 'The Comparative Method in Social Anthropology' (L.T. Hobhouse Memorial Trust Lecture, 1963), in E.-P. *The Position of Women in Primitive Societies and Other Essays in Social Anthropology*, London: Faber and Faber, pp. 13-36.

———, 1965b *Theories of Primitive Religion* (Sir D. Owen Evans Lectures at the University College of Wales, Aberystwyth, 1962), London: Oxford University Press.

———, 1970 'Social Anthropology at Oxford', *Journal of the Anthropological Society of Oxford* 1(3): 103-9.

———, 1973 'Genesis of a Social Anthropologist', *The New Diffusionist* 3: 17-23.

———, 1981 *A History of Anthropological Thought*, ed. André Singer, London: Faber and Faber.

Fardon, Richard, 1990 'Malinowski's Precedent: The Imagination of Equality', *Man* NS 25 (4): 569-87

———, 1999 *Mary Douglas: An Intellectual Biography*, London and New York: Routledge.

Fárová, Anna, 1986 *František Drtikol. Photograph des Art Deco*, (ed.) Manfred Heiting, Munich: Schirmer Mosel.

Firth, Raymond, 1975 'An appraisal of Modern Social Anthropology', *Annual Review of Anthropology* 4: 1-25.

Fleischli, Alfons, 1970 *Franz Baermann Steiner. Leben und Werk*, Dissertation, University of Freiburg (Switzerland), Hochdorf: Buchdruckerei Hochdorf AG.

Fortes, Meyer, 1978 'An Anthropologist's Apprenticeship', *Annual Review of Anthropology* 7: 1-30.

Freud, Sigmund, 1930 *Das Unbehagen in der Kultur*, Vienna: Internationaler Psychoanalytischer Verlag.

Friedmann, Maurice, 1988 *Martin Buber's Life and Work. The Early Years 1878-1923*, London and Tunbridge Wells: Search Press.

Gandhi, M.K., 1946 'Jews and Palestine', *Harijan: a Journal of Applied Gandhism*, 21 July: 229. Excerpted in *The Jewish Chronicle*, 26 July (27 Tammuz 5706).

Gellner, David, 1997 'Preface' to Ernest Gellner *Nationalism*, London: Weidenfeld and Nicholson.

Gellner, Ernest, 1998 *Language and Solitude: Wittgenstein, Malinowski and the Habsburg Dilemma*, Cambridge: Cambridge University Press.

Gilbert, Martin, 1998 *Israel: A History*, London, Moorebank NSW and Auckland: Doubleday.

Gillies, A., 1945 *Herder*, Oxford: Blackwell.

Godwin, Joscelyn, 1979 *Robert Fludd. Hermetic Philosopher and Surveyor of Two Worlds*, London: Thames and Hudson.

Goldberg, David J., 1996 *To the Promised Land: A History of Zionist Political Thought from its Origins to the Modern State of Israel*, Harmondsworth: Penguin.

Goody, Jack, 1995 *The Expansive Moment*, Cambridge: Cambridge University Press.

Gopal, Sarvepalli, 1975 *Jawaharlal Nehru: A Biography, Vol I 1889-1947*, London: Jonathan Cape.

Graebner, F., 1911 *Die Methode der Ethnologie*, Heidelberg: Winter.

Green, Bryan S., 1988 *Literary Methods and Sociological Theory. Case Studies of Simmel and Weber*, Chicago and London: University of Chicago Press.

Habermas, Jürgen, 1985 *The Philosophical Discourse of Modernity*, translated by Frederick Lawrence, Cambridge: Polity Press.

Haddon, Alfred C., 1934 *History of Anthropology*, The Thinker's Library, No. 42, London: Watts and Co.

Hamburger, Michael, 1992 'Introduction', in *Modern Poetry in Translation. Franz Baermann Steiner. With Translations by Michael Hamburger*, New Series, No. 2, 5-21.

Hamburger, Michael and Middleton, Christopher, 1962 *Modern German Poetry 1910-1962. An Anthology with Verse Translations*, London: MacGibbon and Kee.

Hamilton, Ian, 1996 'Life and Letters; An Oxford Union', *New Yorker*, 19 February: 70-74.

Harris, Marvin, 1968 *The Rise of Anthropological Theory. A History of Theories of Culture*, London: Routledge and Kegan Paul.

Hatto, Arthur T. 1995 'Ethnopoetik: Traum oder Möglichkeit?' *Nordrhein-Westfälische Akademie der Wissenschaften, Abhandlungen* 95, *Formen mündlicher Tradition*: 11-25.

Haumann, Heiko, 1990 *Geschichte der Ostjuden*, Munich: Deutscher Taschenbuch Verlag.

Heine-Geldern, Robert, 1964 'One Hundred Years of Ethnological Theory in the German-Speaking Countries: Some Milestones', *Current Anthropology* 5(5): 407-18.

Hermann-Röttgen, Marion, 1988 'Nachwort' in Marion Hermann-Röttgen (ed.) Franz Baermann Steiner, *Fluchtvergnüglichkeit. Feststellungen und Versuche*, Stuttgart: Flugasche, 129-38.

Hirschfeld, Gerhard, 1996 'Durchgangsland England? Die britische 'Academic Community' und die wissenschaftliche Emigration aus Deutschland', in Charmian Brinson *et al.* (eds) *'England? Aber wo liegt es?' Deutsche und österreichische Emigranten in Großbritannien 1933-1945*, Munich: iudicium., pp. 59-70.

Hoensch, J.K., 1987 *Geschichte Böhmens*, Munich: Beck.

Hoffmann, Dierk O., 1982 *Paul Leppin. Eine Skizze mit einer ersten Bibliographie der Werke und Briefe*, Bonn: Bouvier.

————, 1997 'Czech Nationalists Occupy the German Landestheater / Ständetheater in Prague', in Sander L.Gilman and Jack Zipes (eds) *Yale Companion to Jewish Writing and Thought in German Culture, 1096-1996*, New Haven and London: Yale University Press, pp. 390-394.

von Humboldt, Wilhelm, (1836) 1848 *Über die Verschiedenheit des menschlichen Sprachbaues und ihren Einfluß auf die geistige Entwicklung des Menschengeschlechts*, in Wilhelm von Humboldt, *Gesammelte Werke* Vol. VI, Berlin: Reimer, pp. 1-425.

Huntingford, G.W.B., 1955 *The Galla of Ethiopia. The Kingdoms of Kafa and Janjero*, Part II, *North-Eastern Africa, Ethnographic Survey of Africa* (ed.) Daryll Forde, London: International African Institute.

'Institute of Social Anthropology. Annual Report 1948-9', 1949 *Oxford University Gazette* 79, 4 August: 1186-87.

'Institute of Social Anthropology. Annual Report 1949-50', 1950 *Oxford University Gazette* 80, 3 August: 1136.

'Institute of Social Anthropology. Annual Report 1950-1', 1951 *Oxford University Gazette* 81, 26 July: 1199-1200.

'Institute of Social Anthropology. Annual Report 1951-2', 1952 *Oxford University Gazette* 82, 31 July: 1207-8.

'Institute of Social Anthropology. Annual Report 1952-3', 1953 *Oxford University Gazette* 83, 30 July: 1182-83.

Jamme, Christoph and Schneider, Helmut, (eds) 1984 *Mythologie der Vernunft. Hegels 'ältestes Systemprogramm' des deutschen Idealismus*, Frankfurt: Suhrkamp.

Janik, Allan and Toulmin, Stephen, 1973 *Wittgenstein's Vienna*, New York: Simon and Schuster.

Kafka, Franz, 1958 *Briefe 1902-1924*, Frankfurt: Fischer.

Kaiser, Gerhard, 1996 *Geschichte der deutschen Lyrik von Goethe bis zur Gegenwart*, Vol. I, *Von Goethe bis Heine*, Frankfurt: Suhrkamp.

Kapitza, Peter, 1968 *Die frühromantische Theorie der Mischung. Über den Zusammenhang von romantischer Dichtungstheorie und zeitgenössischer Chemie*, Münchener Germanistische Beiträge 4, Munich: Hueber.

Kieval, Hill J., 1988 *The Making of Czech Jewry. National Conflict and Jewish Society in Bohemia, 1970-1918*, New York and Oxford: Oxford University Press.

Kluback, William, 1988 'The "Believing Humanism" of Shmuel Hugo Bergman', *Review of the Society for the History of Jews from Czechoslovakia*, 89: 129-39.

Kolmar, Gertrud, 1970 *Briefe an die SchwesterHilde (1938-1943)*, Munich: Kösel.

Krejčí, Jaroslav and Machonin, Pavel, 1996 *Czechoslovakia, 1918-92. A Laboratory for Social Change*, London and New York: Macmillan Press Ltd.

Kuper, Adam, (1973) 1996 *Anthropology and Anthropologists: the Modern British School*, 3rd edn, London: Routledge.

―――, 1977 (ed.) *The Social Anthropology of Radcliffe-Brown*, London: Routledge and Kegan Paul.

Kuper, Hilda, 1984 'Function, History, Biography: Reflections on Fifty Years in the British Anthropological Tradition', in George W. Stocking Jnr. (ed.) *Functionalism Historicized: Essays in British Social Anthropology, History of Anthropology* Vol. 2, Madison: University of Wisconsin Press, pp. 192-213.

Lang, Bernhard, 1984 'Spione im gelobten Land: Ethnologen als Leser des Alten Testaments', *Ethnologie als Sozialwissenschaft*, Sonderheft 26: 158-77.

Lanternari, V., 1957 Review of *Taboo, Studi e Materiali di Storia delle Religioni* 28 (1): 137-38.

Leach, Edmund R., 1984 'Glimpses of the Unmentionable in the History of British anthropology', *Annual Review of Anthropology* 13: 1-23.

Leppin, Paul, 1905 *Daniel Jesus. Ein Roman*. Berlin [Magazin Verlag] and Leipzig: F. Rothbarth.

Lessing, G.E. (1756) 1973 *Briefwechsel über das Trauerspiel*, in *Werke*, (ed.) H.G. Göpfert, Vol. IV, *Dramaturgische Schriften*, Munich: Hanser, pp.153-227.

Lévi-Strauss, Claude, 1962 *Le totémisme aujourd'hui*, Paris: Presses Universitaires de Paris.

Lewis, Ioan, 1955 *Peoples of the Horn of Africa: Somali, Afar and Saho*, Part I, *North-Eastern Africa, Ethnographic Survey of Africa* (ed.) Daryll Forde, London: International African Institute.

Lichtenberg, Georg, 1968-92 *Schriften und Briefe* (ed.) Wolfgang Promies, 6 vols, Munich: Hanser.

Liebersohn, Harry, 1988 *Fate and Utopia in German Sociology, 1870-1923*, Cambridge, MA and London: MIT Press.

Lienhardt, Godfrey, 1961 *Divinity and Experience: The Religion of the Dinka*, Oxford: Clarendon Press.

―――, 1964 *Social Anthropology*, Oxford: Oxford University Press.

―――, 1974 'E-P: A Personal View. Sir Edward Evans-Pritchard, 1902-1973', *Man* NS 9: 299-304.

Lindenberger, Herbert, 1971, *Georg Trakl*, New York: Twayne.

Lips, Julius, n.d. *Einleitung in die vergleichende Völkerkunde*, Leipzig: Weimann.

Lowie, Robert H., 1937 *The History of Ethnological Theory*, New York: Rinehart and Company.

Mach, Ernst, 1900 *Die Analyse der Empfindungen*, 2nd, rev. edn, Jena: Gustav Fischer.

Malinowski, Bronislaw, 1923 'The Problem of Meaning in Primitive Language', supplement 1 in C.K. Ogden and I.A. Richards *The Meaning of Meaning. A Study of the Influence of Language upon Thought and the Science of Symbolism*, London: Routledge and Kegan Paul, 296-336.

————, 1967 *A Diary in the Strict Sense of the Term*, London: Routledge and Kegan Paul.

Mayer, Reinhold, (ed.), 1963 *Der babylonische Talmud*, Munich: Goldmann.

Melville, Hermann, (1851) 1938 *Moby Dick or The Whale*, with an introduction by Viola Meynell, The World's Classics, London: Humphrey Milford.

Meyrink, Gustav, 1915 *Der Golem. Ein Roman*, Leipzig: Kurt Wolff.

Milbank, John, 1990 *Theology and Social Theory: Beyond Secular Reason*, Oxford: Basil Blackwell.

Murdoch, Iris, 1956 *The Flight from the Enchanter*, London: Chatto and Windus.

————, 1989 *The Message to the Planet*, London: Chatto and Windus.

————, 1997 *Existentialists and Mystics: Writings on Philosophy and Literature*, London: Chatto and Windus.

Neubauer, John, 1978 *Symbolismus und symbolische Logik. Die Idee der ars combinatoria in der Entwicklung der modernen Dichtung*, Humanistische Bibliothek 28, Munich: Fink.

————, 1980 *Novalis*, Boston: Twayne.

Nietzsche, Friedrich, 1954 *Die Geburt der Tragödie*, in *Werke* (ed.) K.Schlechta, Vol. I, Munich: Hanser, pp. 7-134.

O'Brien, William Arctander, 1995 *Novalis: Sign of Revolution*, Durham: Duke University Press.

Orwell, George, 1970 *Collected Essays, Journalism and Letters*, Vol. 1, Harmondsworth: Penguin.

Perckhammer, Heinz, 1930 *Von China und Chinesen*, Schaubücher 28, Zürich und Leipzig: Orell Füssli Verlag.

Pitt-Rivers, Julian, (1954) 1971 *The People of the Sierra*, 2nd edn, Chicago and London: University of Chicago Press.

Plichta, Dalibor, 1961 *Mary Durasová*, Prague: Nakladateství Československých Výtvarných Ulemělců.

Polišenský, J.V., 1991 (1947) *History of Czechoslovakia in Outline*, Prague: Bohemia International.

Primus, Zdeněk, 1990 *Tschechische Avantgarde 1922-1940. Reflexe europäischer Kunst und Fotografie in der Buchgestaltung*, exhibition catalogue, Münster-Schwarzach: Vier-Türme-Verlag.

Radcliffe-Brown, A.R., 1933 'Social Sanctions', *Encyclopaedia of the Social Sciences*, Vol. XIII, New York: Macmillan, pp. 531-34.

————, 1940 'On Social Structure', *Journal of the Royal Anthropological Institute* 70, reprinted in Radcliffe-Brown 1952, pp.188-204.

————, 1951a 'Review' of E.E. Evans-Pritchard 1951 *Social Anthropology*, *British Journal of Sociology* 2: 365-66.

————, 1951b 'The Comparative Method in Social Anthropology', The Huxley Memorial Lecture for 1951, *Journal of the Royal Anthropological Institute* 81: 15-22, reprinted in Adam Kuper (ed.) 1977 *The Social Anthropology of Radcliffe-Brown*, London, Henley and Boston: Routledge and Kegan Paul, pp. 53-69.

————, 1952 *Structure and Function in Primitive Society: Essays and Addresses*, London: Cohen and West.

Raglan, Lord, 1957 Review of *Taboo, Man* 57 Feb: 27.

Ratzel, Friedrich 1885, 1885, 1888 *Völkerkunde* 3 vols, Leipzig: Bibliographisches Institut.

Richards, I.A., 1925 *Principles of Literary Criticism*, London and New York: Kegan Paul and Harcourt Brace.

Rilke, Rainer Maria, 1955 *Duineser Elegien*, in *Sämtliche Werke*, (ed.) Ernst Zinn, Vol. I. Frankfurt am Main: Insel, pp. 683-726.

Ripellino, Angelo Maria 1994 *Magic Prague*, translated by D. N. Marinelli, London: Macmillan.

Ritchie J.M., 1998 *German Exiles. British Perspectives*, Exile Studies 6, New York etc.: Lang.

Rothenberg, Jerome, (ed.) (1968) 1985 *Technicians of the Sacred. A Range of Poetries from Africa, America, Asia, Europe & Oceana*, 2nd edn, Berkeley: University of California Press.

Rothenberg, Jerome and Rothenberg, Diane, 1983 *Symposium of the Whole. A Range of Discourse Toward an Ethnopoetics*, Berkeley: University of California Press.

Rybár, Ctibor, 1991a *Židoská Praha*, Prague: TV Spektrum and Akropolis.

————, 1991b *Das jüdische Prag*, Prague: TV Spektrum and Akropolis.

Ryding, James N., 1975 'Alternatives in Nineteenth-century German Ethnology: a Case Study in the Sociology of Science', *Sociologus* 25: 1-28.

Sayer, Derek, 1998 *The Coasts of Bohemia. A Czech History*, New Jersey: Princeton University Press.

Schapera, Isaac, 1955 'The Sin of Cain', *Journal of the Royal Anthropological Institute* 85: 33-43.

Schiffer, Reinhold, 1979 'Ethnopoetics: Some Aspects of American Avant-Garde Primitivism', *Dutch Quarterly Review of Anglo-American Letters* 9:1, 39-51.

Schmidt, Gilya Gerda, 1991 *Martin Buber's Formative Years*, Tuscaloosa: University of Alabama Press.

Scholem, Gershom, 1941 *Major Trends in Jewish Mysticism*, Jerusalem: Schocken.

————, 1956 'Seelenwanderung und Sympathie der Seelen in der jüdischen Mystik', *Eranos Jahrbuch* XXIV: 55-118.

————, 1963 *Judaica 1*, Frankfurt: Suhrkamp.

Serke, Jürgen, 1987 *Böhmische Dörfer. Wanderung durch eine verlassene literarische Landschaft*, Vienna and Hamburg: Zsolnay.

Sharp, Francis Michael, 1981 *The Poet's Madness. A Reading of Georg Trakl*, Ithaca and London: Cornell University Press.

Sheppard, Richard, 1994 *Ernst Stadler (1883-1914). A German Expressionist Poet at Oxford*. Magdalen College Occasional Paper 2, Oxford: Magdalen College.

Shimoni, Gideon, 1977 *Gandhi, Satyagraha and the Jews: A Formative Factor in India's Policy towards Israel*, Jersusalem Peace Papers, Jerusalem: Leonard Davis Institute for International Relations at the Hebrew University of Jerusalem and the Jerusalem Post.

Simmel, Georg, 1923 *Soziologie. Untersuchungen über die Formen der Vergesellschaftung*, 3rd edn, Munich and Leipzig: Duncker und Humblot.

———, (1900) 1920 *Philosophie des Geldes*, 3rd edn, Munich and Leipzig: Duncker und Humblot.

Sombart, Werner, 1902, *Der moderne Kapitalismus*, 2 vols. Leipzig: Duncker und Humblot.

———, 1911, *Die Juden und das Wirtschaftsleben*, Leipzig: Duncker und Humblot.

Spender, Stephen, 'Amateurs of Poetry: *Poetry London No. Ten: New Poets Number*', *The Sunday Times*, 4 March 1944.

Spiegel, Manka (ed.), 1950 *The Hebrew University of Jerusalem: 1925-50*, Semi Jubilee Volume, Jerusalem: Goldberg's Press Ltd.

Srinivas, M.N., 1952 *Religion and Society among the Coorgs of South India*, Oxford: Clarendon.

———, 1973 'Itineraries of an Indian Social Anthropologist', *International Social Science Journal* 25: 129-48.

Stocking, George W. Jnr, (1968) 1982 *Race, Culture, and Evolution: Essays in the History of Anthropology*, Chicago: University of Chicago Press.

———, (1995) 1996 *After Tylor: British Social Anthropology 1888-1951*, London: Athlone.

———, (ed.) 1984a 'Dr Durkheim and Mr Brown: Comparative Sociology at Cambridge in 1910', in George W. Stocking Jnr (ed.) *Functionalism Historicized: Essays in British Social Anthropology*, History of Anthropology Vol. 2, Madison: University of Wisconsin Press, pp. 106-30.

———, (ed.) 1984b *Functionalism Historicized: Essays in British Social Anthropology*, History of Anthropology Vol. 2, Madison: University of Wisconsin Press.

Summers, Sue, 1988 'The Lost Loves of Iris Murdoch', *Mail on Sunday, You*, 5 June, pp. 16-22.

Thornton, Robert with Skalník, Peter, 1993 'Introduction: Malinowski's Reading, Writing, in 1904-1914', in Thornton, Robert and Skalník, Peter (eds) *The Early Writings of Bronislaw Malinowski*, trans. Ludwig Kryżanowski, Cambridge: Cambridge University Press.

Tönnies, Ferdinand, 1963 *Community and Society*, trans. Charles P. Loomis, New York: Harper and Row.

Troeltsch, Ernst, (1912) 1931, *The Social Teaching of the Christian Churches*, trans. Olive Wyon, 2 vols, New York: Macmillan.

Tully, Carol, 1997 *Creating a National Identity. A Comparative Study of German and Spanish Romanticism with Particular Reference to the* Märchen *of Ludwig Tieck, the Brothers Grimm, and Clemens Brentano, and the* costumbrismo *of Blanco White, Estébanez Calderón, and López Soler*, Stuttgarter Arbeiten zur Germanistik 347, Stuttgart: Heinz.

Unger, Erich, 1930 *Wirklichkeit. Mythos. Erkenntnis*. Munich and Berlin: Verlag R. Oldenbourg.

————, (1928) 1992 'Mythos und Wirklichkeit', in Manfred Voigts (ed.), *Vom Expressionismus zum Mythos des Hebräertums. Schriften 1909 bis 1931*, Würzburg: Königshausen und Neumann, pp. 88-92.

Voigts, Manfred, 1989 'Nachwort', in Erich Unger *Politik und Metaphysik* (ed.) Manfred Voigts, Würzburg: Königshausen und Neumann.

Wagenbach, Klaus, 1958 *Franz Kafka. Eine Biographie*, Frankfurt am Main: Fischer.

Wasserstein, Bernard, 1994 'Their own Fault. Attempts to Shift the Blame for the Holocaust', *The Times Literary Supplement*, 7 January: 4-5.

Weber, Max, 1919 'Wissenschaft als Beruf', in 1951, *Gesammelte Aufsätze zur Wissenschaftslehre*, Tübingen: J.C.B. Mohr.

Whitman, James, 1984 'From Philology to Anthropology in Mid-nineteenth Century Germany', in George W. Stocking Jnr (ed.) *Functionalism Historicized: Essays in British Social Anthropology*, History of Anthropology Vol. 2, Madison: University of Wisconsin Press, pp. 214-29.

Wiemann, Dirk, 1998 *Exilliteratur in Großbritannien 1933-1945*, Wiesbaden: Westdeutscher Verlag.

Wiener, Oskar, 1919 (ed.), *Deutsche Dichter aus Prag. Ein Sammelbuch*, Wien and Leipzig: Strache.

Winter, J.C., 1979 *Bruno Gutmann 1876-1966: A German Approach to Social Anthropology*, Oxford: Clarendon Press.

Wittgenstein, Ludwig, 1960 *Schriften. Tractatus logico-philosophilus, Tagebücher 1914-1916, Philosophische Untersuchungen*, Frankfurt am Main: Suhrkamp.

————, 1967 'Bemerkungen über Frazers *The Golden Bough*', *Synthese* 17: 233-53.

————, (1958) 1969 *Preliminary Studies for the 'Philosophical Investigations'. Generally Known as The Blue and the Brown Books*, Oxford: Blackwell.

Wolff, Kurt, (ed.) 1950 *The Sociology of Georg Simmel*, London and New York: Macmillan.

Wright, David, 1990 *Elegies*, Emscote Lawn, Warwick: Greville Press.

Yates, Frances A., 1982 *Lull and Bruno. Collected Essays*, Vol. I, London, Boston and Henley: Routledge and Kegan Paul.

NAME INDEX TO VOLUMES I AND II

(Page references to Volume I are in italics.)

SUBJECT INDEX TO VOLUMES I AND II

(Page references to Volume I are in italics.)
Note: Franz Baermann Steiner is referred to throughout the index as F.B.S.